Contemporary Europe

READING UNIVERSITY STUDIES ON
CONTEMPORARY EUROPE

Contemporary Europe

Class, Status and Power

Edited by
Margaret Scotford Archer
and Salvador Giner

Weidenfeld and Nicolson
5 Winsley Street London W1

ISBN 0 297 00399 2

Printed in Great Britain by
Cox and Wyman Ltd,
London, Fakenham and Reading

Contents

Preface

There is no doubt that since the end of the second world war the focus of sociological research has geographically expanded to include continents which were until then virtually the preserve of anthropologists. Paradoxically, this has led to a complementary neglect of comparative studies devoted to European societies and even to a shortage of intensive investigations into the social structure of particular European countries. It is characteristic that European sociologists have concentrated on the problems of Brazil and Argentina to a greater extent than on the post-war developments in Portugal and Spain. While other social sciences, from economics to politics and from law to administrative science, have not ignored the issues of European integration, the implications of the Treaty of Rome did little to stimulate sociologists.

This gap is only too apparent to anyone engaged in teaching the sociology of industrial societies. Of course, there are journalistic studies, essays and surveys about 'the social condition of the new Europeans'. Studies by isolated sociologists are also available on the problems of particular European societies. Yet no coherent collection of essays devoted to trends and problems of European stratification existed to date. Hence, it was with a view to having a closer critical look at the relationships of class, status and power in contemporary Europe that the present volume was devised.

We are only too well aware that, in spite of common trends, European societies still differ greatly. While intra-national variations may be as marked as inter-national differences, the national state remains a strong and resilient unit whose political boundaries still delineate distinctive systems of stratification. It is for these reasons that, conscious as we are of the new common denominators of European societies, we have asked most contributors to this volume to give accounts of specific countries, so that a comparative rather than a cross-national picture may emerge. However, it was felt that a fairly detailed study of a limited number of countries was a better starting point than an attempt at covering the whole continent – which would necessarily have been superficial in the extreme. Contributions have been commissioned from individual sociologists with expert knowledge of the society studied which in most cases is that of their country of origin. Each author is alone responsible for the views advanced within his or her own contribution.

However, in a book attempting to study certain aspects of European society as a whole, cross-national analysis could not be entirely neglected. Hence the first chapter gives a critical account of sociological theory and research on the main theme indicated by the title. It is not chiefly concerned with the state of stratification theory in general, but rather with those aspects of contemporary sociological theory and research relevant to the problems of social class, status and power in contemporary Europe. This account is complemented by the concluding chapter in which Professor T. B. Bottomore examines some of the major substantive changes occurring throughout European societies. At the end of the volume, a set of statistical tables has been provided to indicate some of the quantitative differences between European countries which have a direct bearing on systems of social stratification.

Most of the chapters in this book were first presented as papers in a seminar series at the University of Reading during the academic year 1968-9, under the auspices of the Graduate School of Contemporary European Studies. We would like to express our thanks to the Secretary of the School, Mrs Patricia Sales for her sustained help throughout the Series and also to Mrs Audrey Yates and Mrs Audrey Savin from the Sociology Department for their secretarial help. We are most grateful to Dr Michalina Vaughan, of the London School of Economics, for having read the manuscript and given us many useful criticisms; and finally to Dr Stuart Woolf, chairman of the Graduate School, for his continued advice, help and interest both during the Seminar Series and later during the preparation of the present volume.

M.S.A.
S.G.

Contributors

Margaret Scotford ARCHER	Lecturer in Sociology, University of Reading
Michael ATTALIDES	Social Research Centre, Ministry of Education, Nicosia, Cyprus
Thomas B. BOTTOMORE	Professor of Sociology, University of Sussex
Gøsta CARLSSON	Formerly Professor, University of Lund
Colin CROUCH	Lecturer in Sociology, London School of Economics
Luciano GALLINO	Professor of Sociology, Laboratorio di Sociologia, Turin
Salvador GINER	Lecturer in Sociology, University of Reading
John A. JACKSON	Professor of Social Theory and Institutions, Queen's University, Belfast
René KÖNIG	Professor of Sociology, Institut für Sozialforschung, Cologne
David MARTIN	Reader in Sociology, London School of Economics
Herminio MARTINS	Lecturer in Sociology, London School of Economics
Nikos MOUZELIS	Lecturer in Sociology, University of Leicester
Pierre NAVILLE	Director of Research at Centre National de la Recherche Scientifique, France

Frank PARKIN	Lecturer in Sociology, University of Kent
Kaare SVALASTOGA	University of Copenhagen
Michalina VAUGHAN	Senior Lecturer in Sociology, London School of Economics

1 Social Stratification in Europe

Margaret Scotford Archer and Salvador Giner

1 THEORETICAL APPROACHES

Two types of approach characterize any discussion of past, present or future trends in European stratification, without either of them tending to predominate. It is their differing interpretations of the process and effects of industrialization,[1] rather than differences in the theoretical framework employed for the analysis of stratification which account for their divergence. Both approaches, then, pertain to the school of thought which acknowledges the conceptual and empirical separateness of the various dimensions along which societies are stratified; they differ in their designation of those historical epochs in which it is necessary and useful to regard stratification as a multi-dimensional phenomenon as against those in which, for practical purposes, it can be treated as unidimensional.

Thus the first approach (Industrial convergence theory)[2] postulates that while a relative diversity of bases character- ized the stratification of traditional societies, after industrial- ization other dimensions become subordinated to, and therefore highly correlated with, the occupational hierarchy. The second (Industrial divergence theory), views dimensional superimposition as germane to pre-industrial societies, whereas the positions of individuals on the 'class', 'status' and 'power' dimensions of social structures are less highly associated in the post-industrial period. Thus the frameworks recommended by the two schools for any contemporary and empirical analysis of stratification in Europe differ to the extent that the former tends to regard social ranking as unidimensional (and hence recommends a concentration upon comparisons of occupational structures), while the latter insists on the necessity of investigating social ranking as multidimensional (and hence recommends the cross-cultural comparison of several kinds of hierarchies and the relationships between them). Similarly, differences arise at the level of interpretation of empirical data, the former tending to stress convergence of stratification systems as industrialization spreads and to classify divergences as 'cultural lags', the latter emphasizing the likely endurance of such characteristics. After having outlined these approaches in a highly abstract and over-simplified manner their precise implications must be examined and assessed.

A   Industrial convergence theory

While there are many theoretical variations on this theme, the view is shared that an advancing industrial economy tends to standardize social structures through the operation of common occupational imperatives. This approach, which Clark Kerr[3] termed the 'logic of industrialism', assumes the primacy of the economic over other social institutions and the determinant role of occupation in stratification. Although not defending it under all circumstances, Runciman grants that the use of a multi-dimensional framework of stratification is often unnecessary in developed economies.

The analysis of social stratification in terms of occupation is equally justifiable whether it is the causes or the consequences of the nature and distribution of occupations which are to be assessed. To explain the distribution of occupations is largely to explain the social inequalities found in industrial societies, and to explain its consequences is to explain how these are modified or preserved. Occupations are the mechanism by which the influences of natural endowment, upbringing and education are translated into differences of wealth, power and prestige. . . . Whether occupation or some more elaborate measure of 'socio-economic status' is used, there is little need to sift out the separate elements of class, status and power in any of the usual areas of social research. . . . The fit is too close, and a composite indicator is too useful, for it to be called for.[4]

If acceptable, such a theory would have the effect of considerably reducing the empirical problems involved in making cross-cultural comparisons of stratification systems by limiting them to the (still highly complex) task of comparing occupational structures in convergent societies. Basically, then, the 'industrial convergence theory' assumes that the study of stratification can be reduced to the analysis of strata. There are at least two conditions which such a theory must satisfy. *Firstly* it is insufficient to point out similarities in the division of labour, consequent upon industrialization, in several societies, since these are only indicative of a common form of differentiation, not of stratification. For the latter to hold 'the metaphor of high and low must be appropriate'[5] and a cross-cultural similarity found between those occupations assigned to high and low categories respectively before convergence can be assumed. As Inkeles and Rossi state, 'There is, however, no clear-cut imperative arising from the structure of the factory as such which dictates how the incumbents of its typical statuses should be *evaluated* by the population at large.'[6] Thus cultural variations may lead to differences in the prestige ranking of similar occupations. Neither is there any imperative stemming from a common division of labour that there should also be a common system of differentiated rewards associated with it, whether these be defined in terms of remuneration, working conditions, or 'psychic rewards'[7] derived from jobs. Thus neither the normative nor the factual rankings of occupations can be assumed to be dictated by the industrial division of labour since, hypothetically, they may vary with cultural differences. Hence, any degree of cross-cultural variation in subjective and objective occupational ranking, which cannot be attributed to the stages of economic development attained, will be sufficient to show that there is no *logical* association between occupational differentiation and social stratification, but only one of contingency. Furthermore, if the latter relationship were found to prevail the investigation of the two phenomena in a number of countries might produce some estimation of its extent and aid in the specification of those cultural factors which constitute sources of variation.

Secondly, even if a logical relationship or a very high empirical correlation were established between occupational differentiation and occupational ranking (subjectively and objectively defined), this would be insufficient reason in itself to abandon a multi-dimensional framework for the analysis of stratification systems. It would be wrong to say that just because all industrial societies adopt a similar ranking of occupations, they cease to rank individuals along other dimensions which are unrelated to it, without the production of evidence to this effect. However, as Goldthorpe[8] has indicated, those endorsing the 'logic of industrialism' point to mechanisms operating in developed economies whose effect is to reduce traditional bases of stratification to the status of variables dependent upon the occupational structure. The result of this process is a general tendency towards 'status crystallization' or 'equilibration' for individuals, since the industrial society more than any other facilitates adjustments being made in the non-congruent elements. (This involves various assumptions which will be examined later, namely that incongruence is universally perceived, universally held undesirable and that there is a universal attempt to reduce it when conditions permit.) The factors accounting for this dimensional superimposition are those leading to the open or so-called meritocratic society, to the attainment of valuable and valued social positions through achievement rather than ascription. Thus it is held that as social mobility increases, the avenues through which this occurs narrow down to the single channel, education, which is best adapted to the structural and functional imperatives of the technologically determined division of labour. Hence any evidence pointing to enduring 'status incongruence' or to a multiplicity of avenues leading to social promotion would be sufficient to indicate the necessity of retaining a multi-dimensional framework for the analysis of European stratification systems.

Occupational ranking procedures current in the United States have been criticized for confusing several dimensions of occupational prestige, and in particular for not separating the factual from the normative ratings of jobs.[9] While this is certainly true of many rating scales, much of the persuasiveness of such American research and much of its affinity to the Industrial Convergence Theory lies in the fact that high correlations have been found between subjective assessments of occupational prestige and objective factors such as income received and skill required. Thus the early work of Hatt on ranking began from the assumption that occupational 'prestige is estimable and that it lies in the opinions of others rather than in the occupation itself or any specific rewards attached to that position'.[10] However, the NORC scale of occupational prestige, developed from this research was found to correlate highly with median income level (0·85) and median level of educational attainment (0·83).[11] Structural-functionalists of course interpreted such findings as demonstrating 'the way in which functional needs are given moral support'.[12] This tripartite relationship has been expressed in the statement that 'Occupation, therefore, is the intervening activity linking income to education',[13] in an industrial society. To pass from this description of how occupations are ranked in the United States to the assertion that this represents the chief pattern for all industrializing countries requires evidence that other societies, as they move towards an advanced economy, replicate American occupational rankings, defined subjectively by prestige ratings and objectively by skill required and remuneration received.

I. Subjective rankings. One of the first cross-cultural investigations, carried out by Inkeles and Rossi, using data on matched occupations in six industrialized nations,[14] tended to give great support to the convergence theory or, as termed in the study, to 'structuralism' rather than 'culturalism'. Very high correlations were found between the rank orders of occupations or the prestige scores assigned to them indicating a marked agreement on relative prestige despite cultural variations. Only agricultural and some service occupations yielded a degree of disagreement setting them apart, but it was claimed that some of this variability could be attributed to differential degrees of development.

Surprisingly, sociologists extending this research design to the underdeveloped economies of India, the Philippines and Uruguay found occupations ranked in a way very similar to that of industrial ones, which hence 'contradicts a very heavy stress on the industrial system as the major or predominant factor in producing similarities in the occupational-prestige hierarchies of different countries'.[15] This conclusion was checked by taking GNP as a crude measure of industrialization and attempting to see whether its increase accounted for different degrees of similarity with the United States occupational rankings. 'The findings suggest that it is impossible to argue, at least for newly developing countries, that similarities in levels of industrialization induced similarities in the hierarchical evaluation of occupations, since without any substantial progress towards industrialization, many "new nations" have achieved a structure of occupational evaluations quite similar to that observed in the United States.'[16] Thus it appears that while some degree of convergence is taking place at least at this subjective level, the process of industrialization cannot account for it. It would then be the institutional apparatus of the nation state which, as it tends greatly to predate the development of the economy, is considered responsible for such similarities.

Despite obtaining an average correlation of 0·83 between the occupational rankings of twenty-three countries and that of the USA, this study registered some of the lowest degrees of association obtained to date (0·62 for Poland). In addition evidence suggested that over all countries there was less agreement on the ranks to be assigned to blue-collar occupations than for white-collar jobs. The explanation advanced for this returns to the industrialization hypothesis in considering that because blue-collar occupations are related to the 'modernization' process they are less standardized than white-collar ones which serve central social needs. Yet, if level of economic development accounts for this, it would seem strange that the similarity of blue-collar ranking is closest to the USA in New Zealand (0·92), is only 0·54 for Great Britain and 0·42 for Germany; it appears more likely that different cultural values are being reflected.

Polish research tends to support this conclusion since Wesołowski suggests that pre-war occupational prestige rankings were not strikingly different from Western scales, whereas contemporary hierarchies place skilled manual workers significantly higher than in western Europe.[17] The prestige of this group is estimated as second only to the intelligentsia (corresponding roughly to the liberal professions) and above such white-collar occupations as accountant, senior official and nurse, regardless of age, sex and social origin of raters. This change is accounted for by a change in value systems 'The incorporation of some elements of socialist ideology into the universally held value system . . . the high rating of skilled workers undermines the view, generally held until recently that in our society any type of physical work is still less esteemed than any type of intellectual work'.[18] Thus Wesołowski claims that while pre-war values stressing educational qualifications have proved resistant to ideological pressures for raising the prestige of unskilled workers (still at the bottom of rating scales), the opposite is true for skilled occupations. Such findings coincide with Mitchell's suggestion that changes in politics and ideology can over time affect the prestige of particular occupations while others remain stable.[19]

Thus research on subjective occupational ratings appears damaging to the 'Industrial convergence theory' on two grounds. Firstly, because the degree of cross-cultural similarity found cannot be attributed to the inception of an industrial division of labour since in many cases it predates economic development. Secondly, because ideological or political change at least appear capable of modifying any imperatives the economy is assumed to exert over prestige ratings. Hence there is clearly no logical association between occupational differentiation and social stratification (measured in this way) – the relationship between economic development and occupational evaluation is too complex to be captured either by simple 'structuralism' or simple 'culturalism'.

II. Objective rankings of occupations, generally in terms of income received or skills required, since they are capable of diverging from subjective estimates of prestige could theoretically show a greater degree of cross-cultural convergence. As the differences in subjective rankings were greatest between the United States and Poland, this would provide a good test case for the occurrence of convergence in objective rankings. Unfortunately no such direct comparison of rank order of occupational remuneration exists for the two countries in question. However, since it was the high evaluation given to the skilled worker in Poland which accounted for much of the divergence between Polish and American subjective rankings, some supportive evidence for objective convergence would be provided if such a group received lower remuneration than prestige in Poland. Sarapata's investigation of the objective correlates of prestige indicated, however, that the scale of remuneration and prestige for skilled workers roughly coincided.[20] This evidence is clearly too slight to serve as anything other than an indication that political policy can influence industrial remuneration as well as occupational prestige. (It would be erroneous to conclude from this that income determines prestige since in the Polish study several groups, particularly those engaged in the private sector, had lower prestige than remuneration.) The relatively high correlations found in the study mentioned above [21] between subjective occupational rankings and educational qualifications in both America and Poland indicates either that the notion of 'qualification' is itself culturally relative or that job titles (e.g. electrician or engineer) have been imperfectly standardized for the two countries. Although the latter case may certainly hold, it is significant in this connection to note that while high positive associations have been found between level of human resources development and level of economic development (measured by GNP per capita),[22] there is considerable variation *between* countries at the same stage of industrialization. This would seem to indicate that increased national wealth facilitates the expansion of education without constraining the direction of its growth. 'It is significant that there is very little correlation between the percentages of students enrolled in scientific and technical faculties in higher education and GNP or any of the

Table 1

Country	Composite Index* of human resources development	Per capita GNP in US $ 1957–8	Higher education % enrolled in	
			Science and Technology	Humanities, Law, Arts
Spain	39·6	293	16·8	55·6
Portugal	40·8	224	25·2	36·3
Greece	48·5	340	24·5	31·3
Italy	56·8	516	25·1	37·9
Yugoslavia	60·3	265	27·6	32·8
Poland	66·5	475	52·8	14·5
Federal Republic	85·8	927	24·7	29·2
France	107·8	943	32·1	46·1
United Kingdom	121·6	1,189	33·5	34·5

Source: Abstracted from F. Harbison and C. A. Myers, 'Education, Manpower and Economic Growth', pp. 47–48.

* The arithmetic total of enrolment at secondary level as a percentage of the age group 15–19, adjusted for length of schooling and enrolment at the third level of education as a percentage of the age group, multiplied by a weight of 5.

other measures. The same is true of the percentages enrolled in humanities, fine arts and law faculties.'[23] This can be clearly seen from the preceding table covering the countries included in this volume (although some have semi-advanced and others advanced economies).

Thus politico-cultural variations influence the direction of educational investment to some degree, independently of economic influences. It should not therefore be surprising to find different types or even levels of qualifications attached to the 'same' posts in different countries (the most obvious examples being those of 'manager' and 'administrator').

Thus again it appears that while a relationship of contingency exists between objective ratings of occupations and degree of industrialization this is not a logical association. Absence of adequate data prevents one assessing whether objective rankings show any greater or lesser degree of convergence than subjective ratings. However, to deny the simple determinism of industrial convergence theory by pointing to intervening variables which prevent the direct reflection of occupational differentiation in social stratification is not to criticize its complementary hypothesis that occupational positions (however gained and however esteemed) largely account for the distribution of inequalities in modern societies. In other words, to doubt the theory of convergence of stratification systems is not to deny the possibility that stratification may be largely unidimensional.[24] This statement will be initially examined from the point of view of its opponents.

B Industrial divergence theory
Those stressing a relationship of contingency rather than necessity between industrialization and uni-dimensional stratification have accepted that

> Occupation, by definition, cannot possibly be taken as describing esteem; moreover, when it is used as an index, position in one structure is substituted for a sum of positions in many structures. Its value as an index of position therefore must be established in spite of its inability to describe in detail the relevant areas of esteem and multi-structural position.[25]

However, the industrial divergence theorists doubt the existence of dimensional superimposition which is a necessary condition for occupation to function as an index of social position.

To Dahrendorf, such superimposition is located firmly in the earliest phase of industrialization, but does not survive it. During this phase, economic and political power tend to coincide, in the sense of being held by the same group, and law is directed towards the protection of property; class and status are similarly related since large-scale financial differentiation precluded overlapping 'life styles'.[26] On the other hand, advanced industrial societies are characterized by pluralism and segmentalism – as social stratification becomes increasingly multidimensional, status congruence begins to decrease accordingly.

There is many a compensation for those who are excluded from the exercise of power in contemporary European society . . . a combination of factors . . . have provided many of those who have no share in political power with a 'second chance' in other social institutions: economic, educational, voluntary. *There is no longer any one social position which determines all others, as was the case with occupation for many in nineteenth and early twentieth century Europe . . . The scales of power, prestige do not coincide any longer.*[27]

Similarly, Lipset and Zetterberg underline the need for distinguishing between class and status as distinct dimensions.

The changes which have occurred in many Western countries in recent years in the income of different occupational groups points up the necessity to consider consumption class as a distinct stratificational category. . . . An interesting result in many countries having a long-term full-employment economy combined with a reduced working-class birth rate is that a large number of families headed by men in low prestige occupations receive higher incomes than many middle-class families in which the wife does not work, and the children receive a prolonged education.[28]

Thus such theories specifically deny the consistent primacy of the economic dimension over the others in industrial society and refuse to view status and power as functions of occupational position.

There are then two main areas in which the theories of industrial convergence and divergence express contradictory expectations amenable to comparison with some empirical data. While the former postulates increased status crystallization, the latter anticipates growing status incongruence; convergence theory predicts the narrowing of methods for gaining social mobility to a single mode, while divergence theory foresees the maintenance of a multiplicity of channels.

Status Crystallization, as an objective phenomenon,[29] posits a closeness of fit between the three dimensions of stratification, such that knowledge of an individual's position on one scale enables the accurate prediction of his position on the other two. However, before a uni-dimensional framework can be adopted, one must not only show that this phenomenon *increases* with industrialization, but that the fit has become very close indeed. To consider the latter point first – it is presumably sufficient to ask if the degree of status congruence is large enough in the *most* developed economies to employ a uni-dimensional framework for practical purposes, *at the present time*. While the United States is frequently cited as a case of twentieth-century growth in status crystallization it may be doubted whether a very high degree of superimposition in fact obtains. From data collected in 1950, Duncan concluded that 'In a sample of the general population – or more strictly speaking the entire male experienced civilian labour force – one must expect the incidence of "status disequilibrium" to be fairly high or the degree of "status crystallization" to be low'.[30] Aggravation of the ethnic problem in the interim may have had the consequence of maintaining the status dimension distinct from others. While little comparable data exists for the Soviet Union, implicitly the interpretation of the Party bureaucracy as a 'new Class' endorses a growth in congruence, while the controversy surrounding this statement suggests that such dimensional superimposition is not seen as clear cut. In this case, it could not be assumed that less advanced European societies, some with substantial primary sectors of the economy, coercive or monistic political systems and traditionalistic prestige hierarchies, would be more amenable to this approach. While there are undoubtedly areas of social research in which the closeness of fit between the dimensions is sufficient to dispense with differentiation between them, this by definition cannot apply to the comparative study of social stratification.

Channels of social mobility. The possibility remains that a process of convergence and unification is occurring, such that a common mode of appointment to valued social positions on all dimensions is predominating within and between societies. While much research has emphasized the increase of inter-generational at the expense of intra-generational occupational mobility as the importance of educational qualifications grew and the possibilities of advancement through promotion, private business and emigration declined, these appear to be characteristics of the later phases of industrialism rather than the industrial revolution itself. Hence a greater diversity of modes of occupational mobility are found in the less-developed economies of southern Europe.[31] However, even if a trend towards occupational achievement promotion were accepted uncritically it neither follows that positions of power and prestige are similarly awarded nor that those whose positions on the latter two dimensions are incongruent with their occupational standing have the desire or the means through which to bring about equilibration.

Although monistic political systems may not be opposed to occupational promotion through tested educational merit, the distribution of power positions tends to be a reserved sector in which criteria of orthodoxy and commitment outweigh others. It is significant that in such societies suspicion and antagonism are greatest between the intelligentsia and political cadres. Where equilibration occurs it is coercively engineered from above through the various methods leading to occupational dismissal rather than individually achieved from below. Furthermore the endurance of ascriptive recruitment to positions carrying power in the north-western democracies of Europe has proved resistant to the increased demand for educational qualifications. It can be shown, for example, that appointments to the Higher Civil Service in England, France and Germany discriminate against certain social origins of graduate *applicants*.[32] It is certainly the case, however, that greater opportunities for equilibrating occupational positions with power exist in such countries – advisory committees to government, voluntary services, constituency politics, the magistracy and union activities may indirectly serve this function at different occupational levels. But before such means are employed to increase crystallization, status incongruence must be 'realized'. If, as Malewski has stated, 'the incongruence of status depends on normative expectations which have been formed in other men'[33] one would not expect such means to be employed for this purpose unless one could point to a normative expectation of economico-political congruence in the countries concerned. While there may be diffuse expectations that the incumbents of certain occupational roles play a more active part than others in national (bankers, financiers) or local politics (teachers and social workers) it is both difficult to view this as normative rather than descriptive and also to extend examples beyond a small range of jobs. Indeed it is almost a concomitant of large-scale democracies that a majority accept the lowest common denominator of political participation, the vote, as defining their position on the power dimension. Even if only a significant minority did so, this would be sufficient to designate at least one group not seeking equilibration between occupation and power.

In the same way it appears unlikely that the life styles related to social status, at a particular time in a given society, are narrowly associated with occupational positions gained through contest. It could be argued, of course, that since symbols conferring status must be both scarce in supply and highly valued by society, the more affluent a nation becomes, the greater the probability that desirable life styles involve more expenditure. If this were so, remuneration attached to posts would place a limit on the styles attainable to their holders. However, as Lipset and Zetterberg stressed, the income of many working-class families theoretically enables their life styles to surpass that of many middle-class households with a single salary. If this occurred, the outcome would be increased status disequilibration, whether considered as *embourgeoisement* or investment in consumer durables for their own sake. In addition, there are a number of enduring status-conferring attributes which expressly cannot be gained from holding a job (but which may have aided its being secured in a partially ascriptive structure), such as lineage, family background and, in some cases and countries, accent. Finally, while there are many examples of groups seeking to pull up or keep up on this dimension (the *nouveaux-riches* and the Joneses) it seems doubtful whether many of those concerned with status are not more involved in emulation than equilibration. In other words, there may be social groups, perhaps mainly those with blocked occupational mobility who actively seek status incongruence as representing a way to improve their overall social position.

2 THE DIFFICULTIES INVOLVED IN CROSS-CULTURAL COMPARISON OF STRATIFICATION SYSTEMS

While a multi-dimensional approach to social stratification in Europe appears indispensable in theory, each of the three traditional dimensions, 'class', 'status' and 'power' in practice presents analytical and empirical problems within this limited cross-cultural framework. In the case of each traditional facet of stratification, there seem to be obstacles inhibiting international comparisons, and thus precluding, for the time being, their treatment as variables.

Despite the theoretical controversy surrounding the concept of social class and its corresponding variety of synonymous associations, 'relations to production', 'life chances', 'rewards associated with positions in proportion to the contribution of the positions to system goals and maintenance',[34] there appears to be virtual agreement that occupation is a most important determinant of class placement. Whether primarily concerned with ranking positions (and deriving a person's rank directly from his occupational position) or with ranking persons (and subsequently using occupation as an index of class placement), two further assumptions tend to be held in common. Because of their efficiency in empirical investigations and consistency with major theoretical postulates, the family is generally considered a solidary unit of equivalent evaluation and, secondly, the head of household's occupation is taken as the best single indicator of the family's class position. While Watson and Barth[35] have underlined the deficiencies in such assumptions for studies of stratification in the United States, these are both intensified and increased in number when extended to Europe.

To view the family as a solidary unit of equivalent evaluation involves at least three subsidiary propositions, controversial in many regions and some European societies – the prevalence of the nuclear family, of strict conjugal role division, of a single 'head of household'. This outlook is itself an intrinsic part of Industrial Convergence Theory which posits the universal post-industrial development towards this type of family organization.[36] Such a view neglects the differential impact of early industrialization upon the different social classes, which to some extent strengthens extended kinship ties in the upper classes (for reasons of capital conservation)[37] and the lower classes (for reasons of mutual welfare aid),[38] only weakening them in the socially and geographically mobile professional/managerial groups.[39] Another neglected factor is that many wives work out of economic need and, that as productivity develops in scope and complexity, the economy needs more women to join the labour force. Both factors preclude strict role division and a single head of household in some sectors of the industrial community.

The number of male household heads who are not in fulltime employment in conjunction with the number of homes headed by women, lead Watson and Barth to estimate that 40 per cent of American families fall within this category and hence that 'the patriarchal family model with husband working full time at an occupation, which underlies much of stratification theory, is not an adequate model for contemporary society'.[40] In addition, growing female participation on the labour market presents two distinct problems. Firstly the multiple-wage family improves its 'life chances' or 'rewards' by cumulation relative to single wage-earner households even if its overall 'relations to production' remain stable through all sharing roughly similar occupational positions. Not only is the common practice of excluding married women's occupations as indicators of social placement thus theoretically indefensible in the case of *at least* two synonymous associations of the concept 'class', but also it would result in cross-cultural distortions of great magnitude. This becomes clear from the differences in percentage of *Women Active in Labour Force* (see Table 2).

While it is certainly true that for all countries the peak of female employment is between the ages of 20–24, that is the pre-marital or early married years, this percentage has not been halved in the 50–54 age group in Poland, Yugoslavia, France, the Federal Republic, Greece and Spain. Furthermore, since the importance of woman power is everywhere

Table 2

Country	%
Poland	40·1 (1960)
Federal Republic	31·4 (1961)
Yugoslavia	31·1 (1961)
United Kingdom	29·3 (1961)
Greece	27·8 (1961)
France	25·5 (1962)
Ireland	20·4 (1961)
Italy	19·8 (1961)
Spain	17·5 (1960)
Portugal	13·1 (1960)

Source: ILO *Yearbook of Labour Statistics*, 1967, p. 30 ff.

increasing this is not a theoretical difficulty which is or will be empirically resolved by their withdrawal from active employment on marriage. The existence in Europe of such large differentials not closely related to level of economic development (though possibly associated with rate of economic growth), aggravates the problem in the absence of cross-tabulated data on marital status, level of employment and husbands' occupation.

Secondly, a working couple may differ from one another in terms of all three associations of the concept 'class'. The 1960 United States Census indicated that husband's occupational status was similar to wife's in only 22 per cent of cases, his exceeding hers in 36 per cent, and hers his in 42 per cent. Of such couples, 40 per cent were characterized by one white-collar spouse (usually the wife) and one blue-collar spouse (usually the husband).[41] If holding to the same extent in Europe, this throws some doubt on the expectation that the standing of family 'is more likely to reflect the occupation of the husband than that of the wife if both are employed'.[42] It again tends to the more conservative proposition that family placement in such cases is mutually determined.

Finally, a specific European problem, stimulated by labour mobility within the Common Market countries, is presented by the family of the emigrant worker. In these cases, particularly if the wife is employed or works the landholding, the 'householder' is difficult to determine. In the case of this still being considered the husband, is his occupation abroad to be assessed in relation to his host or home country? This again raises the question of international comparability, which those stressing the importance of 'work situation' as a component of class tend to answer in the negative. Such authors point to 'the need of recording not only occupational class but also *occupational setting*, that is, the kind of social system in which the occupation is found'.[43] Even supposing such scruples overruled, a variable proportion of a nation's occupations could be matched cross-culturally, comparisons of international prestige ratings only dealing with jobs, both shared by and well-known in all cultures. The universal exclusion of agricultural employment, with its enduring emphasis on property rather than occupation[44] from such studies, would have the effect of omitting over 30 and sometimes as much as 57 per cent of the economically active population in Spain, Greece, Ireland, Poland, Portugal and Yugoslavia.

Thus it appears that, leaving aside theoretical questions about the relationship between occupation and any of the synonymous associations of the term 'class', there are sufficient empirical difficulties to preclude its present usage for cross-cultural investigation in Europe. It is interesting to note with reference to Industrial convergence theory that among the three main obstacles to employing occupation in this way – working wives, international labour mobility and the endurance of the primary sector of the economy – only the latter tends to decrease with economic development, while the former two are stimulated. Finally, of the most frequently employed alternatives or supplements to occupation – income, education and residence – the same three obstacles apply directly to income, rather more indirectly to education, while the second and third are relevant to residence, in addition to the other specific difficulties which each presents in this context.

While many have acknowledged the difficulties involved in cross-cultural comparisons of class structure as insuperable, there is virtual unanimity in accepting this situation for 'status' and 'power'. Runciman has aptly summarized the problems entailed in scaling either dimension. In the former, it would 'be necessary somehow to decide the relative weight to be assigned to one distinction as against another and to measure the social distance by which individuals or strata are accordingly separated'.[45] If achieved, the distribution of the population studied could be plotted and if the scorings related to a common scale, compared with other populations. Yet factors such as variation in criteria by which status is accorded with time and place, incommensurate nature of criteria and absence of a common yardstick by which to compare the social distance separating two groups of superiors and inferiors, preclude the kind of description necessary for subsequent measurement and comparison.

Similar difficulties are related to the dimension of 'power', where in addition to the problem of obtaining a precise ranking of individuals with reference to it, there is also the impossibility of discovering an individual's power without experimental evidence. While such power may be assessed when restricted to a given role in which its scope and limits are specified, this is to ignore a multiplicity of alternative or supplementary sources of power. Furthermore, 'even if a political structure can be clearly described in terms of the power assigned to the various offices within it and the chances of the representative member of any designated group coming to hold one of these offices, it will still be possible to make only a limited and partial comparison between the distribution of power in one society and another. Even in such a relatively simple, relatively homogeneous and relatively well-documented set of cases as the traditional kingdoms of Africa cannot be compared with each other except in very broad and largely qualitative terms. When it comes to societies as large, complex and sophisticated as those of the advanced industrial nations, then the advantage of greater possibilities of quantification within limited areas is more than offset by the intricacy and incommensurability of the other areas which the researcher must take into account if he is to attempt to plot inequalities of power on even the most rudimentary kind of scale.[46]

While it is not intended to imply the ultimate unscalability of the three dimensions or to deny the differential progress made towards international comparability in terms of 'class' rather than 'status' and 'power', the fact remains that contemporary cross-cultural studies cannot treat the various aspects of social stratification quantitatively. The study of European societies is thus still restricted to qualitative appreciations and comparisons of major trends in social ranking, to detecting the presence or absence of attributes in different cultures rather than measuring variables. Because of this, the rest of this paper will be devoted to the discussion of dominant themes in the changing European class structure, variations in the outstanding forms of social distinction and modifications in the major power roles and chances to occupy them.

3 SOCIAL MOBILITY

Two major themes concerning social mobility are dominant in the Industrial convergence theory – the increasing rate of mobility with economic development and the growing importance of achievement rather than ascriptive criteria in social promotion.[47] Since such a theoretical approach, as mentioned earlier, accepts the existence of dimensional superimposition in the stratification systems of developed nations, the two themes are automatically applied to status and power as well as to the more frequently studied occupational structure. The different stages of economic development attained, together with the multiple methodological difficulties characterizing cross-cultural studies of social mobility preclude the discussion of these themes in the European context in other than broad and tentative terms.[48]

A Occupational mobility
The three main aspects of occupational mobility – collective, inter-generational and intra-generational – are empirically difficult to distinguish both in terms of causes and consequences, since individual 'effects' and collective 'effects' are often juxtaposed or compounded.[49] Nevertheless some very general descriptive and analytical statements can be made about the rate and relationship of these three aspects of social mobility, with regard to at least one factor, education.
Collective mobility. It is frequently stated that for the most advanced European economies century-long changes in technology have resulted in a repatterning of the occupational

structure such that the pyramid of early industrialism is converted to a diamond-shaped structure. The types of component structural change involved have been summarized by W. E. Moore[50] to include sectoral relocation, particularly the growth of non-agricultural employment; specialization, the subdivision and multiplication of skills; upgrading, the proportional shifts to higher skill categories; and bureaucratization, the organization of specialized labour into large administrative units. While these are interrelated in the advanced economy, the presence or absence and differential importance of such factors varies with specific forms of economic development. Thus, for example, while there appears to be a tendency in western Europe for the secondary and tertiary sectors to reach parity in the proportion of the economically active population employed, or for the latter to exceed the former, in Poland, Yugoslavia and Czechoslovakia, the rate of employment in the tertiary sector is approximately half that characterizing the secondary.[51] Such variations which can be cited for each element, being partially independent from level of economic development, may lead to quantitative and qualitative differences in collective mobility patterns and in the speed with which the 'diamond' transformation occurs.

Secondly, such changes in occupational structure may proceed independently from any normative change endorsing increased educational qualifications or selection by merit. While for most countries there is some correlation between economic growth and educational expansion it cannot be assumed that the labour market required more instruction in the labour force rather than merely reflecting provisions made on other grounds. Furthermore, there are sufficient discontinuities between educational and economic development to indicate that the relationship is contingent rather than necessary. While at the end of the nineteenth century industrial England had only just begun to develop a national educational system, pre-industrial France had instituted a centralized state system, vocational in content and merit-oriented in selection at the beginning of the nineteenth century. The types of collective mobility occurring in England may have been related to productive skills, but to skills acquired independently from formal instruction.

In this case at least, education was less the 'handmaiden of industrialism'[52] than the reluctant bride.

Inter-generational mobility. Ideally any statements made about the manifestly greater rate of inter-generational mobility in industrial societies should be preceded by an assessment of the proportion of such movements which can be attributed to collective mobility. Marsh[53] has even argued that if such changes in the occupational structure could be 'subtracted', there would be no residue requiring explanation in terms of changed values and norms encouraging mobility. However, while these two possible influences on upward mobility are difficult to separate empirically,[54] an increased rate of downward movements in industrial societies might witness to changes in the distribution of opportunity or accessibility. As Miller has argued, downward mobility is also influenced by changes in occupational and demographic structure, but it may well be a better indicator of social fluidity and is certainly a better index of the openness of societies and/or subsectors of society.[55] It may be significant in this connection that the only aspect of Lipset's thesis[56] that rates of mobility are similar in industrialized nations, to be roughly confirmed in Miller's cross-cultural study, concerned upward mobility rates from manual into non-manual occupations.[57] Apart from this, the two measures of downward movement (non-manual into manual occupations and rates of movement out of the elite strata) varied widely within Europe. Here mobility was not a symmetrical phenomenon, a nation could be high in one measure of mobility and low in another.

Despite these variations in rates, it has been argued that standardization and limitation of channels of mobility has taken place, so that education predominates over traditional methods of ascent. In no country, however, can a complete shift from ascriptive to achievement recruitment be posited. In all, social origin and level of education have an independent influence on the occupational position of sons, but also a combined effect via the relationship between socio-economic status and education obtained. It was recently concluded for the United States that 'The impact on occupational status of education independent of social origin is considerably greater than that of social origin independent of education'. This finding implies that the influence of fathers' socio-economic status on sons' status is largely mediated in the United States by education.'[58] Very similar results were obtained in Sweden and Denmark, while a slightly higher degree of association between sons' and fathers' status was found in Britain.[59] Any further increase in the importance of education will be a function of growing commitment to policies for democratizing instruction and of their effectiveness. Eastern European data tends to suggest that even the operation of negative educational sanctions against the socially 'privileged' is insufficient to destroy the association between social origins and educational achievement. Finally it should be noted that, even if selection by merit were universalized, the historical and political circumstances which have shaped national educational systems may lead to an enduring cultural relativity in the skills and abilities equated with merit.

Intra-generational mobility has been given little attention cross-culturally although some have stressed its increasing importance in the context of economic individualism.[60] Potentially this aspect of mobility could display the greatest international variations, since in industrialized nations it is related to the extensiveness of career structures. As the advantage to be derived from self-employment decreases with the growth of capital investment required for competitiveness of the small enterprise, the vast majority of individuals become dependent on the promotion prospects of their appointments for advancement, and on the possibility of moving between hierarchically organized appointments. The Western pattern appears to have intensified the barriers between appointments, while increasingly differentiating echelons within them in each country. Because of the *specificity* of qualifications demanded on appointment, occupational transferability decreases for all but the manual categories, although the locus of practice may become more varied, i.e. the metallurgist will find it difficult to be employed in any other capacity, but the openings available to him will be more numerous. The *level* of qualification tends to mark off the range of hierarchical movement possible for any individual. Some, however, have argued that the distinction between certain levels of qualifications (e.g. in Britain Secondary Modern and Grammar School-Apprenticeship/'A' levels) represent greater limitations on occupational mobility than others. In this case, a given level of qualification represents a watershed[61] between two distinct and non-overlapping parts of the occupational hierarchy – *le niveau représente la barrière*. Nevertheless, within *both* parts of the distribution career prospects have improved (independently) as job echelons have multiplied with increasing specialization. This would appear to be equally true of professions[62] as of trades. Hence, while initial appointment will depend heavily on level and type of qualification, echelon promotion in the West will be less dependent on both. It may be this factor which accounts for Blau and Duncan's finding that the maximum influence of education on occupational level is at thirty years of age and decreases thereafter.[63] The post-war eastern European policy attempted to increase echelon promotion, while leaving the whole range of hierarchical movement open to those showing merit through practice rather than qualification. As the perceived utility of formal qualifications increased following the discouraging results gained by promotion from the ranks, the western pattern tends to be replicated throughout socialist economies.[64] Interestingly an analogous occupational watershed appears to exist between those whose educational qualification is limited to a general secondary school-leaving certificate and those who acquire a specific professional qualification at secondary or higher level.[65]

B Non-occupational mobility
Many have pointed to an analogous change in power and status such that in the advanced industrial period their distributions are also transformed from pyramid to diamond shape. In the former case, the numerical growth of those placed towards the middle of the power distribution, those who in some capacity are concerned with executing, adjudicating or advising on policy is generally accounted for in two ways. Firstly, a universal factor, the increased division of labour in power, related to the spread of bureaucratization, is held by Dahrendorf to account for the swollen ranks of what he calls the 'Service Class'.[66] Secondly, the growth of political pluralism in the western democracies has resulted in a multiplication of elite positions. With regard to status, the conjunction between increased affluence, lowered income

differentials and a growing communality of 'consumption culture' sponsored by the mass media is often held to facilitate, if not advance, a convergence in life styles. However, the parallel modifications undergone in the distributions of the three dimensions of stratification does not necessarily imply a higher degree of status consistency. The fact that three pyramids have almost simultaneously been transformed to three diamond-shaped distributions *may* reproduce the same lack of consistency between the dimensions in the latter case as in the former. Nevertheless, those who oversimplify by positing that mobility on all dimensions is increasingly determined by achievement rather than ascriptive criteria implicitly endorse growing status consistency as the importance of education develops in relation to all aspects of social mobility. Kahl neatly summarizes this outlook, presenting such changes as dynamically integrated.

Income and prestige now flow from education and occupation (as they used to flow from property ownership). As the middle-ranks on the educational-occupational hierarchy expand, so do the 'middle classes' as judged by consumption styles and patterns of respect and deference. . . . These changes in turn produce political changes: the franchise expands, all adults become citizens, and the complete monopolization of knowledge and power in the hands of a tiny permanent elite becomes impossible.[67]

The more contentious concepts of 'meritocracy' and 'technocracy' are merely special cases of the same outlook, albeit more pessimistic in general. As in the case of occupational mobility such statements about rates of movement and the role of education must now be examined in relation to Power and Status.

Power mobility. Much of the debate surrounding this issue appears to stem from the difficulty of specifying all political positions and roles in a variety of systems undergoing rapid change. Consequently diverse operational definitions tend to be employed in research whose results, understandably, tend to be inconclusive. It would seem useful to avoid confusion by distinguishing between three aspects of power in the following discussion – political power (power as a profession), occupational power (derived from occupation) and influential power (independent from occupation).

The most frequent type of analysis concentrates upon power

as an occupation, examining mobility in relation to political offices in a given nation – representatives, higher civil servants, heads of armed forces, members of the judiciary etc. The thesis of growing meritocracy, which also refers to this aspect of power, postulates that eligibility for recruitment to the political elite, takes place on the basis of formally tested educational merit. Since 'the recruitment process itself adheres to the dominant values of the system',[68] it is unsurprising to find that where ideological orthodoxy is the most important criterion, elite positions may be allocated with only minimal reference to formal qualifications. This is particularly striking in eastern Europe where political positions are significant exceptions to the rule of meritocratic occupational appointment, but also characterizes the Mediterranean region though to a lesser extent. In the northwestern democracies, eligibility for elite positions is clearly wider, without this necessarily resulting in a broad basis of recruitment. Most studies have emphasized the endurance of ascriptive criteria, in many cases despite attempts at democratizing recruitment, in the context of an overall rise in educational qualifications.[69] There are, however, considerable cross-cultural variations in the extent to which ascriptive criteria are, and can be, applied to particular elite roles. For example, the relative prestige, remuneration and prospects attached to a career in the higher civil services in Europe appear important determinants of the way in which German, French and British civil services have remained aristocratic and the Italian, Belgian and Swiss[70] have become more open.

Power derived from occupations refers to those positions, which, while not exclusively concerned with the exercise of power, but with some other primary goal, nevertheless carry a decision-making capacity, potential for influence or advisory role susceptible of affecting the political elite. It is to this aspect of power that the thesis of technocracy relates, 'generalists' by one cultural definition or another, occupying the major elite positions in Europe.[71] Since, historically, the expert and particularly the technologist have both been relatively deprived of power and recruited from backgrounds similarly deprived, any change in influence would represent a kind of collective mobility in terms of power. However, as an occupational group in Europe, scientists and technologists have had no difficulty in becoming managers or even directors, but their political influence often is still felt to be small.[72] Undoubtedly, with increased economic planning and state intervention the role of the expert has everywhere increased, yet paradoxically it is in the most advanced economies in Europe that the greatest checks on his influence are found. Apparently, the greater the degree of political pluralism, the more efficiently the power of technocrats is checked – even though it may have increased relatively speaking. If one considers advisory committees to government there seems to have been a tendency for the expert committee and the representative committee to have developed apace and, on mixed committees, for the deliberate counter-balancing of experts by representatives of organizations, associations, or the general public. This is only one aspect of the wider process by which the growth in unionization and professional associations has paralleled technological advance in the West. Despite the overall growth in influence of this group, their increase in status (from being the educationally despised and rejected whose public image was confused with that of the technicians), appears more striking than their gain on the power dimension.

Changes in power unrelated to occupation nearly always take the form of collective mobility, the main exception being the relatively unexplored area of the non-expert, financially disinterested pressure group.[73] The historical growth of enfranchisement and the more complex development of citizenship rights as a corollary of diverse political changes in Europe have generally preceded rather than followed the extension of education to the groups involved. As far as the Western democracies are concerned the English Chartists appear to have been accurate in their analysis that 'Education will follow the suffrage as sure as day succeeds night'.[74] It would be equally true to say that in eastern Europe the dictatorship of the proletariat has preceded its instruction. Furthermore the existence of authoritarian governments, which in southern Europe curtail the rights of citizenship of the intelligentsia and the rest of society (whose level of in-struction may have risen considerably under such regimes), indicates that while an educated people may be a necessary condition of democracy it is far from being a sufficient one.

Thus it appears that when power is subdivided into these three types a considerable variability in the rates of mobility characterizes the European nations in relation to each of them. It is on the second type – power derived from occupation – that there is most similarity, after having taken the level of economic development into account. Both power as occupation and power unrelated to occupation appear to be responsive to political rather than economic factors and also to show the greatest degree of deviation from achievement criteria in selection procedures or definitions of eligibility for political participation.

Status mobility, the most difficult to measure, refers to a change in life style, from a less to a more socially valued consumption pattern. If evaluative criteria remain constant, mobility on this dimension will depend on either increased objective capacity for attaining the positively assessed life style(s) and/or increased subjective desire to adopt such consumption patterns. It might be argued that the growing urbanization of Europe has been a major agent in standardizing life styles simply by reducing the range of national variation, and of mobility where the national evaluation of the rural way of life was low. However, to claim that in general status is now conferred with greater reference to achieved rather than ascribed styles is to posit a universal shift in the subjective criteria by which status honour is accorded. Such an argument frequently states that in the subsistence economy the lack of surplus material resources tended to restrict status differentiation to a range of ascribed characteristics. With increasing affluence status honour is allegedly redirected to material symbols leading to a growing association between income and status. Such an outlook often confuses expenditure on status 'neutral' objects by many groups with a narrowing of status differentials – it is guilty of the 'washing-machine-is-not-a-washing-machine' fallacy. It also fails to point out the endurance, or possibly even the revaluation, of non-material symbols, as others become more accessible. Hence the continuation, as means of social discrimination of accent in England, of lineage in Republican France, Federal Germany and even in Socialist Poland and the USSR. However, such criteria serve to distinguish traditional elites from the rest of the population, they do not differentiate among the non-elite. Where these are concerned, enduring status differences seem rooted not in lack of objective material ability to adopt superior life styles, but rather in a mass of intangible nuances of tastes affecting dress, furnishings, leisure pursuits etc. – a mass of preferences induced by tradition, supported by culture and transmitted in socialization.

While status mobility is the most difficult of the dimensions to compare cross-culturally, some of its aspects being restricted to specific regions and communities, there would, on the face of it, appear to be little relation between the increasing permeability of status barriers and their penetration by growing numbers. Much further research is however required before any comparisons on rates and avenues of mobility are attempted.

4 THE TRANSFORMATION OF THE PEASANTRY

Although industrial society is European in origin, a traditional peasantry has until the recent past remained relatively immune from the impact of industrialization and continued to affect the politics, economies and cultures of most European countries. After the second world war, as agricultural incomes continued to lag behind industrial ones, rural exodus persisted,[75] and, in the south of Europe, reached unprecedented proportions. The relative depopulation of the countryside, accompanied by the growth of provincial centres, has been paralleled by the penetration of industry in rural areas and the industrialization of agriculture. As a result, the rural population has acquired new status and occupational characteristics in becoming the rural strata of industrial society.[76] Simultaneously, rural migrants have been integrated into other sectors of the economy. They have not always been absorbed by the secondary sector, since industrial development and rural exodus have been imperfectly correlated and since the considerable expansion of the service sector (particularly open to women) has become a decisive factor in the restratification of modern societies. Thus Colin Clark's scheme of transfer from agriculture to industry and industry to services posited as characteristic of economic modernization seems inadequate for the post-second world war period. Under modern technological conditions, even economically backward countries can avoid this sequence.[77]

The entry of rural migrants into the other sectors of the economy does not everywhere occur in one single step. As Amassari has recently shown in relation to Italy, 'on the whole the trend is from agriculture and craft or services into urban non-manufacturing occupations: . . . migrants from subsistence agriculture, dying crafts and stationary services increase the urban under-employed who are ready to become industrial workers as soon as the opportunity arises'.[78] This hypothesis of a two-step flow in sectoral re-employment is applicable to southern European countries other than Italy.[79] Consequently, the stratification of the lower classes follows a double pattern: that of advanced industrialized societies where a new working class has already emerged with a distinctive life style and that of less developed economies in which the working class is still a proletariat, a 'dwindling stratum of totally unskilled labourers who are characteristically either newcomers to industry (beginners, former agricultural labourers, immigrants) or semi-unemployables'.[80] While rural migrants swell this proletariat, only the older age group, which is in the minority, is never absorbed by the 'established' working class. Indeed, young migrants view their membership of the unskilled proletariat as strictly transitional. During this transition period, they acquire a preliminary 'occupational socialization', through which they become acquainted with the attitudes and culture of the modern working class, to the detriment of traditional values and community attachments.[81] However, the integration of rural migrants into the working class is not smooth and often is only partial, thus to some extent perpetuating differentiation among industrial workers in terms of geographical origin. As Touraine and Ragazzi have shown,[82] attitudinal differences may be enduring and result both in higher expectations of inter-generational mobility and greater dissatisfaction with the work situation among former rural workers.[83]

In addition, international labour mobility – mainly originating from rural areas – carries this working-class differentiation beyond national borders. In countries like Switzerland, where most menial jobs are consigned to foreigners, the indigenous system of stratification is supplemented by new strata. As a result of ethno-cultural discrimination and prejudice, foreign workers are adopted as negative reference groups particularly by indigenous manual workers, thereby increasing the complexity of the status hierarchies and social distance networks in the whole society. This phenomenon has been insufficiently studied and even less attention has been paid to the return of former emigrants to their countries of origin.[84] Such an occurrence may have been uncommon when migrations were mainly transatlantic, but is bound to become more frequent now that they occur between southern and northern Europe, and to have a corresponding impact on the future modernization of such areas as Sicily, Macedonia or Andalusia.

5 THE RISE OF THE NEW WORKING CLASS: STRATA FORMA-
TION AND STATUS DIFFERENTIATION

It is not only among Marxists that Marx's assumption about the inevitable and increasing homogeneity of the working class has proved durable. Indeed the theory of mass society, so often embraced by right-wing critics of modern industrial civilization, incorporates this assumption and extends it to the whole of society.[85] It was perhaps these dual pressures of Marxism and right-wing pessimism which accounted for the slow recognition by sociologists of the forces counteracting homogeneity during the inter-war period. Empirical studies of the new working class conducted since the end of the war have not succeeded in dispelling this emphasis on homogeneity, and the very entrenchment of this view has cast counter-arguments in a polemic mould.[86]

While the political and ideological connotations of the 'unity of the working class' were bound to influence socio-logical theory, such events as the failure of the *Front Populaire* in France, the rise and the fall of Stalinism, and the institu-tionalization of Communist parties in the political systems of western Europe allowed many sociologists to escape from the synoptic view of the modern working classes. First came the realization of intra-working class occupational differentiation and its corresponding division into three large strata with characteristic life chances and to some extent life styles: the skilled workers and new craftsmen, the semi-skilled workers and the unskilled.[87] The discrepancies between these groups prompted sociologists, and Dahrendorf in particular, to doubt the unity of the working class.[88] In his study published in 1957, Dahrendorf claimed that in modern industrial society the distance between the three strata was too great to be bridged by what class solidarity prevailed among them. He referred to a decomposition of the working class rather than to an extreme form of differentiation.[89]

However, Dahrendorf's opinion appears to be overstated even in relation to the most industrialized areas of Europe. Among other evidence, Popitz and others have shown that subjectively workers of all strata from the Ruhr iron industry tend to view society in dichotomous terms, as divided between 'us' and 'them'.[90] Such subjective perceptions of the class structure should not however blur intra-class and intra-occupational distinctions, of which workers also have a keen awareness and on which they base their own status scales as well as their assessment of merits and rewards. The degree of emphasis on inter- or intra-class distinctions can be seen as dependent on the perspective adopted by the worker or workers at a given time, provided conditions of economic prosperity allow for the coexistence of both types of distinctions. Hence in advanced industrialized societies class consciousness coexists with stratum consciousness, defined as a perception of belonging to an occupational group and, through membership of this group, to the working class. Firstly, stratum consciousness provides the worker with a range of intra-class (positive and negative) reference groups which will largely determine his hostilities and loyalties in everyday life. Secondly, through the essential features of his work situation and of the social connections provided by his occupations, stratum consciousness imposes on the worker a class consciousness, which modern conditions have transformed rather than erased.[91]

Yet discontinuities in occupational ranking and the low degree of status crystallization mentioned earlier prevent stratum consciousness in the working class from becoming well-delineated. Studies of the labour force have shown that there appears to be no linear relationship between occupational roles and social status. Nosow and Form have attempted to enumerate some of the causes for these discontinuities and incongruencies. According to them, in industrial societies:

1. The occupational structure itself is not an absolutely or clearly ordered status continuum.

2. The occupational structure is undergoing very rapid change, increasing the ambiguity of occupational roles.

3. There is a continuous change in the numbers and types of persons entering the labour market, partly because of the changes in the occupational structure, but also because of changing community definitions of what is appropriate behaviour for women, the young, and the aged. In addition, the tremendous amount of geographic mobility in the United States has increased the ambiguities of occupational roles because the status of migrants is often ambiguous.[92]

4. Contradictory values also operate in the community to becloud both the occupational and the general community status structures. Such contradictory values are evinced on the one hand by the community desire to define who is qualified for particular jobs through differential and discriminatory hiring, and on the other by the desire of given firms to maximize the output through hiring the most technically competent.[93]

Technological change and such cultural trends as egalitarianism have resulted in the growth of a complex and fluid occupational structure with a correspondingly complex system of status stratification. The increase in status inconsistency[94] is a concomitant of this fluidity and complexity. It is most frequent among strata bordering on two classes, e.g. among affluent skilled workers. In such a case, while income 'pulls' upwards, occupational role 'keeps manual workers in their place' socially, emphasizing their membership of the working class.

Thus two characteristics distinguish the modern from the traditional working class. They can be viewed as the embodiment of two opposite social trends. On the one hand, the distinctions between the three strata of workers are hardening. This is accentuated as the gulf widens between the most skilled sections of the working class (the 'aristocracy of labour' as Serge Mallet terms them[95]) and the unskilled proletariat, often swollen by rural migrants.[96] Despite ideological statements to the contrary, little solidarity obtains between the strata polarized by skill, and their behaviour patterns when in conflict with other classes, the state and labour organizations are widely different. On the other hand, status groups are sufficiently loose for abundant inconsistencies to exist. The indeterminedness and fluidity of status systems reflects not only the rapid pace of social change, but also the gradual institutionalization of recruitment by merit in modern societies with their universal systems of education.

Class conflict, 'embourgeoisement' and depolitization of the working class

'European sociology after World War II', comments Dahrendorf, 'started with a large number of studies in industrial sociology. Most of these were devoted to the working class and betray the disappointment on the part of their authors with this class.'[97] This disenchantment can be attributed to a dilution in the class consciousness experienced by the working class and a decline in the class conflict in which it engages. Two explanatory concepts were advanced in order to account for this double phenomenon. On the one hand 'the sudden advance of the *embourgeoisement* of the working class'[98] was held responsible for lessened class consciousness, as workers' life styles and aspirations approximated more closely to those of the middle class. This interpretation concentrated on converging patterns of consumption rather than on enduring differences between relations to production. Thus 'discussion on the *embourgeoisement* issue revealed a very one-sided emphasis on the worker as a consumer rather than a producer'.[99] On the other hand, increased affluence was also held responsible for the channelling of working-class militancy into institutionalized forms of economic bargaining and away from class struggle. This *depolitization* is the counterpart on the power dimension of *embourgeoisement* on the status dimension.

Embourgeoisement

Despite some references to the widespread acceptance of this thesis among sociologists[100] and its considerable appeal as fodder for the journalist and reassurance for the conservative reader, recent research has not confirmed the adequacy of this concept. The theoretical assumptions underpinning it have been questioned by Runciman[101] and Dahrendorf,[102] while the empirical findings of Serge Mallet on the *nouvelle classe ouvrière*,[103] corroborated by Richard Hamilton's research on French workers 'after affluence'[104] ruled out any serious claims of *embourgeoisement* amongst the new, highly skilled groups of workers. In studying the effects of affluence on certain skilled sections of the British working class, Goldthorpe, Lockwood and their collaborators have arrived at a similar conclusion.

A certain standard of living, measured simply by income and possessions does not . . . result in any direct way either in participation in different membership groups or in the adoption of reference groups other than those which derived from [the worker's] role as a manual wage-earner. Being affluent does not mean that the worker becomes a member of middle-class society or even aspires to such membership.[105]

Different conditions may obtain in some socialist states. Thus in Yugoslavia, as Frank Parkin observes, skilled workers rank higher (in both social and economic rewards) than the lower white-collar employees. The latter, then, 'do not comprise the tail-end of a more prosperous professional middle-class endowed with greater prestige'.[106]

However, even if economic prosperity has not transformed the aspirations held by workers in the western countries, it is argued that ties with the middle class have become more extensive and are likely to increase in the future. As white-collar employment expands more rapidly than blue-collar jobs, the likelihood grows that workers (and especially their wives) will be absorbed by the tertiary sector[107] – the occupational stronghold of the modern middle classes. It is from the angle of sectorial mobility that one should study the potential *embourgeoisement* of the affluent section of the working class.

Since there has been no evidence of changing values in western European societies in the positive evaluation of non-manual work and the lower assessment of manual occupations, the worker does not pass the barriers imposed by this distinction, no matter how skilled and well-paid he might be. He remains of his class – even though the working class has acquired an unprecedented complexity. While group promotion is thus restricted by the enduring manual/non-manual dichotomy, individual social mobility is facilitated by the increased range of occupations available within the working class itself, especially for its younger members, since a 'career' is now possible within the boundaries of this class. This intra-class mobility has not been accompanied, however, by a similar increase in inter-class mobility. It is a surprising lack in societies characterized by developed educational systems and by an emphasis on achievement in the general value orientation. The obstacle to this form of mobility can no longer be imputed to the 'evil intentions' of the ruling class, which may be interested in self-preservation, but operates in a context of educational, fiscal and economic policies increasingly equalizing opportunity. The most common explanation for class rigidity has been sought in the existence of subcultures. The lower educational aspirations, motivation and linguistic skills of the working class have been held to account for the lower school attainment of its children. This limitation imposed by pupils' class of origin at the time of their schooling may of course begin to be countered by a general trend towards higher 'school consciousness' among the lower classes.[108] The relative 'poverty' of the imagery, vocabulary and thought processes of this class and the inadequacy of its culture in socializing for the universalistic, individualistic and instrumental orientations required for upward mobility, contribute to its isolation from the middle class. It is the maintenance of such barriers which makes the concept of *embourgeoisement* questionable, even in the affluent European societies.

Depolitization

The varying levels of economic development in Europe, both inter- and intra-nationally, the wide range of existing political systems and the ideological implications of any reference to class conflict – particularly in the Iberian peninsula or the popular democracies – have tended to restrict research on this problem, except in the established parliamentary democracies. It can, however, be anticipated that in any political context, regardless of affluence, the endurance of inequalities associated with classes and of barriers inhibiting mobility between them will result in some form of class conflict. Widespread working-class unrest throughout 1969, accompanied in Italy by demands which go beyond the reformism characteristic of post-second world war western democracies, highlights the unstability of the present situation. Moreover, in countries with 'older' class systems, such as Greece and Spain, militant movements advocating an intensification of class struggle are likely to appear in the near future. Indeed the lower strata of their working class continue to grow as industrialization progresses, while tensions are exacerbated by the political rule of non-socialist regimes with a definite class bias.

The alleged depolitization of the working class refers to an institutionalization of class conflict through unionization and the establishment of left-wing parties in politics.[109] In a variety of political contexts, increased affluence has been associated with an attenuation of working-classes militancy proceeding apace with the differentiation of the economic and political organizations of this class. To describe this phenomenon as depolitization, as a deplorable result of the consumer or affluent mass society, is to forget the true nature of political pluralism. Although class warfare in the traditional sense has virtually disappeared in Europe,[110] class conflict has not been fully institutionalized within unions and parties. In fact its outbursts in the form of wild-cat strikes and popular demonstrations have often been directed in several parts of Europe against the union or party which is supposed to represent workers.[111] Such examples indicate firstly, that the double absorption of class conflict by unions and parties is incomplete and secondly, that under circumstances in which class antagonism is exacerbated new militant organization must arise, involving a condemnation of the bureaucratized agencies. The partial loss of control by the CGT in France in May 1968 illustrated this process; the fact that it has largely recovered its earlier position indicates a conservatism among the working class which cannot be attributed to institutionalization alone.

According to Dahrendorf 'class conflict is a form of contest which becomes necessary if large numbers of individuals cannot realize their interests by individual endeavour',[112] and it is precisely the heightened possibilities of individual advancement which have smothered the extreme forms of class conflict. To acknowledge this fact does not imply the existence of social equality or the equalization of opportunities, merely the abolition of cruder forms of class repression in conjunction with wider educational opportunities and better employment prospects in a growing tertiary sector.[113] Thus, as Dahrendorf says, 'since structures of power restrict the individual's chances to realize his interests for himself, solidary action is probably bound to remain one of the vehicles of contest even in an open society'.[114]

6 THE EUROPEAN MIDDLE CLASSES: OLD AND NEW

Differentiation within the middle classes has been perceived and analysed earlier than the complexity of the working classes.[115] This tradition can be traced back to Marx's *Les luttes de classe en France* and paradoxically it is only in recent years that some sociologists have oversimplified the composition of the middle classes.[116] In fact the delineation of this group remains a problem; despite advances in methodology, definition of its borders is still arbitrary to some degree.[117] While both the middle and the working classes are composed of multiple strata, the former are characterized by a more tenuous solidarity, a greater variety of political organizations and a wider range of economic goals, precluding class unity even in times of crisis. Middle-class alliances are ephemeral and sometimes kaleidoscopic, in view of various strata's separate allegiance to the ruling groups and their respective political and economic standpoints. Confronted with this situation, social scientists have tended to formulate negative definitions of the middle classes as that set of strata which is located between manual workers and the ruling class, without belonging to either. While negative definitions tend to be poor, this seems to be the most poverty-stricken of all, such is the variety of the groups lumped under one blanket term. Contrary to most radical predictions, this section of the population keeps growing in size and, since the end of the second world war, in self-confidence.

Efforts to overcome this conceptual difficulty centre on the distinction between the old and the new middle class. While the term 'new middle class' was used by Schmoller in 1897,[118] it is generally attributed to Lederer and Marschak (*Der neue Mittelstand*, 1926)[119] who diagnosed the existence of a new social stratum in contemporary society, which was not an extension of the traditional middle classes. Between the two wars the view that this stratum was substantially composed of 'bureaucratic officials and private employees working for a salary' tended to prevail. While some sociologists maintained that formally such wage earners belonged to the proletariat,[120] this was firmly rejected in the post-war period, as the new middle class continued to grow in size and occupational complexity, and displayed a diversity of outlooks, subcultures and behaviour patterns.[121]

Yet this subdivision into old and new does not constitute a definition of the middle classes; it merely differentiates between occupational roles, assigning shopkeepers, small businessmen and the liberal professions, for example, to the traditional middle classes, and technologists, economic planners and university teachers, together with the medium levels of management, to the new. Consequently, doubts have been expressed about the class character of this complex category. Thus Dahrendorf remarks that 'the new middle classes were born "decomposed" . . . a group that is not a group, class that is not a class and stratum that is not a stratum'.[122] Similar in nature are Hoggart's reference to the 'classless class' and Crozier's to 'la classe sans conscience'.[123] Despite increased opportunities for upward mobility and the consequent intensity of personal involvement with the occupational group rather than with class, members of the new middle classes seem capable of subjectively placing themselves in that category and of assigning many of their fellows to it. Thus the privatization of middle-class individuals does not imply the nonexistence of the new middle classes.[124]

However, the growth of this group has not corresponded to a complementary decline of the traditional middle classes. Although there has been some relative reduction in their size, neither welfare nor socialist policies have been incompatible with their survival, at least in western Europe. Nevertheless it is the new middle classes, Dahrendorf's 'service class'[125] and Bottomore's 'sub-elite',[126] that have attracted most attention in the post-war period. They are not bourgeois in the traditional sense of the word, tending to be other-directed rather than inner-directed,[127] since modern organizations require neither the individualism nor the innovation of private enterprise. In fact there is a *debourgeoisement* of the new middle classes – in paradoxical contrast with the so-called *embourgeoisement* of the affluent workers – in so far as the predominant behaviour patterns, cultural ideals and economic roles of its members differ radically from those of the old-established bourgeoisie.

The heterogeneity of the middle classes
While the new middle classes represent a variable proportion of the middle strata in different European countries, their growth has increased the complexity of social stratification in all these societies, since it has not been accompanied by a complementary elimination of the old middle classes, but has resulted in the coexistence of the two. They may intermingle, but they do not merge. Thus, for example, the development of new professions has not implied their automatic absorption by the old middle class, although the ethos of the traditional liberal professions appeals to the new middle class who imitate it in an attempt to enhance their own status. In this way some occupations whose holders may be classified as 'organization men'[128] (e.g. engineers, company secretaries or patent agents) seek professional status.

Life chances and life styles
Differences in life style and restricted social interaction – commensality, membership of clubs and associations, etc. – demarcate the two sub-classes, although the gradual fusing of the corresponding sub-cultures cannot be ruled out. An integrating influence may be exercised by the common schooling received by children of both backgrounds, whether in state institutions, such as *lycées* or *Gymnasia*, or in private establishments in countries where their prestige is higher. Leaving aside the unstable differences which still exist between the old and the new middle classes, the whole of the middle strata may be characterized by one common trait: it is the locus of the highest degree of individualistic competition, privatization and achievement orientation in society.

Although high rates of social mobility, both upward and downward,[129] are corollaries of competition on the employment market – albeit an imperfectly free one – they are more characteristic of the upper and middle ranks in these classes. On the other hand, the lower strata often differ quantitatively rather than qualitatively from the highest sections of the affluent working class. This gives rise to problems of status indeterminacy which is the counterpart of the possible embourgeoisement of the affluent workers. Thus the lower sections of the middle classes are more fatalistic and less prone to take individualistic risks.

Another limitation on the aggressive and enterprising individualism traditionally attributed to the bourgeoisie[130] is the reliance on family connections and subsidization. Recent research has shown that, far from being a purely personal adventure as the stereotype[131] would have it, both geographical and occupational mobility are financially under-written by the middle-class family. Even when such families are scattered, they display a remarkable degree of solidarity and a strong awareness of the advantages to be derived from mutual aid. Thus the middle-class pattern of financial assistance from relatives is closer to Titmuss's analysis of the upper class than to the personal welfare services customary among the families of manual workers. Another feature of the middle-class family is the willingness to accept financial sacrifices in order to secure educational advantages for its children, improving their occupational opportunities thereby.

Finally, both the life chances and styles of this class are enhanced by the greater propensity of its married women to work. As Viola Klein has noted, 'the activity of women is in direct relation to their educational level'.[132] Female graduates, who are predominantly middle and upper-middle class, show much higher percentages of employment than working-class women. This second wage enables the preservation of social distance in an increasingly egalitarian environment by providing for second cars, holidays, domestic help etc. It also endows the next generation with improved life chances by contributing towards school fees or a lengthier education.

The politics of the middle classes
Without accepting the view that the middle classes are a 'classless class', it is significant to note that political predictions, based on class are particularly difficult for the middle strata of society. The liberal parties traditionally associated with the middle and lower bourgeoisie have lost much of their power and influence, whereas socialist parties of the labour or social-democratic type have increasingly recruited from among these groups, losing their radicalism in the process. In

spite of such vast changes, predictable patterns of middle-class political behaviour are still widespread. It is easy to account for the conservatism of the French *petits commerçants* and their resistance to new forms of taxation, or for the post-civil war apoliticism of the Spanish middle classes which had counted many republican supporters. However, although middle-class political (and religious) movements tend to avoid any cataclysmic view of social change, many forms of radicalism are to be found among its members. For instance, the middle-class roots of several pacifist movements in the last two decades have been obvious. Thus Parkin attempts to account for the 'middle-class radicalism' of the CND movement in Great Britain:

> Given [the] climate of distrust of grand political doctrines and sweeping theories, the anti-Bomb movement was an ideally acceptable vehicle of radical protest. It provided the focus of opposition to the 'Establishment' by concentrating on a single major issue which could be presented as a straightforward choice between good and evil, but which did not at the same time entail the endorsement of a cumbersome set of doctrines, or a specific world view.[133]

Membership of this movement was predominantly from among the liberal and welfare professions, while the managerial and white-collar occupations were vastly under-represented.[134]

The ambiguous voting behaviour of the middle classes has resulted in both left- and right-wing parties courting such 'floating votes'. While at present the specific appeal of given policies to the middle classes remains unexplored, ecological studies, occupational analyses and socio-psychological testing might reveal intra-class regularities. Without denying that middle-class politics are class-bound, it could be argued that under present conditions of lasting prosperity in the West, they are less so than ever before.

While intellectuals have often been described in the past as petty bourgeois in disguise, their political attitudes and activities have emphasized their dissociation from, rather than their allegiance to, this group. Even in countries which possessed a thriving middle class in the nineteenth century,[135] intellectuals have consistently been the leaders of social revolutions,[136] regardless of their own class origin. They have provided 'the crucial ingredient without which social revolutions are impossible – a new ideology to challenge and destroy the existing one'.[137] While this group has been recruited predominantly from among the middle classes ever since the French Revolution, and while this trend has not disappeared, an inflow of intellectuals originating from the working class has begun in western Europe,[138] although it is still small, and is well under way in Communist countries.[139] However, in those countries the behaviour and allegiances of the intellectuals cannot be predicted on the basis of their class origin. Alfred Weber might have been partially wrong about the *freischwebende Intelligenz*;[140] the reactions of intellectuals in the first half of the twentieth century (to such events as Stalinism, the rise of fascism and the cold war) seem to disprove his thesis. However, since 1956 the detachment of intellectuals from large-scale, organized social movements – if not from worthy causes! – is quite remarkable.[141] Intellectuals today may be 'indicative of the class structure of a society in that they betray its rigidity or looseness, its stability or explosiveness, and often its neuralgic points',[142] but their connections with their class of origin tend to be more and more tenuous. However, be it in England or Yugoslavia, in Spain or Czechoslovakia, their behaviour follows interestingly trans-national patterns, especially in a common mistrust of established authority.[143]

7 THE UPPER CLASS AND THE EUROPEAN ELITES

Social change, as it affects the upper classes in Europe, has been relatively neglected in a sociological literature which has concentrated either upon exegesis of Italian elite theory (Mosca, Pareto, Michels, Gramsci) or on studies of the unchanging privileges enjoyed by the traditional upper classes. As Tawney and Titmuss[144] have shown for Britain, this class has not been taxed out of existence under the welfare state. Similarly in all non-Communist countries they have maintained social distance and protected their cherished life-styles against the pressures of egalitarianism. Intermarriage with economically or socially 'useful' members of other classes has been frequent, but it has been a permanent characteristic of the European aristocracy for centuries. Nevertheless class endogamy continues to be a fact, since as Titmuss has shown, it may represent a form of capital conservation. Another trait retained or even accentuated in this stratum is internationalism and cosmopolitanism. The socio-cultural influence of this group endures and represents one of the most impermeable barriers to social mobility.[145]

Traditionally the upper class conformed to Mosca's scheme: it was economically wealthy, politically influential and had a near monopoly on elite recruitment. As Marx put it, the upper class 'owned' the State – this ruling class was the seedbed of elites. However, in contemporary Europe it has gradually been forced into sharing its still considerable power with other groups. In the economic field, the role of the property elite is limited by the development of State-owned enterprises, the introduction of a capital gains tax and the growth of managerial power.[146] In the political sphere, the traditional position of the upper class has been even further eroded. Its monopoly of political power has disappeared in a wide variety of countries, although the causes of this change have been diverse. Thus, in Britain, Germany and Scandinavia, the access to power of social democratic parties and their predominantly middle-class leadership changed the composition of the political elite. In Spain, of all places, the powerful career army remains a typical channel of upward mobility for young men from the middle class in the more traditionalistic areas. In eastern Europe, the Communist party has dislodged the former upper classes and recruited new elites from among the lower and middle ranks.

Consequently a divorce between the upper class and elite groups has taken place in contemporary Europe. In turn, the dissociation of elites from this single class has entailed a degree of mutual dissociation within them. Thus the political, military, economic, ecclesiastic, artistic and intellectual elites – to mention a few – not only show great differences in their degree of association with the upper class, but also differ markedly in their subcultural traits.

The elites in the Welfare State[147]

For the purposes of this analysis, we may leave aside the non-political elites, adopting Aron's definition of an elite as 'the minority which, in any society, performs the function of ruling the community'.[148] The difference between this minority and the traditional political elite in the past has been described in different ways.

Firstly, according to contemporary Marxist sociologists and political scientists, the last decades have merely witnessed a further concentration of power in the hands of the very few. The influence of C. Wright Mills[149] and his model of the power elite dominate this sector of sociological opinion. Secondly, in contrast with this school of thought, European elites have been interpreted, at least in the Western parliamentary democracies, as a more complex phenomenon. The competition model of democracy – as Bottomore named it[150] – represents an alternative to the concentration of power. In this view, political elites are not cut off from their strata of origin and from the institutions to which they owe their position of leadership. A notable degree of elite pluralism is thus accounted for by the constitutional struggle for power of several political parties and by the official recognition of quasi-political bodies, such as trade unions. While some countries displayed this pluralistic pattern earlier, it is the rise of the welfare state which has increased the number of elite groups engaged in political decision-making in western Europe, as Thoenes argues.[151] Thirdly, an intermediary position is taken by those sociologists who have concentrated on the growth of any single elite group in the mixed economies of the western welfare states. Studies of this kind have tended to diagnose an incipient revolution whereby the group observed was about to monopolize power. In this context the ideas of a 'managerial revolution' or of a 'technocratic society' have become popular.

However, the existence of multiple elite groups is an observable characteristic of the northwestern democracies, where the following elites appear to coexist:

1. The political elite composed of parliamentarians, ministers, party leaders and senior officials, and of the main trade union leaders.

2. The functionary elite[152] characterized by technical expertise to which it owes both its appointment and the influence it wields, especially when political elites are unstable.

3. The military elite.

4. The scientific elite whose consultative role has grown and who range from economic advisers to nuclear physicists.[153]

Two more elites could be added: the intellectual and the business-managerial. Both these groups possess influence rather than power: the former affects public opinion through its control of the Press, the mass media and educational institutions, while the latter conducts a variety of effective pressure-group activities. However, it is doubtful whether either belongs to the political elite proper, since what power they possess is influential rather than direct. Moreover, it may be doubted whether either represents a single homogeneous elite. Particularly in the case of intellectuals, ideological heterogeneity impedes the kind of coalescence required for effective political action.

In connection with the plurality of elites, Thoenes described the phenomenon of *verzuiling*, which many consider as 'idiosyncratically' Dutch, but which seems in fact not to be unique. This term refers to an individual spending most of his life in exclusive contact with persons who belong to his own *zuil* or 'column' and possess the appropriate subculture.[154] These columns corresponding to careers cut vertically across strata and develop their own leadership who then strive for prestige, recognition and power at the national level. Throughout western Europe, professional-occupational social systems produce their own powerful elites and every such 'column' attempts or achieves representation within the power elite. A degree of vertical pluralism is thus attained, which parallels the cultural, ideological, religious and even economic pluralism of many European societies.

Though vertical pluralism does not necessarily imply a widespread and harmonious participation in political decision-making, it nevertheless represents a less coercive system than the horizontal monopoly on power of a ruling class, such as e.g. the Portuguese. However, pluralism is still limited by the efforts of each elite (be it military, political, syndicalist, or technocratic) to obtain more power and the consequent unwillingness to compromise. Also and more importantly, pluralism is restricted by the class character of European societies, whose occupational structures and social institutions continue, despite their decreased rigidity, to be shaped by ascriptive status and privilege maintenance – the traditional forms of human inequality and social injustice.

8 CONCLUDING REMARKS

Any statements, even the most tentative, concerning the development of social stratification in Europe depend upon a prior recognition of the two distinct meanings attached to the term 'multi-dimensional' system. In the first place, it may refer to the coexistence within the same society, of two or more stratification systems, founded on different principles. In this case, one may ask whether such societies tend to move away from multiplex and towards a unitary system. On the other hand, within a given stratification system, e.g. either rural or urban, estate or industrial etc., the dimensions along which individuals are ranked may be superimposed, that is 'multibonded' in Sorokin's terms,[155] or relatively independent, that is multidimensional, in the sense employed in this chapter. Here one may ask whether the tendency in societies predominantly characterized by a unitary stratification system is towards multibonding or multidimensionality. As Marshall has put it,

in any advanced society in which economic, political, social and cultural activities are well developed, it is almost certain that several dimensions of stratification will operate. The really important question is not whether they exist – they are bound to – but whether, and to what extent, their products converge. These dimensions may be more or less autonomous in their action, and the hierarchy of groups based upon them may coincide to a greater or lesser degree in size, shape and membership.[156]

Firstly, concerning the possibility of a shift in Europe from multiplex to unitary forms of stratification, it seems clear that while this is a general trend, it is firstly slow and secondly does not map neatly onto the move towards an industrial economy. The resilience of the peasantry in France and Germany aptly demonstrates the latter point, its slow decline over time, the former. Similarly, the coexistence of different social structures within Italy, Spain and Greece indicates that any move towards the unitary may well be delayed in a context of geographic isolation, differential economic development, regional patterning of investment decisions and enduring sociocultural discrepancies. Obviously such qualitative differences are concealed in quantitative indices of economic development, rise in GNP or sectoral reallocation, calculated at the national, not the regional, level.

Since the second question is posed independently, no necessary relationship is seen between the emergence of a more or less unitary system of stratification and its multidimensional or multibonded character. As far as the post-war development of the more advanced countries is concerned, decrease in the traditionally rigid forms of stratification and the conflicts deriving from them has not meant the advent of an open society in which position would be exclusively determined by achievement criteria. Certainly the last two decades have spelt a qualitative change in the traditional class society associated with the Industrial Revolution, but, as has been seen earlier, relative class differences remain, as does conflict arising from social inequality. Similarly, in some countries the recruitment needs of an expanding economy in conjunction with a liberal, egalitarian tradition have led to a shift in emphasis from ascription to achievement, disregarding social class of origin. (The use of achievement criteria within the framework of class for appointment to positions, is of course a common, though frequently forgotten, phenomenon in traditional societies.) Obviously, the dominant conception of merit (i.e. the one to which legal rewards and official social privileges are attached) varies with the prevailing political ideology. Thus, when several societies are said to be converging towards achievement-based criteria of social promotion,[157] they may in fact be widely diverging by rewarding the possession of widely different personal and even group characteristics. Hence, countries whose overall rates of social mobility are increasing, adapt this process to often widely different concepts of merit, originating in political ideologies and economic exigencies, and implemented in educational policies. However, even in nations which have now attained an unprecedented degree of openness, ascriptive factors endure in the attainment of status, power or even occupation. While totalitarian regimes, and particularly the socialist planned economies, also make use of recruitment by merit, backed up by differential rewards, ascriptive ideological criteria are used jointly in appointments. In such cases intense open competition *follows* strong ideological commitment to the party, thus reconciling individual competence with political conformity. In countries whose tertiary development has outstripped the emergence of a strong industrial sector (such as Ireland and Greece) there is an analogous, though less marked, tendency for open competition to *follow* the possession of certain status characteristics.

While all these types of society are multidimensional in the sense employed in this paper, they differ not only in degree of dimensional non-superimposition, but also in which of the three major dimensions, class, status or power can be considered dominant. Two final conclusions follow from the fact that contemporary examples of each form of dominance can be provided. Firstly, doubts are cast on any theory maintaining a unilinear pattern of social stratification, whether based upon the process of industrialization or any other factor. Secondly, excessive optimism derived from observed increases in open competition, minimization of aristocratic privileges and the extension of democratic politics, should be qualified by the recognition that each of these trends can co-exist with a multiplicity of stratification systems, some of whose elements may limit, neutralize or counteract these trends.[158]

NOTES

1   It seems clear that the term 'industrial society' indiscriminately applied to most European countries (including both capitalist and socialist economies) contains a certain ideological bias. Cf. R. Dahrendorf, 'Soziologie in industrielle Gesellschaft' in *Gesellschaft und Freiheit* (Munich, 1961).

2   Here one is not concerned with total national concergence but only with stratification as *one* aspect of social structures.

3   C. Kerr, et al., *Industrialism and Industrial Man* (Cambridge, Mass., 1960).

4   G. Runciman, 'Class, Status and Power?' in J. A. Jackson (ed.), *Social Stratification* (Cambridge), p. 55. Cf. also W. H. Form, 'Occupational and Social Integration of Automobile Workers in Four Countries: a Comparative Study', *International Journal*

of Comparative Sociology, March–June, 1969, Vol. x, Nos. 1–2, pp. 95–116.

5   G. Runciman, 'Class, Status and Power?', p. 28. Cf. also S. Ossowski, *Class Structure in the Social Consciousness* (London, 1963), pp. 19–37.

6   A. Inkeles and P. Rossi, 'National Comparisons of Occupational Prestige', *American Journal of Sociology*, Vol. LXI, No. 3, 1955, p. 329.

7   Cf. P. K. Hatt, 'Occupation and Social Stratification', in A. J. Reiss (ed.), *Occupations and Social Status* (New York, 1961).

8   J. Goldthorpe, 'Social Stratification in Industrial Society', in *The Development of Industrial Societies*, Sociological Review Monograph No. 8, October 1964, pp. 652 ff.

9   J. R. Gusfield and M. Schwartz, 'The Meanings of Occupational Prestige: Reconsideration of the NORC Scale', *American Sociological Review*, Vol. 28, No. 2, 1963, pp. 265 ff.

10   P. K. Hatt, 'Occupation and Social Stratification', p. 248.

11   A. J. Reiss, *Occupations and Social Status*, Chapter IV.

12   Cf. J. R. Gusfield and M. Schwartz, 'The Meanings of Occupational Prestige', p. 267.

13   O. D. Duncan, 'A Socio-Economic Index for All Occupations' in A. J. Reiss, 'Occupations', p. 117.

14   A. Inkeles and P. Rossi, 'National Comparisons'. The countries included were USA, Great Britain, New Zealand, Japan, Germany and Russia (*émigrés*).

15   R. W. Hodge, D. J. Treiman and P. H. Rossi, 'A Comparative Study of Occupational Prestige' in R. Bendix and S. Lipset (eds.), *Class, Status and Power* (New York, 1966), p. 310.

16   Hodge, Treiman, Rossi, p. 320.

17   W. Wesołowski, 'Prestiz zawodow-system wrtosci-uwarswienie społeczne' in A. Sarapata, *Socjologia zawodów* (Warsaw, 1965).

18   W. Wesołowski, 'Prestiz zawodow-system . . .', p. 191.

19   J. Clyde Mitchell, 'Occupational Prestige and Social System', *International Journal of Comparative Sociology*, Vol. v, No. 1, 1964. Following the political crisis in Northern Rhodesia, the African policeman lost prestige over a five years' period, while the rating of other occupations remained largely unchanged.

20   A. Sarapata, *Studia nad uwarstwieniem i ruchliwościá społeczná w Polsca* (Warsaw, 1965), p. 228.

21   See note, 15.

22   F. Harbison and C. A. Myers, *Education, Manpower and Economic Growth* (New York, 1964), Chapter 4.

23   Harbison, Myers, p. 40.

24   About the problems involved in the unidimensional or 'strata' analysis of stratification see K. M. Bolte 'Einige Anmerkungen zur Problematik der Analyse von "Schichtungen" in sozialen Systemen' in D. V. Glass and R. König (eds.), *Soziale Schichtung un soziale Mobilität* (Cologne, Opladen, 1961), pp. 28–53.

25   P. K. Hatt, 'Occupation and Social Stratification', p. 242.

26   R. Dahrendorf, 'Recent Changes in the Class Structure of European Societies' in *Daedalus*, Winter 1964, pp. 235 ff (Stress provided).
27   Dahrendorf, 'Recent Changes . . .', p. 253.
28   S. M. Lipset and H. L. Zetterberg, 'A Theory of Social Mobility' in R. Bendix and S. Lipset, *Class, Status and Power*, p. 563.
29   Cf. A. Malewski, 'The Degree of Status Incongruence and its Effects' in R. Bendix and S. Lipset, 'A Theory of Social Mobility', pp. 302 ff.
30   O. D. Duncan, 'A Socio-Economic Index for All Occupations', p. 143.
31   Cf. Chapters on Italy, Spain, Portugal and Greece in this volume.
32   Margaret Scotford Archer, 'Higher Education and the Recruitment of Higher Civil Servants in Western Europe', report prepared for the Working Party 'Relation between university attainment and employment requirements of administrative and executive posts' by International Social Sciences Council, ISSC/ED/69 W.P.3.
33   A. Malewski, 'The Degree of Status Incongruence and its Effects'.
34   For a critical inventory of modern definitions of social class relevant to this point see G. Gurvitch, *Le concept des classes sociales* (Cours de Sorbonne, Paris, 1954).
35   W. B. Watson and E. A. T. Barth, 'Questionable Assumptions in the Theory of Social Stratification', *Pacific Sociological Review*, Vol. 7, No. 1, 1964.
36   For a more sophisticated statement on convergence in family patterns cf. W. Goode, *World Revolution and Family Patterns* (New York, 1963).
37   Cf. R. Titmuss, *Income Distribution and Social Change* (London, 1962).
38   P. Wilmott and M. Young, *Family and Class in a London Suburb* (London, 1960).
39   Cf. E. Bott, *Family and Social Networks* (London, 1957). F. Musgrove, *The Migratory Elite* (London, 1963). See C. Bell, *Middle Class Families* (London, 1968).
40   W. B. Watson and E. A. T. Barth, 'Questionable Assumptions . . .', p. 13.
41   Watson, Barth, p. 14.
42   O. D. Duncan, 'A Socio-Economic Index for All Occupations', p. 118.
43   S. M. Lipset and H. L. Zetterberg, 'A Theory of Social Mobility', p. 562.
44   Cf. A. L. Stinchcombe, 'Agricultural Enterprise and Rural Class Relations', in R. Bendix and S. Lipset, *Class, Status and Power*.
45   W. G. Runciman, 'Class, Status and Power?', p. 43. See also pp. 43–53.

46 Runciman, 'Class, Status and Power?', p. 53.
47 Cf. Clark Kerr, et al., *Industrialism and Industrial Man.*
48 On the present difficulties for the measurement of social mobility as well as those impeding the construction of a general theory of social mobility see K. M. Bolte, 'Vertikale Mobilität', in R. König (ed.), *Handbuch der empirischen Sozialforschung*, Vol. II (Stuttgart, 1969), pp. 1–33.
49 For a discussion of this general methodological problem see P. M. Blau, 'Formal Organizations: Dimensions of Analysis' in *American Journal of Sociology*, Vol. 63, 1957, pp. 58–69.
50 W. E. Moore, 'Changes in Occupational Structures', in N. J. Smelser and S. M. Lipset, *Social Structure and Mobility in Economic Development* (London, 1966).
51 See Appendix at the end of this volume.
52 C. Kerr, *Industrialism and Industrial Man*, p. 36.
53 R. M. Marsh, 'Values, Demand and Social Mobility' in *American Sociological Review*, Vol. 28, 1963.
54 S. H. Miller, 'Comparative Social Mobility' in C. S. Heller (ed.), *Structured Social Inequality* (New York, 1969), p. 340.
55 J. Frisch, 'Les comportements ouvriers de mobilité', *Année sociologique*, 3rd series, No. 17, 1966, pp. 504–507.
56 S. M. Lipset and R. Bendix, *Social Mobility in Industrial Society* (Berkeley, 1959), pp. 301 ff.
57 S. H. Miller, 'Comparative Social Mobility', p. 339.
58 P. M. Blau and O. D. Duncan, 'Occupational Mobility in the United States' in C. S. Heller (ed.), *Structured Social Inequality*, p. 343.
59 Blau, Duncan, p. 342.
60 Cf. H. L. Wilensky, 'Measures and Effects of Mobility' in Smelser and S. M. Lipset, *Social Structure and Mobility.* . . .
61 This watershed is generally held to map onto the manual/non-manual dichotomy. It is interesting to note that those occupations situated on the divide – clerking and secretarial – appear to have the worst prospects. Even their echelon movement is now being limited more than at the beginning of the century. This factor may be significant both for the feminization of such jobs and also for the concentration or maximizing chances through change of locus, i.e. the change from 'permanent' to 'temporary' employment, lateral rather than hierarchical movement characterizing this occupation.
62 A. Carr-Saunders, *Professions: their organisation and place in society* (Oxford, 1928). The diversification of skills within the major professions is a factor held likely to weaken professional unity by increasing competition among members and differentiation within the association. However the growth of many new professions represents a multiplication of available career structures.
63 P. M. Blau and O. D. Duncan, 'Occupational Mobility in the

US'. The influence of the father's socio-economic status continues to increase until about the age of fifty, p. 343.

64 A study of the background of managers in nationalized industry in Poland shows that between 1949–66 recruitment was almost exclusively on grounds of party allegiance and class origin. When the Six Year Plan was seen to be failing in 1963 this selection policy was gradually modified to increase formal qualifications as a guarantee of competence. Thus between 1955–8 the proportion of managers with higher educational qualifications was doubled and that of managers with incomplete secondary education was halved. H. Najduchowska, 'Managers of Industrial Enterprises' in J. Szczepański, *Przemysł i Spoteczeństwo w Polsce Ludowe* (Wrocław, 1969).

65 Cf. A. Borucki and S. Dziecielska, 'The Social Position and Occupation of Graduates from Secondary Schools in Lodz who do not proceed to Higher Education' in P.A.N. (Polish Academy of Science), *Wykształcenie a pozycja społeczna inteligencji* (Lodz, 1959).

66 R. Dahrendorf, 'Recent Changes . . .'.

67 J. A. Kahl, *Comparative Perspectives on Stratification* (New York, 1968), p. xi.

68 L. G. Seligman, 'Political and Economic Development' in N. J. Smelser and S. M. Lipset, *Social Structure and Mobility . . .*, p. 347.

69 For example, attempts have been made in post-war England and France to democratize recruitment to the Higher Civil Services. In both countries such policies have known only marginal success. S. F. Parris, 'Twenty Years of l'École Nationale d'Administration', *Public Administration*, Vol. 43, p. 965; C. H. Dodd, 'Recruitment to the Administrative Class, 1960–1964', *Public Administration*, Vol. 45, 1967.

70 M. Scotford Archer, 'Higher Education and Recruitment of Higher Civil Servants . . .'.

71 Cf. K. Prandy, *Professional Employees* (London, 1965). Cf. also *La Table Ronde*, No. 253, Feb. 1969, special issue on 'phenomène des "cadres" '.

72 K. Prandy, *Professional Employees*. 'No modern society could properly be described as a "technocracy" in the political sense, nor could one argue that technologists are controllers of industry, although there is little doubt that many of them, particularly engineers, are increasingly to be found in management, even in top management positions', p. 173.

73 For example, in England, religious and cultural pressure groups as well as non-occupational groups lobbying Parliament, like the Anti-Blood Sports League, the Lord's Day Observance Society, the Child Poverty Action Group, the Preservation of Ancient Monuments Society, etc.

74 *Northern Star*, 12 September 1846.

75 Thus the number of farm workers fell from 20 million in 1950

to 15 million in 1960 in the area covered by the European Economic Community, and is down to an estimated 10 million in 1970. In this area, then, on average half a million people now leave the land every year. The rate of stratificational change is bound to accelerate as the number who leave the land begins to include farmers as well as the traditional migrant, the farm labourer and his family. *Agriculture 1980* (European Community Information Service, 1969 pamphlet).

76 Europäische Gesellschaft für ländliche Soziologie *Ländliche Bevölkerungsbewegungen* Bericht des ersten Kongress (Brussels, Louvain) (Bonn, 1959) *passim*. Also H. Kötter, *Landbevölkerung im sozialen Wandel* (Düsseldorf, Cologne, 1958); J. Saville, *Rural Depopulation in England and Wales, 1851–1951* (London, 1957).

77 On these transformations see S. Mallet, *Les paysans contre le passé* (Paris, 1962); J. Martinez Alier, *La estabilidad del latifundismo* (Paris, 1968); F. Langlois, *Les salariés agricoles en France* (Paris, 1962).

78 P. Ammassari, 'The Italian Blue-Collar Worker', *International Journal of Comparative Sociology*, Vol. x, No. 1–2 (1969).

79 Cf. Chapters on Spain and Greece in the present volume.

80 R. Dahrendorf, *Class and Class Conflict in Industrial Society* (London, 1959), p. 50.

81 Ammassari claims that this happens 'even where modern manufacturing is absent', 'The Italian Blue-Collar Worker', p. 21.

82 A. Touraine and O. Ragazzi, *Ouvriers d'origine agricole* (Paris, 1961), pp. 109–18.

83 A. Touraine and B. Mottez, 'Classe ouvrière et société globale' in G. Friedmann, et al., *Traité de sociologie du travail*, Vol. ii (Paris, 1962), pp. 236–83.

84 G. Hermet, *Les Espagnols en France* (Paris, 1967).

85 S. Giner, *Sociedad de masas* (Madrid, 1971); 'Comentarios liminares sobre la llamada sociedad de masas' in *Boletín*, Seminario de Derecho Politico, University of Salamanca, No. 28, 1963, pp. 13–24.

86 Against the Marxian vision sf. Dahrendorf, *Class*, etc.; also G. Gurvitch, *Le concept des classes sociales*, against the mass society conception in its pessimist version T. Geiger, 'Die Legende von der Massengesellschaft', *Archiv für Rechts- u. Sozialphilosophie*, Vol. xxxix, Heft 3 (Bern-Munich, 1951), p. 305, and S. Giner, *La sociedad de masses*.

87 A. Philip, *La democratie industrielle*, quoted by Dahrendorf, *Class*, etc., p. 50.

88 Dahrendorf, *Class,* etc., p. 50.

89 Dahrendorf, *Class,* etc., pp. 51, 61.

90 H. Popitz, et al., *Das Gesellschaftsbild des Arbeiters* (Tübingen, 1961), p. 216; see also article on England in this volume.

91 See below, section on the working classes.

c

92 A statement that also applies to contemporary Europe.
93 S. Nosow and W. Form, *Man, Work and Society* (New York, 1962), p. 113.
94 'Status inconsistency' is used here as the opposite to 'status crystallization', or 'status consistency'. It is not yet a clear and well-delimited concept in theory and research, but must be used for want of a better one. See S. Box and J. Ford, 'Some questionable assumptions in the Theory of Status Inconsistency' in *Sociological Review*, Vol. 17, No. 2, July 1969. J. Goldthorpe, et al. (*The Affluent Worker: Industrial Attitudes and Behaviour* (Cambridge, 1968), pp. 158–9), use 'status incongruency', which is practically a synonym.
95 S. Mallet, *La nouvelle classe ouvrière* (Paris, 1963), pp. 68–9.
96 It can rightly be claimed that, historically, the working class has always been much more differentiated than most external observers have pretended. With the exception of a few privileged groups, however, the majority of the working class in the past (expecially during the nineteenth century) suffered from a common high degree of proletarization which gave its most disparate groups a common ground for complaint, and, to a certain point, a common strategy for action.
97 R. Dahrendorf, 'Recent Changes in the Class Structures of European Societies', *Daedalus*, Vol. 93, No. 1, Winter 1964, p. 257 n. Although the idea that many serious sociologists have accepted *embourgeoisement* of the working class as a fact must be contested, it cannot be denied that working-class affluence coupled with a decline in traditional forms of militancy is an important factor in the 'disappointment' or 'disillusion' of many western intellectuals (including some sociologists) with the fate of revolutionary prospects in the West. (Cf. R. Aron, *Progress and Disillusion* (London, 1969)).
98 R. Dahrendorf, 'Recent Changes . . .', p. 257. The word *embourgeoisement* is used in the text, as it has come to be widely accepted. It seems clear, though, that, as the new middle classes lose some of their traditional bourgeois qualities, another word ought to be applied to the phenomenon.
99 J. Goldthorpe, et al., *The Affluent Worker* . . ., p. 1 and also Vol. ii, p. 1 of their series. Supposedly the wide acceptance they refer to is amongst sociologists, although they do not mention the sociological defendants of the thesis in question (Vol. i, p. 3).
100 S. Mallet, *Nouvelle classe* . . . , pp. 261–66. Simultaneously J. Delcourt and G. Lamarque published their essay *Un faux dilemme: embourgeoisement ou prolétarisation de la classe ouvrière* (Brussels, 1963), in which embourgeoisement was also ruled out. Although their argument is sound, their general presentation of it is faulty.
101 G. W. Runciman, 'Embourgeoisement, Self-Rated Class and Party Preferences', in *Sociological Review*, Vol. xii, 1964.
102 R. Dahrendorf, 'Recent Changes . . .', *Daedalus*, Vol. 93, No. 1.

103   S. Mallet, *Nouvelle classe* . . . , *Ouvrière* (Paris, 1963).
104   R. F. Hamilton, *Affluence and the French Worker in the Fourth Republic* (Princeton, 1967).
105   J. Goldthorpe, et al., *The Affluent Worker: Political Attitudes and Behaviour* (Vol. II of Series), (Cambridge, 1968), p. 47.
106   See article on Yugoslavia in this volume.
107   J. Goldthorpe, et al., *The Affluent Worker* . . ., Vol. II, p. 81.
108   Cf. H. Daheim, 'Soziale Herkunft, Schule und Rekrutierung der Berufe' in D. Glass and R. König, 'Soziale Schichtung . . .', pp. 200–17.
109   'Early forms of action had confused the economic and the political. Then there came a separation between unions and political parties and, albeit with interlocking directorates and memberships, a cooperative division of function. France, Italy and Spain, however, did not achieve this division of labor; while England was developing "Sidney Webbicalism" they developed syndicalism.' V. R. Lorwin, 'Working Class Politics and Economic Development in Western Europe, in *American Historical Review*, Vol. LXIII, No. 2, January 1958. About recent developments approaching the model referred to in the text see the corresponding chapter in this volume.
110   Indirectly connected with this is the problem of the working class conservative vote on which the recent work of R. T. Mackenzie and A. Silver has shed some light (*Angels in Marble: Working Class Conservatives in Urban England* (London, 1968)). But the fact, stressed by these authors, that on no single major factor can differences in voting be established within the working class leaves many questions unanswered. Working class conservative voting is not only a British phenomenon. During the Gaullist period, a sizeable part of the French working-class vote went to the right, if not to the extreme right. (L. Hamon, *Les nouveaux comportements politiques de la classe ouvrière* (Paris, 1962)). It is a well-known fact that in Federal Germany the working class is equally prone as in England to give its vote to the conservative Christian Democrats.
111   It is assumed that extremist revolutionary minorities which have arisen in western Europe in the late sixties do not contradict this assertion, even if their following in some countries (Spain, Italy) is actually or potentially not too small; these countries still possess a considerable proletariat in the classical sense of the word. This does not mean, however, that the existence of a proletariat is taken to be the only cause of class strife. The latter, of course, depends on the patterns of class domination and rigidity, amongst other factors, such as the nature of the polity, that one finds in a given society.
112   R. Dahrendorf, *Conflict after Class: New Perspectives on the Theory of Social and Political Conflict* (The University of Essex, 1967), p. 20.
113   To assume the existence today of class warfare in the forms it

took in Europe up to the end of the Spanish Civil War is quite risky, even if one claims to have 'brought the treatment of the phenomenon up to date', as some writers put it. Cf. M. Bouvier-Ajam and G. Mury, *Les classes sociales en France* (Paris, 1963), Vol. II and N. Poulantzas, *Pouvoir politique et classes sociales* (Paris, 1969) (2nd edn.). On the other hand, sociological parables such as the one contained in M. Young's *The Rise of the Meritocracy* (London, 1958) assume a constant and even progress of individual mobility until new classes are formed along intelligence and skill lines in a manner that seems unwarranted by human behaviour. Quite apart from this, the relative disappearance of large-scale class violence does not preclude in modern Europe all sorts of violence connected with ethnical, cultural and religious groups. Thus, strife in Belgium, Ulster, the Basque Country and similar areas cannot be reduced to class differences, and clashes be explained away as collective sublimations of class frustrations.

114   R. Dahrendorf, *Conflict after* . . . , p. 21.

115   Complex studies of the middle classes can be dated as far back as Aristotle's *Politics*.

116   C. W. Mills, *White Collar* (New York, 1956).

117   G. D. H. Cole, 'The Conception of the Middle Classes', *British Journal of Sociology*, Vol. I, No. 4, December 1950, pp. 275–90.

118   W. Dumon, *De Middenstand als sociologische Categorie* (Louvain, 1963), *passim*.

119   E. Lederer and J. Marschak, 'Der neue Mittelstand', *Grundriss der Sozialökonomik*, Vol. IX–1 (Tübingen, 1962 ed.).

120   A. Menzel in *Encyclopedia of the Social Sciences* (New York, 1938), Vol. p. 412.

121   The late W. Röpke was an exception in this respect: he believed that the expansion of what he called 'mass society' had evidently resulted in the progressive 'proletarianization of the middle classes' in general (*Civitas humana* (London, 1948), pp. 131–49). This conservative writer coincided here with those Marxists who claim that the new types of middle-class people are actually disguised proletarians, or even that the middle classes are on the wane. As late as 1963, two French Communists, M. Bouvier-Ajam and G. Mury, asserted that the 'périclitement [des couches moyennes de la bourgeoisie] saute aux yeux', *Les classes sociales* . . . , p. 322, Vol. II.

122   R. Dahrendorf, *Class and Class Conflict* . . . , p. 51.

123   M. Crozier cited by R. Dahrendorf, 'Recent changes in the class structure of European Societies' in *Daedalus,* Vol. 93, No. 1 Winter 1964, p. 251. R. Hoggart, *The Uses of Literacy.*

124   The contention that the new middle class is not a class at all when lined with the assumption that modern society is basically a middle-class society has become one of the main tenets of a recent stage of the mass society theory. Cf. opening paragraphs

C. W. Mills, *White Collar*, p. 1. The gross oversimplifications implied there need no criticism.

125 R. Dahrendorf, 'Recent Changes . . .', *Daedalus*, Vol. 93, No. 1, pp. 244–52.

126 T. H. Bottomore, *Elites and Society* (Harmondsworth, 1966), p. 11.

127 D. Riesman, et al., *The Lonely Crowd* (New Haven, 1950); also D. Riesman, 'The Lonely Crowd, 20 Years After' in *Encounter*, October 1969, Vol. xxxiii, No. 4, pp. 36–41.

128 The notion of 'organization man' is taken here only for illustrative purposes. An identification of the ideal type 'organization man' with the new professional men of large-scale companies and bureaucracies is not readily warranted by present knowledge of the facts, at least in Europe.

129 Cf. above, section on social mobility. Also J. Frisch, 'Les comportements ouvriers . . .', pp. 504–5.

130 M. Crozier, 'L'ambiguite de la conscience de classe chez les employés et les petits fonctionnaires', *Cahiers internationaux de sociologie*, January 1955, Vol. xxxviii; also D. Lockwood, *The Blackcoated Worker* (London, 1958).

131 C. Moraze, *Les bourgeois conquérants* (Paris, 1957).

132 V. Klein, *Britain's Married Women Workers* (London, 1965), p. 138. Her data in support of this statement refer both to Britain and France.

133 F. Parkin, *Middle Class Radicalism* (Manchester, 1968), p. 56.

134 F. Parkin, *Middle Class Radicalism*, pp. 54–5. The question of middle-class political allegiances under extreme critical situations (such as obtained in Germany, Spain and Italy in the thirties) is not dealt with in our text, as what is relevant in this context is the actual situation of the European middle classes in the fifties and sixties. Cf. also J. Bonham, *The Middle Class Vote* (London, 1954), pp. 19–30.

135 In some economically more backward countries of the past (Russia, Poland) the intellectuals (often together with the whole intelligentsia) were very neatly distinguished from the petty bourgeoisie.

136 A distinction between intellectuals (a culturally creative elite) and the intelligentsia is implicit in these passages. Confusion arises when the latter concept is used as defining intellectual groups. Such seems to be the case with T. Geiger's important *Aufgaben und Stellung der Intelligenz in der Gesellschaft* Stuttgart, 1949).

137 G. Lenski, *Power and Privilege* (New York, 1966), p. 70.

138 T. H. Bottomore, *Elites and Society*, p. 76.

139 J. Szczepański, 'Changement dans la structure et les fonctions de l'*intelligentsia*', *Bulletin international des sciences sociales*, ix, No. 2, 1959, pp. 191–205.

140 A. Weber as quoted by K. Mannheim, *Ideology and Utopia* (London, 1936), p. 137.

141   Thus Lenski's statement that 'ideologies are the stock in trade of intellectuals' must be qualified. (G. Lenski, *Power and Privilege*, p. 70.)

142   R. Dahrendorf, 'Recent Changes . . .', *Daedalus*, Vol. 93, No. 1, p. 259.

143   A problem that falls outside the scope of the present paper. The possibility that intellectuals may form a 'class' of their own in modern society has not been left unexplored. Cf. W. Kraus, *Der fünfte Stand* (Berne, 1966), *passim*. Such a phenomenon seems quite problematic though; as Dahrendorf points out 'many intellectuals all over Europe have not only come to resemble the service class in their profession and general outlook, but they have become members of this class (or, rather, non-class) that is, individuals competing with others for a place in the sun' (R. Dahrendorf, 'Recent Changes . . .', p. 260).

144   R. H. Tawney, *Equality* (London, 1964, 1st ed., 1931).

145   On the enduring maintenance of strength and privilege of the traditional upper class see Inchiesta Shell No. 3 *La classe dirigente italiana*, pp. 65–72; G. N. Copeman, *Leaders of British Industry* (London, 1955); R. V. Clements, *Managers: a Study of their Careers in Industry* (London, 1958) both.

146   R. Aron, 'Social Stratification and the Ruling Class', 2nd part, *Sociological Review*, Vol. 1, No. 2, June 1950, p. 129.

147   The title of this subsection is taken from P. Thoenes, *The Elite in the Welfare State* (London, 1966).

148   R. Aron, 'Social Stratification . . .', *Sociological Review, June 1950*, 1st part, Vol. 1, No. 1, March 1950, p. 9.

149   C. W. Mills, *The Power Elite* (New York, 1963); N. Poulantzas, *op. cit.*; R. Miliband, *The State in Capitalist Society* (1969). All.

150   T. H. Bottomore, *Elites and Society*, p. 113.

151   P. Thoenes, *The Elite in the Welfare State*, II part, pp. 125–225.

152   J. Burnham, The Managerial Revolution (Harmondsworth, 1962) (1st ed., 1942). E. Strauss, *The Ruling Servants* (London, 1961).

153   Only the most obvious elite groups in contemporary Europe have been enumerated. However, a more abstract approach could be used by attempting to draw up a model of the ruling classes *cum* elites (and their corresponding ruled groups) in the new society which is now emerging. It seems though that the construction of such a model would be premature. At least one sociologist, A. Touraine, has attempted it schematically. Cf. A. Touraine, 'Anciennes et nouvelles classes sociales' in G. Balandier, et al., *Perspectives de la sociologie contemporaine* (Paris, 1968), pp. 117–56.

154   P. Thoenes, *The Elite in the Welfare State*, pp. 14–15. Cf. also D. O. Moberg, 'Social Differentiation in the Netherlands' in *Social Forces*, Vol. 39, No. 4, May 1961, pp. 333–7, and the articles in *Sociologische Gids* by I. Schoffer, J. A. A. van Doorn

and J. A. Ponsioen devoted to the *Verzuiling* phenomenon (Vol. 3, 1956).

155 P. Sorokin, Society, *Culture and Personality* (New York, 1962), p. 236.

156 T. H. Marshall, *Sociology at the Crossroads* (London, 1963), p. 132.

157 K. Svalastoga states that, on the face of the present evidence, it may only be concluded that European societies (especially those in the North-west) now tend to resemble each other very closely in their general rates of social mobility. 'Social Mobility: the Western European Model', *Acta sociologica*, Vol. 9, Fascicle 1–2, 1966, pp. 175–82.

158 A. Touraine, 'Anciennes et nouvelles . . .', p. 156, predicts new cleavages and class-bound social movements and conflicts in the emerging social structures of today.

2 Portugal

Herminio Martins

Portugal is not a 'plural' society. A comparative survey of European societies shows that it is characterized by an unusually high degree of national homogeneity. This finding holds good whether racial, ethnic, linguistic, religious or cultural homogeneity aspects are considered. This also holds good whether we compare Portugal with other Mediterranean or north-western European societies, large or small. This important societal property has been obscured by the greater international salience of Portugal's anomalous imperial status. In fact, historically, Portugal has been characterized by a low level of domestic ethno-cultural diversity, at least equal to, if not lower than, that of the other European colonial empires. In contrast to other former imperial nations, it has failed so far to absorb any significant fraction of its colonial or ex-colonial subjects and thus has failed to diversify its ethno-cultural composition. Somewhat paradoxically for an 'oceanic' society, Portugal has been particularly successful at 'exporting' ethno-cultural diversity.

Whilst it is easy to reach agreement on the empirical fact of national homogeneity, its precise bearing on class formation and class conflict is controversial. It might be argued that the virtual absence at the macrosociological level of the kind of horizontal, ascriptive, ethno-cultural cleavages, so widespread elsewhere in Europe, should maximize the pressure of class forces in the social system. This view implies that class situations will become more marked where alternative (non-class) definitions of conflict-situations are not structurally or culturally available. It also implies that class conflict will thrive where the cross-cutting pressures of such primordial bonds as ethnicity, language, religious affiliation, etc. are minimal. However, this view suggests a misleading zero-sum or inverse variation model of the relations between class and status stratification: where class and ethno-cultural cleavages are coterminous concretely (if still analytically distinct), conflict-proneness and conflict intensity may be maximized.[1] Status-inconsistent or rank-disequilibrated collectivities – marked by imbalances between their high rank in at least one scale of social valuations and lower rank in at least one other – are an important source of socially rebellious and politically oppositional elements. Especially when these status-inconsistent collectivities are characterized by indelible or at least visible ascriptive traits – race and ethnicity, language and religious culture – they can become easy targets for repression and oppression which, combined with their social advantages, induces some of their members to identify their cause with that of wholly disadvantaged, consistently deprived collectivities. The contribution of disaffected aristocrats, religious minorities, Jewish intellectuals, etc. to radical and socialist movements is well known: generally at least in the early stages of class-struggle, as of national emancipation, *superordinate* strata must furnish indispensable resources of leadership, ideology and organization to subordinate classes and the paradox is only dispelled when we realize that it is precisely from status-inconsistent or rank-disequilibrated collectivities that these resources typically stem. In a highly homogeneous society, like the Portuguese, these ethnic, religious and linguistic minorities – potential sources of aid to subordinate classes in the early, critical stages of class conflict particularly before the consolidation of strong, autonomous class organizations – have been largely absent. I suggest that this circumstance is perhaps even more important than the greater transparency of class situations resulting from social homogeneity: although it is true that Catholic workers are not separated from Protestant workers on purely religious grounds, or that the antagonism between say Flemish and Walloon workers or between Catalan and Castilian lower strata has no counterpart in Portugal, it is also true that there are no socially distinctive ascriptive minorities to ally themselves with lower or working-class revindications. Of course, a number of intellectuals have participated in the more openly class revolutionary movements and have indeed played an important role in them, but there is no national, structural cleavage which systematically generates this flow of dissidence from any important, distinctive status group. Even if it were argued that such religious, ethnic and linguistic minorities provide targets for the displacement of social tensions so that despotic regimes can manipulate prejudice and particularistic ideologies to organize pogroms and massacres as a means of distracting the oppressed from the real sources of their grievances, one can reply that such unrealistic conflict would constitute a rather different situation from the monotonous absence of overt violent conflict (other than police repression) between social groups in Portugal during the *Estado Novo*. To channel social conflict solely and exclusively into unrealistic violent outlets is very difficult: the possibilities of reverberation and escalation too considerable to be discounted by a regime of 'authority, hierarchy and discipline'. To sum up: class and status cleavages do not necessarily cancel each other out so that homogeneous societies are necessarily more prone to class conflict than heterogeneous ones with important national, ethnic, religious or linguistic minorities. Social homogeneity and the lack of ascriptive status cleavages other than purely class-specific ones may be inimical to class conflict, particularly intense, violent, protracted class conflict. When class, language, religion etc. coincide, class conflict may be maximized; but when class distinctions are not cross-cut at some level by ascriptive status cleavages class conflict may be *under-determined* whereas in the other case it may be *over-determined*.

The homogeneity of Portuguese society is largely the outcome, though not the inevitable outcome, of historical factors such as the almost unbroken eight-centuries-old statehood, the early attainment of national identity and the fact that the existing frontiers have remained substantially unchanged for seven hundred years. Portuguese social stability stems in part from the circumstance that the formation of the state and the definition of national identity took place centuries ago, long before the social crises brought about by industrialization, urbanization and other phases of modernization, in sharp contrast not only to many countries of the Third World but also to a number of European countries whose achievement of statehood and national consciousness is both much more recent and much closer in

time to the rise of industrialism. To have to solve simultaneously the problems of nationality, statehood and economic
development as is the fate of so many countries today is more
stressful, other things being equal, than to tackle the problems
of political participation and economic transformation
taking for granted the existence and scope of the nation-
state as the object of civic allegiance.*

It is against this background that one must assess to what
extent autonomous power-factors have shaped the stratification system, just as we discussed the extent to which major
ascriptive *status* cleavages (or the absence of them) affects the
nature of the Portuguese class system. The existence of the
oldest non-Communist dictatorship in Europe, though
neither preceded nor consolidated by civil war, is perhaps
proof enough that we are not dealing with a 'hegemonic' (in
Gramsci's now classical sense) system of class domination.
But the genus of non-hegemonic, non-totalitarian dictatorships comprises many cases and several species. A useful
classification appears to be that of Andreski who distinguishes
between 'apparatic' and 'classist' dictatorships, the former
being characterized as the rule of a terroristic and predatory
nucleus which eventually minimizes calculability for the
privileged strata of the property and market system (although
not the calculability *of* private property since this type of
dictatorship is by definition non-revolutionary).[2] The political
elite of a classist dictatorship will not be composed of plebeian
or socially marginal elements: in the case of Portugal access
to the political elite is determined by social origin, by
recruitment through highly selective, prestige-conferring,
educational and military institutions, or both; through
formal organizations and informal connubial and convivial
relations it is thoroughly identified with the upper class. The
economic policy of the regime has been avowedly 'neo-
liberal': budgetary balance, monetary and price stability, a
'hard' currency, etc. Through a regressive tax-structure (60
per cent of government revenue is derived from indirect

* Cf. Dankwart A. Rustow, *A World of Nations*, Washington, DC,
1967. It should be noted that the identification of the colonial empire
with nationalism in Portugal provides a kind of functional equivalent
to the divisive nation-state issues that rend so many countries today.
However, a fuller discussion of this issue would take us too far afield.

taxation), special administered prices (wheat price supports which have boosted the economic position of the big southern landowners) and restrictions on competition, the regime has sought to foster a capitalist order. An indication of the 'classism' of the regime (of the fact that it is based on massive national class formations rather than on a narrow exclusive corporate 'apparatus' of violence) may be found in the fact that despite the administrative and political preferment of the officer corps, the size of the armed forces, the officer corps or the military budget did not (until 1961) show a constant tendency to rise in absolute or relative terms. In addition to these limitations on the corporate privilege of the Army, the main avenues to wealth have not been through political office or military rank. An indicator of the extent to which economic surpluses are available through the market or 'civil society' is the degree of fiscal dependence on taxes on external trade: the higher are taxes on external trade the lower become the former. Whereas in 1937 47 per cent of government tax revenue came from such taxes, this proportion had fallen to 23 per cent by 1967.

The dominant version of class theory ties social class both conceptually and empirically to market situations. It has been inferred that classes in this sense cannot exist in command economies, their 'functional equivalent' being some other type of social formation. However, 'pure' market economies only exist as ideal types. In the Portuguese system, at least three factors should be taken into account as 'qualifying' the market economy: (i) the labour-repressive system[3] whereby physical sanctions are used by political authority to curtail labour associations and to prevent or terminate strikes; (ii) particularistic recruitment to white-collar, bureaucratic employment, restricted in law and to some extent even now in practice to the politically loyal; (iii) kleptocracy: the use of public office for gain, or conversely the purchase of political and administrative favours, in a systematic and sustained fashion. Now the term 'kleptocracy' can be used in a 'strong' or a 'weak' sense, i.e. either as a basic type of economic system, analytically related to the concepts of 'command', 'market' or 'customary' economy[4] – or at least to such subtypes as 'market socialism' or 'state capitalism' – or, alternatively, as a secondary determination of market relations without the coherence and comprehensiveness of a society-wide economy. On the whole, it seems best to view these three factors (and others, such as the strength of particularistic-ascriptive value-orientations which are structurally incompatible with rational bourgeois capitalism) as determinations of the market system. In other words, we regard the economy as market in essence, and secondarily labour-repressive and kleptocratic by 'accident' to use the Aristotelian terminology: and consequently, the stratification system as primarily of a class type.

* * *

The Portuguese upper class comprises the following segments: latifundists, financiers, leading industrialists and other businessmen; the upper echelons of the officer corps, the civil service and the professoriate; the Catholic episcopate and the top ranks of the liberal professions. It is much closer to the ideal-type of the 'concrete', established elite, a multi-bonded collectivity unified by common social origins, endogamy, a common education and culture, than to the 'abstract' elite whose members share nothing but the incumbency of leading positions.[5] Its 'established' character does not mean social closure: there is empirical evidence concerning intergenerational mobility into the business elite and the conspicuous co-optation of Salazar and Caetano via the professoriate exemplifies the role of co-optive institutions. Within the upper class a wide 'functional' spectrum is found, economic, political, cultural; diverse economic interest groups; social distinctions between aristocrats and bourgeois, old and new rich, owners and managers; political distinctions between monarchists and republicans, etc., precisely because it is not a specialized power elite. Some of these components correspond to distinct classes in other systems ('landed aristocracy', 'financial aristocracy', 'industrial bourgeoisie') and hence one should speak of 'compression' as much as of 'concreteness' in characterizing the upper class.

The small size of the upper class, at least as far as its economic groups, stems in part from the high level of concentration and centralization of economic power. Portugal certainly conforms to the empirical generalization that a curvilinear relationship obtains between levels of economic development and degrees of concentration of economic power. This high concentration exists in all major fields of enterprise – agriculture, industry and finance. The available indicators are extremely crude and under-assess the real state of affairs. Thus in agriculture 0·3 per cent of farms (less than 3,000) occupy 39 per cent of the acreage, while 95 per cent of farms occupy one-third, whereas in industry 1·4 per cent of factories (not firms) employ 44 per cent of industrial workers. In terms of income, 1·9 per cent of landowners earned 45·8 per cent of agricultural income, whilst 89·5 per cent of farmers earned 32·4 per cent of farm income; in industry and the services, the top 1 per cent of enterprises earned 42 per cent of income, whilst 83 per cent earned 10·6 per cent. The six leading banks hold 60 per cent of total deposits and of the commercial and private credit. In both industry and agriculture a small number of large enterprises confront vast unorganized masses of petty enterprises. These monopolistic or oligopolistic structures are reinforced by the existence of a few geographically far-flung industrial-financial-commercial cartels whose policies affect macro-economic decisions and which are themselves controlled by a small number of families.

Latifundism – as elsewhere in Mediterranean Europe – is characterized by extensive cultivation, monoculture, absentee ownership and extensive leasing. What concerns us here is its importance as a base for class-formation and class-domination. Latifundism is often rather mechanistically regarded as the *fons et origo* of all social and political evils wherever it exists. However, instead of considering it as a cross-national invariant, a variable coefficient of latifundiary dominance should be posited and its value determined empirically in each case. The value of this coefficient for Portugal appears to fall below that attained elsewhere, as a result of the following constraints: (i) relative ecological isolation, latifundia largely concentrated in the south; (ii) lack of control over a monoproduct or oligoproducts crucial to the earning of critical foreign exchange reserves; (iii) want of patrimonial authority over large, captive clienteles; (iv) the relatively small size of the population under latifundiary control (8 per cent of the population in 1960); (v) lack of direct control over the means of violence (no private armies or Mafia), though the State's own police has been at the latifundists' disposal.

In spite of these constraints the 'staying power' of the latifundists should not be underestimated. Though industry has long replaced agriculture as the prime contributor to gross national product, and the stagnation of agricultural production and productivity have become a current subject of concern for progressive public opinion, thereby undermining the social prestige of the rural upper strata, it remains an important source of private wealth. The main latifundist districts have the most unequal distribution of income within the category of surtax payers in the country and two of these have the highest percentage of surtax payers outside Lisbon and Porto. The diffuse influence and weight of the values and ideological orientations congenial to the material and ideal interests of the latifundists are less easy to pinpoint. The orthodoxy of 'agrarian fundamentalism' (the view that agriculture is the 'sacred' way of life, all the others being as it were 'profane'), of what we might call national agrarianism (the view that Portugal is an essentially agricultural country) and of official ecological pessimism (the view that Portugal's natural resource endowment is so poor that substantial improvements in agricultural production or productivity are not feasible) no longer hold sway. Yet latifundists enjoy other social and value assets: they have important links with finance capital, a stake in urban wealth through real estate investment as well as finance, and the 'monetarist' economic policy of the regime is most congenial to their material interests. They have important personal connections with the aristocracy, the monarchists, the officer corps and the public bureaucracy. The bureaucratic-landowning linkage operates not only through landownership by bureaucrats, but also through value convergence: thus amongst university students, the sons of landowners and the sons of higher civil servants show a very similar pattern of faculty choice, both groups being disproportionately concentrated in Agriculture and Law Schools and forming a high proportion of the student body in each. Thus a significant proportion of landowners' sons choose law – a major avenue to politics and administration – and form a high percentage of all students reading law, thus acting as landowner value carriers in the politico-administrative elite. Conversely, a significant proportion of civil servants' sons choose farming and form a high percentage of all students reading agriculture, which indicates a prior stake or affinity with landowning, as agriculture is overwhelmingly an upper or upper middle-class choice, more so than other faculties of the universities.[6] The interpenetration of the landowning stratum and the politico-administrative elite is reinforced by the sparseness of the middle class in rural areas, so that local government tends to be keyed to landowning interests and by the fact that agriculture is exclusively represented by the large landowners in the corporate state order. These two circumstances help to account for the relative weakness of the State and of the technocrats in advancing rational economic policies in agriculture. (The latifundist stratum is not, of course, homogeneous: it is not, for instance, uniformly characterized by a *rentier* economic ethic, but even when guided by the canons of private economic rationality, serious discrepancies arise between this and social or collective economic rationality which raise again the question of the distribution of political power and the political leverage for transforming agrarian structures.)[7]

The industrial business elite is still predominantly familistic: more than half the controllers of large enterprises (defined as those with more than 500 employees) are heirs or founders and in general the larger the enterprise, the greater the number of relatives in the firm. Over half of industrial businessmen are themselves the sons of businessmen, according to a 1966 sample survey.[8] As secondary and higher education have been amongst the scarcest and most unequally distributed goods in this stratification system, the educational background of industrial businessmen is particularly revealing, no matter which set of data is considered:

Table 1

| | Educational standard of businessmen (in %) | | |
	a	b	c
University	20	21·8	48
completed	—	19·5	37
Secondary	43	44·6	37
Primary or less	37	34·6	15

Sources: For *a*, 1960 Census; for *b*, 1961 Manpower Survey; for *c*, H. Makler in R. Sayers (ed.), *Portugal and Brazil*.

The industrial business elite is not only 'over-educated' in relation to the active population as a whole (or that of the urban centres), but also in relation to the business elites of countries with similar levels of development, like Spain, let alone industrial societies where at least secondary education is much more widely available.

The very fact that such a high proportion (perhaps as much as half) of the industrial business elite has been exposed to the universities, which in Portugal have hardly been in the vanguard of modernization, but have acted as carriers of traditional value and cognitive orientations, would indicate a low level of value autonomy for this stratum. However, amongst graduate industrialists, well over half of those in Makler's sample survey had graduated in engineering and only 19 per cent in Law, the arch-traditional subject (this finding contradicts the impressionistic judgment that on leading company boards non-engineers tend to be over-represented). Similarly, the children of large industrialists and other businessmen show a markedly low preference for law at university. Emerging bourgeoisies can lose their hegemonic 'vocation' by aristocratization or by bureaucratization (or indeed by a mixture of the two as in the case of the *noblesse de robe*), the two forms of the 'parasitic involution of capitalism'. Politico-bureaucratic parasitism in Portugal has been fostered by the State policy of legal monopolies, the importance of State contracts, loans and concessions, and by the nexus of familistic oligopolies with their easy access to the politico-administrative elite. Lately, the Lisbon region has become by far the most important industrial area, so that in a sense political and economic power have never been closer in modern Portugal than now. Aristocratization has taken the form of a propensity to marry into the aristocracy, to adopt the aristocratic norm of large families (hence a curvilinear class-fertility pattern, similar to that obtaining in Spain, although less pronounced), to seek social acceptance by the aristocracy, to indulge in conspicuous consumption, etc. The presence in the capital of the Portuguese and other royal families, of leading Portuguese and other European aristocra-cies, of a nucleus of cosmopolitan rich and super-rich has reinforced the strength of 'ostentatious display patterns' (to quote Veblen). The unusually high proportion of national expenditure on building, private or corporate, betokens a non-bourgeois pattern of 'conspicuous construction'.

The behaviour of the industrial elite is in part a function of ecology. In the Porto area, chronologically the first and now the second industrial district in scale and economic weight, the business elite has enjoyed more limited aristocratization and kleptocratic chances than the counterpart in the capital. It has been more socially distinctive, indeed exclusive, and more prone to Republican affiliations (a symbol of the refusal of aristocratization). Mobility into the business elite has been significantly less than in central Portugal, even holding size of enterprise constant. This familism together with the technological conservatism, economic retardation and provincial social climate of Porto suggest the habitat of burghers rather than of Schumpeterian entrepreneurs. If we turn from comparisons in space to comparisons over time, the fast rising 'functional weight' and indeed primacy of industry in the national economy (including a majority of exports) suggest a potential for autonomy in the business elite which has in part been actualized. (The wealthy industrialists, for example, now have their own places of recreation, whereas formerly the aristocrats set the tone of upper-class social life.) While the dependence on finance capital may not have substantially decreased, the aristocratic presence in the leading banks is far less intrusive than in Spain. The prestige of industrial enterprise in the current climate of growth-oriented evaluation accrues not only to owners, but also to top management: the managerial controller or presumptive controller has become a figure of importance. The primacy of the cartels and of the five or six leading families (which all antedate the regime, indicating considerable generational continuity) has not been challenged, however. Under present circumstances the range of kleptocratic opportunities is perhaps wider than ever, so that the growth of rational bourgeois capitalism is rather problematic.

The political elite at Cabinet level is recruited from three more or less (numerically) equal segments: the military establishment, the professoriate and other civilians, the professoriate enjoying a slight numerical lead. The professoriate enjoys high occupational prestige, the role being assessed by the business elite as having most prestige, more so than the leadership of large industrial enterprises.[9] As perhaps befits potential ministers, senior academics are paid the same salary as the highest civil servants (the directors-general), the top military (generals and admirals) and minister-plenipotentiaries, and only less than such officials as Cabinet ministers and the most senior judges. Although the professorial prominence (over half of all civilian ministers) in the Cabinet has perhaps no counterpart in Europe at present, the same cannot be said of the prominence of lawyers. Well over half the civilian Cabinet ministers during the period 1932–68 graduated in Law; a similar proportion probably holds for senior civil servants; the role of Law as an avenue to power is recognized by the law students themselves, who are also characterized by the highest degree of self-recruitment among the university population. These and other findings corroborate Dahrendorf's generalization that the 'real continental equivalent to the Public School as an avenue to power is the study of law',[10] the military channel of access being perhaps the single biggest alternative in Portugal. The prominence of law is associated with the diffuse character of legal education and its high potential for role-substitution. Together with the military, the professoriate supplies the most versatile component of the upper strata, facilitating the role-substitution, multiple career pattern and institutional interpenetration which elsewhere are more exclusively associated with lawyers. Both the professoriate and the military are involved in business as well as political and bureaucratic roles (the 'directorships craze' has particularly affected the military in recent years). Socially the various strands of the upper class have been consistently marked by high permeability in terms of connubium and convivium, as well as institutional co-optation through the university and the Army. Role-substitutability is therefore accompanied by multi-bonding in terms of sociability, intermarriage, and common education at least for succeeding generations (as the growth of exclusive private secondary schools indicates). Caetano, successor to Salazar as Prime Minister, may be regarded as a 'representative man' of the upper class, through co-optation (a conservative monarchist of non-upper class origin, he had a distinguished academic career in Law) via the professoriate, whence he joined the Cabinet, and played other political roles – exemplifying role-pluralism; and by marriage into a leading Republican business family whose wealth and Republicanism date back several generations, exemplifying multi-bonding.

The size of the upper class can be estimated in various ways. Educationally, the university formed (in 1960) 1·2 per cent of the active population. In terms of market power, as we have seen, the top 1 per cent of enterprises in industry and services were paramount. In terms of combined income and occupational criteria, the sub-categories of surtax payers corresponding to the occupational groups which we have identified as constituting the upper class comprised in 1962 about 0·5 per cent of the number of families in the total population. This is probably the most reliable estimate of the size of this class.

* * *

The size of the middle class is often taken as corresponding roughly to that of the tertiary sector (services), although this is of course no more than a rule of thumb estimate (the proportion of middle-class occupations within this sector depends itself on the level of economic development). In any case the pattern of employment has a close bearing on the shape and span of the stratification system. The following table affords a picture of the scale, pace and direction of change in the allocation of the labour force:

Table 2. The Portuguese labour force (in %)

	Year			
Sector	1940	1950	1960	1970
Primary	49·3	48·4	42·8	29·8
Secondary	20·4	24·9	29·5	36·7
Tertiary	30·3	26·7	27·7	33·5

Source and note: Data for 1940–60 are taken from the Censuses of Population. The figures for 1970 are estimates by FDMO, the Government manpower study agency. The sectoral profile for 1970 may be represented as *stp* (where 'p' stands for 'primary sector', 't' for tertiary and 's' for secondary and the order of listing indicates the rank-order of employment size of each sector). The profile had changed in 1960 to *pst* and in 1970 to *stp*.

So far, Portugal has shifted from the sectoral profile typical of the most backward countries – *pts* (the rank-order of employment) to *pst* by 1960 and later if the 1964 estimate is to be believed to *spt*. Two alternative development models appear to have been avoided so far. One is the Greek model, which has registered considerable economic advance maintaining the *pts* pattern and consequently a high proportion of employers and self-employed in industry and the services. This proportion has declined slightly in Portugal to about 14 per cent in 1962 with a very slight increase in absolute numbers in the five years prior to that date. To this extent the entrepreneurial familism and compressed segmentation of petty enterprises in the non-agricultural economy is less generalized than in Greece. The other model is the Latin American one of countries with a similar level of GNP and GNP per capita, but characterized by the sectoral profile *tps* involving a high level of 'bureaucratization' of the economy: only 12 per cent of the active population in the non-primary sectors were public officials (although a quarter of the labour force in the tertiary sector) employing a very liberal definition of 'State bureaucracy' to include the judiciary, teaching staffs of State schools, etc., as well as civil servants in the narrow sense. The ability to contain the growth of the tertiary sector is of course closely related to urbanization.

Although in 1950 Portugal had a smaller proportion of its labour force working in agriculture than either Spain or Greece, the level of urbanization then was still significantly below the other southern European societies and has remained so. Thus *circa* 1958 the Portuguese urbanization coefficient ('urbanization' meaning here population living in centres with 20,000 people or more) was 16·4 per cent, compared with Spain's 39·8 and Greece's 26·8. However, the substantial fertility differentials between urban and rural areas have meant a 'demographic vacuum' left by the urban middle strata, so that, until the 1960s at least, the increment in urban population was mainly due to rural migration rather than to the natural increase of the urban population itself. Thus between 1950 and 1960, the urban population grew by 21 per cent, whilst the total population grew only by 4·5 per cent. Even so, it is plausible to argue that a higher level of urbanization (and we know that levels of urbanization are not uniquely and completely determined by economic growth or industrialization) would have been more conducive to equality and mobility. Lerner[11] has suggested an urbanization coefficient of 10 per cent as the 'critical minimum' and of 25 per cent as the 'critical optimum' for modernization because of the pressures to increased literacy and media participation arising out of urbanization. Since urbanization is defined in this model as population in centres of 50,000 or more and as the Portuguese coefficient up till 1960 fell below 13 per cent, this indicates the size of the 'urban gap'.

It is almost unnecessary to say that the low level of urbanization does not stem from the ascriptive immobility of the rural strata. Immobilizing factors certainly exist: mass illiteracy (36 per cent of the active population in rural areas – 'rural' being defined as living in centres of less than 10,000) and low level of schooling (76 per cent of the active population enjoyed less than four years of schooling); ecological isolation (30 per cent of the total population live in centres inaccessible by road); isolation from the market economy (only 15 per cent of gross agricultural product is marketed); low level of exposure to the mass media (cinema attendance in Portugal has lagged very substantially behind that of other southern European countries), etc. Portugal has, of course, been a high-emigration country even by southern European standards. The rural exodus, however, has shown a consistent propensity to be inter- rather than intra-national: only 22 per cent of rural migrants during 1950–60 moved to the cities, the bulk of the rest going abroad.[12] As a result of emigration, Paris is now the third, if not the second, largest Portuguese city in Europe: this is particularly striking since the absence of cities of 50–300,000 population is one of the most persistent features of Portuguese urban distribution. Potential urbanization can perhaps be measured by emigration which to the extent that it has hindered the move to Portuguese towns can paradoxically be regarded as a ruralizing force (although it is most often described as 'rural exodus'). Of course, urbanization and emigration can be combined in various ways: (1) low urbanization and low emigration; (2) high urbanization and low emigration (Latin America in general); (3) high urbanization and high emigration (Greece); (4) high emigration and low urbanization, as in Portugal, where urbanization and emigration appear to have 'competed' in the last two decades.

A higher level (or faster tempo) of urbanization would not necessarily diminish either the unevenness of urbanization in terms of size-frequency categories (the absence of middle-sized cities) or its territorial asymmetry. This results from the 'dualism' characterizing Portuguese society, which generally tends to increase in the early stages of economic growth: a narrow strip of the western seaboard contains the bulk of 'modern', 'central' or 'Northern' Portugal. There reside the bulk of the urban population, of the university and secondary educated, of the professional and other skilled groups. Generally, all social assets – economic resources, human capital, political power – tend to be very unevenly distributed between the two sectors. This concentration and agglutination of superior assets in a rather sharply demarcated and exiguous area of the country tends to persist over time and indeed to increase during early industrialization through the 'brain drain', the 'perverse' capital flows from the backward to the privileged areas and many other similar mechanisms. This 'dual society' syndrome has led a number of sociologists to reconsider class theory or its applicability to 'dual societies'.

Three logically distinct revisions of class analysis have been put forward in this context. The first interprets the 'dual society' cleavage, owing to the extent, diversity and resilience of the social inequalities involved, as a system of territorial stratification existing in dual societies which is perhaps more consequential than 'class' stratification (particularly the class structure within the 'modern industrial' sector). This type of argument should be distinguished from a second thesis which holds that territorial inequalities are a major *aspect* of classes in 'dual societies', but not their defining property or their primary attribute. The third or 'strong' version of theory holds that in 'dual societies' territoriality, or rather belonging to the 'centre' or the 'periphery', in spatially bipolarized societies is the *criterion* of classes or the basis of class-formation. It is this 'strong' version that draws most on an analogy with the international stratification system, not only for analytical or heuristic purposes, but also for the sake of its moral rhetoric, since the characteristic expression 'internal colonialism' calls upon the most potent moral symbols in the world today. Of course the more 'ideological' versions of the international stratification theory have sought to replace the category of 'class' by the category of 'nation' in the analysis of international behaviour, or to construe nations as 'classes'. Similarly, theories of 'internal colonialism' have sought to subordinate social class concepts, at least as conventionally understood, to the master-cleavage of the 'dual society'. It would certainly be difficult to object to this approach if one adopted Dahrendorf's class-criterion of membership of superordinate or subordinate statuses in authority structures, for this would largely coincide with the 'dual society' cleavage in underdeveloped or semi-developed societies as well as with market-situations, holding territoriality constant. It would be perfectly legitimate therefore to regard the 'dual society' cleavage as involving the distribution of power in the society as a whole, as a basis for 'class'-formation and a potential for 'class' conflict.[13]

In any case two territorially based stratification systems emerge as a result of these structured disparities.[14] The stratification system of 'Northern' Portugal is in part the 'Southern' one shifted upwards – with a higher floor and even a higher ceiling. However, it is also characterized by a more egalitarian shape resembling a hexagon or diamond rather than a truncated pyramid. Without being conceptually or empirically identical with class structure, occupational distribution provides a rough approximation to it. This statement can be specified by considering the distribution of the labour force by sectors and by regions.

Table 3. *Portuguese labour force by sectors and by regions 1960 (in %)*

Sector	Lisbon	Porto	Other Northern Range	Southern Range
Primary	14	18	34–38	41–76
Secondary	32	49	38–43	10–40
Tertiary	54	33	19–28	13–26

Source: Computed from 1960 Census of Population.

Portugal's eighteen districts can be classified occupationally as follows. One shows the occupational profile *tsp* (Lisbon) characteristic of the most advanced industrial societies, such as the US or the Netherlands. One has the occupational profile *stp* (Porto) characteristic of industrial societies. Two are characterized by the occupational profile *spt* (Aveiro, Setubal) which has recently come to characterize the country as a whole. The occupational profile of six *pst* corresponds to the national profile in the same year. The occupational profile of the remaining eight districts – *pts* – is characteristic of the most backward economies with such well-known 'deviant' cases as Greece: some of the districts in this category do in fact have the lowest incomes per capita in the country and rank equally low in terms of a number of social indicators, but two are quite well-off (and therefore 'Greek-like'). Even though these five occupational profiles do not coincide with income per capita variations within the country, they correspond roughly to five levels of cross-national economic development. It is noteworthy that the three occupational profiles of 'Northern' Portugal correspond to stages of economic development not yet attained by the country at that time, whereas one (*pts*) corresponded to a stage already overcome by the national economy. In this way variations in space can be translated into temporal terms, into retrospective and even prospective stages. (Our criterion of 'Northern' here was that the primary sector should be smaller than either the secondary or the tertiary.)

In order to substantiate our thesis concerning the existence of territorially based stratification systems, it is important to consider not only the occupational 'mix' of the labour force, but also the structure of educational opportunity as a pointer to life-chances and to the prospective flow of upward social mobility. A crude means of assessing educational opportunity is to compare access to secondary and to higher education in different districts in relation to the national averages in each case.

Table 4. Access to secondary and higher education

Type	Access to secondary education	Access to higher education
I	high	high
II	high	low
III	low	high
IV	low	low

Type I districts were relatively 'democratic' in educational access: they include Lisbon and Porto and one other (Coimbra). Type II involving high access to secondary education only is, as it were, a 'populist' district with a high level of access to technical, terminal secondary education (with high concentration of modern industry). Type III is an 'elitist' district with high access only to higher education (but two other districts are much more favourable to higher education relatively speaking than to secondary education by comparison with the national situation). Type IV which includes most districts is the 'backward' one with low access to both (although four are close to Type II in that they are proportionately more favourable to secondary than to higher education rather than being equiproportionately disadvantaged for both modes of education). These four types correspond again to cross-national levels of educational development or to the several Portugals. Nevertheless the main gap is still between the relatively 'developed' (Types I and II) and the relatively 'underdeveloped' Portugal (Types III and IV). The two districts of Lisbon and Porto alone accounted for 46 per cent of university students in 1963–4: the significance of this datum can only be understood if we realize that the regional distribution of graduates is much more unequal than the regional origin profile of university students, indicating a constant transfer for talent from 'underdeveloped' to 'developed' Portugal (much the same is true of the secondary educated and secondary schoolchildren).

The foregoing tables suggest some general propositions concerning the social ecology of class in Portugal. First, the sparseness of the middle class in 'peripheric' Portugal, where until 1960 at least 70 per cent of the population lived: the 'backwash effects' of economic growth at this stage magnify and accelerate the contraction not only of actual, but also of *potential* middle strata in it. The hiatus between middle and lower strata in 'peripheric' Portugal is so deep (to take only one indicator – in 1950 only three out of 18 districts had a lower illiteracy rate than that for the country as a whole, viz. 40 per cent), as to seriously impede effective class leadership by the middle class in the bulk of the country. Middle-class leadership roles, 'culture broker' functions or power and influence 'banks' can hardly take root under such structural and cultural conditions. The greater centralization of the State apparatus under the current regime and its reliance on the clergy as the chief agents of non-coercive rural social control, ruling out organized competition for local leadership and representation, have further inhibited middle-class formation in 'peripheric' Portugal. Second, a squirearchy or landed gentry have never developed but whilst a national upper class does not need to be in direct personal control of local polities, this cannot be said of a middle class with hegemonic pretensions.[15] Third, a 'sturdy yeomanry' has not developed: the smallholding peasantry despite numerical growth until 1960 has experienced a steady decline in its economic position. As the 'dual society' cleavage has worsened, no militant social class has a direct stake in the reduction of the 'duality' of Portuguese society. In northwestern Europe, even holding ethno-cultural diversity constant, social ecological differentials and imbalances may provide new foci of class conflict. Touraine goes so far as to say that 'the part formerly played by attachment to craft is now played by attachment to space',[16] but such a struggle for 'territorial justice' as a new and more salient form of distributive justice presupposes an already well organized and militant class, which is precisely what is lacking in 'peripheric' Portugal.

The most important single point about education in relation to class in Portugal is its extreme scarcity: as late as 1960, 30 per cent of the active population were illiterate. Portugal until quite recently lagged much further behind Greece and Spain in all quantitative educational indicators than in economic ones. Apart from the absolute scarcity of education, there is a relative scarcity of secondary education which represents the biggest bottleneck. Not only is education scarce and maldistributed, the educational system is also extremely inefficient in view of the high drop-out and failure rates at each of the multiple examination hurdles (starting with the first year of primary school where the rejection rate between 1950 and 1960 did not fall below 30%).[17] This is a pervasive feature of the entire educational system considered vertically or horizontally, by level or type of school or college.

The secondary school system is bifurcated into lycées, organized as ante-chambers to the universities and technical schools, defined as terminal educational institutions and of course there is a big gap in prestige between the two. Enrolment in the former has consistently exceeded enrolment in the latter, although by a small margin; moreover, the private secondary schools (mostly lycées and Catholic institutions) attract larger numbers than the relatively inexpensive State lycées. Taking the three categories of secondary schools, the more expensive the education, the greater the enrolment, a 'counter-economic' phenomenon which appears to contradict the laws of supply and demand. This is explicable in terms of the higher social selectivity of recruitment and because secondary education is largely geared to the universities rather than valued for the sake of distinct educational and occupational goals. Furthermore, the lag in expansion and the strong geographic concentration of the State lycées has fostered the growth of private secondary schools with the double function of maintaining lycée education as a middle-class monopoly and of aiding the recatholicization of this class.

The expansion of secondary and higher education does not necessarily involve increased inter-generational vertical mobility: it is noteworthy that the expansion of the universities has taken place without any significant increase in the small number of scholarships, so that the bulk of students remain wholly or largely dependent on their families financially. Thus what may be occurring is not increased mobility so much as the educational upgrading of the middle class and the reduction of status inconsistencies between occupation and education, in line with the greater national emphasis on educational certificates and formal universalistic criteria. Whilst 95 per cent of students are recruited from the upper and middle strata – occupationally defined – the educational profile of their fathers is much less inegalitarian:

Table 5. Educational background of fathers of university students and that of the active male population (in %).

	Active males 1960	Fathers of university students 1963–4
University	1·2	27·5
Secondary	3·9	36·1
Primary	37·0	32·7
No school diploma	58·0	2·7

Source: *Situação e opinião dos universitários*, p. 198.

The basic orientation of the secondary and university systems is of course towards the conferment of diffuse elite status. In Portugal, as in most of southern Europe, the historical weakness of the middle class has meant that the universities never lost the monopoly of training for the higher professions and have been able to maintain their aristocratic ethos, their scholastic pedagogy and archaic cultural mentality. They have therefore acted as agencies of cultural immobility rather than of social mobility.[18]

The size of the middle class can be estimated in various ways. The fiscal criterion – the size of the direct taxpayer category – measures it to be about 15 per cent of the active population. Those enfranchised constitute about 20 per cent of the active population. The size of the middle and upper occupational strata is about 25 per cent of the active population, the maximum reasonable estimate.

*   *   *

Subordinate strata in Portugal, like typical subordinate strata everywhere, constitute quasi-groups whose conflict-potential hinges on the opportunity for communication, sustained occupational and communal interaction, autonomous association and organization. Three levels are pertinent here: the national level, marked by limited, discontinuous communication and low social mobilization (disclosed by such indicators as urbanization, physical mobility, mass media, etc.); the inter-stratum level, where three ecologically and culturally distinct strata emerge: the smallholding peasantry, the farm labourers and the industrial workers whose life-situations are as yet distinct and non-homogeneous (the 'lower class' in Dahrendorf's sense, viz. the incumbents of subordinate statuses in all authority structures,[19] who thus constitute a quasi-group of quasi-groups); the intra-stratum level, at which wide gaps emerge between the maximum and the modal patterns of ecological or occupational integration or social isolation. Comparing the three strata in broad terms, the farm labourers and industrial workers have been consistently more militant than the smallholders, as one might expect if the intervening variable, communication, were decisive in translating the pressure of market situations into instrumental group conflict. Within each stratum, the most militant sectors have been precisely the most nucleated, concentrated or occupationally organized: the north-eastern highlanders in the case of the smallholders, the southern *latifundia* labourers in the case of rural workers, and the workers in the heavy industrial concentrations and dense ecological aggregations south of Lisbon in the case of the industrial workers. However, at the inter-stratum level of analysis, we must take into account characteristics other than the extent of communication. Property of course differentiates the smallholding stratum from others, but the Census categories of 'farm labourers' and 'industrial workers' yield little detailed information on the actual incidence of property-lessness. This may be of some importance, as even a property right of low value may play an anchoring function in the stratification order. Since 'disguised unemployment' rather than trade cycle or mass conjunctural unemployment has characterized the Portuguese economy, it is the latifundia labourers who have been most affected by a 'shifting and insecure' labour market, the extremely seasonal character of labour market fluctuations being similar to that of other Mediterranean latifundia. In addition, there is also a differential incidence of secularization which is partly due to a territorial-cultural north-south cleavage and partly to the impact of early industrialization. In any case the present 'religious geography' already obtained in the early twentieth century, the bulk of the northern peasantry being Catholic or clerically led and the majority of *latifundia* labourers and industrial workers being detached even from the minimal Catholicism of the basic rites of passage.

Since the industrial workers have partly been recruited from the peasantry, one has to take into account both the logic of their present work and market situations and the existence of 'situationally inappropriate' values and motivations of workers who are not only ex-peasants, but also prospective peasants in terms of their aspirations and life-goals. Three sets of variables are relevant here: the extent to which situations (structure) can alter values and identities (culture); the extent to which the shift to urban-industrial life-situations is genuinely discontinuous and unmediated; the rate of flow into the industrial worker category and the ratio between the core of workers with a distinctive 'class ideology' and the new class recruits. There is some evidence that industrial-urbanization has been highly mediated, through the slowness of urbanization – in 1950 over half the workers in industry and construction lived in rural localities with less than 2,000 inhabitants – through serial urbanization (movement from small towns to the big city), through particular occupations (building), supportive kinship structures, etc. In so far as either relative gratification (using rural conditions as the yardstick) or a low threshold of 'absolute gratification' prevail, the class-frustration of the new workers should be minimal (even though agricultural wages have risen fast since 1958 and at a rate greater than urban-industrial ones, they still fall significantly short of the latter). The social heterogeneity of the industrial workers is shown by the existence of either relative intra-class deprivation or a higher level of desired absolute gratification among one group even after the rise in real incomes during the last decade. This section of industrial workers accounts for one of the streams of Portuguese emigration (urban skilled workers who are in short supply). Previous mention of the flow into industry draws attention to the fact that the learning of industrial occupational roles and working class-identities need not involve a large cultural 'jump'. Nevertheless a cross-sectional picture of Portuguese industry shows a moderately high level of bureaucratization of the labour force in terms of organizational contexts: 83 per cent of industrial workers were employed in production units with more than 5 employees, 55 per cent in plants with more than 10 employees, 44 per cent in plants with more than 100 employees (data refers to 1959). Historically, the industrial working class developed in the context of highly ascriptive and particularistic social values since the upper strata in Portugal entertained a dichotomic vision of the class system in which the expression '*o povo*' designates a vast, undifferentiated ascriptive mass.[20] The prevalence of such values virtually ensured the dominance of the labour movement first by anarcho-syndicalism and later by Communism (encompassing both the industrial workers and the *latifundia* labourers in each case). Thus both industrial and latifundia workers were trebly disfranchised: they are disenfranchised because of limited suffrage (literacy and tax requirements), because their allegiance is often to the Communist party which is illegal (and not even allowed to present candidates at the so-called elections, when some non-Communist candidates are allowed to stand for office, although never elected), and because the dictatorship distorts the electoral process and manipulates the voting results.

By far the most difficult feature of lower-class behaviour in Portugal to explain is the political apathy of the peasantry (excluding the southern 'rural proletariat' which, however, is not distinctive of our own time alone, but characteristic of the entire historical epoch since about 1850). Yet the small-holder has been subject to multiple and severe economic strains: the shrinking size and increasing fragmentation of farms, the 'price scissors' (i.e. increases on the sale prices of farming products tending to lag behind increases in the prices of goods bought by farmers such as tractors, fertilizers, consumer durables or semi-durables), monopsonistic or monopolistic exploitation in the commodity, land and capital markets, etc. In 1954, only 31 per cent of small farms were self-sufficient, the others being forced, for instance, into extensive leaseholding with its onerous, unregulated rent-contracts. Many compensatory mechanisms have operated, including the persistence of customary rights and of the non-market principles of reciprocity and prestation, dependency on patron-client relations, limited social differentiation within the village community, etc. But the most important mechanism is surely emigration.

Although emigration particularly since the early sixties has become much more evenly spread geographically and occupationally, it has been historically most closely associated with the peasantry. In particular it has been typical of the propertied peasant, since it involves a minimum level of resources and was therefore largely closed to the destitute. Since 1945 about a million people have emigrated from Portugal; the annual rate has sharply accelerated since 1961, exceeding in 1966 the natural increase of population, and, since 1964 exceeding the natural increase of the labour force. As regards both scale and impact of emigration, Portugal is second in Europe only to Ireland. In the logic of the situation, emigration is a fairly *rational* behaviour pattern: unlike other forms of striving for individual or collective mobility or class action, it is hallowed by tradition, legitimated by moral authorities like parish priests, and not liable to the same punishments as 'subversion'. Moreover, given a secular trend in emigration, the virtual certainty of everyone having close contacts with emigrants, the extensive communication system surrounding emigration (Portugal has a very high flow of overseas letters per capita, like other high-emigration societies) with a high degree of 'redundancy', it is an easily *learned* pattern of behaviour, more easily learned than efficacious instrumental group action or other structural alternatives. Emigration represents the standard horizon of social expectations as well as of dreams and hopes, which means that, whether rationally or irrationally, most people will entertain an emigratory project, and that the emigratory alternative is continuously suggested by many sources.

The stabilizing function of emigration has already been implied, but it involves a number of different aspects. Firstly, the aggregate level, the scale of withdrawal from the labour force and the property system. Secondly, the differential class incidence: as the smallholding peasantry has been the least militant of all the lower classes in Portugal (under market-conditions which have elsewhere generated violent expressive group conflict), and is the most emigration-prone it appears that emigration impinges maximally on this class. Thirdly, the intra-class selectivity of emigration, involving the loss of potential leaders. Fourthly, the economic support provided by emigrants. Fifthly, the reduction in urban migration. Sixthly, the impact on the structure of social consciousness: both high and continuous emigration and the permanent possibility of emigration, involving anticipatory socialization to an emigratory solution to life problems, have resulted in a type of consciousness which is neither politically 'utopian' nor religiously ideological (other worldly) but rather *heterotopian*, oriented to an 'elsewhere', an extra-national substitute opportunity structure. In the peculiar topology of emigratory space, Caracas or Paris may be closer to the village – their opportunity structure more visible and appealing – than Lisbon or Porto. Clearly if the emigratory perspective is ever-present, the calculus of social and political action is altered: even while physically present, one is already a potential non-member of the society or the class or both. In this sense, emigration provides a functional equivalent to the belief in openness which, however contrary to fact, mitigates class feeling in other societies and is in some ways less subject to reality-testing, since by definition it is not open to local surveillance. In addition, successful emigration, unlike local social mobility, need not involve occupational mobility: it can be achieved via occupations which, if engaged in at home, would bring about derogation and shame.

At the general societal level, we have to consider how far Portugal's imperial status has stabilized the stratification order. Whether it has or not, it is certain that *de*colonization would be *de*stabilizing: the absence of major historical discontinuities both within the society and in the society's interaction with others makes Portugal almost unique within Europe. It is one of the few European nations which within the last forty years has failed to experience civil war or defeat and occupation by another power or both. Neither has it experienced major inflationary bursts or major balance of payments crises. Urbanization, industrialization, increases in media density, access to secondary and higher education and the granting of minimal social rights have kept pace in a fairly synchronized and harmonious fashion.[21] Of course the granting of political rights (the illiterate have never been enfranchised) and of social rights, like the right to strike, hardly matches a labour-scarce economy – a fact which should facilitate the struggle for occupational role upgrading and citizenship. Although the colonial wars have failed to destabilize the system, the sharp increase in the 'military participation ratio', now perhaps the highest in the world, must be expected to exert levelling pressures, through raised aspiration levels, greater national identification and civil awareness, etc. It can of course be argued that the sense of membership in an imperial country is a 'collective good' or 'indivisible benefit' which compensates for the maldistribution of scarce, divisible assets.[22] However, since emigration to or immigration from the colonies has been so limited, this common ascriptive gratification must perforce be a relatively 'abstract' one, quite unlike that enjoyed by, say, the 'poor whites' through myriad daily acts of 'concrete' face-to-face domination in the South. Admittedly prestige and importance gained in the international stratification system can be seen as an 'input' into the domestic stratification system, even though the lower strata in the latter only possess limited cognitive maps of the situation. However, such positive cross-stratification effects are shrouded in ambiguity and uncertainty.

It is now generally agreed that modernization does not typically involve a cross-nationally uni-variant path leading up to a single final outcome. Paradoxically the early stages of economic growth may bring about not only development, but also, in a kind of dialectical unity of opposites, traditionalization through a number of typical agencies. (i) 'Lagging social emulation':[23] returned emigrants, for example, now as in the past, often seem primarily oriented to the purchase of land and the emulation of the traditional aristocratic land-owning life style. Formerly such conduct was 'appropriate' to a stable social order but in an industrializing society it is anachronistic. (ii) Access to facilities through economic growth, without institutional change, is likely to lead to either manifest or latent aristocratization even by urban middle-class strata. This is the case, for instance, with increased access to largely unchanged educational institutions: the universities now have more law students but also a higher proportion of them in the total student body than ten years ago, tending to make it more 'aristocratic' in its composition and symbolic associations as the law faculty is a bastion of traditional political power orientations. (iii) The 'fusion effect':[24] received aristocratic life styles may combine with international mass consumption standards to displace social conflict onto the expressive field of consumption. (iv) In particular, as market forces in the present conjuncture have led to increased real labour incomes without concomitant political, legal and value changes or greater opportunities for instrumental conflict, intense sumptuary competition may occur in the provinces (tourism may have a salutary effect in this respect, as it legitimates a relatively sober sumptuary pattern by linking it to presumptive high social status). (v) Economic growth without institutional change widens the kleptocratic opportunity structure: in fact, rational-capitalist and kleptocratic-parasitic or political-capitalist modes of appropriation may grow *pari passu*, a trend reinforced by the fact that Portugal is a predatory imperial power.

Nevertheless market forces even within a resistant institutional framework can be instrumental in the struggle for distributive justice and citizenship. At least some segments of the lower strata have taken advantage of their new market powers not only to exact higher wages, but to demand the upgrading of occupational roles (including their renaming) and new ceremonials of civility, a matter of some import particularly in a highly formalistic culture in which modes of address are so closely tied to the expression of a rigid status hierarchy; the social gains have been largest in the case of roles which traditionally required maximum personal subordination, such as rural labourers and domestic servants – both rapidly shrinking occupations. Furthermore in the sphere of consumption, many symbolic correlates of middle-class status have been appropriated by the lower strata, so that the 'trickle effect'[25] – the continual catching up with the old and being overtaken by the new consumption symbols of the upper strata – is now definitely in operation. Whether in fact it can perform the same stabilizing function as in advanced industrial societies is doubtful. These changes however have not been endorsed by new moral symbols, partly because of the repression of secular political ideologies. Even in the religious sphere, new movements within Catholicism such as Christian Socialism and the upper-class-led, but formally egalitarian, *cursilhistas*, and the Protestant fundamentalist sects, although testifying to a deepened sense of moral equality, have had limited impact. Thus the major obstacles even to attaining the level of 'citizenship' already achieved in north-western Europe remain located in the political system and the dominant values.

NOTES

1   Cf. Fallers in Geertz (C) (Ed), *Old societies, new states*, 1963 : 'The period of greatest class consciousness in the American labor movement coincided with the period of mass immigration . . . ethnicity played a role in American stratification somewhat analogous to that of class culture in Europe.'
2   S. Andreski, *Parasitism and Subversion in Latin America*, 1964.
3   B. Moore, *Social Origins of Dictatorship and Democracy*, 1966.

4   J. Hicks, *A Theory of Economic History*, 1969.
5   R. Dahrendorf, 'The education of an elite: law faculties and the German upper class', *Transactions of the Fifth World Congress of Sociology*, 1964.
6   Codes, *Situação e opinião dos universitarios*, 1967.
7   R. Dumont and M. Mazoyer, *Développement et socialismes*, 1969.
8   Makler in R. Sayers (Ed.), *Portugal and Brazil*, 1968.
9   Makler in *Portugal and Brazil*.
10 R. Dahrendorf, 'Recent changes in the class structure of European Societies', *Daedalus*, Winter 1964.
11 D. Lerner, *The Passing of Traditional Society*, 1958.
12 A Alarcão in *Analise social*, 7–8, 1964, 511–73.
13 P. Casanova, 'Internal colonialism and national development', *Studies in comparative international development* (1965).
14 The best account of dualism in Portugal is by A. Sedas Nunes, *Sociologia e ideologia do desenvolvimento*, 1968, pp. 195–256.
15 G. W. Domhoff (*Who Rules America?*, 1967), tries to show that ' "pluralism" on the local level is not incompatible with the idea of a national upper class' (p. 1).
16 A. Touraine, 'Anciennes et nouvelles classes' in G. Balandier (Ed.), *Perspectives de la sociologie contemporaine*, 1968, p. 137.
17 OECD, *Mediterranean Regional Project, Portugal*, 1968.
18 J. Ben-David, 'The growth of the professions and the class system', *Current Sociology*, 12 (1963–4).
19 R. Dahrendorf, *Class and class conflict in an industrial society*, 1959.
20 Cp. S. Ossowski, *Class structure in the social consciousness*, 1963, where the dichotomic vision of society is imputed to lower strata only.
21 Cp. D. Lerner, *The passing of Traditional Society*, on the idea of 'balance'.
22 H. Johnson (Ed.), *The economics of nationalism*, 1968, on the theory of 'public' or 'collective' goods.
23 E. Friedland, 'Lagging emulation in post-peasant society', *American Anthropologist*, 66, 1964, pp. 569–86.
24 G. Germani, *Politica y sociedad en una epoca de transicion*, 1963.
25 The concept, formulated originally by L. Fallers, has been further discussed by M. Levy, *Modernization and the structure of society*, 1966.

3 Italy

Luciano Gallino

The general approach that will be followed in this chapter
for studying social classes and class structures (i.e. the prevailing relations between classes) is one that assumes that
they are or may be important historical *actors* in any society.
Their actions shape the pattern of growth or evolution of a
society; they conflict with each other; form alliances against
the challenges posed by other classes, by industrialism, by
agricultural and commercial revolutions. Moreover, a class
may be a collective subject of action, not only when it is
already a class *for itself*, that is, when it has developed a
common consciousness working as a binding and cohesive
force, but also when it is still a class *in itself*, provided that its
component members have developed common orientations
towards shared problems. In the latter case, however, its
actions will usually be less effective.

All this is common stock in the classical tradition of
sociological thought; from Comte to Marx to Weber, most
sociologists who shaped the central problems of sociology
considered social classes as the main actors of history.
Contemporary sociology, on the other hand, has broken
away from this tradition. It has rather centred its attention –
and its large research funds – on fragmentary aspects in this
area, such as distribution of social rewards, local patterns of
stratification, the changing outlook and life style of the
working class, the influence of class on individual behaviour,
the images of classes held by different sets of people.[1] Because
the present approach is different from, and rather strongly
opposed to the main approaches now at the forefront in the
sociological study of classes, a short discussion of a few of
them – which are held to be representative of the best in the
field – will be in order before tackling specific Italian problems. The point to be stressed is that social classes do act as

single actors within the nation, as the study of (at least European) history should show; and if that is so, the factors accounting for their engagement in action must be explained. None of the approaches shortly discussed – Lenski's, Runciman's and Dahrendorf's[2] – seems to cope satisfactorily with the tangle of problems raised by this consideration or by the fact that being historical products classes have different ages and thus can constitute different class structures *within the same society.*

Lenski defines a class as 'an aggregation of persons in a society who stand in a similar position with respect to some form of power, privilege, or prestige'.[3] These criteria, he says, do not have the same relevance: power is by far the most important, and 'class' is subsequently used by the author as short for 'power class'. This is not due simply to the greater importance of power, but also to the fact that 'the distribution of privilege and prestige seem largely determined by the distribution of power, at least in those societies in which a significant surplus is produced'.[4] Moreover, power rests on various foundations, which differ according to the stage of development reached by any given society. In industrial societies, for example, such foundations are provided by politics, property, occupation, education, racial, ethnic and religious affiliations, sex and age – the last five being less important than the first four. Provided that several sets of people are usually hierarchically ranked in terms of any single criterion among those listed above, this means that in a given society there are several class systems, i.e. the political class system, the property class system, the occupational class system, the ethnic class system, and so on.[5] Of major importance for our argument is the conclusion drawn by Lenski that 'every member of American society [or, for that matter, of any advanced industrial society] holds simultaneous membership in some class within the occupational, property, racial-ethnic, educational, age and sexual class systems.'[6]

Although this approach can usefully explain several minor problems in the theory of social stratification, to the present writer it seems powerless to explain the major ones, such as the way classes act in times of decision. In Italy, for instance, the decision of the landed upper class and the class of business managers to join forces against the working classes, thus opening the road to fascism, can be in no way explained if one assumes that each individual is torn apart by his affiliation to several different classes – occupational, property, educational, etc. The same can be said, to take a case from eighteenth-century England, about the nobility and the rising commercial and industrial classes forming a coalition directed against the labouring classes in both town and countryside.[7] Situations such as these can only be explained if the social phenomenon of 'class' is seen as having one – and only one – major foundation. This means that in a society there can be only *one* class system, though in countries – such as Italy – which are multiple-society countries both one dominant or contemporary class system can be observed together with the remnants of an older system and the elements of a future system. Thus Lenski's approach, by assuming a rather close association between power, privilege and prestige after erroneously taking them as foundations of class, instead of considering them as *dimensions* of it, neglects the problem of what brings about class action – a problem whose solution can be sought precisely in the various kinds of inconsistencies or inverse relationships between these dimensions of class.[8]

In his important essay on 'Class, Status and Power?' Runciman spends the largest part of his argument in examining the necessity and the interest of making the distinction between 'class', status and power (that is: wealth, prestige and power) as separate dimensions of stratification. The main reason frequently advanced for rejecting the distinction – which I take, on the contrary, to be crucial for any discussion on class structure – is that it is so difficult to assess the real meaning and weight of *each* dimension, taken separately, that any attempt to combine them in order to rank people in ordered sets is bound to be hopeless. Two other reasons are, first, that the distinction is often unnecessary 'because of the closeness of fit between the three dimensions alike in industrial and pre-industrial societies. Wealth, power and prestige tend to go together, and this tendency itself is reinforced by a continuous feedback.'[9] Second, this 'three-dimensional framework' is often irrelevant because it is of no use in the study of many central problems. However, in the final section of the paper, Runciman maintains that in many cases, particularly 'those where there is not simply a lag which is in due course either personally or institutionally remedied, but a permanent discrepancy [between the three dimensions]',[10] the distinction is not only relevant but indispensable. This is especially true when the prestige of a person or group is not in line with their power or wealth. In such cases it would be impossible to understand the origins and the nature of the inequalities involved without keeping separate the three dimensions of stratification.

Despite Runciman's conclusions, the reasons he himself has put forward as to why any one of the three dimensions, but especially 'class', can be used to predict the other two, seem well-grounded, so that after all one is left with the idea that any independent analysis of these is likely to be pointless, or at least wasteful. It should be added that the very cases where the distinction *is* relevant according to Runciman, are by far the most important in the study of classes, whereas many of the cases for which it is claimed to be irrelevant, are rather marginal to the study of stratification. At any time in modern history, in any developed society, each class is, in effect, either suffering because of some permanent degree of discrepancy between the three dimensions, or because of some permanent threat to their present congruity. The main springs of class action, which in turn represent the main features of class structures, derive from conflict over reducing this discrepancy between or maintaining the existing consistency of the three dimensions.

Dahrendorf's *Class and Class Conflict in Industrial Society* (1957) is one of the ablest attempts to characterize the new class structure emerging in advanced industrial societies, and it will be taken as representative of a whole series of socio-logical studies undertaking the same problem. His book on German society, *Society and Democracy in Germany*, develops further his model of class structure and adds a host of refer-ences to empirical situations, though, mostly ones specific to Germany. Neither the empirical validity of the general model nor its specific application to German society are contested here, but only the usefulness of applying to a whole 'society', especially to a European 'society', a homogeneous model of class structure. Actually, in Dahrendorf's model account is taken of older classes or strata (author's term), but they are compounded within the same framework. The structure of German society is thus seen as an organic whole which is slowly passing from a less to a more modern shape along a continuum, each point of which is comparable to a given stage of evolution in a living system. This is reflected in a pictorial model made up of seven 'rooms', ordered in a thrapezoidal pattern which makes evident both the fact that a fraction of class X can have a higher position in comparison with the majority of class Y, while the largest part of class X has a position lower than class Y, and that opportunities for mobility of 'circulation' exist among the different strata.[11] Attention also is given to the survival of traditionalism in attitudes and personal behaviour within modern, rational social structures. However, the model is basically meant to picture the *whole* of German society; it is, in other words, a uni-dimensional model of structural change.

On the contrary, for well-known historical reasons, European societies should be considered as 'multiple' or 'plural' societies, whose pattern of structural change is not only saw-shaped, but may be quite different from region to region, from level to level *within* the same society. This is to say that within any country or national state one finds in a very definite sense different 'societies', or, for reasons given in the next section, 'social formations'. Each of them has different historical origins, and consequently its own class structure. Thus, the total class structure of a national society is made up from a number of partial class structures whose origins are to be found in subsequent stages of development in that society. In spite of its care for historical depth, Dahrendorf's model winds up by flattening the class structure, robbing it of variations both on the horizontal (or territorial) and the vertical levels. This line of criticism of unidimensional or one-front models of structural change does *not* mean any leaning towards Lenski's 'multi-dimensional approach', for such criticism implies that the basis of classes is, within each society, one and the same: the function of a set of people in the social organization, considered as a whole. This is in line with the classical approach to the study of classes, and opposed to contemporary approaches involving ranking within compartmentalized political, religious, educational, property systems.

A dynamic interpretation of change in class structures, i.e. one which does not restrict itself to a comparison of two snapshots of a given structure, taken at different times, requires at least three points of reference: (a) a definition of the *bases* of classes as objective categories, independent from the consciousness of their members; (b) a choice of *dimensions or indicators* of class; (c) a theory of class *motivation*, or in Benthamite terms, 'a table of springs of action'. While it is not intended to add anything new to these huge topics, since this would be out of place in this paper, it seems necessary to be explicit about the choices made on each point to aid the reader in following and criticizing the argument.

The *bases* of class are taken to be the functions that a set of people has in the whole organization of society – not simply in the economic sector, although this does go a long way to shape the overall pattern of organization. Often organizational functions constitute the control and/or transformation of productive resources: materials (including land), means of production (and destruction), capital, information and human beings. Apart from the use of force, a common way to control the latter is through the patterning and manipulation of their motives. From the combination of productive resources come the goods, services and organization, which, together with their symbolic meaning, constitute the social rewards usually offered to a given set of people for yielding a fraction of the resources it controls. The degree of total development characterizing a society, as measured by any parameter of physical, political or cultural development, obviously depends upon the stage reached by the 'productive forces' (means of production, skills of people and level of scientific information), though not upon its type or direction of change. However, social organization is made up not only of norms regulating the use of means of production but also of services and symbolic forms of action. The functions of producing and circulating these latter elements represent the bases of several other classes, which will be discussed later.

Having to choose between a host of class dimensions or indicators, it is held that the most useful combination is still the classical, and by now common one which includes wealth or income, prestige or social evaluation and power or control. This set of indicators is akin to the Weberian triad of class, status and power, but reserves the term 'status' to cover the total sum of social rewards (roughly income, prestige and power) offered to the holders of different social positions. All these indicators must be considered from a *societal*, not an individual point of view; it is the income 'typical' of any class in comparison with other classes in society, the prestige received on average by members of a class wherever they go, the power enjoyed by them in and over the total social organization, which is involved here.

The theory of class motivation I refer to could be considered as a *collective* theory of status consistency.[12] It has a number of facets and starts from three very common observations; unremittingly people compare their status (on its separate dimensions) with that of others; people do have a definite idea, which is obviously culture-bound, of the rewards their social position warrants and of the desirable relationship between the different dimensions; people do not like to see the products of their efforts consumed by others. Thus the main motives of class action can, from this, be summarized under the headings of *comparison, frustration* and *exploitation*. From this standpoint, to say that a class has economic and affective interests[13] means not only that it wishes to maintain a constancy of rewards (including prestige), but also that it likes to improve consistency between dimensions to attain a situation of overall balance. A few key propositions which are backed up by historical evidence, can be derived from these starting-points.

a. Classes strive to bring and to maintain their position on the three dimensions of class at the same level. If their income is high, as happened with early merchants and entrepreneurs, they will strive to gain greater power and prestige, as they did in England, France and Japan during their respective industrial revolutions.

b. In whatever 'social formation' it is embedded, each class seeks to bring its overall status to, or maintain it at, the level attained in the formation where it is or was most rewarded. This is the conservative aspect of any class which is uppermost in political action because, for reasons which will become clearer below, if it is to have a minimal probability of success, efforts *must* be directed towards maintaining the whole social formation to which it has an 'organic' relationship.

c. Classes strive to improve their overall status in relation to other classes in the same social formation. That is, they constantly seek a distribution of social rewards which is more favourable to them regardless of its effects on other classes.

The probability that a given class takes a given action as well as its strength, coherence and effectiveness are closely associated with the development of class consciousness and organization.

In order to present a dynamic scheme of Italian class structure, with a particular eye to post-war changes, the fact that Italy, to a greater degree than other European nations, is not one society but several societies in one, must be taken into account. In terms of almost any sociological parameter it appears a bewildering complex of several very different societies or parts of them. In order to disentangle this situation it seems useful to employ a revised concept of 'social formation'. The origins of this concept go back as far as Marx, but there is no space here to recapitulate the stages of its revision and enlargement to satisfy the needs of contemporary sociology.[14] Let us simply say that here 'social formation' is taken to mean an 'organic' societal system, associated with a given historical period and not necessarily co-extensive with State or nation. It is made up of four aspects which tend to be mutually consistent to a high degree: a social system whose main components are the economic, political and kinship sub-systems; a culture whose main patterns support and are supported by the social system; a set of basic personality structures, influenced by the interaction between culture and the social system, and in turn supporting both of these as a result of value internalization; an ecological system whose main components are the demographic structure of the population, its genetic composition, the distribution and size of territorial settlements. The degree of consistency attained at any time between the four aspects may be very high, but the actual degree of consistency is less important than the pressures towards it in every formation.

It is held that in Italy there are at least three different social formations, each of which struggles to shape and adapt the total society to itself, i.e. each struggles to become or to remain co-extensive with the whole country and to mould it to its unique pattern. They are termed for short the Traditional, Modern and Contemporary social formations. The main basis of the traditional formation is agricultural property and production; of the modern, free-competition capitalism; of the contemporary, oligopolistic capitalism. There is no assumption of 'economic determinism' implied here. Taking the economic sub-system as the main feature and basis of every social formation simply means an acceptance of the hypothesis that if this feature has developed, many other changes consistent with it must have preceded and will follow in the other sub-systems and layers of social reality. Thus the economic sub-system is the best indicator of the overall structure of a social formation, although it cannot be said to have 'determined' it.

It would take too long to engage upon a detailed description of each social formation in Italy – suffice it to say that all of them have different historical and local origins. The locus of the 'traditional' social formation was mainly central and southern Italy, where the large landholdings of the Church and nobility underwent important changes during and after the decade of Unification (1860–70), their control largely passing into the hands of the upper bourgeoisie. This class rapidly increased agricultural productivity while leaving virtually unchanged the feudal patterns of social and economic relationships with the peasantry. The locus of the 'modern' formation has been the northern regions, where in the last third of the nineteenth and first decade of the twentieth century the overdue Italian industrial 'revolution' started, with the growth of entrepreneurial activities financed by savings from many small banks which had drained them from the advanced agriculture of the area. Lastly, the 'contemporary' formation developed between the two world wars, and particularly after the second, in the north-western region with branches reaching the upper-central area. *All* the giant Italian companies recently ranked by *Fortune* among the largest 200 industrial companies in the world and outside the United States (Fiat, Montecatini, Italsider, Olivetti, Snia Viscosa, Alfa Romeo, ENI) originated and expanded in this part of the country,[15] instigating a process of social change – think only of internal migrations – which is still increasing in momentum. From a geographical point of view, the traditional formation is now shrinking, whereas the modern and contemporary are expanding, but from a sociological viewpoint the picture is much more balanced. All formations are becoming interpenetrated as large numbers of people increasingly live part of the time in different social formations. The plant they work in may be contemporary while the family or community they return to at night, only modern or traditional. But they belong to a single class according to the functions they have in the societal organization. It is to the complex class structure emerging from the coexistence of different social formations, each with its own characteristic class structure that we must now turn. In order to present a complete model of Italian class structure today, three steps have to be taken: each class must be defined and its internal changes over time marked, i.e. its path must be followed through the different social formations; the class structure distinctive of each social formation must be sketched, if only for the main classes; finally, the total class structure of the present day must be outlined with an emphasis on post-war changes and on the potential action of the main classes.

In the period considered, which is little more than a century, it is possible to trace a number of classes which are present in almost every social formation, although their size and relative strength differ over time. The main classes appear in the following list which is neither exhaustive nor in order of importance:

Landed proprietors	Industrial workers
Independent entrepreneurs	Rural workers (propertyless)
Service class ('professionals')	Independent farmers
Business managers	Craftsmen, shopkeepers
Professional politicians	Intellectuals
State bureaucrats	Technicians

1 *Landed proprietors*

While holding property rights over large acreages of land, they never engage in agricultural labour, are seldom involved in farm management, but usually collect rents from tenant farmers. At the time of national unification, by far the largest part of fertile land was owned by the nobility and the Church. Social relations in the countryside were almost everywhere of the feudal type: the master drew various levies on the produce of peasants and small farmers living on his domain, as well as on their services: the latter, though heavily exploited, enjoyed some degree of security which was to be lost in the next stage of capitalistic agriculture. Between 1865 and the end of the century a dual development took place. In the central and southern regions, the growing bourgeoisie acquired almost all the lands which were formerly owned by the Church, on the abolition of its privileges over landholding (*manomorta*), whereas the estates of the nobility remained almost untouched. However, in the north, it was by slicing out large chunks from the domains of the nobility that the bourgeoisie acquired land. These developments made for the conservation of feudal relationships in the south, even on bourgeois-owned lands, whereas in the north the way was opened for the 'modern' pattern of relationships between capitalist farmers and propertyless rural workers.[16] Thus the main characteristic of the 'traditional' social formation is the endurance in rural areas of a social order handed down from the feudal epoch; landed property is the main source of wealth, prestige and political power. In the 'modern' formation, the class of landed proprietors who are unwilling or unable to turn into agricultural entrepreneurs are under pressure from the expanding bourgeoisie. Although its rents may remain very high, its prestige is shrinking as compared with that of the entrepreneurs, and its political power is challenged with overwhelming force by the rising bourgeoisie. Where and when the 'contemporary' formation develops, the landed proprietors are at their lowest ebb: their rents are cut both by taxes, by competition from modern commercialized farming and by an increase in labour costs: their prestige, as that of those who are not involved in business management, declines, while landowning is restricted to the local level and becomes dependent on personal relations of patronage and clientele.

2 *Independent entrepreneurs*
This class of people who directly control and manage a small-to medium-sized industrial, commercial or agricultural

enterprise, owned largely or wholly by themselves or their relatives, was numerically insignificant until the last third of the nineteenth century and was mainly concentrated in the northern regions. Being a little island of entrepreneurship in the sea of the 'traditional' formation, this class established contacts with the European mainstream of capitalist development. It already had a sizeable income, but its prestige and power was almost nil. As had happened almost a century earlier in England and fifty years earlier in France and Germany, this inconsistency stimulated a forceful drive for improvement on these dimensions. In less than four decades the situation prevailing in Italy was thus reversed. Between 1870 and 1910 this class might not have been the wealthiest, though it was perhaps second only to the landed proprietors, but it was certainly awarded the highest prestige in the national culture and was politically the most powerful group. Its interests were represented by a large majority of parliamentarians and government members; almost all bills or State policies potentially favourable to this class were enacted or adopted as a result of pressures made on its behalf. This was the 'modern' Italy of hard work, internal tariff cutting but national customs barriers, and 'enlightened' right-wing policies. The social relations, personality types and cultural patterns consistent with the interests of this class and characteristic of the modern formation were the most salient aspects of Italian society in the northern and upper-central regions. This class was only forced into a defensive position by the rapid growth of oligopolistic capitalism – the main trait of the 'contemporary' social formation after the second world war. In terms of prestige, it has been overtaken by business managers, professionals and career politicians; its power is being undermined by the growing strength of corporations and trade unions; its wealth is reduced by the comparatively lower productivity of its firms. It is still, however, a large and important class whose membership numbers hundreds of thousands and is still increasing. It still employs approximately *eighty per cent* of the total industrial labour force and its power is still great enough to control the *Confindustria* ('the employers' organization) and to shape its labour policy despite divergent pressures from the large corporations.

3 *The service class*

This class includes all those who offer highly skilled services – legal, administrative, financial, insurance and possibly medical. Since it was the provider of services required by landed proprietors for the management of their estates, as well as a connecting link with the local community, it was already sizeable in the 'traditional' formation, as compared with entrepreneurs, business managers or intellectuals, and is still a feature of this formation. However, in the 'modern' formation this class becomes the main mediator between the powerful entrepreneurs and the State, since it aids in the framing of legislation and also in its subsequent interpretation to the advantage of the dominant class. It is within this formation that the service class strikes the best balance between wealth (or income), prestige and power. In the 'contemporary' formation its members begin to be hired by the corporations on to their growing administrative staffs. The average income of the professional will go up, but gone is the image of the 'free', independent professions. On the power dimension, it is only possible to participate in decision-making at corporate level by relinquishing professional activities for managerial ones: a choice which is in fact made by some.

4 *The business managers*

These trained and/or experienced individuals run the largest companies in every sector of the economy. They often have a share, e.g., stock shares, in the business they help to manage, but their position is founded on their function or role in the enterprise rather than on property. As a class they have almost no place in the 'traditional' formation. In the 'modern', they began a troubled existence as big industry and finance belatedly and clumsily developed. It was only towards the end of the nineteenth century that steel, chemicals, and large-scale banking started in Italy, aided by State protection, and developed for the next thirty or forty years under cover of protective tariffs, with the stimulation of war production and the advantage of a very favourable labour market. Their structural weakness was demonstrated in the 1930's when the whole of the Italian economy was brought to the verge of collapse. The State intervened, taking control of an important part of big industry and banking through the foundation of the IRI (Institution for Industrial Reconstruction). In relation to the 'modern' formation, then dominant in Italy, this class was on the defensive. The personal incomes of its members declined, as did their prestige and power. Only a small elite at its apex, comprising only a few dozen managers, had any real weight on the political scene. After the war and within little more than a decade, the 'contemporary' formation became dominant in Italian society. The 'economic miracle' was apparently brought about by a much younger group of managers, going to and fro between Turin, Milan, Genoa and Harvard or MIT, and possessing a wide network of personal and business contacts throughout Europe. The 'clumsy' factory plants of the 1930's gave way to industrial and financial giants on a world scale, whose investment decisions have had an enormous impact on Italian society, threatening to 'disrupt' northern society for ever, while leaving the south in a perpetual state of backwardness. On the dimensions of wealth, prestige and power, this is *the* dominant class of 'contemporary' Italy.

5 *The professional politicians*

It may seem strange to lump together in a single class the representatives of different interests and ideologies, but in Italy those who spend most of their productive life in national politics, and often derive a livelihood from their political activity, have always had more features in common as politicians than dissimilarities as members of competing parties. Since the opposition's trade mark has long been a conspicuous political sterility, professional politicians appear to have a higher stake in their positions than in the social implications of their action, whatever their ideological platform. Whenever opposition parties have entered the government, their reforming spirit has been lampooned and dampened by the conservative majority. Such has been the fate of the Socialists. The Communists, by contrast, have insisted on policies that have constantly kept them out of power, whilst they were also incapable of influencing the government's line. Thus, judging from the *objective* consequences of their policies, professional politicians appear to have a higher stake in their occupation than in the social effects of their actions *qua* politicians, whatever their ideology. It is precisely this common interest which is a foundation of class.

The split between the governing class and the people, the 'popularity gap' so often mentioned today, dates back to the very beginning of the unification process, to the foundation of the Kingdom of Italy in 1861. In the elections of that year voters totalled only 417,000 (including the islands) since the franchise was restricted to the upper income and educational brackets. Thus less than two per cent of the Italian population voted in the 'Historical Right', a political class composed of landowners and members of the upper bourgeoisie, who based the new State's budget on indirect taxation, shifting the burden to the poor. The 'young Left', representing for the first time the interests of entrepreneurs and the service class, won the elections of 1876. Politics was still a face-to-face or inter-group affair, incomprehensible to the vast majority of the people, to whom the State meant mostly the tax man, the 'carabinieri' enforcing the draft into the national army, or the soldiers repressing the first labour strikes. There was little change in the country as a whole despite the political class having moved from a 'traditional' to a more 'modern' basis. Most Italians discovered that they belonged to a single, united country only during the first world war.

During the fascist period (1922–43), the class of professional politicians coincided with the upper layers of the Fascist party hierarchy, mostly of bourgeois origin. When the war was over and fascism with it, there followed a short interlude of leftist governments until a mildly conservative political class, with middle or lower service class or intellectual backgrounds, emerged. This 'new' political class has been governing the country since 1947, when the first government without Communist members was formed by De Gasperi. This class includes the higher regional and national officials of the 'democratic' parties (Christian Democrats, Socialist – there are several, Republican and Liberal), their representatives in the House, senators, members of the Government and a sizeable fraction of the officials, representatives and senators from the Communist Party. Their interests and identities are first and foremost political in the context of a parliamentary system run by the national councils and secretariats of the parties. The split of this class from the people endures and its overall goal is to remain in power. This has been achieved by aptly selecting from its ranks the men best suited to the changing mood of the electorate.

This 'contemporary' political class is far less homogeneous than it ever was in the 'modern' or 'traditional' situations and it is also characterized by a greater degree of status incongruence. Its income remains as low as before, but its prestige has been seriously damaged by its inability to bring in any major reform. At the same time, its actual and potential power has never been so great, both because of State control over huge nationalized industries and because of private industry's reliance on State support in the face of world competition, monetary crises and general political unrest.

6 *The state bureaucrats*

The 'contemporary' State bureaucracy is the outgrowth of the Piedmontese civil service, which developed in the middle decades of the nineteenth century and was modelled on the French and Prussian civil services. As a result of these origins, it is still one of the most rigid administrative bureaucracies, i.e., it is totally committed to a scrupulous allocation of financial resources to legally defined goals. At the beginning, in the 'traditional' foundation, it was a very small and homogeneous class originating from the middle layer of the bourgeoisie. Over time its composition has changed and it is now mostly recruited from the lower-middle bourgeoisie. In Italy, the position of the State official is unassailable: he cannot be dismissed or transferred without extremely painstaking procedures which are seldom resorted to. By virtue of its permanence, this class has acquired a power of administrative veto. It can be a strong support to any regime, as it was to the fascists, but it can also block or dilute any unpalatable reform, starting with that of the State administration. There is a special ministry for its reform which has achieved nothing in fifteen years. As State intervention extended to new fields before and after the second world war – banking and insurance, shipbuilding and pensions schemes, steel and medicare, land reform and regional development – this class has become very large and internally differentiated. The number of State employees has reached two million, of whom hundreds of thousands belong to this class. It was in the 'modern' rather than in the 'contemporary' formation that its members had higher incomes relative to other groups and prestige superior to that of most classes, with the exception of independent entrepreneurs and professionals. Moreover, tenure and social security benefits were more valued before the onset of the 'contemporary' formation.

7 *The industrial workers*
The growth in size and strength of this class is of course directly related to the stage of national or local industrial development. In 'traditional' situations it is small, fragmented, heavily exploited and poorly organized. Its power is practically non-existent, its income very low, although its prestige is somewhat higher than that of rural workers or independent farmers. This still applies in many 'traditional' areas in the south and the Islands. In the 'modern' formation, its size increases sharply, so that at the turn of the century there were already two million industrial workers. However, its organization remains sectorial and corporative. Differences of skill, culture and political maturity separate the elites of the typographers and tool-makers from the mass of the workers. In the 'contemporary' formation, a new increase in size occurs, while a decrease in internal differentiation takes place, as both the proportion of heavy manual jobs and traditional skills shrink under the impact of automated technology. The level of organization reaches its peak and consequently so does the power of this class. Now that the huge unions are following a unified policy, this is the most consistent and self-conscious class in Italian society.

8 *The rural workers*
Propertyless rural workers (agricultural labourers and rural wage-earners) are by and large the product of the capitalist transformation of agriculture. Unsurprisingly, from the turn of the century to date, the mass of labourers was concentrated in the north-eastern regions, especially in southern Veneto and Romagna, as a result of the capitalist rationalization of cultivation in Lombardy and Emilia and of the massive land reclamation around the Po delta. In the south, where few peasants were expelled from former feudal domains, this phenomenon is less extensive. The labourers are often

independent farmers crushed by debts or sons of impoverished families who have to seek a living which their own barren land does not provide. Although this class has shrunk in size after the war, it has not undergone structural changes during that period nor has it made the transition through the different social formations. Since the prestige enjoyed by agricultural labourers has never been lower than now, increased remuneration has to be offered by commercial farmers to obtain manpower and consequently the average income of this class has risen. The moderate increase in education and standard of living has facilitated a higher degree of political organization, which is beginning to spread southward.

9 *The independent farmers*

According to the last agricultural census (1961), there were in Italy 3·5 million farms operated by a little less than 2 million farmers, aided at best by members of their families. Two-thirds of these farms (more than 2·35 million) had less than 3 ha. (7·2 acres) of land each, yet extensive cultivation predominates. Although the absolute number of farmers may have diminished since, it was somewhat higher in 1961 than at the end of the war. This was mostly due to the Land Reform Bill which, for political reasons, established in the early 1950s tens of thousands of small (7 to 12 acres) farms in the north-eastern, west-central and southern regions. The Christian Democrat Party held that the transformation of labourers into independent farmers would result in a sizeable transfer of votes from the extreme Left to its own side, particularly in the 'red' areas of the Po delta. Not only was this policy a partial failure in political terms, but also on economic, technical and social grounds, with a few exceptions in the cases where the best lands had been redistributed. This class was and is heavily exploited in the 'traditional' formation by the landed proprietors and the commercial system, which is by far the most archaic feature of Italian agriculture. Within the 'modern' formation it has usually enjoyed a higher relative income, since industrial wages were on average low and since more than fifty per cent of them were spent on foodstuffs, while the output of independent farmers still kept up with that of commercial farming and markets were mainly restricted to the local community. In the 'contemporary' formation, this class loses out in both absolute and relative terms, as it is under pressure from the competition of commercial agriculture, expanding markets (see the European Common Market) and changing cultural values. Income is lower than that of every group with the exception of rural workers in 'traditional' rural areas. There is no protection from market oscillations or bad weather, as no form of economic co-operation has developed between farmers. The attractions of urban living have further reduced the prestige attached to farming. However, in an indirect way the influence, and hence to a certain extent the political power of this class, have increased over the last two decades mainly through the efforts of the Christian Democrat Party. This party has very ably penetrated the countryside and succeeded, by passing the Land Reform Bill and by other forms of intervention, to cast itself as the best defender of the independent farming interest. Through the capillary activity of the party-controlled *Federconsorzi*, a giant organization established with the manifest function of providing subsidiary services to small farmers and the latent function of channelling farmers' votes to the party, this class has built up in the 'contemporary' formation a cohesiveness and a political strength which – although they are still relatively small – exceed any it has ever possessed before.

10 *The craftsmen, shopkeepers and small merchants*
This class has always been disproportionately large in Italy and remains so, despite increasing competition from industry, commercial firms and supermarkets. While there are about 1·3 million individually owned shops, they average 1·6 labour units each, which generally means the head of the family with some help from a relative or a hired boy. This structural feature, characteristic of societies with a large 'traditional' formation, has not changed appreciably in the later formations.

11 *The intellectuals*
Membership of this class is defined by reference to a conscious participation in the production and transmission of formal culture; therefore it includes teachers and professors as well as novelists and scientists. As a class, the Italian intellectuals

have always had the problem of establishing an 'organic' connection (Gramsci's term) with other classes endowed with greater functional importance, so as to become more deeply rooted in society. In the 'traditional' formation, their loyalties went primarily to the governing classes, the landed proprietors and the professionals. Throughout the 'modern' formation, they have been largely uprooted, giving for instance a very scant contribution to the development of a strong 'liberal' ideology fitted to the needs of a rising entrepreneurial class – as a cultural phenomenon. Italian liberalism has had mainly agrarian support. After the war, most intellectuals have taken more and more leftist attitudes, but there has been a noticeable change with the passing of generations. The older intellectuals, who had participated in the war, felt bound to offer their loyalty and services to either the old Socialist or the Communist party, considered as the true leaders of the revolutionary struggle. Younger intellectuals, however, are dissatisfied with the sluggish political action of all parties and, stirred by student movements, have gradually come to seek a direct relationship with the industrial workers. Partly a new edition of vacuous populism, partly a genuine political development, the attitude of intellectuals since the end of the cold war is insufficiently consolidated for one to assert that this class has found a new basis for unity.

12 *Technicians*

This class is more 'contemporary' than all others, except the business managers, being largely an outcome of the advanced system of production in the latest stage of capitalism. It includes those who design and keep running the technical equipment of the economy. While it is not yet a class 'for itself', it may well become so before long. In the original 'traditional' formation, there was almost no distinction between the role of the craftsman and that of the technician – the technique was, as it were, built into the craft – and could not be detached from it. In the 'modern' formation, the part of the technician is played either by the skilled worker or by the entrepreneur himself. True, there is the 'ingegnere', a university graduate with higher technical training, but he – a very scarce human resource at the time – is generally the man who plans and designs the product, while the plant is maintained by the foreman and supervisors who are usually older skilled workers. However, in the 'contemporary' industrial and service sectors, a class of specialists develops, whose function is differentiated from that of the skilled worker – the technical supervisor or project engineer. Industrial designers, system analysts, O and M specialists, production and organization planners, operational research specialists, microcircuitry designers, these new experts are needed to organize and control production, and to keep the plant running smoothly. The project engineer, a sort of lonely inventor, is replaced by the inter-divisional project team where each member works on a small fraction of the total task; the skill gained from experience is replaced by external or internal technical schooling. At the end of the war this class was very small, since the largest part of Italian industry remained in the 'modern' formation. However, it has grown faster than any other class and now represents the core of the main industrial sectors, as well as of many service sectors, where advanced technology is applied, e.g., banking and air transport.[17]

The classes specified do not offer an exhaustive description of the Italian population. For instance, priests have not been included since they are not a class in the sense applied here. However, the main component parts of Italian class structure have been included.

In each of the three social formations currently coexisting in Italy, a different class structure prevails. When they first appeared, the 'traditional' and 'modern' formations had a 'pure' class structure, namely one which was well adapted to the overall structure of the corresponding formation. Now that the two older formations intermingle with the 'contemporary', both their overall structures and their class structures have an unstable and fragmented composition. Thus each formation has an 'impure' class structure which will be analysed with special emphasis on recent changes, prior to describing the resulting patterns. As the earlier definition of class structure emphasized that the relations between classes are never in a steady state, the main purpose of the present analysis is to investigate the past developments and probable evolution of inter-class relations in Italy.

The 'traditional' formation originally had a very simple,

almost dichotomous social structure. The dominant class was obviously the landed proprietors; the dominated or under-privileged classes were the rural workers and independent farmers. A tiny service class mediated between them and the propertied class and State bureaucracy (again a very small class). In regional and provincial areas, such as parts of the south and Sicily, where the 'traditional' formation still survives, though in impure form, the relationships between the classes have changed somewhat in the post-war period. The class consciousness and unionization of rural workers have considerably increased, although they still lag far behind the 'modern' stage. On the other hand, the propertied class is to some extent on the defensive, being under the joint pressures of State intervention through land-reform agencies (inefficient and erratic as they are), of an enlarged and more demanding service class, and of industrial competition on the labour market. In the last decade it has also largely lost the support of organized violence from underground criminal associations, such as the *mafia* in Sicily and the *camorra* in Campania, not because these have dissolved or renounced violence, but because their activities are directed towards the new and more fruitful fields of building, domestic appliances retail, commercial patents, etc. Landed proprietors, however, still constitute a powerful class in the south which largely controls local politics and thus undermines all attempts at modernization – that is all opportunities for rapid transition from the 'traditional' to the 'modern' or 'contemporary' formations.

In the pure 'modern' social formation, the main feature of the class structure was the relationship between the entre-preneurial class and the industrial workers. Important also were the landed proprietors and rural workers belonging to commercial farms. It was the coalition of the entrepreneurial class and of the landed proprietors against the abortive alliance between industrial workers in the north and rural workers in central and southern Italy, which was a key factor for the success of fascism in the 1920's. The 'modern' sector has been expanding very rapidly since the war, especially in the regions surrounding those where the first spurt of entre-preneurship started almost a century ago. This first wave had been limited to the larger towns and a few provincial areas in

Piedmont, Lombardy and Liguria. The second wave has now spread to the bordering regions of Veneto (where three-quarters of the new domestic appliances industry is concentrated), Tuscany and Emilia-Romagna, and filled the previously unindustrialized parts of the earlier industrialized regions. This new entrepreneurial class is extremely bold, self-assertive and imaginative. With a minimum of technical culture (or any other, for that matter), a scant knowledge of languages, a shaky financial backing and amazing stamina for business trips abroad, it has pushed onto world markets all kinds of Italian products. There is, however, a cleavage between the entrepreneurs engaged in the newest industrial sectors, such as domestic appliances, scooters, light electronics, and the entrepreneurs of the older sectors, such as textiles and mechanical industries. Whereas the former are expanding, profitable and free – for the time being – from oligopolistic competition, the latter are in a state of semi-permanent economic decline, like textiles, or dominated by local corporations which contract out the manufacturing of many standard components for their products. Correlative discrepancies in interests make for a less cohesive attitude in this class, undermining its potential for concerted action.

This entrepreneurial class is confronted by the class of industrial workers. Until the 1950s and even later in some regions, the power of the latter was almost nil. Those who got jobs felt themselves to be lucky and did nothing which could endanger their tenure. Unions were regarded as nuisances by entrepreneurs and those shop committees which existed at the time were little heeded. Throughout the 1950s and the early 1960s workers tended to leave jobs in small firms whenever they could secure employment in larger ones. Thus the turnover in small-scale, independent enterprises was often up to thirty or even fifty per cent of their labour force. In the last five years or so a change has begun, as unionists and the political efficacy of unions have increased even in relation to smaller firms. More and more the entrepreneurs have had to accept that they can no longer control firms at will, as they used to do in the past.

The entrepreneurial class[18] is currently as opposed to State intervention and State bureaucracy as it ever was, but it has gradually been forced into an ambiguous position. On the one hand it tries as before to evade the network of rules imposed by the State bureaucracy: on the other, it needs the support of the State bureaucratic machinery since its expanded national and international role increasingly depends upon licences, permits, information, tax refunds and supranational regulations. The politics of this class are thus ambiguous, demanding at the same time more and less State intervention in the economy.

In the class structure of the 'modern' formation, the service class plays a more passive part. The individualistic ideology of the liberal professions and their very structure are factors conducive to widespread fragmentation which renders unlikely any form of independent unitary action. However, this class is functionally indispensable as a mediating link between a class – the entrepreneurs – whose only aptitudes lie in the field of 'buying at lower and selling at higher prices',[19] a State bureaucracy which is intrinsically hostile to any form of entrepreneurial activity, i.e., of deviation from formalized rules, and a class – the industrial workers – forced by its historical situation indiscriminately to demand more rather than elaborating cultural alternatives to the existing way of life. It is from this central position that the service class derives a unique consistency between its high income, prestige and power.

The class structure of the 'contemporary' formation is intrinsically the most complex, quite apart from intermingling with the structures of the older formations. Its dominant class is constituted by business managers, with or without property interests. Still large and powerful, though less so than before, is the class of independent entrepreneurs. While the service class has grown richer, its prestige and influence have declined in relation to the previous formation. Professional politicians are the 'coming' class, a class endowed with responsibilities which it does not seem very fit to bear. The State bureaucrats have lost in prestige, but are still capable of postponing or defeating attempted reforms, particularly in such sectors as education or central administration. The expanding ranks of industrial workers are more schooled, more skilled and more organized than ever, and emboldened by full employment. Rural workers get somewhat better and more regular wages, but while better organized they are steadily declining in numbers. Independent farmers are extremely vocal and have directly or indirectly acquired greater influence over the professional politicians. The intelligentsia are more numerous than ever and in the age of mass communication they are sought after, hired and well paid as consultants or experts. Thus they are employed to search, elaborate and transmit information by the very industry whose de-humanizing function they condemn. Finally, technicians are growing more numerous and diversifying their functions.

The network of class interests (not all of which are economic) serves to unify the business managers, the service class and the independent entrepreneurs, despite the latter's internal divisions and their frequent opposition to the ruthless expansionist policies of the big corporations. The unification of industrial and rural workers has still a long way to go, although these two classes are now closer than they were in the 'modern' formation because the role and work situation of the agricultural labourer in advanced 'contemporary' farming is becoming more akin to that of industrial workers. A small part of the intellectual class – about ten per cent of university students – is making an effort to establish some 'organic' link with industrial workers, without achieving much visible political influence. As yet the technicians have remained uncommitted, tending to act in accordance with the interests of the business managers, but increasingly showing signs of unrest.

It is professional politicians who have proved most adaptable, thereby matching the requirements of the 'contemporary' formation characterized by rapid social change. In twenty-odd years in power, this class has produced leaders and governments responsive to the prevailing national mood though often the response has lagged behind. It produced centre-right men, governments and policies in the late 1940s and early 1950s, when the Cold War and fear of Communist advance in eastern Europe brought the Christian-Democrats forty-eight per cent of the votes in 1948.[20] In the middle 1960s, it started to pick out 'leftist' men and to produce 'leftist' governments, at the time of increased labour unrest under conditions of full employment (at least in some regions), of the crisis in the universities and of growing public dissatisfaction with a long list of administrative deficiencies – all of which seemed to demand a more progressive policy. While the platform of professional politicians seems to endorse moderately left policies to various degrees, it is more realistic to acknowledge that their motives are opportunist – with hopes of vote-catching. This class is thus demonstrating a flair for steering a safe political course, but for how long can it endure on the basis of expediency is hard to tell.

Before embarking on an analysis of the main changes in the social stratification of post-war Italy, changes in the position of each class on all three dimensions throughout the three formations are summed up in table form. The main features of the post-war period have been: (a) a 'slide' towards the 'modern' and later the 'contemporary' formation; (b) internal modifications of the older classes; (c) an increase in the number of classes participating fully in national life; (d) the the growth of new classes, for instance, professional politicians and technicians. In the light of earlier comments on class motivation and of coalition theory,[21] an attempt will be made to predict future relationships among the main classes, with special reference to the stable coalitions which might develop in the near future. The problem is twofold: is it possible for a class to adopt a common stand at the national level, in spite of the internal differences which characterize it within each formation? Secondly, if it is, what class coalitions are possible or likely?

Some twenty years ago, the answer to the first question would have been negative for most classes, but many of them now are capable of adopting common stands. The main reason for this evolution is that many pressures are made on all classes to adopt a national frame of reference. Increased geographic mobility, the omnipresent mass media, the unifying influences of technology, unionization – all these influences have undermined the local or regional community as an exclusive or even a major reference group. People are more and more likely to make cross-regional comparisons and to feel frustrated or exploited when they compare their lot with that of their counterparts in the rest of Italy. This is not to say that the situation of a class in the local community no longer matters, merely that its frame of reference for

Table 1. Classes in Italy

'Pure' Social Formations			Landed proprietors	Independent entrepreneurs	Service class	Business managers	Professional politicians	State bureaucracy offices	Industrial workers	Rural workers	Independent farmers	Craftsmen, shopkeepers	Intellectuals	Technicians
Traditional		I	+++	+	+						−	+	−	
		Pr	+++	−	+		++	+	+		−	+	+	
		Po	+++	−	−		+	−	−	−	−	+	−	
Modern		I	+	+++	+++	++		−	+++	+	+	+	−	−
		Pr	+	+++	+	++	++	++	+++	+	−	−	+	++
		Po	+	+++	+	−	+	+	+++	−	−	−	−	−
Contemporary		I	+	+++	++	+++	−	+	+++	+	−	+	+	++
		Pr	−	+	+	+++	+	+	+++	+	+	−	±	++
		Po	+		+	+	+	−	+	−	−	−	±	−

I = Income
Pr = Prestige
Po = Power
+ or − means mainly *diachronically* relative Income, Prestige or Power. No attempt to measure the size of present differentials between classes has been made.

assessing its own opportunity costs has become wider and more diverse, since it extends beyond the local level to other formations. Thus many situations which would have passed unnoticed only two decades ago can now rapidly polarize the feelings and actions of a whole class, despite inter-formational differences.

The independent entrepreneurs are obviously apt to take a unitary stand as a class, and so are the business managers. The former are an old class with a long past and thus tend to look backward, from the 'contemporary' to the 'modern' formation, from which they derive the collective individualistic image of society which guides their behaviour. It is above all this shared philosophy which accounts for the consistency of this class in its dealings with labour and the State. Thus its actions are concerted without being necessarily planned. On the other hand, business managers are united by similar origins and direct personal relationships (this class is still a small one). Such a group has so little interest vested in the past, and so much at stake in the 'contemporary' formation, that it is bent on destroying the older social formations as fast as possible in order to make the 'contemporary' dominant throughout the country.

Professional politicians and State bureaucrats are increasingly inclined to act each as a single actor in view of motives which distinguish them from other classes. Increasingly, Italian politics have become national, since it is only at this level that a politician can make the moves and propagate the image which will perpetuate his career. While the electoral district, with its distinctively local problems, is the launching-pad, it is only by tackling national problems, at least verbally, that a candidate acquires sufficient party support to achieve a parliamentary career. Moreover, Italian parties have strong permanent machines which are heavily centralized. All this makes for a very cohesive political class, commuting between its 'traditional', 'modern' or contemporary constituency and Rome, and sharing a common will to stay in power regardless of variations in local demands. Similarly, the bureaucratic class is totally dependent upon the State which makes for common outlooks and forms of behaviour, despite the differences between geographical regions or historical formations in which they have to work. This is particularly striking within the 'contemporary' formation, since top bureaucrats tend to be traditionally oriented.

Both industrial and rural workers, although to a higher extent in the case of the former, appear well launched on the road towards unitary policies of conflict and defence, despite the different social formations in which they are embedded. The major factor accounting for this has been the development of unionization, although it represents only one aspect of class solidarity. Up to the early 1960s, there was a marked split between the unions affiliated to the Communist-oriented *Confederazione Generale Italiana del Lavoro* (CGIL), and those affiliated to the Christian-Democrat-oriented *Confederazione Italiana Sindacati Lavoratori* (CISL), or to the Social-Democrat-oriented *Unione Italiana Lavoratori* (UIL). Conflicts between the three of them were not infrequent. The situation has altered gradually in the last few years, as the largest unions in key productive sectors have adopted a common policy which is proving durable. This appears to represent a structural change rather than simply a temporary shift in practice. Paradoxically this is not a sign of increasing power of unions over the working class, but rather of a decline in such power. Unions are worried by the protesting minority of left-wing young workers who oppose the decisions of national headquarters and dare to denounce even the CGIL as the pawn of management. These attitudes encourage the unions to step up their demands in order to contain the extremist left within and outside their ranks.

Whatever its causes, the impact of newly found unity among industrial workers, on the one hand, and rural workers, on the other, has already been felt by business managers, entrepreneurs and landed proprietors in several significant areas – elimination of national basic wage differentials, radical improvement of State pension schemes and the tough bargaining in 1969 for a new three-year contract in the mechanical industry. If, as Simmel thought, cohesion brings about yet more cohesion, these classes seem likely to adopt unitary stands on major countrywide issues.

Compared with other classes, it is difficult to assess whether independent farmers adopt a unitary stand in the various formations, although they do have an association, the *Coldiretti*, and common interests at stake. For example, the crisis in the agricultural sector of the Common Market is hitting at the relatively affluent farmers in north-eastern Piedmont and south-eastern Lombardy, as well as the much poorer farmers in Campania and Puglia, although the former are involved in the 'contemporary' formation and the latter in the 'traditional'. However, their social function being localized, their frame of reference correspondingly tends to be more local than that of other classes. Furthermore, the communication flow leading from farm to farm and from region to region makes for a slow and episodic transmission of information about outside conditions, thus reducing unitary class action. It is only when forced by the behaviour of other classes to focus their interest on nationwide problems, such as farm ownership and management, that this class begins to unify regardless of differences between the three formations.

It is more difficult to determine which coalitions are likely in the near future. In all major decisions, the independent entrepreneurs have so far ranked themselves with the business managers: there appears to be no *structural* reason why they should switch alliances. Though they believe themselves to be, and often are, damaged by competition with large-scale industry they are nevertheless the class best off after the business managers in the 'contemporary' formation. In addition, anything which would hurt the business managers, such as a higher share of workers' control within the factories, would be detrimental to themselves. To a lesser extent this applies also to the landowners. This triad has been and may again be a coalition of classes consciously adopting common collective stands, taking the same decisions and employing the same strategies. This form of mutual support must be distinguished from electoral alliances formed between them and including other partners when the ballot takes place. Thus the service class is likely to vote for this coalition, although in non-electoral situations this class has little unity in view of the individualistic functions its members perform.

The industrial workers are the main opposition to this coalition and, despite the better standards of living enjoyed by the majority of them, compared with their position in the 1950s, their antagonism has never been so pronounced. The theory of relative deprivation, which can be traced back at least as far as de Tocqueville, has rightly been used to account for the increase in lower classes hostility as social distances shrinks.[22] While objectively the likely partners in an alliance would be the rural workers, the necessary conditions for the implementation of this coalition have not yet been fulfilled. Industrial workers are more than ever an urban class; they know little about the problems of the countryside and tend to interpret them in the light of their own. Moreover, there has been a numerical decline among agricultural labourers in the last twenty years and they now total little more than 1·5 million. Consequently their attractiveness as allies has reduced over time. Finally, there is no serious political attempt under way towards providing a common frame of reference for the two classes.

However, through their independent activities, these two manual classes have proved strong enough to check the bourgeois classes and to improve their own lot. Yet they are too weak to force the opposition into granting any major modernizing reform. Thus the class structure is so balanced as to perpetuate a complex and frustrating situation. Hence change depends upon the stand adopted by three intermediary classes: the independent farmers, the technicians and the professional politicians. The independent farmers constitute the most conservative class in the country and, as previously indicated, are insufficiently cohesive to adopt an autonomous stand. Therefore they are most likely to support the party presenting least threat to their vested interests and providing greatest rewards for their support. Obviously it is improbable that the workers, with their more or less explicit labour ideology, should support farmers' interests in private property, individual farm management and higher food prices.

Therefore the potential partners to *any* coalition which would seem to offer them better rewards are the two un-committed classes with the greatest degree of status incongruence in Italian society, namely the technicians and the professional politicians. Pretty well off in (relative) income and prestige, technicians are now seeking power, i.e., influence over the plant they operate and the uses towards which it is put in terms of social goals. They also seek to improve their own chances of upward mobility. They are not yet a class 'for itself', but their status incongruence, coupled with their uncommitted position *vis-à-vis* the two opposing coalitions, with potential gains to be derived from joining either, is likely to speed up the process of structuration. For the time being, it is still very unlikely that they should rank themselves *as a class* against the business managers and entrepreneurs. It is even more improbable that they should oppose the industrial workers.

While their income is low, professional politicians use their (relatively) high power in a bid for increased prestige, asserting the independent social value of the political function conceived of as an ethical rather than a purely technical activity. This outlook leads them at present to take a stand against business managers and independent entrepreneurs who have continuously denied or denigrated the importance of this function in a parliamentary democracy. Such an attitude is already apparent in the decisions and speeches directed by the government against industries involved in contract renewal in such sectors as manufacturing and the chemical industry. But this policy seems to be restricted to the verbal level, as an attempt to dampen the 'leftist' stirrings in the country. In fact the unco-ordinated and contradictory interventions made by the government to meet the frantic and unselective demands of the unions contribute in the end to preserving the existing balance of power between the classes, or even result in a shift to the right as a reaction against populism. This ambiguous behaviour of the Italian political class – demagogic declarations on the one hand and inability to carry through any serious reform on the other – possibly provides the key to forthcoming changes in the Italian class structure.

NOTES

1   Most representative of the non-structural and 'non-actional' approach to the study of class are the works by W. L. Warner. See W. L. Warner and P. S. Lunt, *The Social Life of a Modern Community* (New Haven, 1941); W. L. Warner, et al., *Social Class in America: the Evaluation of Status* (New York, 1949). For an intensive discussion of distribution processes see the papers, replies and counter-replies by Kingsley Davis, W. E. Moore,

M. M. Tumin and others now collected in Reinhard Bendix and S. M. Lipset (eds.), *Class, Status and Power* (2nd edn., New York, 1966). H. T. Gans's *The Urban Villagers* (New York, 1962), is a well-known work on the effects of class affiliation. A good sample of American, British, Polish, German and Argentinian papers on the subjective perception of class is given by Massimo Paci (ed.), *Immagine della società e coscienza di classe* (Padova, 1969). To British readers, the works by David Lockwood and John Goldthorpe on the 'new' working class are surely known. The list could still be very long, but the result would not change: classes as collective, historical actors do not seem to deserve much attention from contemporary sociologists.

2　The works mainly referred to are Gerhard Lenski, *Power and Privilege: a Theory of Social Stratification* (New York, 1966); W. G. Runciman, *Relative Deprivation and Social Justice* (London, 1966), especially Chapter III; id. id. 'Class, Status and Power?', in *Sociological Studies*, 1, 1968, pp. 25–61; Ralf Dahrendorf, *Class and Class Conflict in Industrial Society* (London, 1959); id. id., *Society and Democracy in Germany* (London, 1968).

3　Lenski, *Power and Privilege* . . . , pp. 74–5. Emphasis in the text.

4　Lenski, *Power and Privilege* . . . , p. 75.

5　Lenski, *Power and Privilege* . . . , pp. 79 ff.

6　Lenski, *Power and Privilege* . . . , p. 80. See also Chapters 10, 11, 12 on class systems within industrial societies.

7　The latter case is dealt with by Barrington Moore, Jr., *Social Origins of Dictatorship and Democracy* (Boston, 1966), Chapter I.

8　One could object that Lenski's purpose is to explain the distributive processes in society, so why should he bother with class action. The trouble is, he *equates* social stratification, i.e. class structures, with distributive processes only. Thus, no room is left for a unitary structural approach – a prerequisite for studying the distributive processes *and* the class actions stirred by them.

9　Runciman, 'Class, Status and Power' in J. A. Jackson (ed.), *Social Stratification* (Cambridge University Press, 1969), p. 54.

10　Runciman, 'Class, Status and Power', p. 57.

11　See Dahrendorf, *Society and Democracy* . . . , Chapter VI, and the diagram therein appended.

12　The effects of *individual* status inconsistency have been largely discussed under a variety of headings. For a sample of the most recent literature, see E. F. Jackson, 'Status Consistency and Symptoms of Stress', *Amer. Sociological R.*, 27 (4) 1962; E. E. Sampson, 'Status Congruence and Cognitive Consistency, *Sociometry*, 26 (2) 1963; J. C. Kimberly, 'A Theory of Status Equilibration', in Berger, Zelditch and Anderson (eds.), *Sociological Theories in Progress* (Boston, 1966); H. M. Blalock, 'The Identification Problem and Theory Building: the Case of Status Inconsistency', *Amer. Sociological R.*, 31 (1) 1966; J. A.

Geschwender, 'Continuities in Theories of Status Consistency and Cognitive Dissonance', *Social Forces*, 46 (2) 1967; Patrick Doreian and Norman Stockman, 'A Critique of the Multi-dimensional Approach to Stratification', *The Sociological Review*, 17 (1) 1969. Though it is apparent that several propositions developed by the theory of status inconsistency do apply to classes to no lesser degree than to individuals, the literature on the effects of *collective* status inconsistency is very poor. One of the best treatments is still E. E. Hagen, *On the Theory of Social Change* (Homewood, 1962), where the phenomenon of 'status withdrawal' (which it would be better to call inconsistency) is taken as a mainspring of economic growth.

13   A very good analysis of economic *and* affective interests is given by Parsons in *The Social System* (Glencoe, 1951). See the references under 'interests' in the subject index.

14   The English reader can find a very useful introduction to the problem in Eric Hobsbawm's Preface to the first English translation of Marx' *Pre-capitalistic economic forms* (London, 1964). For a good summary of the whole discussion see Oskar Lange, 'Modi di produzione e formazioni sociali. Concezione materialistica della storia', Chapter II of his *Economia politica* (Rome, 1962). See also R. S. Warner, 'Die Methodologie in Karl Marx' vergleichenden Untersuchungen über die Produktionsweisen', *Kölner Zeitschrift für Soziologie und Sozialpsychologie*, 20 (2) 1968.

15   'The 200 largest industrial companies outside US' by the editors of *Fortune*, July 1969.

16   The best analysis of this part of Italian social history is Emilio Sereni's, *Il capitalismo nelle campagne: 1860–1900* (Turin, 1947, 2nd edn., 1968).

17   This is not the 'technostructure' in Galbraith's sense. See his *The New Industrial State* (Boston, 1967), Chapter VI. The technostructure includes a much larger group of people, and its boundaries are rather hazy.

18   This class would also be included in the technostructure, I suppose, making up as it were, its lower stratum. But admitting that within it there are at least two classes casts serious doubts on the usefulness of taking this term to mean a single collective actor, as Galbraith does.

19   For a discussion of the relations among Mafia and landed property in 'traditional' society see Anton Blok, 'Mafia and peasant rebellion as contrasting factors in Sicilian latifundism', *Archives européennes de sociologie*, X (1) 1969. Some hints about the class structure in 'traditional' situations of today can also be gleaned from such works as E. C. Banfield, *The Moral Basis of a Backward Society* (Glencoe, 1958), Chapter 4; and Joseph Lopreato, *Peasants No More: Social Change in an Underdeveloped Society* (San Francisco, 1967), especially part two.

20   It must be noted that 48 per cent of votes given to a single party

is an extremely high figure in a multiparty political system such as Italy's.

21 My thinking on this subject has been stimulated by Theodore Caplow, *Two against One: Coalition in Triads* (Englewood Cliff, 1968).

22 See W. G. Runciman, *Relative Deprivation and Social Justice: A Study of Attitudes to Social Inequality in Twentieth-Century England* (London, 1966).

SOURCES ON THE SOCIAL STRATIFICATION OF ITALY (Compiled by the Editors)

Ammassari, P., 'The Italian Blue-Collar Worker', *International Journal of Comparative Sociology* (Vol. x, Nos. 1–2, 1969).

Banfield, E. C., *The Moral Basis of Backward Society* (Glencoe, Free Press, 1958).

Bergonzini, L., *La stratificazione demografico-sociale in Italia* (Milan, Feltrinelli, 1963).

Cappelletti, L., *Burocrazia e Società* (Milan, Giuffrè, 1968).

Gramsci, A., *Opere* (Turin, Einaudi, 1953, 3rd edn.).

Inchiesta Shell, *La classe dirigente italiana* (Rome, Shell, 1964).

Lopreato, J., *Peasants No More: Social Change in an Under-developed Society* (San Francisco, 1967).

Luzatto-Fegis, P. P., *Il volto sconosciuto dell' Italia* (Milan, Giuffrè, 1966).

Neufeld, M. F., *Italy: School for Awakening Nations* (Ithaca, Cornell University, 1961).

Morandi, R., *Storia della grande industria in Italia* (Turin: Einaudi, 1966).

Romano, S. F., *Le classi sociali in Italia* (Turin, Einaudi, 1965).

Salvemini, G., *Scritti sulla quatione meridionale 1898–1955* in *Opere* (Turin, Einaudi, Vol. 1, 1955).

Surace, S. J., *Ideology, Economic Change and the Working Classes: The Case of Italy* (Berkeley, University of California, 1966).

4 Spain

Salvador Giner[1]

Class conflict is one of the inherent elements of all civil wars, no matter what the chief issues at stake might be. Historians and sociologists, though, do not always have an easy time when attempting to determine the class loyalties, cleavages, and ideologies which come into play during such conflagrations – so many exceptions tend to run counter to a neatly drawn class interpretation of civil wars. The class nature of the Spanish Civil War, however, can be considered to be now firmly established, even if exceptions and special cases were also present in it, as if to belie the many oversimplified versions of it that have been fashionable ever since.[2]

When the three-year long conflict ended, in 1939, a government came to power which was the expression of a general right-wing alliance, which meant, in turn, that it was firmly based in the upper classes. For a series of historical causes, moreover, these upper classes were particularly reactionary in outlook. Their right-wing extremism was now exacerbated by the struggle which they had been so operative in provoking.[3] That they had lacked enough popular support was quite obvious: a mercenary Moorish army and massive fascist foreign intervention were needed from the start for them to succeed. Foreign fascist help largely explains the prominent role of one of the few sources of 'popular' rightist recruitment: the Falange. Volunteers and new party members swelled its ranks during the first months of the war from 75,000 to nearly a million towards the end of 1939.[4] Although many had belonged to a right-wing Catholic party[5] until then, they were not all upper class; thus, the final victory brought to them all manner of political and economic rewards. In exchange for them, of course, Falangists were demanded to drop whatever 'revolutionary' claims the Falangist doctrine might have had at the time the Falange was reluctantly admitted to join in the secret preparation of the uprising.[6] A more genuine source of popular support was provided by the Navarrese countrymen, whose ultramontane Catholicism and somewhat populist Carlism prompted them to action against the hated 'masonic' and 'corrupt' Republic. Paradoxically for the people of Navarre, they found themselves fighting the side of centralism and in favour of a monarchist restoration of old-fashioned absolutism that would never take place.[7]

At the end of the Civil War the patterns of class dominance were extremely clear cut. The upper classes were everywhere in power: the threat of agrarian reform had ceased to be a nightmare for the great *latifundia* landlords, while the industrialists and the financial bourgeoisie had nothing to fear from a working class whose leaders had been decimated, driven into exile or imprisoned, and their political and trade union organizations outlawed. They had to share power with the military, without whose help the victory of a 'reactionary Spain' would have never taken place and, for the time being, with the top leadership of the Falangist party. A vast 'service class' of rank-and-file Carlists and Falangists, middle-class conservatives and leaders of Catholic organizations now controlled the machinery of the state and occupied any post of public responsibility. Vast purges and sustained terror kept any potential opposition at bay. Guerrilla warfare against the regime, which reached substantial proportions after the end of the second world war, was successfully repressed. The liberal intelligentsia, who had backed the Republic to a man, was exiled or completely silenced.

The 'years of hunger' – as they are now called – that is, the period following the end of the Civil War, witnessed a deliberate attempt at reverting to the past as conceived by Spain's new rulers. From the point of view of social stratification this simply meant that the modernization of society, which had begun to gather momentum under the auspices of the Republic, came to a halt. Agrarian reform was shelved. Any social conflict that could be remotely related to class was ignored and to this end a 'vertical' or corporatist trade union organization, the *Sindicato Vertical* was set up. The idea of help and charity to the needy supplanted the true spirit of welfare state action that had imbued the social policies of the republican years. In a word, social change in the direction of a more open society was everywhere halted.

Yet, no regime coming to power in Europe in the middle of the twentieth century could do so on a simple-minded programme of 'refeudalization'. Although much official rhetoric went into convincing the impoverished and exhausted nation that Spaniards were an ascetic people of 'soldiers and friars', it was obvious that Spain would hardly achieve the imperialistic goals set to her by her new rulers without developing a very strong economy. Moreover, the new regime had to prove that its economic policies were more efficient than those of the Republic. (In this, the government failed thoroughly: by 1945, five years after the regime had come to power, the per capita income of Spaniards had sunk and, until at least 1951, stagnation of the economy – if not regression – was total.) The general policy upon which the government embarked was that of fascist autarchy. The rationale was that the Spanish economy had to be liberated from foreign domination, and that self-financed industrialization had to be achieved at all costs for Spain to recover her ancient might. Thus, in 1941, the *Instituto Nacional de Industria* (INI) was created. Its chief overt goal was to fill the gaps left by private enterprise in the country, and help in a general drive towards *sustitución de importaciones*, i.e. producing those commodities which could only be obtained abroad. The INI had additional aims such as setting up heavy industries away from the Basque Country and Catalonia, whose loyalty to the regime was shakier than that of the other parts of the Peninsula. But in practice the whole project became wasteful and was doomed[8] from the start – although it had important, if originally unintended, economic effects later on. The second world war was raging, and Spain could hardly obtain all the materials and machinery needed for such autarchic policies. During the first world war, the Spanish economy had boomed in an unprecedented fashion, helped by neutrality and a sudden international demand for Spanish products by the belligerent nations. However, during the second world war Spanish neutrality was not so complete and the country, after a terrible civil war, was in no position to supply the more sophisticated goods required.

As a result of the self-financed policies of this period,

Spanish banks acquired uncommon powers which today make them stand out in the world of European banking.[9] Moreover, the INI grew into an industrial giant, soon to be coveted by private enterprise in a country whose nationalization policy had been implemented less than half-heartedly. As fascism was not eradicated from Spanish soil after 1945, and economic isolation tended to linger on, autarchic policies had to be enforced for another decade. Although the government tried to break-out of forced isolation, especially through the so-called Franco–Perón pact with the Argentine, large-scale aid of the Marshall Plan type was not available. By the time of the Spanish–American agreements (1953) autarchic policies were well entrenched. In fact, from about 1951, the self-financed industrialization, 'imports substitution' and inflationary policies had been intensified. The critical ceiling was reached only in 1958 for the more foreign aid the regime received during those years after the American pact, the more it persevered in its specific forms of interventionist, bureaucratic and inflationary development. Because of this precedent, the 1959 package deal with the International Monetary Fund and the United States – which rescued the regime from a financial disaster – introduced at last a series of reforms which were imposed on the government. These reforms meant the return of Spain to greater economic liberalism, and led to the economic pragmatism of the 1960s.

Ideologically, parallel processes were taking place, although their pace was uneven. After 1945 the regime began slowly to shed its fascistic rhetorics and paraphernalia, while substituting for them the hedonistic and technocratic doctrine embodied in the idea of *desarrollismo*, or 'developmentism'. *Desarrollismo*, championed today by the Opus Dei elements in the power elite, calls for economic efficiency and 'sane' neocapitalist policies. In turn, such new attitudes have produced substantial effects: the new faculties of economics have been providing public and private enterprises with new waves of less incompetent economic advisers; in 1959, a successful programme for stabilizing the economy was enacted; mergers were later encouraged, and later still, small business firms were left unprotected; permitted rates of foreign participation were increased to the point of raising well-founded protests against the 'colonization' of the economy by investors from abroad; tourism, which had soon become an apparent source of stability for the balance of payments, was encouraged.

After 1959 the country definitely embarked on a new phase of economic expansion. The *desarrollista* ministers and their teams have consistently claimed that such expansion has been inspired and channelled by their two four-year Economic Development Plans. Yet, as reliable economists have shown, this is far from being so.[10] However continued, if enforced, peace, technological change, hard foreign currency from tourism and, above all, the enduring trends of urbanization and industrialization which date back to the first world war, have borne some fruit at last. Of course, to speak of a 'Spanish economic miracle' is ideological gibberish – the results of present expansion are far less spectacular than those of, say, Japan. But by 1968, the average per capita income had reached $650 ($362 in 1958). By 1969 Spain's rate of industrial production was above those of the United States, Great Britain and, more significantly, Italy.[11] By 1969 the gross national product per head was $872. In spite of all this economic development was very unevenly distributed throughout the country, although urbanized areas of great prosperity were no longer confined to very small regional pockets.

At the end of the Civil War, Spain presented a plurality of stratification systems, all widely different, under the cover of one small power elite and of one 'service class' of this elite. The regime that then came to power, for all its centralism, helped to maintain the local and traditional patterns of class domination. Its policies largely explain what has happened in Spain and also much of what has not taken place. Thus, in the case of contemporary Spain an interpretation of stratification must, to be correct, stress the power dimension more than the status or class dimensions. There is little doubt that the 'logic of industrialism', that of urbanization and continued economic growth have had their share in shaping the present patterns of occupational mobility, working-class and middle-class expansion, as well as increased achievement-orientation in the distribution of status and social rewards. However, their belated and restricted development, together with the maintenance to this very day of traditional as well as of 'spoils of war' criteria of privilege can only be explained politically.

The transformation of rural society

Very deep changes have occurred in the rural society of Spain since 1940. In the 1940s rural overpopulation led to undernourishment and poverty, as well as to intense, endemic social tensions between landowners and the landless. The internal migratory movements which accompanied industrialization rocketed during the following years and have changed this situation to a great extent. Yet the 'agrarian question' is still one of the greatest social problems confronting the country as a whole.[12] However, in less than a quarter of a century, from 1940 to 1946, the farming population fell from more than one-half of the total labour force to slightly over one-third. From 1960 to 1968 – in a country of just over 30 million inhabitants – more than one million abandoned agriculture. More significantly, over 80 per cent of them belonged to the rural proletariat, while the rest were landowning peasants many of whom were of course quite poor.[13] Although the proportion of active population engaged in agriculture in 1950 was the same as that of pre-second world war Italy, or France half a century earlier, its steady decline in the 1960s continued at a very quick pace. Thus socioeconomic gaps between Spain and more advanced European nations were not bridged, but began to be narrowed. This is shown in the following table – which is also intended to acquaint the reader with the distribution of active population over the three main sectors of the economy, and their fluctuation over the last few years.

It is predictable that by 1975 the proportion of active population in agriculture will be about 20 per cent of the

Table 1. Percentages of Active Population[14]

	1960	1964	1966	1968
Primary sector	41·7	34·9	32·2	31·2
Secondary sector	31·8	34·8	36·0	36·4
Mining	1·6	1·3	1·2	1·1
Manufacturing	22·4	25·0	25·9	26·0
Building	7·1	7·8	8·2	8·6
Electricity, gas, water	0·7	0·7	0·7	0·7
Tertiary sector	26·5	30·3	31·8	32·4
Trade	8·2	9·3	9·9	10·5
Transport	4·6	4·8	5·0	5·0
Other services	13·7	16·2	16·9	16·9

total.[15] It is harder to predict the figures for the total rural population, which were still extremely high according to the 1960 Census (54·64 per cent of the population lived in communities of less than 20,000 inhabitants). But the mass flight from the land, or *éxodo rural*, continues unabated.[16] Thus, severe depopulation of the countryside is taking place over vast areas. Not surprisingly, it mostly affects those regions where the two extreme forms of landed property, the southern *latifundio* and the north-western *minifundio*, are to be found. The geographical distribution of population is not, by itself, a variable which patterns social inequality in a given society. Nevertheless, in Spain, rural exodus is now seriously affecting the traditional class ratios in precisely those areas which have been notorious in the past for their 'archaic' stratification systems.

As stated above, Spain is a country which presents a plurality of stratification systems. The sharp differences between them is nowhere clearer than in rural society. It is therefore inaccurate to speak of one Spanish rural world. It would also be unjustified to reduce the diverse types of rural property and hierarchy to a couple of main types. Thus, while a brief classification must be attempted here, the following basic morphology of Spain's rural society should be read with these objections in mind. Basically, there are three main stratification systems, each characterized by wide internal variations, some of which will be pointed out.

A Traditionally integrated rural society

It covers those areas – generally in the northern half of the Peninsula – where middling and small landowners predominate. A great variety of landownership is in fact to be found there, along with a plurality of systems of social integration. In some areas, as in Catalonia, the family estate is protected by the right of primogeniture – the *hereu* of Catalan law; in others, such as Old Castile and Galicia, all children have some access to the deceased parent's property. In these, fragmentation of property ensues, and often, extreme poverty. In both cases, however, personal ties to the land and the local community (which tends to be of small size in this area, often less than 5,000 or even 2,000 inhabitants) act as strong integrative factors: these are not the typical areas of traditional peasant revolts.

In spite of its relative stability, it is in such an area that one finds Spain's extreme case of rural poverty: the Galician countryside. Its land fragmentation into small plots (*minifundio*) and its archaic laws of subinfeudation (*foros*) are the chief cause of this state of affairs. More than half of the Galicians deserve to be called utterly poor. They remain scattered over their hilly and humid country, attached to their grotesquely minuscule plots of land, showing a remarkably low degree of class consciousness and posing no real threat to the ruling classes of Galicia. As a result in that area rural exodus, now across the Pyrénées, formerly overseas, is combined with acute *marasmo rural* or stagnation of rural society.[17] It is significant that only since 1952 has the government tried to tackle the problem of 'plot atomization'; in this, however, it shows no particular hurry: by 1967 only 23 per cent of Spanish lands susceptible of some improvement had been somewhat affected by planned concentration of scattered *minifundio* plots.[18]

The varied forms of social hierarchy are very striking in all these areas. Thus, the Galician peasants show a higher degree of traditional subservience and awe in front of the urban and semi-urban upper classes, and of course, in front of the local bosses. On the other hand, Catalan and Basque peasants, often more secure in their prosperous farms (the Catalan *mas*, the Basque *caserío*), tend to demand a more egalitarian treatment, and often show a great pride in their status as farmers.

B Latifundio society

With the exception of Catalonia, the Iberian medieval kingdoms did not possess a fully-fledged feudal system of stratification.[19] It is in the areas which conformed least to the conventional idea of 'feudal society' that one finds today social relationships reminiscent of feudalism – though no form of vassalage, even disguised, is encountered. The possibility of *mafia* or *camorra* style organizations was soon ruled out by a powerful (Castilian-built) state. This southern area – roughly covering Andalusia and Extremadura, and, cutting across modern borders, also the Portuguese Algarve and Alentejo, is characterized by extensive properties or *latifundios*, intensively cultivated wherever irrigation is possible, and otherwise, half abandoned. The *latifundios* cover the best quality land, leaving some marginal arable land to small owners who must alternate their work with that seasonally rendered to the landlords. These are often absentee noblemen or descendants of nineteenth-century bourgeois. Their haciendas hire great numbers of seasonal labourers, who are idle for many months and during bad harvests. For all these reasons, social stratification is relatively simple: landless peasants, often living in the Andalusian agrotowns, waiting for work most of the year; a very high upper class composed of nobility and grandees; an intermediate class of retainers, servants and administrators – the service class of the powerful and rich. Throughout the system status consistency is very high; status is ascriptive and fatalistic social values quite common. In the past, periods of stagnation have alternated with the revolts of millenarian character typical of anarchism in Andalusia.

In the *latifundio* area, however, the gradual introduction of modern technology and some changes in the mentality of the landowner – i.e. the adoption of a more entrepreneurial, capitalistic outlook – have had some interesting effects: fertilizers and machinery have come to the rescue of the landowner who saw his peons disappear, lured by industrial work; in turn, greater efficiency means that he now is less dependent on labour. In spite of his insistence on maintaining his aristocratic and traditionalistic social image, the *latifundista* has to satisfy certain new cultural demands by appearing as an efficient 'agricultural entrepreneur', rather than as an idle landlord. Such changes have not been fully accomplished, since vast areas are still given to the breeding of fighting bulls, or lie practically fallow, as hunting grounds. Yet, change has gone far enough to guarantee the future stability of *latifundismo*.[20] The question of the optimum size agricultural unit is relevant in this connection, for it makes the old anarchist hopes for redistributing land in small plots (*reparto*) look even more utopian. Basically this transformation results from the slow penetration of a more efficient type of capitalism into the most resilient Spanish agricultural institution, the *latifundio*. Its traditional stability as an economic unit has been consolidated (and therefore is a potential source of trouble, while *latifundios* are owned by the very few and employ a rural proletariat living in agrotowns). However, the rural-class antagonisms – which in themselves may not have lost intensity – have ceased to affect society at large as they used to in the past. Such antagonism may remain acute, but the importance of the *latifundio* has decreased in today's Spain, and will decrease further. Accordingly, this group will have to share the political arena with the forces of the growing industrial class.

Yet, rural class tensions in Spain should not be under-estimated. It is still a country where 1·8 per cent of landowners possess more than half the cultivated land,[21] and where the landowning class also belong to the political ruling class, deeply committed to an anti-democratic state. This is aggravated by the fact that in Andalusia, with its higher population growth, the rural population has in fact increased. Thus, only 13 per cent of Andalusian agricultural workers enjoyed fixed employment by 1963.[22] No less than 700,000 peons and labourers in Andalusia must still be defined as rural proletarians, bound to an archaic system of landed property.[23] The state, partially controlled by the landowning class, has only tried to come to terms with these problems by creating industrial 'poles of development' and some agricultural projects, whose showcase effect is often ex-cellent. The actual socio-economic results of policies em-bodied in development projects such as the Plan Badajoz, the Plan Jaén, the Campo de Gibraltar industrialization programme, interesting as they are, are still marginal, so great are the cleavages and the inequalities of the agrarian societies of Andalusia and Extremadura, amongst other regions.[24]

C Industrialized agriculture zones

These small circumscribed zones are worth mentioning because of their presently expanding characteristics. Fully industrialized areas of rural society are hard to find on the Spanish map, simply because the availability of cheap labour in the neighbouring more backward areas blurs the picture. However, industrialized exploitations of agricultural resources have made considerable strides in significant sectors (cotton, tobacco, sugar-beet, poultry, etc.) spurred by the new market demands of a much more urbanized Spain and by the vast hotel and tourist industry. Yet, even here one finds important differences: next to the 'model' farm not hard to come by in, say, Catalonia, one finds highly competitive and industrialized agricultural regions – such as orange-growing Valencia – still hampered by old-fashioned labour-management relations, firm fragmentation, and lack of foreign marketing co-ordination. Moreover, government-sponsored irrigation plans have often distributed land on a familistic, small-plot basis, thus hindering mechanical cultivation and high returns. Mechanization of the land in general continues though. And Spain has now attained a growing rate of agricultural production.[25] Since all this is occurring by and large within the traditional patterns of ownership, it is too early to predict the final outcome for the structure of the Spanish rural society of the future.

URBANIZATION, INDUSTRIALIZATION, AND THE WORKING CLASS

Recent migratory trends have reinforced the pattern of population distribution inherited from the eighteenth century, that is, a concentration of the highest densities along the coastal fringes, with an isolated cluster of high density in the centre of the Peninsula.[26] Thus, by 1963 the average density in the interior was of forty inhabitants per square kilometre, while that of the periphery was of 106 inhabitants per square kilometre.[27] However, the natural population growth of the coastal fringe is lower – a fact related to industrialization and the urban way of life. Madrid conforms to this pattern too and, as usual, is a special case. Centralist and authoritarian governments have artificially created all the necessary conditions for its phenomenal growth (and for its particular types of prevalent occupational structures and status hierarchies). Madrid increased its population by 70 per cent between 1950 and 1964 alone. At present it is growing at the rate of more than 100,000 inhabitants per year.[28] By the same token, Madrid has now finally become an industrial city, although it is still an oasis in the desert of the Castilian high plateau.[29] It now has a sizeable industrial bourgeoisie and a developing managerial stratum, as well as high working-class districts. On the other hand, the Barcelona conurbation (the only one in Spain) shows no signs of slackening its growth. Finally, several provincial towns in non-industrial Spain, have also begun to grow, absorbing the neighbouring rural population and thus greatly increasing the overall index of urbanization. At the beginning of this century only 8·9 per cent of the population lived in cities of more than 100,000 inhabitants; by 1960 27·8 per cent lived in such cities.[30] Until recently, in many areas, urbanization often took place unaccompanied by corresponding industrialization.

In the 1960s, however, the industrial working class has grown practically apace with urbanization and the decline of rural population. This underlines the fact that external migrations have not substantially affected the overall volume of the industrial working class. The half a million or more workers who, between 1959 and 1964 crossed the Pyrénées to find jobs abroad eased, if anything, the anti-government pressures, by not aggravating the situation of growing industrial disputes. (By contrast, the presence of hundreds of thousands of Spanish workers in other European countries – as well as Greeks, Yugoslavs, Portuguese, Italians, must have some effect on the stratification systems and socio-cultural patterns of these countries.[31] Basically, the existence of a European labour market points to the fact that the multi-national social structures of European countries and their trends can hardly be explained in isolation from each other.) These migratory trends are, of course, very sensitive to economic fluctuations, both at home and abroad. Thus, by 1965 migrants to European countries were almost nearing the 200,000 workers' mark. In the course of that year, though, the *net* emigration figures were beginning to decline because of the growing numbers of emigrants who returned home. During the following year and up to the present, the balance has been negative, more workers returning to Spain than leaving for other European countries.[32] It is too early to predict the effects that the return of these tens of thousands of men with several years' experience in Germany, France or Switzerland will have on Spanish labour attitudes, working-class subculture and political behaviour.[33]

While, in the 1950s and 1960s, the numbers of workers in

industrial areas have increased, many rural towns throughout the country – including some Andalusian agrotowns – have become partially industrial. The new and vast industrial working class differs from its counterparts in other western countries in several respects. For a start, a great part of the working class in Spain consists of a proletariat (poor and unskilled). Given varied systems of social stratification characterizing the country, the proletarian-to-skilled-labour ratio sharply contrasts from the less to the more developed areas. Thus Spain has entered the second half of the twentieth century with a proletariat which often fits the classical image: its living conditions are deficient, its salaries are extremely low, its educational background is feeble, and its political rights are negligible.[34] Yet, this situation is in a state of flux; if the numbers of those employed as unskilled labour is still growing, so is that of skilled labour, and not altogether unconnected with this, the size of the white-collar population is also expanding. Assuming that most urban workers are industrial workers, let us look at the following table:

Table 2. *Occupational Distribution in Urban Areas, 1950 and 1964*[35]
(*percentages*)

	1950	1964	Difference
Professionals, technicians, etc.	4·8	1·3	−2·7
Entrepreneurs, managers, etc.	1·8	2·7	0·9
Small entrepreneurs, independent business-men	6·4	11·0	4·6
Clerks, administrators and other white-collar workers	8·0	12·2	4·2
SKILLED WORKERS	15·4	22·0	6·3
UNSKILLED WORKERS servants, unemployed, etc.	15·4	16·7	1·3
Total	100·0	100·0	
	(10,793,057)	(11,707,600)	

The trends have continued, with a steady increase in the skilled labour population. However, a tendency for the greater growth of technical and administrative jobs is already present: from 1964 to 1969 the active population in the industrial sector has grown by 7·8 per cent, while the services have grown by 11·1 per cent.[36] Thus, by 1971 the predicted non-manual urban population will be 37 per cent of the active population (28 per cent in 1966). If the present trends and rates of growth continue, white-collar workers will catch up numerically and later overtake other workers in the 1970s. It is only then that Spain will *begin* to converge towards the present western European pattern. This can be safely predicted because – even under the political conditions which have dominated the country after 1939 – literacy and technical skills have steadily increased amongst workers. Even the present Spanish regime needed to justify itself by a *política social*, which includes some elements of progress towards the open society. Thus, workers may have been skilfully barred from higher education through their redirection towards the so-called 'labour universities' as well as various types of training schools, but these, in turn, have raised the technical knowledge of countless people.

Whatever rates of upward mobility one detects in the working-class and in upper working-class recruitment into the new middle classes,[37] these are statistically counter-balanced by the steady growth of the lower strata of the working class. Such growth will lose momentum as soon as the rural exodus begins to slacken, for intensive depopulation of the countryside cannot go on for ever. Besides, it must be emphasized that the lower strata of the urban and industrial working class are not at rockbottom of the Spanish stratification systems: the segment of poor landowners in the north-west, the *minifundistas*, and the southern peons or *jornaleros* rank even lower: they see their transfer into the urban proletariat as a promotion. From the standpoint of their living standards, the middle and upper working classes are better off than the lower levels of the rural middle class, for they are often in possession of refrigerators, television sets, and so on. This is not due to the fact that they are better off economically, but to their being more integrated in the incipient 'consumer society'[38] of urban Spain, where hire purchase methods of trade came into full swing in the 1960s.

As regards the political activity of the working class, it is the workers with the highest salaries and/or employed by the biggest and most modern plants who are most outspokenly rebellious – a pattern not unfamiliar in other countries. For the government, this means that they have to come to grips not only with the traditional trouble spots – Asturian mines,

Catalan textiles, Basque steel works – but that they now have to face opposition from industrial areas created by their own economic policies, such as the INI plants and the Madrid industrial belt. In society as a whole, workers' opposition to the regime has been only equalled by that of the students and, later, by Basque separatists. (More recently, other groups have joined in the unrest, such as Carlists and disgruntled Falangists.) The traditional revolts of the peasantry having become impossible after the war, the new, swollen proletariat has taken the initiative in class strife. The government has retaliated by some marginal changes in its own, fascist-like *sindicato vertical* but, above all, by tolerating certain 'non-political' strikes as well as by introducing collective bargaining in industrial conflict. All government measures though have been half-hearted and have failed to meet the most elementary claims of the workers,[39] but such minimal concessions have been enough to avert greater threats. A more important stabilizing factor – under a dictatorial right-wing regime – is the fact that an enormous number of workers are employed by small firms: in 1958, more than half worked in firms employing less than 100 men; by 1968, more than 80 per cent of firms were employing 10 or less workers each. Middling firms, employing from fifty to 500 workers, covered only 18 per cent of the total, excluding the firms with less than 10 workers. This compares very badly with Great Britain (56 per cent) or France (46 per cent) and shows the vast changes in industrial structure which Spain has still to undergo, if she is to bridge the gap which separates her from the more advanced countries of Europe.[40] The trend, however, is towards industrial concentration, even if it is doubtful whether at the present rate of industrial modernization the country will soon be prepared to join the Common Market with a minimally up-to-date industrial structure.

Today's class rigidity coupled with the rapid expansion of a still largely proletarian working class could explain the persistence of a revolutionary Spain in the future. However, the seeds of a western style 'consumer' economy are already planted in the Peninsula and Spain's high rate of industrial production after 1959 could in the long run modify the strategies of the revolutionary elements. Thus, *Comisiones obreras*, the semiclandestine workers' organizations so active in the late 1960s, have tended to be less revolutionary in their demands than wages-minded, but this could be a sign of their tactics. Both the outlawed parties and the syndicalist organizations will certainly step up the range of their demands under less repressive conditions. All these questions about the future of class conflict in Spain depend also very largely upon the politics of groups stemming from the middle classes. And it would be unwise to assume that these will only act as a break or cushion to class conflict, as certain forms of middle-class radicalism are a phenomenon of long standing in the history of the country.

THE MIDDLE CLASSES: OLD AND NEW

The slow transformation of the old middle classes and the emergence of a new middle class is one of the most outstanding features of contemporary Spain. The old middle class, with its heterogeneous composition (small merchants, civil servants, administrators, teachers, military officers, and so on) still exists. In fact, following the pluralistic form of stratification to which constant reference must be made, they should be subdivided into at least two groups: the first includes the middle classes of non-industrial Spain – small rentiers, professionals, civil servants, churchmen, merchants. Significantly many of the families appertaining to this class still maintain strong links with rural society. Their outlook is very conservative and provincial. Thus, they can be defined as a preindustrial middle class.[41] The second type of the old middle class is to be found in industrial Spain: the Catalan *menestralia*, hard-working, conservative and yet achievement-orientated, reasonably well-off, is perhaps the typical example of the lower ranks of this middle class; it also comprises the prosperous middle-class strata of the Iberian periphery, based on trade and industry. In terms of status and prestige, these strata must now compete with new groups of skilled workers, technicians, small managers, professionals, owners of small new-type enterprises (bars, hotels, garages, etc.), often connected with the pervading phenomenon of tourism.

Just like in many other countries, the Spanish middle class must be spoken of in the plural. As elsewhere, the differences in values and attitudes between middle-class subclasses are notable. Of these, the new middle-class strata deserve special attention. Their growth, largely connected with the industrial development which began in the 1960s, must be related above all to educational trends, as the occupational structures of the new middle classes – and their intra-class mobility – can be largely explained by reference to these trends. The expansion of education was halted by fascist repression in the aftermath of the Civil War as well as by rampant clerical obscurantism. The built-in needs of industrialization, international opinion and the ideology of *desarrollismo*, however, have accounted for expansion after that period. (The fact that clerical-technocratic groups, such as the Opus Dei or others, at earlier times, the Jesuits, have attempted to get as large a share of control over education as possible, raises different questions.) Thus, there were less than 50,000 pupils in technical schools – both of intermediate and higher education – and universities combined, in the years immediately after the end of the Civil War. In the academic year 1967/8, however, there were already 152,000 students at the higher level. Since 1964, the government has belatedly tried to tackle some of the problems which chronically beset higher education in Spain, opening new faculties and universities, founding new chairs and research units, and so on. Although its policies in this field often seem doomed to failure,[42] some interesting consequences can be detected. Universities are producing a socially ambitious youth, much less fatalistic in outlook than their predecessors of other generations, much more rationalistic and technically minded, more secularized, and often less cynical about politics than other young men and women in other occupational groups.[43] More and more students go into engineering or economics, relatively fewer to the law schools. Women are also much more numerous now in higher education – they were already one-quarter of the student body in 1969. These facts are, of course, related to the socio-cultural traits just mentioned. Yet, the whole process must be qualified by the fact that the expansion of higher education still rests more upon changes occurring within the old middle classes than upon the upward mobility of the lower. To this day, Spanish universities are the prerogative of the middle and upper classes.[44] Under the new social conditions, they must, nevertheless, be considered as very important sources both of intra-class social mobility and of occupational expectations, as well as of new political attitudes among the educated population.

Spanish sociologists concerned with the contemporary class structure of their country have engaged in a debate on the actual size of the middle classes.[45] In general, the most reliable findings seem to indicate that the various middle classes together cover less than a quarter of the entire population, though their size is slowly increasing. For a relatively long time to come, then, the middle classes will find themselves squeezed between the vast lower classes and a not inconsiderable upper class. To aggravate this situation, the lower middle classes, for all their urbane dignity so typical of their country, still are the *sufridas clases medias*, painfully making ends meet by skilful administration of the family budget and by *pluriempleo*. As long as having several jobs in order to meet basic expenses, or *pluriempleo*, is well established for heads of families, the lower middle class in Spain will be substantially different from its counterpart north of the Pyrénées. This stratum of the middle class includes salesmen, employees in banking and administration, some shopkeepers and merchants and smaller groups, such as shareholders in small production co-operatives. In 1960, using the census as a guide, their size could be put at 12·2 per cent of the entire active population. The upper middle class, composed chiefly of entrepreneurs and members of the liberal professions, would account for 7·7 per cent of the active population of that year. Thus, following such a criterion, the middle classes would represent 20 per cent of the total population of Spain in 1960. With the present rates of growth and mobility, one may venture to guess that, in 1970, the middle classes corresponded to a quarter of the total population.

SOCIAL MOBILITY, PATRONAGE AND THE OCCUPATIONAL STRUCTURES OF CONTEMPORARY SPAIN

Transformations in the occupational structure have been the main source of social change in contemporary Spain. The numerical decline of the peasantry, the increase of skilled labour, the multiplication of university and technical school graduates, the growth of employment in the service sector, have all occurred without causing the least discomfort to the wealthy and the powerful – whose immunities from taxation and whose political privileges have been so remarkable since 1939.

Because of the political organization of the country, and also because of traditional cultural patterns and inherited systems of property, networks of patronage – often hiding sheer class dominance – are an important feature of the Spanish social structures. Networks of patronage, of course, also exist in modern class societies, but they must constantly meet the challenge of upwardly mobile individuals whose claims are not based on lineage, privilege, contacts, or friends. Spain is far from this situation. Although there is evidence that a new picture is emerging and that younger generations are gaining confidence in the possibility that personal merit and effort may be rewarded, this is still quite low. Traditional belief in luck, family influence, powerful contacts and so on, are strongly entrenched.[46] The historical causes of this attitude are much older than the Civil War, but there is no doubt that its outcome, by institutionalizing privilege instead of competitive achievement, reinforced the old patterns of favouritism and networks of patronage. Thus, today, when the ordinary Spaniard has to solve some official business his first reaction usually is to look for influential recommendations, if he cannot think of other inegalitarian means, such as presents, or taking personal steps which are entirely unnecessary 'on paper'.

Under post-Civil War circumstances, with no political parties and without a dynamic polity, the traditional networks of patronage have hardened into official and semi-official hierarchies. Of these, the Falange and the Opus Dei have been the most notorious, the army being a separate case because of its fuller identification with the state. During the later phases of the regime, the Falange and the Carlists have lost a great part of the central power, though not all of their economic privileges and local power. The Opus Dei, which has risen to full power during the *desarrollista* period, culminating in the 1969 government reorganization, has clearly not worked towards the establishment of a democratic state. Therefore it has contributed to the process of institutionalizing patronage hierarchies and its own network of avenues of social mobility based on favouritism in the midst of a class society already noted for its rigidity. Since class boundaries were hard to cross while social promotion and mobility were much needed in a country entering a dynamic phase of its social history, the Opus' systems of patronage have provided channels to high status, even if at the price of deep ideological commitment in their recruits.[47]

When ideologically oriented patronage structures are as politically institutionalized as they are in Spain, they also have important effects in hindering certain kinds of social mobility. Thus, because of these groups, a great number of talented and capable people have been unable to take their due part in public life or in the division of labour. In a sense, the exile of the intelligentsia did not stop after the great 1939 diaspora. Notable numbers of 'liberal' intellectuals and scientists have not applied for university chairs, for instance, knowing that the old-fashioned *oposiciones* which lead to them are more often than not thoroughly rigged. Many have gone abroad. Professors and teachers have recurrently lost their posts when too vocal against the regime. Ruthlessly and systematically the neofeudal[48] and now 'technocratic' polity has made marginal all those who did not show enough loyalty (the invariable, official, word for it is *adhesión*) to the vague 'principles of the National Movement' and, more concretely, to one of its networks of patronage. For all these reasons, such 'marginalization' can be understood as a form of internal exile or confinement. Its ideological and political consequences are clear, for the victims of such process, jobless and disgruntled, soon embrace left-wing radicalism.

Having said all this about the institutionalization of patronage in contemporary Spain, a set of occupational groups which are very revealing for the country may be taken as illustrations of trends in mobility, status and power.

1 *Entrepreneurs and managers.* One may now speak of a neo-capitalist generation of Spanish entrepreneurs, eager to imitate the attitudes and approach of their foreign counterparts, and struggling against the inertia of the majority of the other *empresarios*. In some places they have even grouped themselves in clubs with pressure-group ambitions – as is the case with the Barcelona *Círculo de Economía*. Tension with

the old-fashioned and timid *empresariado* class can also be viewed as another aspect of the acute intergenerational conflict which now cuts across the whole of Spanish society. The new entrepreneurs, ready to collaborate with technicians, to appoint competent managers, and to make ample use of marketing and productivity methods is, of course, more frequently found in the more modern sectors of the economy, although interestingly enough, it is in the more depressed sectors of industry that managers are most acutely aware of the national problems of the economy, such as the rural-urban disequilibrium and the 'agrarian question'. In general, though, the old-fashioned type of *empresario* thinks that his task is carried out if he successfully maintains his firm as a going concern, without introducing change or 'adventurous' reorganizations.[49] The protectionism that went with the autarchic policies left him unexposed to foreign market competition for a long time and goes some way in explaining his smug contentment. It is doubtful, however, that under present pressures of change, he will be able to maintain it for long. (As a matter of fact, many of these old-type entrepreneurs are showing a remarkable willingness partially to sell their firms to foreign capital.)

In spite of its familistic and closely-knit structure, the *empresariado* somewhat deviates from the pattern of association characterizing other upper-class strata, as about one-third of them came from non-entrepreneurial families in the early 1960s.[50] Business acumen and technical competence have now been broadened as channels of access to the upper classes. The recent widening of the *numerus clausus* in the traditionally elite schools of mining, engineering, and others is related to this trend, and is bound to have effects on the size and mentality of future entrepreneurs and managers: in the academic year 1950/1 there were 2,972 students in the higher technological schools; by 1962 there were 17,604. Over the decade 1952 to 1962, the percentage of advanced technologists employed in industry passed from 41 per cent to 52 per cent. Most of these students are of middle-class origin, but are soon able to join the lower ranks of the upper class. A loss of the status enjoyed by engineers and technologists is already noticeable in connection with the great numerical increase. The new generations of economists must be added to this group: they now man numerous planning bodies (public and private) and find easy access to the higher echelons of big industry, banking and the public administration. These new cadres are giving certain areas of Spain's economic life an air of professionalism, competence and efficiency which is quite unprecedented. Furthermore, their effect on stratification has already been felt: their rise has coincided with an incipient loss of the prestige enjoyed by career officers (this is true at least for the lower ranks), the old-type bureaucrats and even the old-fashioned rentiers. Yet, it must be emphasized that these trends are now only beginning to be felt.

II *The military*. This professional group has diminished in numbers as the Civil War has become a thing of the past, but this reduction has been slow and the number of officers continues to be exceedingly high for the size of the armed forces. For many years, about 300 cadets received their commissions annually at the Saragossa General Military Academy, a very high figure indeed. They joined an officer corps already swollen by the uncommon expansion due to the war. Laws passed in 1953 and 1958, however, increased the numbers of officers who went into the reserve and, more significantly, the numbers of admissions to the General Academy went down to 220 in 1966.[51]

In the early 1960s, nearly 70 per cent of the new officers in the Saragossa Academy were sons of soldiers and officers, with lower percentages for the Navy and the Air Forces. There is evidence that a strong *esprit de corps* prevails at the entrance examinations and favours inbreeding,[52] although access to the forces is relatively open. The highest proportion by far of recruits to this profession comes from Old and New Castile and from the areas immediately surrounding the military academies, where the armed forces are still generally regarded as an excellent means to improve one's station in life. As could be expected, Basques and Catalans provided by far the lowest numbers of applicants to the military schools.[53]

The armed forces remain an important channel for upward mobility. However, access to the highest posts of stage power is still strictly determined by past Civil War allegiances. As a result many civil provincial governors, heads of civil ministry departments, presidents of state-run enterprises and members of boards of companies are military men. Out of a total of sixty-seven ministers from the time the government was organized in the war until 1964, twenty-six, or 39 per cent, were military men,[54] amongst them the chief of state and, almost invariably, the men who were second in command to him. From the point of view of political power, the upper ranks of the military have reaped the greatest benefits from the Civil War. This cannot be said of the overstaffed[55] middle and lower officer ranks whose problems as regards salary and status seem to be much the same as in earlier times. However, they have been for a long time a dependable group for the rulers to rely on, as the past civil strife thoroughly committed them to the new forms of authority.

Finally, the numerous men who compose the rank and file of the Civil Guard and the *Policía Armada* can be defined as lower class, although they are severed from it by their allegiances to these corps. In the most depressed agricultural areas, however, they are looked as ranking above the status of peons and seasonal labourers. Amongst the peonage, joining either of these police bodies means a step forward. Of the two, the Civil Guard ranks higher, with its traditions, its degree of apoliticism, and its 'aristocratic' isolationism and characteristic life style. It is a more in-bred body, not always readily available to the poor peasant.

III *The 'Funcionarios'*. The problem of quantifying this occupational set of categories in Spain is thorny. The number of civil servants employed by state, state-controlled and local authorities could be put at well over 600,000 in the 1960s.[56] They were first severely reduced by extensive political purges after the Civil War. Replacements occurred, but it is clear that bureaucratic inflation started later than 1940, perhaps towards 1945. However, it is very likely that bureaucratization has been halted by the ideological and political guarantees demanded by the state when recruiting prospective *funcionarios*: the slightest sign of possible deviance in the candidate was met with outright rejection. For a long time, posts were given simply as political rewards without a check on the technical competence of the candidate. In 1939 a decree had reserved 80 per cent of all *funcionario* posts in the central administration to demobilized veterans of the winning side. Moreover, the administration was puffed up with a host of bureaucratic bodies, often staffed by Falangists, such as the huge *Sindicatos verticales*. By and large, *funcionarios* suffered a great deal of penury – unless they were in strategic posts where good bribes, as opposed to mere tipping, could be extracted. Their low salaries did not measure up to the middle-class respectability they aspired to, and this – as in past times – was their curse. It is this group that has, more than any other, resorted to *pluriempleo* to keep up with its status-bound standard of living.[57]

The nature of the regime – partially based on a politics of factions, not of parties – has favoured the *altos funcionarios*, in contrast with the lower ranks of their occupational groups. Ministers, and even the chief of state have often had to seek the support of highly placed administrators, as they could not count on the backing of a political party. Accordingly, the high civil servants have increasingly wielded more power within the state.[58] An inflation in promotion to high posts has occurred in this connection. The possibility for top civil servants to gain rewards, coupled with an excess in sheer numbers and inefficient, obsolete procedures, has fostered a remarkable degree of friction between the several departments of the administration, while enhancing loyalty to the central sources of power.[59] The fear of the quick and heavy hand of the executive has kept the whole apparatus united as a going concern.

Since about 1960 *funcionarios* too have felt the effects of technocratization. Higher levels of competence began to be required, and a state school for higher administrative training was opened. Loyalties to the new influential group, to the 'modern-minded' Opus Dei, also began to count, whilst strict apoliticism became relatively acceptable in some jobs. Economic development plans, new ministerial departments and new statistical offices required a much better-trained personnel. The second, *desarrollista* phase, of the regime has encouraged competent and apolitical young men from non-industrial Spain (where most bureaucrats, judges, and higher civil servants come from) to join the administration. To a certain degree, then, the old-type *funcionario* is in decline, while the new generation of civil servants are finding promotion strictly based on efficiency somewhat less difficult than in former times.

IV *The clergy.* The numbers of this occupational group have steadily, if unevenly, decreased since the middle of the eighteenth century, following western patterns of secularization more closely than superficial observers of the country usually assume. In 1769 there was one priest for every forty-one inhabitants; in 1962 there was one for every 1,228. By 1965, in many areas one priest corresponded to well over 2,000 inhabitants. The clericalist regime has not been able entirely to reverse such a trend after several decades in power, although some recovery is noticeable during certain years or short periods. Thus, while in 1925 there were only 0·5 seminary students for the priesthood per thousand inhabitants, by 1954 the average only improved to 0·69 per thousand. Massive help from the government came after 1945, and by 1949 the country was reaching its peak of enforced clericalism, much to the Church's satisfaction, while the Falange and the *Führerprinzip* began to be displaced from the public eye. This process, used by the ruling elite in its search for new sources of legitimation, meant much more than cultural and ideological shifts. The chief of state nominated the bishops, with Rome's invariable acquiescence (until 1969), establishing a political clientele at the top of the Church hierarchy and binding it to the ruling elite. Access to certain political bodies (such as the Cortes) also gave the dignitaries a taste of secular power. In the systems of class domination, the Spanish Church had a central role at least during the period between 1945 and 1951; up till 1968, it still had a share of power and influence. From then on, however, fissures have become too clear for observers not to make important distinctions.

A few years before the II Vatican Council, a new generation of priests and lay catholics already began to oppose the ultramontane Church. By 1968 they had become a sizeable and vigorous part of post-Council Spain, actually imposing liberalization in the attitudes of the Church, and a more neutral policy towards the state. By the end of 1969, open disagreement with the government was being voiced by the usually ultramontane elements of the hierarchy.[60] Tensions and strife between the two main trends, the *conciliares* and the *integristas*, have become quite serious, and have followed definite generational lines. Although the old-fashioned

F

Church seems to be on the losing side (in the long run), one must remember that upper-class congregations, such as the Opus Dei, have been remarkably skilful in blending *integrismo* and *desarrollismo,* thus satisfying the specific demands of the Spanish state.[61]

In spite of these developments, numbers of priests have not grown substantially, let alone soared, as was intended. Priests tend to be recruited amongst the lower layers of the society, especially the peasantry, although the Jesuits and the Opus Dei have been successful in recruiting members amongst the bourgeoisie and certain segments of the intelligentsia.[62] The same changes in mentality which are transforming the middle classes and the more prosperous part of the working classes have often undermined the Church's sources of recruitment and the loyalty of seminarists and priests who leave their profession. This situation is aggravated by the rural exodus and the steady pressure on the Spanish hierarchy to send missionaries overseas and to chronically understaffed countries. The vast campaigns carried out by the Church with full governmental backing, to sponsor 'vocations' for the seminaries, have produced meagre results. It is safe to add, moreover, that priests have also lost status in areas where a more hedonistic value system is penetrating.

THE UPPER CLASSES AND THE RULING ELITES: PATTERNS OF CLASS DOMINATION

For 1960, the size of the upper classes of Spain could tentatively be put at about 4 per cent of the total population. Using the Census as a criterion – for lack of better sources – it is found that the high entrepreneurial class, the prominent landowners, the main directors of banks, industry and trade and the superior cadres of administration put together add up to a 3·73 per cent of the total active population. Again, tentatively, one can add another 0·25 of prominent military men – actually wielding political power – similarly placed churchmen, and very influential people not included in the latter census categories, such as, for instance, the leaders of the *Opus Dei* who are not members of the government. But the sizes of classes and their mutual ratios are only a primary, if often revealing, datum. What matters particularly in the

Spanish context is the extent to which the upper classes encompass power, privilege and high status, that is, the extent to which they are the exclusive seedbed of national elites in every field.

Every serious observer of the social structure of Spain, past and present, has remarked on the extent to which unchecked power has been and still is concentrated in the hands of the few.[63] Although sociologists have often been rightly mistrustful of the 'one hundred families' or 'two hundred families' approach to the description of upper classes anywhere, in countries such as Spain after 1939, where the usual patterns of upper-class isolationism are combined with an unchallenged possession of the political apparatus, such an approach does not seem entirely out of place.[64] To give an idea of the concentration of economic power in the hands of the very few, it suffices to say that about half the capital of all private companies in Spain is held by the people who happen to sit on the executive councils of the five most powerful banks. (And private banking is, in Spain, by far the main centre of economic power.)[65] In Spain, policies must always first satisfy upper-class groups, be they Andalusian landowners, Valencian citrus growers and exporters, Catalan textile industrialists, Madrid financiers *cum* politicians, or Basque steel-mill owners. More often than not, 'egalitarian' policies are either strategic concessions to officially unrecognized social movements – students in revolt, workers' wage claims – or part of the 'social and economic' development plans of the official ideology, carefully worked out to increase the per capita income of the average Spaniard without upsetting the present distribution of power and privilege in the hands of the military and the high bourgeoisie.

Changes and shifts have taken place in the structure of contemporary upper classes, but they have never been drastic. Thus, the considerable displacement of the Falange party from power has not always meant total ostracism for its formerly powerful members, let alone impoverishment. As has been pointed out, Opus Dei members in the top governmental posts have often come a relatively long way up through the class and status hierarchies before they got there.[66] Yet, basically these examples of downward or upward mobility have coincided with necessary reorientations of policy and/or struggles amongst factions, which have left the upper classes and the core groups in the dictatorship (the chief of state and his chosen friends) unruffled in their respective positions[67] of either class domination or dictatorial political power. There are, of course, other upper-class groups who, in the midst of economic change have increased their size or influence. Such are, for instance, the so-called technocrats or *desarrollistas* in government departments and the high entrepreneurial class. The upper ranks of the *empresariado* have strengthened their traditionally firm position and acquired an even greater say in spheres of political power. Except for the *arrivistes* and new men who got to high posts as a result of the Civil War and kleptocratically carved fortunes for themselves while in power, the very high industrialists and bankers directly share in political power. By the same token some non-industrialists also wield private economic power: thus, large companies found it convenient to place at least one army general on their boards of directors. (However, all this has its long traditions: the financial bourgeoisie of Madrid have for a very long time been accustomed to draw a considerable income from state-sponsored projects inspired by themselves.)

Not surprisingly for a country whose government has been determined for more than three decades by the outcome of a Civil War, it is in the ruling elite and the political posts generally that one finds striking cases of upward mobility, starting with the head of state himself.[68] Upper-class people did not *have* to take sides, whereas many – notably amongst the military and other groups, such as the Falangists – took enormous risks during the conflict. Those who survived, as in any other civil war in any country, found exceptional rewards in the end. This is not to say that *all* the ruling elites of the country are staffed by formally mobile individuals, but that these are a substantial part of the whole.

Corruption, confusion in one person or group of different kinds of power, nepotism, political favouritism and the like are not, of course, exclusive to Spain. Nor can these traits be confined to pre-modern societies. Many countries – rich and poor – perhaps show these evils to a greater degree, while the so-called 'establishments' of some prosperous countries have been found to be remarkably prone to such practices. What happened in Spain with the outcome of the Civil War, however, is that they came to be institutionalized by the political system, as most economic, cultural and political power and influence were confined to the ranks of a backward-looking upper class for several decades.

SOME CONCLUDING REMARKS

From the above descriptions and analyses several basic conclusions about the nature of stratification in contemporary Spain may be drawn. In the first place, it is clear that Spanish society presents a variety of stratification systems[69] in the same manner as the other two Mediterranean peninsulas. No European society has proceeded towards 'modernity' by a linear process, nor have all regions in a given polity equally participated in the process. In countries like Italy or Spain, however, disparities have been greater than elsewhere. In both countries, moreover, ethno-cultural areas have often coincided with stratification systems. In Spain, this correlation still holds, but it is being eroded. While local upper classes still vary in their outlook and in their sources of power and wealth the alliance between say, Andalusian landowners and Catalan businessmen is no longer uneasy. Under the umbrella of a remarkably oligarchic regime, they have finally found a common ground and a common consciousness of kind. On the other hand, traditionally non-industrial areas are increasing their level of urbanization and industrialization; that is to say, an ample middle class and an ample non-rural working class are ceasing to be the exclusive traits of culturally distinct (and economically prosperous) areas such as Catalonia and the Basque country. In contrast to France, the pluri-national system of Spain has not been reduced to a mere set of regional distinctions. Catalans, Basques and Galicians may retain their identities in the future, but there are reasons to doubt whether the stratification structures that set them apart from the other areas in the Iberian Peninsula will remain untouched.

Under the cover of a great amount of political immobility, serious changes have been occurring that run counter to the equilibrium established by the regime: on the one hand, one finds an officially sanctioned power and status system based on authoritarian and dictatorial conceptions of public life, which openly favours the confusion of economic, cultural and political powers which have been clearly distinguished earlier on. On the other, for the reasons mentioned earlier, because of the developments already explained, an achievement-oriented society, favouring at least equality of opportunity, a secularized and universalistic system of values and generalized political participation in public life is also making great strides in a number of significant areas. (This, of course, is not new, it rather represents the revival of a process which came to a head under the aegis of the Republic.) Groups and individuals within the official system have tried to reconcile both trends and the regime itself has attempted to blend its own intrinsic characteristics with what one could call a more forward-looking attitude. Yet workers' unrest, separatist activities, students' rebellions, intellectual disaffection are of such import that the cleavage between the two conflicting conceptions of the polity (and the two corresponding stratificational systems) cannot be bridged by the continuation of the present regime. This regime is too committed to the identification of power with class, and privilege with high status (the characteristics of traditional societies) to be able to allow serious changes towards the open society, with its political pluralism, high secularization, and varieties of independent and competitive occupational structures, not to speak of the basic freedoms of speech and opinion. As important trends in the economy and the culture of the country – as well as in its unofficial politics – point towards a more open society, a serious conflict – often in the form of class conflict – can be expected to oppose the strata connected with these trends and the traditional and power groups committed to the specifically Spanish form of a closed society. It might seem paradoxical to state that the intensification of conflict will come about with either a greater disintegration of a regime incapable of institutionalizing substantial political changes or with a democratic polity – yet in either case repression would play a lesser role and dissent would cease to be a criminal offence.[70]

NOTES

1 The author of this paper has already done some work on the same subject, parts of which have necessarily been incorporated here, though often in a revised form. Cf. S. Giner, *Continuity and Change: The Social Stratification of Spain* (University of Reading, 1967); 'The Structure of Spanish Society and the Process of Modernisation' in a forthcoming issue of the *Sociological Review* (Monograph Series); chapter on 'Spain' in M. S. Archer (ed.), *Students, Universities and Society* (London: Heinemann, 1971). The author wishes to express his gratitude to Sr. E. Pinilla de las Heras, of the Laboratoire de Sociologie Industrielle, École Pratique des Hautes Études, Paris, for his continued advice and criticism. Some of his publications have had an important bearing on my data and opinions. Cf. his 'Estructura y procesos de cambio en la sociedad española contemporánea' in *Mañana*, Paris, Nos. 9 and 10, 1965, under the pseudonym *Steparius*; also 'Crise de la société rurale espagnole' in *Systèmes sociaux et systèmes d'éducation dans les pays mediterranéens*, Fascicule IX (Dubrovnik, 1965), and *Los empresarios y el desarrollo capitalista: el caso catalán* (Barcelona: Peninsula, 1967). In spite of Sr. Pinilla de las Heras's active role in the composition of this paper, the author alone is responsible for its judgments and data.

2 Cf. P. Broué and E. Témime, *La révolution et la guerre d'Espagne* (Paris: Editions de Minuit, 1961) for a 'class' interpretation of the Civil War. Also I. Fernández de Castro, *De las Cortes de Cádiz al Plan de Desarrollo* (Paris: Ruedo Ibérico, 1968), pp. 159–207; and R. Soler, 'The New Spain' in *New Left Review*, No. 58, Nov.–Dec. 1969, pp. 3–27.

3 On right-wing 'provocation' of the Civil War see G. Brenan, *The Spanish Labyrinth* (Cambridge University Press, 1960, 2nd edn.). Also I. Fernández de Castro, *De las Cortes . . .*, pp. 217–28.

4 H. Thomas, *The Spanish Civil War* (Penguin, 1961, 1965), p. 445.

5 For the social composition of the Falange during its early phases, H. Thomas, pp. 99–102; also S. G. Payne, *Falange* (Stanford University Press, 1962).

6 The waverings of military and civil conspirators about accepting straight fascist (i.e. Falangist) help show the upper-class traditionalist roots of the power elite. For them, even the Falangists were too revolutionary. But it soon became clear that their corporatist ideology would prove most useful in the 'justification' and 'reasons' that had to be given for the uprising, as well as in the consolidation of what they called the 'new State'.

7 The Navarrese peasants were qualitatively very different from the rural proletariat of the south. Their regionalism was duly

rewarded at the end of the Civil War. In the strongly centralist State that emerged, a degree of administrative autonomy was granted to the stronghold of Carlism, Navarre. In recent years, though, the anti-centralist tendencies of Carlism have again become very apparent.

8 Thus, it was clear that some investment in the already industrialized areas would have produced quick results; even investment in the underdeveloped ones would have been more beneficial had it been backed by agrarian reform. That the new men in power were economically naïve was shown when costly refineries (*sic*) of bituminous slate were opened in New Castile with the vain hope that petrol would flow from it.

9 Only towards the end of 1968, and after several serious attacks from left-wing economists, have the Cortes shyly tried to tackle the problem of the all-powerful Spanish banks. *Cuadernos para el diálogo*, esp. issue, April 1968, *passim*.

10 R. Tamames, *Introducción a la economía española* (Madrid, Alianza Editorial, 1967), pp. 454–84. As Tamames has shown the collection and study of the data used by the Plans were not reliable; the different committees that drew them up lacked co-ordination; great economic issues, such as the perennial *latifundio* question, have remained unmentioned. Both Plans pretended to be merely indicative, and even in this they failed.

11 Banco de Bilbao, *Informe económico de 1968* (Zamudio: Eléxpuru, 1969), pp. 88, 121.

12 'The fundamental problem in Spain: the agrarian question and its relation to industry', so did G. Brenan start the part of his book devoted to the condition of the working classes (*The Spanish Labyrinth* (2nd edn. Cambridge University Press, 1960) p. 87). His analysis is based on legal considerations, an approach which was correct at the time. Today juridical problems of land distribution and ownership have become secondary to question of agrarian development and financing. Cf. X. Flores, 'La Propiedad rural en España' in Cuadernos de Ruedo Ibérico, *Horizonte español 1966* (Paris: Ruedo Ibérico, 1966), Vol. I, pp. 129–48; R. Tamames, *Cuatro problemas de la economía española* (Barcelona: Península, 1965), pp. 151–96.

13 Official estimates *España Semanal* (*Servicio Informativo Español*), No. 369, 3 November 1969, p. 6.

14 Banco de Bilbao, *Informe Económico de 1968*, p. 174. The percentage of women within the active population was of 17·5 per cent, according to ILO sources for 1967 (13·5 per cent in 1960). In the same year it was 19·7 per cent for Italy. For Portugal, 13·1 per cent in 1960. (*ILO Labour Statistics*, 1968.)

15 Estimate in FOESSA, *Informe sociológico sobre la situación social en España 1970* (Madrid: Euramérica, 1970) p. 169.

16 During the 1950s, forty provinces out of the fifty into which Spain is administratively divided sent emigrants to the other ten. (R. Tamames, *Cuatro problemas de la economia española*

(Barcelona: Peninsula, 1965), pp. 99–148.) Of these forty provinces, eighteen were actually losing population in absolute terms, the 1960 Census informs us. Cf. also A. G. Barbancho, 'La emigración y la población agraria en Espana', in *Boletín de Estudios Económicos* (Bilbao, XIX, Jan.–April 1964, No. 61, pp. 100–11).

17 A. Míguez, *Galicia: éxodo y desarrollo* (Madrid: Edicusa, 1967), pp. 57–104.

18 A. Drain, *L'Economie de l'Espagne* (Paris: PUF, 1968), p. 107.

19 The hypothesis that – to put it schematically – 'the greater the degree of feudality in the past, the greater the degree of later capitalist development' which has been applied to Europe and Japan. Cf. R. Coulbourn, *Feudalism in History* (Princeton University Press, 1956) seems to have at least some confirmation in Spain. When, during the eighteenth century 'modernization' began to spread in Spain, only ex-feudal Catalonia possessed a European-type middle class and bourgeoisie. Cf. P. Vilar, *La Catalogne dans l'Espagne moderne* (Paris, SEVPEN, 1962, and *Crecimiento y desarrollo* (Barcelona: Ariel, 1964), pp. 139–74, 249–399.

20 As J. Martínez Alier has shown in *La estabilidad del latifundismo* (Paris: Ruedo Ibérico, 1968).

21 *Anuario estadístico de España*, 1964.

22 M. Capelo Martínez, *Fudamentos del desarrollo económico de Andalucía* (Madrid: CSIC, 1963), p. 91.

23 A. C. Comín, *España del Sur* (Madrid: Tecnos 1966); G. Hermet, *Le problème méridional de l'Espagne* (Paris: Armand Colin, 1965).

24 In the southern regions, however, income per head often grows at rates higher than the national average, as was the case between 1956 and 1960. But the rate of growth does not give any indication that the gap with the richer regions is going to be bridged.

25 Index of final agricultural production 1953/4: 100; 1961–5 average: 139·3; 1967 provision index: 162·2 (of which, final livestock production index: 209·2). OECD Economic Surveys, *Spain 1969*, p. 54.

26 José Gentil da Silva, *En Espagne* (The Hague: Mouton), pp. 191–214, esp. maps and tables after p. 202.

27 R. Tamames, *Estructura ecónomica de España* (Madrid: SEP., 1965, 1st edn. 1961), p. 10.

28 FOESSA-Cáritas Diocesana de Madrid-Alcalá, *Informe sociológico sobre la situación social de Madrid* (Madrid: Euramérica, 1967), pp. 39–46. If this is maintained, the city may surpass the five-million mark by 1980, in a country whose period of intensive population growth (as J. Nadal has pointed out) will probably be over by then. (*La población española* (Barcelona: Ariel, 1966), p. 222.)

29 Asociación Católica de Dirigentes, *Informe Social 1968* (Barcelona, 1969), pp. 86, 87, quoting Professor García Barbancho.

30 1960 Census.

31 During recent years, the public in some countries – especially in Switzerland – have become acutely aware of the presence in their midst of a new lower-class stratum of foreign workers, vitally necessary to their economy and yet discriminated against as a result of ethnocentric prejudice.

32 At this stage, it is too early to say whether the downward trend will persist. Thus as a result of the renewed expansion of Germany more workers left Spain in 1968 (about 88,000) than in 1967 (59,000). The migratory balance, however, was still negative, as no less than 100,000 workers returned in 1968. (Provisional figures, Instituto Nacional de Emigración, in Banco de Bilbao, *Informe Económico*, p. 177; and OECD, *Spain 1969*, p. 57.)

33 A study along these lines has been carried out by Angels Pascual; Barcelona: Nova Terra, 1970, under the title *El retorn dels emigrants*. For attitude changes of Spaniards in France see G. Hermet, *Les Espagnols en France* (Paris: Editions Ouvrières, 1967); J. Marsal (*Hacer la América* (Buenos Aires: Instituto di Tella, 1969) also tackles this problem, but from the point of view of overseas emigrants.

34 Cuadernos de Ruedo Ibérico, *Horizonte Español* (Paris: Ruedo Ibérico, 1966), Vols. I and II.

35 FOESSA, *Informe sociológico sobre la situación social en Espana* (Madrid, 1966), p. 55. The negative difference of the first item may be explained by the expansion of the sectors represented by some of the other items.

36 *España Semanal*. Official Estimates.

37 Instituto Nacional de Estadísica, *Encuesta de equipamiento y nivel cultural de la familia* (Madrid, 1968), p. 108.

38 By 1969 there were 60 private cars and 124 telephones per 1,000 inhabitants. OECD, *Spain 1971*.

39 J. García Nieto, J. Estivill et alii, 'Relaciones laborales en España' in *Boletín Informativo*, ESADE-Instituto de Estudios Laborales, Barcelona, 1968, Nos. 4–5; also J. Estivill and M. Molins, *Evolución de las relaciones laborales en España desde 1939 hasta nuestros días* (Barcelona: Esmela de Ingenieros, 1969).
    J. M. Maravall, *Trabajo y conflicto social* (Madrid: Edicusa, 1967).

40 A. López Muñoz, J. L. García Delgado, *Crecimiento y crisis del capitalismo español* (Madrid: Edicusa, 1968), p. 156.

41 J. J. Linz and A. de Miguel, 'Within-Nation Differences and Comparisons: the Eight Spains' in R. L. Merrit and S. Rokkan, *Comparing Nations* (New Haven: Yale University Press, 1966), p. 290.

42 M. Tuñón de Lara, 'Le problème universitaire espagnol' in *Esprit*, May 1969, No. 5, pp. 848, 850.

43 J. L. Pinillos, 'Actitudes sociales de los universitarios españoles' amongst other unpublished material by him. (Yet, cf. *Time* magazine, Vol. 67, No. 3, 16 January 1956.) Also his 'Actitudes

sociales primarias', *Revista de la Universidad de Madrid*, 1953, No. 7.

44 Instituto Nacional de Estadística, *Encuesta de gastos de enseñanza de las economías familiares* (Madrid, 1964).

45 Among other publications, cf. F. Murillo, 'Die Spanische Mittelschichten' in R. König, (ed.), *Probleme der Mittelklassen in Entwicklungsländern* (Cologne: Westdeutescher Verlag, 1964), pp. 55–97; J. J. Linz and A. de Miguel, 'Within-Nation Differences . . .'; J. Cazorla Perez, 'Un ensayo de estratificación social española de 1957', in *Revista española de la opinión pública*, No. 1, 1965, pp. 91–105.

46 Cf. M. Kenny, *A Spanish Tapestry* (New York: Harper, 1966, 1st edn. 1961); FOESSA, *Informe Sociológico (España)*, 1966, p. 293.

47 These patterns of hierarchical inequality are by no means incompatible with the typically Spanish brand of egalitarianism. As Kenny says, partly commenting on a text of Pitt-Rivers, '. . . egalitarianism among Spaniards in general . . . has always been noted with surprise by foreigners. The distinction which villagers and townsmen alike make between personality and social position overrrides the concept of class, and has been expressed as "a respect for human personality rather than for human rights". Such a distinction has as its basis a system of social values linked to the ideal behaviour by which a man is judged', *A Spanish Tapestry*, p. 76.

48 About modern Spain developing 'neofeudal' social structures, see J. Costa, *Oligarquía y caciquismo como formas actual de gobierno en España*, 'Ecuesta', Ateneo de Madrid, 1901. Also the studies and essays on Spanish society by G. de Azcárate and A. Posada.

49 E. Pinilla de las Heras, *Los empresarios y el desarrollo capitalista*, pp. 228–9.

50 J. J. Linz and A. de Miguel, 'La cantera de los futuros empresarios'; 'Estructura ocupacional de España'; both articles mimeographed by the Delegación Nacional de Asociaciones del Movimento, 1964. Also, by the same authors, 'Características estructurales de las empresas españolas: tecnificación y burocracia', in *Racionalización*, Nos. 1 to 4, Madrid, 1964.

51 J. Busquests, *El militar de carrera en España* (Barcelona: Ariel, 1967), p. 30. Parallel trends have been detected in the Navy and the Air Force. Training has notably improved with regard to technological knowledge, especially after 1954.

52 Busquests, *El Militar . . .* , pp. 83–5, 87.

53 Busquests, *El Militar . . .* , p. 99.

54 J. J. Linz, 'An authoritarian regime: Spain' in E. Allardt and Y. Littunen, *Cleavages, Ideologies and Party Systems* (Helsinki, 1964), pp. 241–341.

55 The numbers of military and militarized men (*funcionarios militares*) are difficult to assess. Estimates for the period between

1955 and 1962 oscillate around the 150,000 figure. See below Note 56.

56   It is impossible here to give an idea of the confusion surrounding this matter. For estimates which are often contradictory see: L. Jordana de Pozas 'Formación y perfeccionamiento de los funcionarios públicos', *Actas, Coloquio Internacional de functionarrios públicos* (Madrid: BOE, 1960); S. Royo Villanova, *La función pública en la Administración pública y el Estado contemporáneo* (Madrid: IEP, 1961); A. Carro Martínez, 'Reivindicación y reforma del funcionario español', *Documentación administrativa* (Madrid, April 1963); J. R. Herrero Fontana, 'La remuneración de los funcionarios públicos', *Actas III Semana de estudios para la reforma administrativa* (Madrid, 1963); A. Gutiérrez Reñón, 'Estructura de la burocracia española', *Rev. esp. de la Opinión Pública*, No. 3, March 1963. Some authors include amongst the *funcionarios* the members of the clergy who are paid by the State. Teachers and professors might be included, whereas attorneys and property registrars, whose functions are public and state regulated, might not be included by either authors or official publications. According to the Opus Dei weekly *Mundo* (1 September 1968, p. 21) the number of *funcionarios* in the central administration – including the military – was 406,890. From the above sources, as well as others referring to local administration (such as the *Anuario estadístico de las corporaciones locales* (Madrid, 1964)), the following picture emerged for 1963:

Civil servants:	Central administration	431,000
	Autonomous state bodies	111,000
	Local corporations	150,000
	Total	692,000

57   A. Perpiñá, *¿Hacia una sociedad sin clases?* (Madrid: Euramérica, no date (?1957)), p. 160.

58   K. Medhurst, 'The political presence of the Spanish bureaucracy' in *Government and Opposition* (Vol. 4, No. 2), Spring 1969, p. 236.

59   Medhurst, 'The political presence . . .', pp. 247–8.

60   Cf. proceedings of XI Plenary Assembly of the Spanish Episcopate, Madrid, December 1969, as reported in *Le Monde* (over first fortnight of month). It was the first time that the *ultras* in the episcopate spoke against the government.

61   I. Fernández de Castro, 'La Iglesia de la Cruzada y sus supervivencias' in *Horizonte Español*, Vol. I, pp. 207–23.

62   H. Thomas, 'The Spanish Church as a Power for Progress', *New Society*, No. 135, 29 April 1965, p. 11.

63   J. Vicens Vives, *Historia económica de España* (Barcelona: Teide, 1959), p. 560.

64   J. Velarde, 'El profesor Bernís ante la economía española' in *Revista de Economía Política* (Madrid, December 1960). Equipo de jóvenes economistas 'Las 100 familias españolas' in *Horizonte*

español, Vol. I, pp. 47–120; P. Marcos Santibáñez, 'La familia "F" ', *Horizonte español*, Vol. I, pp. 121–7. (A study of the private possessions of General Franco's family.)

65 R. Tamames, *La lucha contra los monopolios* (Madrid: Tecnos, 1966, 2nd edn.), p. 431.

66 D. Artigues, *El Opus Dei en España* (Paris: Ruedo Ibérico, 1968).

67 One must then disagree here with those sociologists who have interpreted Spain's regime as merely paternalistic authoritarianism, and not as a dictatorship; they point out that in Spain the chief of state has left a wide area of discretion to his ministers. This has not been the case in fact. These authors confuse the technical division of labour necessary in a country as complex as Spain with power distribution. The latter has remained dictatorially concentrated, as events in 1969 have sufficiently shown, in the hands of one man. Cf. J. J. Linz, 'An Authoritarian Regime: Spain' in *Cleavages, Ideologies. . . .*

68 A. R. M. Carr, 'Spain: Rule by Generals' in M. Howard (ed.), *Soldiers and Governments* (London, 1957), pp. 133–48.

69 Cf. J. J. Linz and A. de Miguel, 'The Eight Spains' in R. L. Merrit, S. Rokkan (eds.) *Comparing Nations* (New Haven: Yale University Press, 1966), pp. 267–319; also by J. J. Linz, the role of ecological differences in the different contexts of Spanish stratification: 'Ecological Analysis and Survey Research' in M. Dogan and S. Rokkan, *Quantitative Ecological Analysis in the Social Sciences* (Boston: MIT Press, 1969), pp. 91–131.

70 Some publications relevant to Spanish social stratification have appeared since this chapter was written. The most important is FOESSA's *Informe, 1970* (see note 15 above). I am grateful to Sr A. de Miguel for allowing me to see the data of the censored chapter on politics. See also the special issue *Cuadernos para el diálogo* on *España: Realidad y política*, supplement no. 6, 1969; J. M. Maravall, *El desarrollo económico y la clase obrera* (Barcelona: Ariel, 1970); J. Estivill et al., *La partici pació dels treballadors a la gestió de l'empresa* (Barcelona: Nova Terra, 1970); J. Ynfante, *La prodigiosa aventura del Opus Dei* (Paris: Ruedo Ibérico, 1970); C. W. Anderson, *The Political Economy of Modern Spain* (University of Wisconsin Press, 1970). While these publications increase information on the subject, no major changes seem to be called for in the present chapter.

5 Greece

Nikos Mouzelis and Michael Attalides

INTRODUCTION

Although a European society linked to the Western Block of alliances, modern Greece differs in striking and fundamental ways from the highly developed societies of western Europe. These differences do not refer simply to and cannot be explained fully by the relatively low degree of industrialization in Greece. There are some fundamental structural differences in relation to western European societies which would persist even if Greece were to reach the same level of economic development as its Common Market partners. Such structural characteristics reflect the fact that Greece, unlike Western countries, has emerged as a modern nation from the disintegration of a patrimonial empire without experiencing a feudal past, at least not in the manner and to the extent common to Western societies. Some of the main features of the Greek class structure, which are constant throughout history, can only be understood by analysing their formation and persistence, i.e. by examining class struggles and developments during the Ottoman rule and the Greek war of Independence at the beginning of the nineteenth century. Thus Part One of this chapter will deal in a highly selective manner with key events in Greek history, crucial for explaining some persistent characteristics of the two most important classes, the bourgeoisie and the peasantry. Against this background, the second part will attempt to assess the changing post-war class structure in the economic and political context of modern Greece.

An analysis of the relationship between class structure and economic development in Greece, indicates that the major concepts and theories prevalent in this field are largely inapplicable. Such theories can be roughly classified under two major, diametrically opposed approaches.

On the one hand, highly empirical studies of stratification examine the distribution of various characteristics in a population and therefore use the concept of class as a convenient pigeon-hole for categorizing people according to certain criteria (income, occupation, consumption patterns etc.). This approach eliminates class as a concrete group, susceptible under certain conditions, of acquiring a corporate reality – i.e. of becoming an active and unified collectivity facing issues and adopting policies. The class structure ceases to be a system of interrelated groups or quasi-groups and becomes a fictional configuration of statistical boxes which, while of use in static analysis, cannot deal with problems of social change and development.

On the other hand, Marxist theories of class, although avoiding these shortcomings, often overemphasize the importance of classes as collective actors, thus denying the relative autonomy of groups in non-economic institutional spheres (like the political, the religious etc.).[1] For instance, many Marxist theories see the political sphere as a mere reflection of the infrastructure. Any political event is therefore automatically reduced to the relevant class struggles which allegedly brought it about. Again this approach seems unsatisfactory for analysing the Greek class structure. For instance, when referring to the growing dominance of bourgeois classes in Greek society, the authors do not imply that the Greek political elite is exclusively recruited from bourgeois strata; nor do they assume a cohesive and omnipotent group of merchants to be 'pulling the strings' behind the political scene. By the dominance of the bourgeoisie they mean (a) its importance in setting the pattern of economic activities in society, and (b) its early impact on the dominant value system and on the fundamental institutional structures of Greek society (religious, educational etc.) which, to a great extent, account for the sort of problems debated in the political arena or left outside it. Thus, except in very limited periods of Greek history, political struggles have been confined to a framework in which certain issues fundamental to social change, for example the issue of the ownership of the means of production, have been underemphasized or systematically excluded from political debates. In that sense the 'dominance' of the bourgeoisie takes a much more indirect form than some Marxist historians of modern Greece would suggest. This dominance does not automatically imply a perfectly organized and omniscient social group controlling in a Machiavellian way, everything and everybody; it rather implies a *limiting framework* of values and relationships which only allow for certain social choices and exclude others.[2]

I THE GREEK BOURGEOISIE AND PEASANTRY: SELECTED ASPECTS OF THEIR HISTORICAL DEVELOPMENT

The development of the Greek Merchant class under the Ottoman Empire

The Turkish elite, principally engaged in military conquest, had very little inclination for administrative and commercial activities. While their religion was not opposed to economic ventures, for the Turkish elite, commerce, especially foreign commerce, was to some extent a degrading activity. This hostility was mainly cultivated by various religious and political groups which were apprehensive of the corrupting influences contact with foreign cultures could have on the faithful. The Greeks, because of their geographical position and long maritime and merchant traditions, did not hesitate to take advantage of this favourable situation, and managed rather quickly to play a dominant trading role not only within the Ottoman Empire but on a wider scale.

An important reason for the ascendancy of the Greek Orthodox merchant concerns the *Phanariotes*. The *Phanariotes*, who took their name from a district in Constantinople called Phanari, could almost be defined as a '*noblesse de robe*' of the Ottoman Empire. Most claimed to be direct descendants of Byzantine aristocratic families, but a considerable number of them accumulated their wealth as traders in the Aegean, the Danubian principalities and Russia before they settled in Constantinople. The Phanariotes managed to expand their activities to the political and administrative field. Their organizational skills, their knowledge of languages, their education and urban sophistication made them the indispensable advisers and technical experts of the *Porte*. They managed not only to occupy and maintain for generations key positions in the Ottoman Administration (like

Dragoman of the *Porte* and Dragoman of the fleet), but also a handful of *Phanariote* families, through their political influence, gained control over most financial and banking operations in the empire. Moreover, they acquired the right to appoint from among their members the governors of the Danubian principalities and had a strong influence in the highly powerful Greek Orthodox Church.

This formidable urban patriciate, a strange combination of financial and administrative elite, by simply protecting and promoting their own interests, through their considerable political power, contributed to the rise of the Greek Orthodox merchant in the Balkans.[3]

Another major factor explaining the importance of the Greek merchant under Turkish rule is the Greek Orthodox Church. As the Turks were practising an 'indirect rule' system of government, the Orthodox Church from the beginning of the Ottoman occupation constituted the main link between the Sultan and his Greek subjects. In that sense the church although subjected to strict central control, not only had a high degree of autonomy in religious and cultural matters – it also acquired a large number of political functions. Indeed, together with local Greek notables, the church was responsible for the running of all municipal affairs. Moreover, the power of the patriarchate was not limited to the Greeks alone: to a lesser extent it was exercised over all the orthodox subjects of the empire – at least up to the date when the non-Greek orthodox nationalities fought for the establishment of national churches. Thus, if one compares the position of the church during the Byzantine empire with its position under the Turkish rule two major points can be made: on the one hand the church increased its power over lay members, whether Greek or non-Greek; on the other hand the autonomy of the church from the temporal power was drastically reduced – the patriarch having to submit unconditionally to arbitrary sultanic rule.

The subjugation of the church by the Ottoman administration explains to a great extent the venality of its highest offices; for the Sultan the device of putting ecclesiastical positions on auction was a convenient way of increasing his revenue. Since such positions were extremely expensive, the high clergy was dependent on the financial support of wealthy merchant families. Usually the transaction took the form of loans advanced to members of the clergy with the understanding that once the office was acquired the debt would be repaid from the considerable income attached to the post. As a result of this situation many Phanariote families could, for instance, nominate bishops at will and could even influence the nomination of the Patriarch. This being, in very crude terms, the relationship between the Greek bourgeoisie and the Orthodox Church, it is understandable that the latter through its spiritual and political influence was advancing Greek economic interests, both in relation to the Porte and to Balkan trade competitors. In addition, this 'secularization' of the orthodox church helped Greek commerce by prompting an extremely lenient attitude to such matters as usury and the accumulation of excessive wealth.[4]

Greek dominance. There were many other factors which favoured the development of Greek commerce during the Ottoman rule: for example, the hostility between Venetians and Turks which ended the commercial hegemony of Venice in the Mediterranean, the closing of the Black Sea to all ships from outside the Ottoman Empire (1592–1774), the economic blockade during the Napoleonic Wars, etc.[5] Some of the above factors favoured not only Greek merchants, but also other nationalities like the Serbs and Bulgarians. However, because of the long trading traditions of Greece, its crucial geographical position and most importantly, the power position of the Phanariotes and Patriarchate, Serb and Bulgarian merchants appeared much later and their importance was secondary even in the eighteenth and nineteenth century. If the dominance of the Greek church made Greek the language for culture and education in all Balkan societies, the dominance of Greek merchants made it the language of commerce as well. This culminated in a process of gradual hellenization of the Orthodox Balkan merchants.[6] Increasingly it was a sign of upward mobility and prestige for a Slav trader to speak Greek and to be considered as a Greek. (Only the Serb merchants opposed these hellenizing influences to some extent, but even their resistance waned towards the end of the eighteenth century.) Thus previous to the nationalist wars of independence and the emergence of autonomous Balkan states – which abruptly ended this hellenizing process – Balkan merchants were united through Greek language and culture; they constituted a very cohesive class, cohesion being another important factor in its ascent under Ottoman rule.

Non industrialization. A final important factor which explains not only the development of Greek business, but also its specific form relates to the customs and manufacturing policies of the Ottoman Empire. During the years of Turkish rule there was a reasonable balance between the development of trade and of manufacturing in the Empire. Thus the rapid growth of urban centres during the sixteenth century was linked with the development of important craft industries and textile manufactures in the large cities.[7]

During the late eighteenth century, Western industrialization shattered this balance between commercial and craft development. The expansion of towns, population and industry in the West increased the demand for such Balkan products as wool, cotton, tobacco and maize. This growing demand and the ensuing spectacular rise of agricultural prices led to an intensification of agricultural production which had repercussions in the social and economic organization of the Balkan system of production.

At the same time western Europe was demanding Balkan agricultural products – it was of course pressing for the introduction of its own industrial goods. The Ottoman Government, already in a state of decline, was unwilling and/ or unable to implement a mercantilist policy which could protect and further develop its already existing industry.[8] Indeed, with the extension of 'capitulations' (special trading privileges) to an increasing number of western European countries, the existing industry in the Empire disappeared. Internally there was no great pressure on the Sultan for the adoption of a protectionist policy. The powerful landowners were, for obvious reasons, satisfied with the *laissez-faire* policy of the administration as were the powerful Greek merchants who, very quickly, took control of both maritime and land trade between the Empire and the West.

The Greek Bourgeoisie during and after the War of Independence. On the eve of the War of Independence the Greek peasants had reached the extremes of poverty and degradation. The radical changes in agriculture which were brought about by the increasing Western demand for Balkan agricultural products contributed to the very rapid commercialization of agriculture. The trend combined with the end of Ottoman territorial expansion, the weakening of the central government and the attraction of urban speculators to agricultural ventures caused profound changes in the relationship between landlord and peasant in the Balkans.

The old 'timar' system of production gave way to the 'chiflik' system. Under the 'timar' system the landlord was strictly controlled by the central government and the peasant, whether moslem or Christian, had a number of important privileges, for example the hereditary right to the land. Under the 'chiflik' system both governmental control and the customary rights of the peasant, the two main mechanisms protecting against the landlord's arbitrariness, were removed and the peasant found himself at the complete mercy of the landowner.[9]

Thus the gradual dominance of the *chiflik* system and the ensuing exploitation of the Greek peasant by both Greek and Turkish landowners explain to a great extent the revolutionary tendency of the peasantry at the beginning of the nineteenth century. Actually the majority of the Greek peasants were less interested in political independence than in a return to the good old days when a strong Ottoman Government could safeguard their traditional rights and could check the rapaciousness of landlords and officials.[10]

It was at this crucial point that the bourgeoisie played a decisive role in the overthrow of the Turks. While the Greek peasantry provided the energy source for the revolution, the bourgeoisie and the intellectuals managed to direct this energy towards nationalist goals. The merchants helped the popular revolt not only by providing leadership and material resources, but also by disseminating French revolutionary ideas and more generally Western culture in a society dominated by the formalism and oriental obscurantism of Christian Orthodoxy. Together with intellectuals, teachers and other professionals educated abroad, the bourgeoisie constituted the catalyst which started the whole revolutionary process and gave it direction.[11]

The Church, the *Phanariotes* and the Greek landowners were ambivalent towards the revolution. The church, especially the high clergy, was at the beginning clearly hostile to any idea of overthrowing Turkish rule under which it occupied a privileged position. The Patriarchate exercising political and spiritual power over all the orthodox subjects of the empire, whether Greek or non-Greek, quickly realized that the emergence of a new autonomous nation would not only fragment Ottoman power, but its own as well. Moreover, as the Greek nationalist movement was influenced by the Western enlightenment, this provided an additional reason for opposition. On similar grounds the Phanariote aristocracy, although initially responsive to Western ideas,[12] was opposed to the Greek nationalist movement. Their privileged position within the Ottoman administration, their close links with the church and their cosmopolitan orientation explain their reluctance to join the revolution. The Greek landlords were, of course, initially opposed to any idea of nationalist revolution – being afraid that the exploited peasants would unavoidably demand land redistribution. Once the revolution gained momentum, these groups finally threw their weight on the side of the revolutionaries and contributed to its final success.[13]

The leading role of the bourgeoisie before and during the War of Independence explains to a great extent why the merchant class became the value originator and the standard setter of Greek life; it explains why from the very start national life was organized along liberal bourgeois lines. Thus, for instance, the first Greek constitutions were totally inspired by the French experience and although Capo d'Istria and later King Otho tried to implement an absolutist model of government, their efforts were ultimately frustrated.

During the War of Independence both class and regional differences were so acute that no social group or elite was powerful enough to impose unity and to integrate the country.[14] Intestine quarrels almost jeopardized the whole movement of Independence, which was finally salvaged by the intervention of the Great Powers imposing the Monarchy in Greece. This is highly significant for understanding the exceptionally low political autonomy of Greece in relation to more powerful nations and the crucial role of the monarchy in Greek society.

The throne constituted the nucleus around which the

Greek *Tzakia* or 'establishment' was formed. This grouping of landowners, wealthy bourgeois and families whose ancestors played an important military or political role during the War of Independence, was crucial in shaping Greek politics and culture. However, it should not be seen as a continuously cohesive and self-conscious group. Although capable of unification when fundamental issues threatened its very existence, it was otherwise torn between competing factions.

Throughout the nineteenth and twentieth centuries the domination of the bourgeoisie seems to have gradually increased at the expense of the throne, the landowning[15] and other more traditional elements in society. Thus the revolutions of 1843, 1862 and 1909 restricted the power of the throne and in an *indirect way* strengthened the power position of the bourgeoisie.

The commercial character of the Greek bourgeoisie. The Greek bourgeoisie had and still has a predominantly *commercial character*; investments in the secondary sector are minimal in Greece. Most capital is channelled to the service sector which creates a hypertrophical and parasitic body of commercial intermediaries who usually prosper at the expense of the direct agricultural producer and the final consumer. The commercial character of the bourgeoisie explains to a great extent the weakness of the industrial working class in Greece. As industrial organizations are few and of small size, the workers are weak both numerically and in terms of class consciousness. Therefore it is not surprising that the trade union movement was from its beginnings under governmental control.

The factors accounting for the persistently commercial character of the bourgeoisie and its incapacity to transform itself into an industrial elite include those common to all underdeveloped countries (i.e. competition with already industrialized countries, political instability, dependence on Great Powers etc.), but can also be related to the Turkish legacy, which shaped the dominant modes of thinking and acting of the Greek merchant class. Despite its influential position *vis-à-vis* the Ottoman administration, the bourgeoisie lived under the constant threat of arbitrary governmental interference in its affairs; the threat of total destruction of life and property was always present, especially during the declining years of the empire when sultanic arbitrariness reached its zenith.

Under such circumstances the Greek merchants had to buy their security. Political bribery was the only institutionalized channel for conducting serious business in the empire. However close the Greek merchants were to the centre of power, they were still subject to the same arbitrariness. Even when they were officials and influential advisers to the *Porte*, sultanic disfavour was a constant possibility. Unceasing flattery and propitiation were therefore basic for survival.

Their position can be contrasted with the autonomy western European merchants enjoyed. For instance, the burghers of north-western Europe, profiting from the antagonism between king and nobility, secured a high degree of autonomy for their urban communities – a factor which, as Weber shows, contributed greatly to the development of Western capitalism. No similar urban centres existed in the Ottoman empire. Towns looked more like large villages and they usually had no autonomy whatsoever *vis-à-vis* the Sultan. Even the guild organizations in Constantinople were under his direct control.

For all these reasons two basic patterns developed among merchants:

a. *A servile attitude* towards authority coupled with total *mistrust* of government and a constant attempt to propitiate it by bribery.

b. *Short-term and opportunistic orientation* towards economic activities; under circumstances of constant insecurity, the merchants' aim was maximum profit in the shortest possible time.

These patterns which were fully developed during the Turkish occupation, are still detectable today. They are certainly relevant for explaining why Greek entrepreneurs would refuse extremely favourable governmental loans for industrial investments which could be very profitable in the long term. Thus one can argue that the character of the Greek bourgeoisie is such that, even if all other factors necessary for rapid industrialization were present, this merchant class would hardly transform itself into an industrial elite.

Agrarianism and the Greek peasantry. Despite Greece's early urbanization and the commercialization of agriculture, the peasantry[16] is still numerically the most important class – approximately 50 per cent of the working population is still occupied in the primary sector. The most striking feature of this social category is its inability to organize itself politically. Indeed, during the *interwar period*, when all other Balkan countries had extremely important agrarian movements and developed strong agrarian parties, Greece, was the only exception. The Greek agrarian party was numerically and otherwise insignificant at a time when the creation of a '*Green*' international was contemplated and agrarianism seen as an East European challenge to both capitalism and socialism.[17]

The type of landholding and property relationships among peasants seems important in accounting for the lack of peasant radicalism in Greece. However, the predominance of small property ownership, resulting from the land reform in the 1920s, was not only prevalent in Greece; similar land reforms took place at approximately the same time in all Balkan countries. Thus small landholdings were dominant in Bulgaria and Yugoslavia, two countries with very important agrarian movements. An adequate explanation for the lack of agrarian movement in Greece must take into account three interrelated factors. The early commercialization of the peasantry, the early independence of Greece in comparison with its Balkan neighbours and the nature of its village communities.

Early commercialization. The reasons which account for the early development and the clear dominance of the Greek merchant class in the Balkans also explain the early commercialization of the Greek rural economy. Indeed, the Greek peasant was exposed to the influence of the money economy much earlier than his northern neighbours. At a time when the Bulgarian peasant was completely immersed in the Zadruga family system which protected him from market forces, the Greek peasant was fully exposed to the vagaries of a money economy.

As in all similar situations, the introduction of the cash nexus in a previously subsistence economy had the following well-known consequences on the peasant's mode of life:

Increasing individualism.
Less attachment to the land which is increasingly
seen as a marketable commodity.
Imitation of urban styles of life and increasing
desire to migrate to the city.
Rising aspirations and the development of a
consumer's mentality.
Chronic indebtedness to urban moneylenders or
state banks, etc.[18]

In other Balkan countries this process of commercialization
took place much later and in fact never reached the same
proportions as in Greece. Thus for instance in the early
1920s whereas the percentage of the total labour force
employed in agriculture was approximately 80 per cent in
Yugoslavia, Bulgaria and Rumania, it was only 50 per cent in
Greece. This remarkable difference between Greece and the
other Balkan countries has been maintained up to the second
world war.[19]

This contrast can be illustrated by the difference in life
styles between peasants of Greek and Slav origin, both living
in Greece. Thus the Peloponnesian peasants, growing cash
crops, do not try to raise animals or to make their own
clothes, but rely on grocers and merchants. Their free time is
spent at the coffee house smoking, drinking and discussing
politics. They are chronically indebted to the National Bank
and, having no savings, depend entirely on a good crop and a
favourable market situation for their subsistence. On the
other hand, the Macedonian peasants of Slav origin in
northern Greece who, at the beginning of the twentieth
century, were still cultivating the land within the Zadruga
system were showing the opposite characteristics: sobriety,
frugality, minimum dependence on the market, high savings,
strong attachment to the land.[20]

The village community. The nature of the village community is also relevant in accounting for the absence of agrarianism in Greece. During the Turkish occupation the village
community was a highly developed and cohesive form of
social organization. Its leadership, usually a combination of
priests and local landowners, performed crucial functions
both in the economic and the political sphere. The main
reason which explains this remarkable flourishing of

communal institutions during that period was the highly decentralized system of Turkish government. The community, for instance, was responsible for the collection of taxes and it was the task of the communal leaders, the so-called *Cotsambassides*, to decide how much each member would pay. If the quota fixed by the administration was not reached, all members of the community were collectively responsible.

Not only was the village community highly self-contained in terms of functions performed – it also had a high degree of cohesion. Indeed, whether the communal political system was aristocratic (*Eftanissa*), democratic (*Psara*) or plutocratic (most Aegean Islands), all villagers were united in sharing a precarious position in relation to the conqueror. Furthermore, although there was social stratification within the village in terms of wealth, prestige and power, these differences were limited as the Turks held most of the land and wealth of the country.

The strength of the village community was first undermined by the early commercialization of Greek agriculture and was destroyed when, after independence, the administration of King Otho completely disregarded this intricate piece of social organization. The highly centralized Bavarian system of government was introduced, stripping the village community of its most vital functions. This is a classic example of an attempt to transplant Western institutions to a less differentiated social setting. While the early commercialization of the countryside reduced the self-sufficiency of the peasant and placed him under the control of the merchant, the decline of the village community (which could operate as a protective mechanism and as basis for an autonomous co-operative movement) had further reduced peasant autonomy and increased dependence on the central government and the politicians.

Early independence. A final crucial factor which can account for the lack of Greek agrarianism lies in Greece having gained its independence much earlier than the other Balkan countries. This means that during the period when agrarianism was spreading all over the Balkan peninsula, the Greek political formations (predominantly bourgeois parties) were much more entrenched and well established than were their

Bulgarian equivalents. Thus in the 1930s the Greek bourgeois parties had a much stronger hold over the peasants than their counterparts in other Balkan countries, managing to channel peasant demands through their own political agencies and thus preventing the rise of a strong peasant party. The precise mechanism through which this was achieved was the patronage system, consisting in a straightforward form of exchange whereby politicians provided mediation services between the peasants and the state and received their votes as remuneration.[21] This process, which is quite widespread in many underdeveloped countries, takes a particular significance in the Greek context because of the language barrier between officials and peasants, all governmental business being conducted in '*katharevoussa*', a form of archaic Greek completely incomprehensible to the uneducated peasant.[22]

In view of the chronic indebtedness to the State banking system of the Greek consumption-oriented peasant, it is not difficult to understand the effectiveness with which the patronage system works in Greece. Moreover, merchants help politicians considerably in this process of vote catching. Indeed, if politicians receive votes in exchange for mediation services, merchants, on whom peasants are often utterly dependent, are able to buy peasant votes in a more direct way.

Thus, in conclusion, it is thought that the patronage system, very early entrenched in Greek political life, in combination with the early commercialization of agriculture and the destruction of the village community, account to some extent for the present position of the peasantry; they explain why a class which contributed so much to the overthrow of the Turkish conqueror was unable a century later and up to the present day to organize itself and protect its collective interests.

This sketchy analysis attempted to indicate some of the reasons which explain

    (a) the predominant position of the bourgeoisie in modern Greek society;

    (b) the lack of autonomous political organization among the peasants. Obviously this explanation is by no means sufficient and requires supplementing by more detailed historical analysis than the scope of this paper would permit.

II ECONOMIC, POLITICAL AND SOCIAL DEVELOPMENTS SINCE THE SECOND WORLD WAR

The economic and political context of the Civil War

It may appear paradoxical that given the structure of Greek class relations, especially the inertia of the peasantry in politics, there should have been, during the war and after, a revolutionary movement which came close to altering Greek society. Peasant participation was a major force behind the Greek Civil War, yet previously the peasantry had been under the control of bourgeois parties by means of the patronage system. This system was disrupted in 1936 by the establishment of the Metaxas right-wing dictatorship which put an end to parliamentary institutions.[23] Patronage based on the exchange of services for votes, disappeared with political parties. The German occupation in 1941 resulted in economic anarchy, and eliminated the other mechanism by which peasants were bound to the bourgeoisie, i.e. the commercial middleman. The link between the peasant participation in the Civil War and the decline of commerce and of the patronage system seems to be substantiated by the fact that provinces which gave most support to the Communist-oriented Revolutionary National Liberation Front (EAM)[24] were those previously most dominated by patronage and most highly commercialized – Thessaly, Thrace and Macedonia.[25] However, in contrast to Yugoslavia, which otherwise presented similar political features at the end of the war.[26] Greece was placed in the Western sphere of influence.[27] This enabled Britain and the United States to successfully intervene and to defeat the EAM.

After the Civil War Greece was literally in ruins.[28] The task of economic reconstruction and development with which the country was faced had a double aspect. The rationalization of agricultural production[29] and the development of the industrial sector to absorb the unemployed population of the towns and the labour force which agricultural rationalization would make redundant in the countryside.

Economic development (at least in the form of balanced growth of *both the agricultural and the industrial sector*) can be achieved either through a highly planned economy within which the state assumes the major responsibility for investments; or, as in the case of England, it can be achieved through the initiative of private entrepreneurs with the state providing a favourable framework for such activities.[30] After the second world war Greece's northern neighbours followed the former course; Greece as a result of the civil war has adopted the latter.

Post-Civil War economic developments: slow industrialization
On the basis of some economic indicators, Greece might appear to have been advancing rather steadily since the end of the civil war, the national income increasing at an annual rate of about 6 per cent since 1949.[31] This increase, however, although it has serious implications for Greece, did not lead towards the industrial development of the country. In fact, the main reasons for the post-war doubling of national income are: American aid, the development of tourism,[32] attractiveness of the country to shipowners once a right-wing government was secure[33] and remittances from the increasing number of Greek emigrants.[34] Thus the urban prosperity achieved after the war is not an 'economic miracle' – in the sense that the economy develops along lines which in the long term aggravate rather than solve the social and economic problems of the country. In fact, if one compares Greece with some of its Balkan neighbours in terms of a few indices of industrialization, it is quite clear that developments which are taking place within Greece are not leading to industrialization. The comparison is made more striking by the fact that before the war Greece was the most industrialized country in the Balkans.[35]

Table 1. Index of manufacturing production

	1938	1948	1959	1965
Greece	52	34	101	155
Yugoslavia	28	44	114	226
Bulgaria	10	21	121	272
Rumania	24	20	110	248

(1958 = 100)

Source: United Nations Statistical Yearbook, 1966. Extracted from Table 50.

Table 2. Distribution of labour force[36]

GREECE	1920	1928	1951	1961
Agriculture	49·6	53·7	48·2	55·3
Industry (and Construction)	16·2	15·9	19·4	19·7
Commerce and Services	21·1	18·3	26·5	24·2
YUGOSLAVIA	1921	1931	1953	1961
Agriculture	82·2	78·7	70	58·4
Industry (and Construction)	11·0	11·1	16	22·6
Commerce and Services	6·8	8·9	12·9	15·3
BULGARIA	1920	1934	1946	1956
Agriculture	81·9	80·0	75·5	64·2
Industry (and Construction)	8·0	8·0	10·3	18·7
Commerce and Services	9·5	9·6	11·8	17·4

Source: T. Deldycke et al., *The Working Population and Its Structure* (Brussels, 1968), Table A.2.

The figures of these two tables indicate clearly that the rate of growth of the Greek manufacturing sector is comparatively very slow. If one considers the crucial importance of this sector for generating self-sustained and durable economic growth and for solving the balance of payments and un-employment problems, one can realize how unsatisfactory the present structure of the Greek economy is.[37]

If one looks at the same picture from the angle of economic actors (i.e. in terms of class structure) the prospects of industrialization are rather discouraging, judging from the post-war performance of the Greek bourgeoisie.[38] Two decades after the civil war, the Greek bourgeoisie has shown no signs of losing its pronounced mercantile character. It remains consumption oriented and persistently shows a marked reluctance to invest its capital in the industrial sector. Although considerable resources are extracted from the rural population[39] they are not directed to productive channels, but consumed. Thus, not only is the peasantry impoverished, but industrial productivity is not stimulated. Due to pro-tectionist policies, the prices of industrial products are high and the rate of exchange between industry and agriculture is unfavourable. This is aggravated by the relative importance of indirect taxation which penalizes small incomes and thus further squeezes the peasants.[40] Moreover, the innumerable commercial intermediaries between the agricultural producer and the final consumer minimize the share of the former and increase the income of merchants.[41] Thus in Greece only 10 per cent of the national income is productively invested, as against 17 per cent in Rumania and 27 per cent in Bulgaria.[42] Thus in 1951 the strictly manufacturing investments were only 19 per cent of total capital investment in the economy. In 1961 the proportion declined to 10 per cent.[43] These figures are congruent with Tables 1 and 2 indicating the slow growth of the manufacturing sector in Greece.

What is more serious is that despite strong governmental incentives (subsidization, extremely favourable credit facilities, protection from internal and foreign competition, tax exemptions etc.) private capital is still unattracted to the manufacturing sector.[44] According to a Greek civil servant, 'the greatest obstacle to the further development of the country is the weakness of the productive private investment. However, the fiscal concessions are so generous that it is difficult to extend them further.'[45] Thus, the Greek bourgeoisie, partly for the reasons outlined in Part One, persists in its old ways of thinking and acting.

The Common Market. If the present degree of industrialization is unfavourable future prospects are even worse. The entry of Greece into the Common Market in 1962 has brought an unhappy recurrence in Greek economic history. Under the Turkish empire, the weakness of the state and the lack of a protectionist policy led to the destruction of the existing handicraft industry and to the subsequent commercial development of the Greek and Slav bourgeoisies. A similar pattern is likely to occur again. Although some provisions have been made to temporarily safeguard the existing industrial production in Greece,[46] in the long term, as custom barriers disappear, it is highly improbable that Greek industrialists will be able to compete with their Western counterparts.

These considerations imply three future trends of development for Greece.

(a) The chances of successful industrialization will be minimized as it will even become difficult for already existing industrial establishments to survive.

(b) Greece will be a source of labour recruitment for western Europe (already in 1963–4, 60,000 to 70,000 workers a year were leaving for Germany).

(c) The commercial bourgeoisie will go on flourishing in Greece – if tourism expands at its present rate.[47]

Post-Civil War political developments. The failure of the bourgeoisie to solve the economic problems of Greece is coupled with the state's inability to take the initiative and to participate in a much more direct and vigorous manner in the task of industrialization. This inability can be accounted for by the post-civil war political structure of Greek society. The main feature of post-war politics was an extreme right-left polarization which was taking place within an institutional framework reflecting the victory of the right-wing conservative force. Indeed, the right-wing forces, after the civil war, with the help of their American supporters, established a limited parliamentary system. It was 'limited' in the sense that the Communist party was banned and Communists as well as fellow travellers were systematically persecuted.[48] Within this parliamentary context an acute right-left antagonism developed which strengthened and consolidated the forces at the two extremes and at the same time hindered the development of strong parties in the middle of the political spectrum.

At one extreme, since the Communist party was illegal, its followers articulated their demands through EDA (United Democratic Left). Its main support came from the urban working classes,[49] from a part of the intelligentsia and from Asia Minor refugees.[50] Peasant support for EDA was not strong as peasants had been reintegrated into the main stream of bourgeois politics through the patronage system.

At the other extreme, strong personal leadership and a skilful use of anti-Communist propaganda accounted for the strength and unity of ERE (Radical Union), the right-wing party, which governed continuously for a period of eleven years (1952–63).[51] Its policy and practice have been the creation of a framework of suitable conditions for private enterprise, the attraction of foreign capital, the suppression of Communism and the development of closer links with

NATO and the United States. Through the skilful use of the patronage system and sometimes of even more coercive methods, ERE succeeded in drawing a large portion of peasant vote. Its organization followed classical patronage lines and it relied for active organizational and financial support on the upper levels of the bourgeoisie.[52] Thus, on the whole, the Radical Union represented those very groups whose interests have to be curbed for successful industrialization (drastic curbs in consumption and drastic measures forcing the bourgeoisie to invest in industry being necessary preconditions for industrialization). This explains why the right-wing party has not been a force for rapid industrialization despite its great involvement in the economy.

Between these two cohesive and antithetical political forces, the moderate parties of the centre remained divided, never managing to present a stable common front in the political arena. This rigidly polarized political framework could hardly deal with the rising aspirations of large social strata. Neither ERE nor EDA could articulate the demands of an increasing number of people for radical but peaceful changes of the status quo (e.g. a more equal distribution of income). Although the post-war economic developments had not been leading to industrialization, the national income of Greece could not double without consequences. With increasing urbanization,[53] the size of the relatively prosperous lower middle class increased.[54] The paraphernalia of 'Police Democracy' – arbitrary manipulation of elections, political discrimination in employment, ubiquitous police files, unrepresentative trade unions – connected as they were with the depths of the civil war became even more incongruous with the Greek cultural identification with the Western democracies. It is in the context of the above changes that one should locate two more recent political developments which pointed towards a less polarized, more differentiated political system.

The first development was the formation of the Centre Union Party which brought together all the small liberal parties of the centre. The Centre Union, under the leadership of George Papandreou won two successive elections in 1963 and 1964. In the 1964 election it managed to gain the unprecedented majority of 53 per cent, drawing votes from both

G

the right and the left wings. Thus, for the first time since 1952, the moderate forces managed to challenge successfully the continuous dominance of the right and to consolidate their position between the two extreme poles. This significant change in the power structure of the parties resulted in the decline of political extremism and the gradual liberalization of the regime (i.e. gradual release of political prisoners, end of political intimidation in the countryside etc.).

The second and more recent political development was a further differentiation within the Centre Union. A 'left' wing emerged under the leadership of Papandreou's son Andreas, whose rising and unexpected popularity was a clear indication of the gradually emerging demand for a genuine alternative to the communist-anti-Communist deadlock of the post-war period.

These trends constituted alternatives to political extremism and, in the long term, could even present a challenge to the dominant merchant group through the formulation of a more effective policy of industrialization. The military coup of April 1967 has interrupted this evolution, and has brought the country back to the polarized situation of the late 1940s.

III SELECTED ASPECTS OF THE CONTEMPORARY SOCIAL STRUCTURE
The dual system of social stratification. Like other largely agrarian societies, Greece has a dual but interrelated system of stratification, corresponding to the urban-rural dichotomy and based on the criteria of property and education. The present stage of economic development makes property the more important criterion of the two, although society has changed sufficiently for education, and through it occupation, to be increasingly significant in urban areas. For the rural population, property is sometimes a means of acquiring education for the next generation who then become both geographically and socially mobile. Because of this inter-relationship social differentiation in rural communities rests largely on property. Since there are no great landowners, relatively few propertyless workers, and a small range of variation in the size of holdings, the system of stratification in the countryside is one of fine gradations. In Greece 88 per cent of all farms are between 2·5 to 12·5 acres in size.

Within these narrow limits further differentiation occurs along the dimensions of power and prestige, resulting in the following strata in the larger than average village.

1. The upper stratum consists of the most prosperous peasants, large storekeepers or merchants and professionals (the doctor, teacher, governmental official etc.).

2. The middle stratum consists of the bulk of farm owners, small storekeepers and the few skilled workers who exist in the village.

3. Propertyless farm labourers together with the few persons who are, for various reasons, not quite acceptable to the village community (i.e. the 'dishonoured', the mentally disturbed) occupy the bottom of the prestige ladder.[55]

In the urban areas, on the other hand, the system of stratification is more complex and its range is much wider. The highest and lowest levels are clearly defined by the ownership or non-ownership of property and the difference between them, as in most developing societies, is vast. In between, there is a less clearly defined sphere where educational and property hierarchies run parallel or merge. The strata of urban Greece could be enumerated as follows:

1. The upper stratum is composed of shipowners, bankers, big merchants and industrialists. This is broadly the group previously referred to as the 'bourgeoisie'. One should also include a few very successful and wealthy professionals and administrators.[56] One can further differentiate two substrata within this category. The first substratum consists of a few descendants of families which played an important role during the War of Independence, of *phanariot* families and of pre-land reform big landowning families which have managed to retain some of their wealth; their origin, in combination with their wealth, gives them the implicit claim of being an 'aristocracy'.[57] Their offspring, after attending the few elite secondary schools in Greece, usually study abroad. This imparts to the subgroup a distinct cosmopolitanism which is perhaps the main cultural feature differentiating it from the rest of the bourgeoisie. The latter consists of families which have been rich for one or at most two generations and are therefore, less 'cultivated' (i.e. less 'Westernized') and cosmopolitan. However, the barriers between the two substrata are very fragile as the less 'aristocratic' subgroup tries

to give to its offspring exactly the same education as the aristocratic one. Thus, when a family succeeds in retaining its wealth for the second or third generation, the life styles of its members become identical with those of the 'aristocracy' and the former are easily accepted by the latter.

2. The middle strata are composed of professionals, senior officials, executives and lesser entrepreneurs. This class, together with the lower middle class (small merchants, shopkeepers, clerks, civil servants, craftsmen) compose the majority of the urban population.

3. Finally, the lower strata groups all those who possess neither property nor education. This is a diverse category composed of labourers, factory workers, diverse domestic servants and others providing numerous minor services.

It is impossible to calculate the exact magnitude of these groups, since the property element cannot be deduced from available statistics. However, some rough idea may be obtained from the following classification which heavily emphasizes degree of skill.

Table 3. Occupational classification of the active population in Greece.[58]

Occupational Category	Number	Per cent of total labour force
Professional, Managerial and Technical	136,190	4·1
Clerical and Sales	411,410	12·6
Skilled and Semi-Skilled Workers	581,000	17·8
Unskilled Workers	408,600	12·5
Farmers and Farm Workers	1,722,100	52·8
	3,259,300	

Source: OECD 'The Mediterranean Regional Project: Country Reports, *"Greece"* ', Paris, 1965, Tables 52–9.

As to the distribution of income among the urban strata, the only available information is that provided by the consumer surveys of the National Statistical Service of Greece. The following table shows the distribution of urban households according to six income classes.

Table 4. *Income distribution for urban households*

Weekly cash income of Household in Drachmae 1 Pound = 80 drachmae	Per cent of all Households Failing in income class		Given
	1957–58		*1960–62*
1. Under 250	13·0		9·9
2. 250–449	23·4		17·6
3. 450–799	30·9		34·8
4. 800–1099	14·8		15·1
5. 1100·1599	9·4		11·8
6. 1600 and over	8·5		10·8

Source: J. Crockett, 'Consumer expenditures and incomes in Greece', Centre of Planning and Economic Research, Athens, 1967, p. 88.

The table indicates that between the two time periods there is a decrease of the proportion of households in the two lower income classes and a corresponding increase in the other income classes, especially class 3. However, this improvement is partially nullified by a rise in consumer prices of 6·1/2 per cent approximately. According to the same source in 1957–8 the highest sixth of the households (in terms of income) accounts for over 40 per cent of the total cash and about 33 per cent of total cash purchases plus receipts in kind. On the other hand, the lowest third of the households accounts for just over one-tenth of total cash income and about one-sixth of total cash purchases plus receipts in kind.[59] In all these computations one must take into account the systematic tendency of the respondents in the upper-income brackets to understate their income.[60] Finally, one must also bear in mind that these figures refer to urban incomes only. If rural incomes were considered the income differential would have been much greater.

Urban rural differences. The rural and urban stratification systems having been contrasted, the relationship between them must be outlined. In this connection the discrepancy in standards of living as well as the geographical and social mobility between town and countryside require consideration.

The following table, which shows the difference in per capita gross product between the various geographical regions of Greece, gives a rough idea of the great differences between rural and urban areas:

Table 5. Per capita gross regional product, 1962

Regions	Gross Regional Product per Capita (In Drs.)	Regional Indices	
		(Greece–100)	Attica–100)
Attica	18·801	156·30	100·00
Rest of Central Greece	9·215	76·60	49·00
Peloponnesos	10·658	80·60	56·70
Thessaly	8·913	74·10	47·40
Epirus	6·846	56·90	36·40
Macedonia	11·137	92·60	59·20
Thrace	8·605	71·50	45·70
Crete	7·938	66·00	42·20
Aegean Islands	8·229	68·40	43·70
Ionian Islands	6·944	57·70	36·90
Greece	12·028	100·00	64·00

Source: Centre of Planning and Economic research *Draft of the five year economic development plan for Greece (1966–1967)*, Athens 1965, p. 146.

These figures show that the per capita gross products of Attica (Athens area) and such regions as Epirus and Crete are in the ratio 2·5 to one. Such differences are reflected in the higher standards of living in Athens (whose population constitutes a little less than a quarter of the total Greek population) compared with the rest of the country. The following table provides indicators of the difference in standards of living between Greater Athens and such economically backward regions as Thrace and the Ionian Islands.

Taking into consideration the rural–urban gap it is not surprising that there is considerable internal migration from the countryside to the urban centres. Thus, according to a report of the National Statistical Service of Greece the number of internal migrants between 1 January 1956 and 19 March 1961 amounted to 645,000. Of all internal migrants 63·4 per cent moved to the urban centres, mainly Athens and Salonica.[61]

In 1920 the Athenian population amounted to 453,000 people. In 1961 it had risen to 1,802,000, a rise of more than

Table 6. Some indicators of regional differences in standards of living

Indicators	Greater Athens	Thrace	Epirus	Ionian Islands
1. Per capita consumption of electric energy (1962)				
i. Total (Kwh)	833	34	48	66
ii. Domestic use (kwh)	290	9	16	22
2. Private Cars (1961) (per 10,000 inhabitants)	168	8	7	12
3. Shower or bath installed (1961) (% of total households)	30	2	2	6
4. Drinking water installation (1961) (% of total households)	72	21	18	20
5. Inhabitants per (1962)				
i. one doctor	305	3,293	1,576	1,505
ii. one dentist	963	7,751	5,780	7,330
iii. one hospital bed	70	588	398	184
6. Illiteracy (1961) (% of total population)	10	30	22	25

Source: Draft of the five year economic development plan for Greece, (1966–7), Athens 1965, p. 147.

400 per cent. This influx to the capital cannot always be explained in purely economic terms. For instance, it is not the poorest areas of Greece which have the largest number of migrants.[62] But whatever the reasons, this exorbitant growth of the capital, which various governmental attempts at decentralization failed to check, creates all sorts of economic imbalances.

The fact that almost a quarter of the Greek population is concentrated in the Athens area is directly relevant to the economic and cultural decline of the provinces. Moreover, there is a striking imbalance between rates of migration and rates of industrialization. Despite the fact that most industries are concentrated in the Greater Athens area, because of Greece's low degree of industrialization and because of low skills of the migrants, Athens cannot absorb the incoming labour force in an economically sound manner. Consequently most of them are employed in a highly unproductive manner (small street sellers, shoe shiners etc.), and live under the most appalling conditions.[63]

Social mobility

The degree of commercialization of the Greek countryside in conjunction with the high level of migration implies that urban values often intrude upon and influence traditional peasant systems. Values emphasizing the advantages of a large family as a source of household labour gradually give way to a preference for fewer children with the sons being educated to the highest level possible. This change of emphasis is illustrated by the fact that whereas only 10 per cent of urban workers' sons register for university studies, 14 per cent of peasants' sons enrol despite the greater obstacles that the latter encounter.[64] Indeed, financing a son through university represents a considerable hardship for an average peasant family (although education is free in Greece, there is no governmental provision for the maintenance of students); but there are compensations. The expenditure is gradual and is taken into account when the family land is subdivided. So education for at least one son may be partly a means of limiting extreme land fragmentation and of dealing with the need for the daughter's dowry.[65] Since the doctor, the lawyer and the teacher are at the top of the village prestige hierarchy, to have a son in one of these professions confers prestige on the whole family. As Lambiri-Dimaki points out, the peasant who is away from the urban centres tends to underestimate the serious shortage of jobs for university graduates. Due to the remoteness of the urban governmental bureaucracy from the peasant, the education of a son and his settlement in Athens or Salonica with perhaps a civil service job is an asset in bringing the family a little nearer to the distant and imcomprehensible hierarchies of power. A member of the family who at least understands the bureaucracy will guide other members through the tortuous procedures always necessary for conducting family business in relation to the government. Moreover, the son who moves further and achieves a professional administrative position is expected to use his influence in order to improve the lot of the whole family. Thus it could be argued that, contrary to what happens in advanced industrial societies, in Greece and other developing countries social mobility for one member of the family does not operate as a factor of divisiveness and estrangement from his kin. Family ties and other relationships of patronage promote movement between stratum lines and help to blur to some extent cultural distinctions between the different status groups. Of course the importance of family and patronage does not end with higher education. In business and professional circles, '*mesa*' (literally 'means') is a crucially important determinant of advancement and is widely acknowledged as such. Thus, when a sample of Athens University students were asked 'Do you think that in our country, genuine ability alone can enable a young man or woman to succeed?' 82 per cent of the men and 86 per cent of the women replied in the negative.[66]

Although the statistical evidence is very scant, in terms of some indices bearing upon social mobility Greece appears to be a relatively open society by Western standards. Thus the rate of enrolment in educational institutions is surprisingly high. Almost 90 per cent of children complete the compulsory six years of elementary education. Of these almost half go to secondary schools and 40 per cent successfully complete the course. Forty-three per cent of these graduating from

Table 7. Percentage distribution of total population and of students in higher education by socio-economic group, 1961

Socio-economic Group	A % total Population	B % of total University Students	Index of educational opportunity $C = \dfrac{B}{A}$
Professional workers, top managers, rent earners, and teachers	4·5	21·2	4·71
Clerical workers	4·0	11·0	2·75
Sales workers including small working proprietors	6·2	12·6	2·03
Farmers, Fishermen and Miners	55·8	29·2	0·52
Transport and communication workers	3·2	3·7	1·16
Craftsmen, skilled and unskilled labourers	19·4	10·8	0·66
Service trade workers and permanent personnel of armed forces	6·9	6·2	0·90

Source: OECD 'The Mediterranean Regional Project', *Greece*, p. 67.

secondary schools proceed to university.[67] These figures are an indication of the strength of the belief in education as the key to wealth and status. This emphasis, together with the patronage and family aid, helps to account for the fact that, though as in all societies the lower strata are under-represented among university students, the degree to which they are in fact educated is striking, given the highly inegalitarian nature of Greek society in other respects (such as income distribution).

Thus, 40 per cent of the students at university are the sons of farmers, fishermen, miners, craftsmen, skilled and unskilled labourers, i.e. 'the lower urban and rural strata'.

It should be noted, however, that educational 'openness' is not in itself a good indicator of social mobility, unless accompanied by an increasing capacity of the economy to absorb those who acquire this education. Greece, like many other developing countries, has a pool of frustrated university graduates who cannot find jobs appropriate to their training. Thus, while the educational system is relatively open, the fierce competition for jobs among graduates means that those lacking wealth or social influence will find difficulty in gaining social promotion.

Apart from education, the second major avenue of mobility in Greece is through business and the acquisition of property. This process is facilitated by the relatively small size of enterprise in Greece. Other things being equal, small size and the low degree of bureaucratization of enterprises are favourable to intra-generational mobility. One study has indicated that 40 per cent of the more important Greek industrialists today were the sons of peasants, craftsmen and small shopkeepers.[68] However, as the present trend is towards larger economic units and as bureaucratization increases, this type of mobility will certainly decrease.

NOTES

1   This bias is particularly accentuated in the writings of the Greek Marxist historian G. Kordatos, *The social significance of the Greek Revolution of 1821* (in Greek), (Athens, 1946), and his 5

volume *History of Modern Greece* (in Greek), (Athens, 1957). See also G. Zevros, *A short study of modern Greek History* (in Greek), (Athens, 1945).

2 Gramsci's concept of hegemonic class implies such a theoretical approach. See G. A. Williams, 'Gramsci's concept of Egemonia' in *Journal of the History of Ideas*, 1960, Vol. 21, No. 4, pp. 589–99. Among non-Marxist writers the work of Barrington Moore Junior has a similar theoretical framework. See his *Social Origins of Dictatorship and Democracy* (London, 1967).

3 T. Stoianovich, 'The conquering Balkan Orthodox merchant' in *Journal of Economic History*, 1960, pp. 269–73.

4 This was reinforced by the well-known practice of wealthy Greeks donating a considerable amount of their fortune to the Church, a custom which in a slightly different form still exists today. Interestingly, there is no contradiction in the minds of the faithful between this type of philanthropy and the usually dubious manner by which wealth was acquired, e.g. piracy or brigandage. This can be explained if one takes into account some of the salient characteristics of the Greek Orthodox Church which are as valid today as they were a few centuries ago. One of the most distinctive features of Greek Orthodoxy is its extreme formalism. From the point of view of the Orthodox believer, faith has very little to do with moral problems or metaphysical questions. There is very little soul searching and very little internalization of ethical principles. For the Greek Orthodox, even the sophisticated one, to be a good Christian means primarily to follow as strictly as possible rules governing church attendance, fasting etc. Also one has to consider the temporal powers of the Church and the fact that despite its corruption and exploitation it contributed more than any other body to the maintenance of the Greek language, culture and national identity during the four centuries of Turkish occupation. From the point of view of the believer, the Patriarch was not simply a spiritual leader, he was also the ethnarch, the leader of the Greek nation. Therefore it is not surprising that even for a modern Greek, religion and nationalism are inextricably linked, to be a good Christian is to be a good patriot and vice-versa. Thus one can argue that the formalistic and temporal character of the Greek Orthodox Church was relevant to the development of Greek commerce. Indeed, the Orthodox economic 'ethic', if not favouring economic activities in the direct and active way of the Protestant ethic, at least did not hinder them, as did some other-worldly types of religion. For the general position of the Church under the Ottoman Empire, see T. H. Papadopoulos, *Studies and Documents relating to the History of the Greek Church and People under Turkish domination*, (Brussels, 1952), and G. G. Arnakis, 'The Greek Church of Constantinople and the Ottoman Empire' in *Journal of Modern History*, 1952, pp. 235–50.

5 G. Kordatos, *Introduction to the History of Greek capitalism* (in

Greek), (Athens, 1930). See also Stoianovich, 'Balkan Orthodox Merchant. . .'.

6   For instance, during the eighteenth century two very important trading groups appeared in the Balkans. The famous maritime merchants of Hydra, Spetsai and Psara who were originally Albanians, and the land traders of Macedonia, Epirus and Thessaly who had predominantly Vlac and Macedonian origins. By 1800 the wealthy members of both groups were completely hellenized.

7   Thus there were flourishing Greek and Jewish textile manufacturers in Salonica, Bursa and Constantinople. Later very important craft industries developed in many parts of Greece, mainly in places enjoying a relatively high degree of political autonomy. Handicraft centres like the Ambelakia and the Zagorochoria were selling their products not only in the Empire, but in western Europe as well. See K. Koukkidis, *The spirit of co-operation among modern Greeks and Ambelakia* (in Greek), (Athens, 1948).

8   There were several attempts at implementing such a policy, but they did not succeed. For instance, in 1703 the Grand Vizier Ramis Mohamed Pasha worked out a plan for the improvement of industry and the founding of new textile industries in Salonica, Andrianople and Constantinople. Mohamed Pasha soon fell and the project 'to establish cloth and silk fabric manufacturers in the States of the Grand Seigneur fell with him', according to the French ambassador who had definite instructions to hinder any attempts at creating textile competitors in Turkey. See Stoianovich, 'Balkan Merchant', pp. 259–83.

9   For an analysis and a bibliography of the shift from '*timar*' to '*chiflik*', see Stavrianos, *The Balkans since 1453* (New York, 1963), Chapter 9.

10   Stavrianos, *The Balkans since 1453*, pp. 144 ff. See also his 'Antecedents to the Balkan Revolution of the 19th century' in *Journal of Modern History*, 1957, pp. 335–72.

11   For instance, most of the members of the 'Philike Hetairia', the secret revolutionary society which played a crucial role in initiating the 1821 revolution, were merchants. See C. W. Crawley, 'John Capodistria and the Greeks before 1821' in *Cambridge Historical Journal*, 1952. For short biographies of the leading members of the society, see S. Melas, *Philikoi* (in Greek), (Athens, 1960). However some merchants, including the shipping magnates of Hydra, were initially opposed to the revolution. Moreover in Peloponnesus, commerce was controlled by local landowners who were initially against any violent uprising. See M. Sakellariou, *Peloponnesus during the second Ottoman rule* (in Greek), (Athens, 1939). Yet many merchants, especially those living abroad, supported the revolution for the following reasons: (a) the increasing lawlessness during the declining years of the Ottoman Empire which was hindering commerce, and (b)

the growing contact between Greek traders and the West. See Stavrianos, *The Balkans since 1453*, p. 335–42.

12 N. Svoronos, *Histoire de la Grèce moderne* (Paris, 1953), pp. 30 ff.

13 For the role that the Church, the *Phanoriotes* and the landowning class played during the revolution, see D. Tsakonas, *The Sociology of Modern Greek Culture* (in Greek), (Athens, 1968), pp. 99–103. For a comparison with other Balkan countries, see T. Stoianovich, 'The social foundations of Balkan politics' in C. and B. Jelavich, *The Balkans in Transition* (Berkeley, 1963), pp. 297–345 and L. S. Stavrianos, *The Balkans 1815–1914* (New York, 1963), pp. 17 ff.

14 For an account of social fragmentation and the interrelations between regional and class differences in the early nineteenth century, see Tsakonas, *The Sociology of Modern Greek Culture*, p. 100 ff.

15 The landowning classes never achieved in Greece the power and prestige of their counterparts in western Europe. Greece, apart from a few exceptions (Crete and the Ionian Islands), did not develop an indigenous feudal aristocracy. Moreover, under the Ottoman rule, as Turks owned most of the land, the Greek landowning classes were relatively weak both in political and economic terms. See Sakellariou, *Peloponnesus*. For a discussion of the landowning classes and differences within this group, see Tsakonas, *Sociology . . .* , p. 84 ff.

16 The terms 'peasant' and 'peasantry' as sociological concepts are by no means without ambiguity. Thus one could argue that because of the early commercialization of agriculture, one should speak rather about Greek 'farmers', not peasants. However, in this essay we have adopted a broad definition of the term 'peasant', as given by H. Landsberger in his article 'The role of peasant movements and revolts in development: an analytical framework' in *International Institute for Labour Studies Bulletin*, 1968, pp. 8–15.

17 R. L. Wolff, *The Balkans in our time* (Cambridge, Mass., 1956), pp. 101–90; H. Seton-Watson, *Eastern Europe between the wars* (Cambridge, 1945); Stavrianos, *The Balkans since 1453*, p. 598 ff; G. M. Dimitrov, 'Agrarianism' in F. Gross, *European Ideologies* (New York, 1948), pp. 369–451; J. Tomasevich, *Peasants, Politics and Economic Change in Yugoslavia* (Stanford, 1955).

18 For an account of the impact of early commercialization on Greek peasant life and social organization, see K. Karavidas, *A comparative study on the economic and social morphology of Greece and of the neighbouring Slav countries* (in Greek), (Athens, 1931).

19 T. Deldycke, et al., *The working population and its structure* (Brussels, 1968).

20 Vasmaltzidis, a technical superintendent of the Greek Agricultural Bank, who studied in detail a great number of Slav peasant families concludes his report as follows: 'Thus the Zadrouga

gives the impression of a social organisation with very strong and deep roots, whereas on the contrary the majority of all other agricultural enterprises in Northern Greece give the impression of social formations without roots whose foundations could be shattered by the first strong wind.' He goes on to say that the Slav peasants are the only ones in Greece whose outlook shows 'a steady and real peasant conscience. They are the only wheat growers in Greece whose enterprises are not in deficit.' (Authors' translation.) D. Daniilides, *Modern Greek Society and Economy* (in Greek) (Athens, 1934), pp. 126–42.

21   J. K. Campbell, *Honour, Family and Patronage* (Oxford, 1964).

22   G. Kordatos, *The History of our Language Problem* (in Greek), (Athens, 1943).

23   An analytical account of the establishment of dictatorships in the Balkans between the wars can be found in T. Stoianovich, 'The social and political foundations of Balkan politics 1750–1941', in Charles and Barbara Jelavich (eds.), *The Balkans in Transition* (Berkeley, 1963).

24   By the summer of 1943 almost four-fifths of the country was controlled by the EAM, see B. Sweet-Escott, *Greece: a political and economic survey 1939–1953* (London, 1954), p. 21.

25   UK Foreign Office, *Greece, Basic Handbook* (London, 1943), p. 25.

26   For an account of the situation in Yugoslavia, see R. L. Wolff, *The Balkans in our Time*, pp. 206–13.

27   For a detailed account of diplomatic events at the end of the war, see S. G. Xydis, *Greece and the Great Powers 1944–47* (Thessalonika, 1963).

28   At the end of the war 9,000 villages and 23 per cent of all buildings had been destroyed. See C. A. Coombs, *Post-war Public Finance in Greece* (London, 1947).

29   Mainly through mechanization and the concentration of an owner's small and scattered strips of land into more compact holdings which can be worked as a unit. See I. T. Sanders, *Rainbow in the Rock* (Cambridge Mass., 1962), p. 68.

30   Barrington Moore Junior, *Social origins of dictatorship and democracy* (London, 1967).

31   H. S. Ellis, et al., *Industrial capital in Greek development* (Athens, 1964), p. 237.

32   From 37,000 in 1950 to 737,000 in 1967 according to the Greek Statistical Yearbook.

33   Greek shipping tonnage increased from 1,500 in 1952 to 7 million in 1962. See J. Meynaud, *Les forces politiques en Grèce* (Paris, 1965), p. 375.

34   Emigration reached a rate of over 100,000 per annum in 1963–4. OECD, *Manpower Policy and Problems in Greece* (Paris, 1965), p. 32, Table 19.

35   N. Spulber, 'Changes in the economic structures of the Balkans 1860–1960' in Jelavich, *The Balkans in Transition* (Berkeley,

1963); PEP, *Economic Development in South-East Europe* (London 1945).

36 From T. Deldycke, et al., *Working Population . . .*: 'Agriculture' includes forestry, hunting and fishing, 'industry' includes extractive industries, manufacturing industries, electricity, gas, water and sanitary services, 'services' includes commerce, banking, insurance, real estate, transport, storage and communication services.

37 G. Meier and R. Baldwin, *Economic development: theory, history, policy* (New York, 1963).

38 For the sake of clarity the distinction should be made between the broad term 'middle classes' which is often used loosely to denote all non-manual occupations and the term 'bourgeoisie'. A bourgeoisie is distinguished by the fact that its members are independent entrepreneurs. Furthermore, unless one speaks of the 'petty bourgeoisie', small shopkeepers, artisans etc., the term refers to the economic elite of the country (big shipowners, financiers, important commercial intermediaries between urban and rural Greece and between Greece and the developed countries etc.). Among this group the 'mercantile' element predominates. The 'industrial' bourgeoisie is weak, both in economic significance and because of its dependence on a framework of State protection.

39 The two-thirds of the population who live in agricultural areas receive one-third only of the national income. See A. Gregoroyiannis, *The economic development of Greece* (in Greek), (Athens, 1959), p. 40.

40 Meynaud, *Les Forces Politiques . . .* p. 376.

41 For a detailed account of different techniques by which merchants extract usurious interest from the Greek peasant, see A. Godart, 'Problèmes sociaux du développement' in *Revue de l'Institut de Sociologie*, 1966, 3, pp. 538–44. It has been frequently pointed out that the peasant class always bears the cost of successful industrialization – as illustrated by Germany, England and the USSR. The situation in Greece indicates that the peasants bear a no-smaller burden in the case of arrested industrialization.

42 Figures for 1954, see Gregoroyiannis, *Economic Development of Greece*.

43 In fact, even in absolute terms investment in manufacturing was lower in 1961 than it was in 1958. See H. S. Ellis, et al., op. cit., p. 237. For a study of the social origins of Greek industrialists, see A. Alexander, *Greek industrialists* (Athens, 1964). Contrary to the author's conclusions (pp. 128–30), we believe on the basis of our historical analysis that it is not possible to explain the slow growth of industrial entrepreneurship in purely economic terms.

44 J. Meynaud, *Les Forces Politiques . . .* , pp. 381–3.

45 D. Poulakos, 'Problèmes actuels de l'économie hellénique' in *Reflets et Perspectives* (August, 1964), p. 258.

46   Exports from the Six of products which are also manufactured in Greece will not be allowed to enter the country until 1984. All other goods will become duty-free ten years earlier, by 1972. OECD, *Greece*, p. 12.

47   S. Triantis, *Common Market and Economic Development*, Centre of Planning and Economic Research, (Athens, 1965).

48   For a summary of police restrictions in Greece, see P. Williams, *Athens under the Spartans*, Fabian Research Series, 264 (London, 1967), pp. 12–13.

49   The Greek working class developed during the inter-war period of industrialization. Since the country industrialized slowly, the working class remained weak in numerical as well as organizational terms. The quasi-craft organization of most Greek industries does not favour trade-union formation and the development of class consciousness. A third of all people engaged in manufacturing are either owners or relatives of owners. In addition, a half of the labour force engaged in manufacturing is employed in workshops with a staff of under ten people. See G. Koutsoumaris, *The morphology of Greek industry*, Centre of Economic Research monograph no. 6 (Athens, 1963), pp. 66–7. Under such circumstances it is not surprising that the trade-union movement was always strictly controlled by the government. F. Venenci, *La participation des ouvriers à la vie politique en Grèce* (unpublished thesis for the University of Paris, 1961), p. 88 ff; G. Kordatos, *History of the Greek workers' movement* (in Greek), (Athens, 1956); C. Jecchines, *Trade-unionism in Greece* (Chicago, 1967).

50   The Asia Minor Greeks settled in mainland Greece after the total failure of the Greek Asia Minor expedition in 1922. D. Pentzopoulos shows the continuing relationship between refugee settlements and Communist support until the late 1950s, in *Balkan Exchange of Minorities and its impact upon Greece* (Paris and The Hague, 1962), pp. 190–5.

51   For a more detailed discussion of the Radical Union and also of the other major Greek parties, see Meynaud, *Forces Politiques . . .*, pp. 195–306; G. Daphnis, *The Greek Political Parties 1821–1961* (in Greek), (Athens, 1961); G. D. Daskalakis, *Political Parties and Democracy* (in Greek), (Athens, 1958).

52   To the list of ERE's *relatively* stable supporters one must of course add such extra-parliamentary formations as the Palace, the Church and the Army. The Army's role in modern Greek history was not always conservative. It played a major part in the overthrow of the monarchy and the establishment of the Greek Republic (1924–36). It was with the Metaxas dictatorship and the dismissal of the republican officers that the Army acquired a clearly conservative orientation. See M. Wheeler, 'Greek Political Perspectives' in *Government and Opposition*, Vol. 3, No. 3, 1968, p. 341.

53   For some figures on the exceptionally high rate of urbanization in

Greece, see V. Michel, 'Y a-t-il des régions économiquement sous-développées en Europe? Aperçu de la situation économico-sociale actuelle de la Grèce' in *Les dossiers de l'action sociale catholique* (July–August 1959), p. 470 ff.

54 On the rise of the lower middle classes and their political role, see T. Charlier-Yannopoulou, 'A propos de la crise politique grecque' in *Revue française de science politique*, Vol. 17, No. 1, 1967, p. 53 ff; F. Venencie, op. cit., p. 29.

55 This classification is partially based on J. Photiadis's study of a Macedonian village, reported in I. T. Sanders, op. cit., p. 279 ff.

56 According to J. Cambel and P. Sherrard, this group probably numbers one thousand families. See their *Modern Greece*, (London, 1968), p. 370.

57 Perhaps one should include in this group all persons who belonged to the pre-coup Palace entourage.

58 The percentages do not add up to a hundred since they have been rounded. Moreover, a large number of the 'sales' workers and 'skilled' workers are very different from groups which are formally classified under the same labels in the more developed European countries. A large proportion of the former are small shopowners and traders and of the latter, craftsmen.

59 J. Crockett, *Consumer Expenditures and Incomes in Greece* (Athens, 1967), p. 89.

60 *Crockett*, pp. 85–7.

61 S. Hazoglou, 'Internal Migration' (in Greek) in *Spoudai* (Studies), No. 4, 1965–6, p. 579.

62 C. Moustaka, *The Internal Migrant*, Social Sciences Centre monograph (Athens, 1964).

63 From a report of the Greek Statistical Service it appears that of migrants established in Athens only 29·6 per cent and 10·5 per cent are respectively absorbed by industry and commerce. A further 31 per cent are grouped under the residual label 'other services', which refers to the unproductive occupations mentioned earlier. See Hazoglou, 'Internal Migration', pp. 587–8.

64 See J. Lambiri-Dimaki, 'Les chances d'accès à l'enseignement en Grèce' in R. Castel and J. Passeron, *Education, développement et démocratie* (Paris, 1967).

65 E. Friedl, 'Dowry and inheritance in Modern Greece' in *Annals of the New York Academy of Sciences*, Series 2, Vol. 22, 1959, pp. 49–54.

66 Unpublished study by J. Lambiri-Dimaki quoted in C. Safilios-Rothschild, 'Class position and success stereotypes in Greek and American cultures' in *Social Forces* (March 1967).

67 Cambell and Sherrard, *Modern Greece*, p. 384.

68 Alexander, *Greek Industrialists*, pp. 44–53.

6 Ireland

John Jackson

An understanding of social stratification in Ireland[1] rests upon the notion of a dependent society which is a reflection of the continuing dependence of the economy. The caste distinctions maintained and developed during the dominance of the Protestant Ascendancy, and still to be observed in Ulster, have remained in spite of the relative decline of the Protestant minority. The dependence of the economy on British markets, migration to Britain and externally owned industry supports this dependent quality. In terms of the political development of a new nation it must be explained by the failure of any political revolution to follow the achievement and attainment of independence. As Humphreys observes with some force about the period between 1922 and 1951:

> In the history of Europe, Ireland's revolution surely is among the most un-revolutionary. To be sure the fighting involved in it and in the Civil War which followed it, seems bloody and costly enough. But self-government, once achieved, led to no radical or violent uprooting of established institutions. Rather, these thirty years were marked by a general institutional continuity, by conservatism in policy and by change, which though steady was slow[2].

A recent article by Patrick Lynch on the Irish economy underlines this sense of dependent status that has acted, in part, to vitiate the development, not merely of political consciousness, but also of a consciousness of a distinctive leadership among the majority Catholic population of the country. He writes about the period following the death of Arthur Griffith (a leader in the Easter Rising and after whose journal the Sinn Fein movement was named) that

> gradually the idealism (of *Sinn Fein*) gave way to a despondent national mood marked by self-laceration expressed in puritanical

political and social legislation, and in economic policies that seemed to have little relevance to the objectives of Pearse and Connolly. The middle class was on the stage, and those who thought that the Irish struggle for independence had other ideals were stranded helplessly in the wings.[3]

Certainly in the economic theories and government and administrative forms which were developed by the new state there was little alteration from the British pattern. The long history of economic ties established since the Act of Union in 1800 might be broken at a political level but it was a different matter when it came to the economy. In a real sense Ireland remained Britain's breadbasket and Britain remained Ireland's banker. Geographical proximity, the distribution of raw materials, the simple facts of an agricultural economy dependent on exports underlined the reality and in the early governments of the Free State *laissez-faire* liberalism remained the prevailing philosophy. As Lynch has it: 'The money of Irish investors flowed out to be invested in Britain, where it secured a better return, and Irish workers sought jobs in Britain, where they got better wages.'[4]

Emigration in particular has served a convenient function in limiting already high levels of unemployment but more significantly as 'a godsend to the politicians. It is the great safety valve which prevents the emergence of a politically conscious working class.'[5] This peculiar feature of the Irish situation must be seen in relation to three inherent strains towards conservatism within the society itself. The first lies in the rural social structure; the second stems from the fact that the initial problem of government following the Civil War was to establish law and order and the third lies in the influence of the Catholic Church.

The transfer of political power to Dublin left a ruling elite drawn from the older professions, an established merchant class and a group of large farmers. The administrative structure and its senior civil servants remained essentially unaltered. It was after all a society which though it had emerged as independent had lost many of its potential leaders in the struggle and much of its fire in the bitterness of the Civil War.

This preamble to a discussion of social structure in Ireland since the war is necessitated by the fact that subsequent development has been substantially conditioned by the style that was set by the new state in its early years. The period of stability and standstill which characterized it in the 1920s was followed by significant policies of rapid industrial development during the 1930s combined with the application of selective tariffs. Although many of these policies, largely attributable to Mr Sean Lemass, had the effect of enormously increasing the contribution of industry to the economy, it was developed within a protectionist framework dependent on the import of raw materials and essentially conservative in its implications. The interesting fact that much of the industry that was developed during this period was by public enterprises should not lead to the assumption that this was inspired by a socialist political philosophy. As Lynch and other observers have pointed out although Ireland has probably a greater share of its economy in the public sector than any other country in western Europe 'radicalism, either in ideas or policies has not been a conspicuous feature of Ireland since independence'.[6] It has only been in the last decade that there has been a significant shift away from these prevailing tendencies and a lively social critique which has begun to question some of the assumptions of the middle-class monopoly. As Lenin makes clear, expectations for Ireland as the trigger society for revolution were sadly disappointed in the event.[7]

Polarization along class lines has been inhibited in political terms by the essential similarities of policy of the two major political parties which drew their basis of support essentially from divisions of the electorate based on loyalties established during the Civil War period. The initial dominance for thirty years of the Fianna Fail party and the continued influence of de Valera served to develop a mood of cynicism which became associated with patronage and personalities rather than a structured 'party' identity. To a large degree political life has exhibited those principles of a carefully blended system of exchange by which power in the centre is essentially ascriptive in character and, as Eisenstadt defines it, more oriented to a closed tradition.[8] This finds reinforcement in the operation of traditional political affiliation, the power of the church, the external source of economic and political power especially as expressed in the ascriptive status aspiration both to the wider context of British economy and society and to the still evident reference group of the aspirant elite – the Protestant Ascendancy.

Two further features of this general structure may be stated briefly. The first lies in the effect of proportional representation as an electoral system, the complex mechanics of which have served to encourage 'personality' rather than 'party' and have thereby inhibited the development of any mass parties in Duverger's terms.[9] The second can be seen in the essential inability of the Labour Party, which only recently has defined itself as socialist, to attract either a trade union or proletarian basis of support.[10]

Although Ireland is a society where the past still dominates the present to an often obsessive degree it is also true that the approach to history tends to be particularistic rather than general. A sense of historical perspective has been less apparent than the continued significance of a series of symbolic and emotionally loaded reference points which have prevented the emergence of a larger view or a more cohesive sense of the relationship of the past to the present. The result is that any aspect of Irish life is characterized by a variety of often inconsistent overtones. So far as social stratification is concerned, these overtones, not by any means subtle, as recent events in Northern Ireland have demonstrated, necessitate a constant awareness of the significance of religion, kinship links, specific political genealogies, and regional identities in addition to the more 'objective' indicators of social class. These variables must be taken into account in addition to the fact of the extensive development of local status systems so characteristic of rural communities, necessarily self-sufficient and divided by distance from larger social centres.

Regional variation, perhaps the most straightforward of these factors, demonstrates clearly the need to avoid assumptions of a unitary society in attempting an analysis of this kind. Not only have the differences between the eastern seaboard and the west coast led to a contrast between rich and poor farms acutely reflected in heavier emigration from the west during the last two hundred years, but such long-established differences in resources have been exacerbated by recent industrialization. Although the national figure for those employed in agriculture was 30·9 per cent in 1966, the figure for the County of Dublin was only 7·7 per cent and for County Louth 17·1 per cent, while in the three western counties of Leitrim, Roscommon and Mayo over 60 per cent still have agricultural employment.[11] Within the past decade there has been an especially rapid shift away from agriculture in the country as a whole and a consequent increase in those employed in industry and in the tertiary sectors of employment. In the five years between the census of 1961 and that of 1966 there was an increase of 25 per cent in the managerial and employers group and rises of 18·5 per cent and 20·1 per cent respectively in the higher professional and skilled manual categories. Such changes in the economic and social balance of a society of no more than 2,882,000 people (1966) are bound to create important shifts in the patterns of social stratification and cause changes in the class structure.

The difficulty with all studies of social class is to establish a relatively stable base against which changes of this kind can be estimated. Within highly industrialized societies it is possible to define a fairly comprehensive framework for analysis based on industrial occupational categories, but this must still omit, or treat distinctly, such primary producers as farmers, or dependants. These groups may be less of an embarrassment in, say, Britain where 90 per cent of economically active males are earning wages and salaries. Where the proportion of 'employees' is lower as in Ireland, it is clear that it is far less satisfactory to rely on an analytical model which assumes a clustering of the attitudes of social class around the variable of employment.[12] If, as is the case in this volume, some attempt is being made to consider social class in a number of European countries the difficulties of comparison become even more acute and one must rely on necessarily crude statistical outlines such as that in Table 1 to indicate the broad dimensions that distinguish a particular society. Economic factors are themselves only part of the outline from which an analysis of social class can be constructed but they do still serve to set limits within which the more ephemeral elements can be described.

The low proportion of industrial employees in Ireland is made up for the most part of those working in small firms employing 300 workers or less. Only six manufacturing firms

Table 1. *Employment sectors of the male work force, 1966*

	Agriculture	Industry	Tertiary Sector
Ireland	31·9% (38·5)	27·9% (24·1)	40·2% (37·4)
United Kingdom	4·6	54·5	40·9
Italy	23·8	44·4	31·8

* Figures in brackets refer to 1956.

in the major industrial areas employ more than 1,000 people.[13] The relatively small scale of Irish industry has a number of important results. The most striking consequence from the point of view of social stratification is the lack of any large units of employment which might provide an industrial base for working-class proletariat.

However, even if occupational classifications were to provide a ready guide to Irish social classes, a difficulty would be presented by the large number of those employees who in addition own land and may derive a certain amount of income from their landholding. Of the total of gainfully occupied male landholders one-sixth (36,880) are not employed directly in agriculture but hold land.

Table 2. *Landholders distinguished by occupational status and size of holding*[14]

	All Holdings	Under 5 acres	Over 5 acres
Farmers*	69·3	6·7	83·1
Others Gainfully Occupied*	18·5	56·3	10·2
Not Gainfully Occupied*	12·2	37·0	6·7
	100·0%	18·0	82·0

* Both males and females have been grouped together for this table.

A further factor which inevitably affects the analysis of the social structure of Ireland is the continuing importance of emigration. With free movement of labour between Ireland and Britain, emigration has been heavy during the last twenty-five years and has been principally directed to Britain rather than to the USA. Emigration has had two main effects. In the first place it has provided a means whereby young men and women could break with the relatively narrow range of opportunities available to them at home. Secondly, it has provided a source of funds in the form of remittances which have served to support the economy of small farms and shops and has consequently often acted to retain and preserve those very elements in the social structure which partly contributed to the factors that necessitated the emigration itself. A third effect is also important. Emigration has provided even in the most rural areas a cosmopolitan frame of reference by virtue of those known overseas or the large proportion of those in the community who have been emigrant themselves (about 25 per cent).[15] This cosmopolitan perspective can act as a basis for transvaluing the local and consequently allows alternative avenues for those who feel especially disadvantaged by the social structure.

Although there is a marked decline in the number of people employed in agriculture the influence of the farm family and its dominant position in the social structure of the country remains decisive. In a society in which links are retained with the land to such a considerable extent and where the process of urbanization has developed only to a slight degree this is bound to be true. But, the influence of the farm is more dominant and far reaching than these reasons alone would suggest. It is responsible for the institutional character of marriage and for status attributions which continue into the urban society of Dublin and provide the basic framework for analysis.

There has been very considerable modification of the patterns described by Arensberg and Kimball in their study of County Clare.[16] However, most rural areas still retain the basic features of the traditional pattern which rotates around the ownership of the farm, the dowry system and the maintenance of uncertainty over the inheritance which underlies the father's authority and status. Late marriage, the high proportion of bachelors and spinsters and the strong incentives for temporary or permanent emigration are all derived from these structural features. They are all supportive of a rural class structure in which the farmer has enjoyed a key position of authority and status by virtue of his ownership of land on the products of which the whole community is dependent for its welfare and economic viability.

In that Ireland remains fundamentally an agricultural country it is then as well to start our detailed analysis with the plough rather than the stars. This is not to deny the importance of the urban elite in the society but merely to emphasize the perspective from which the society is viewed by the large majority of those living in its midst. In some shape or form agriculture defines the material condition of the Irish people, their economy is based on it, their politics are agrarian, their demography is related to patterns of land tenure and the urban population for the most part, is less than one or at the most two generations from the soil.

Within the framework of the characteristic rural community the farm is the locus of a stratification system based on size of holding and contribution to the essential economic matrix of agriculture. Unlike the situation in southern Italy where those who work on the land live in urban settlements from which they go out to till their fields, the Irish farmer lives on his land distinct and separated from his neighbour. This 'scattered' pattern emphasizes the farm community's separation from the town which has for him a primarily marketing function, while the occasional clustering of cottages around a crossing are hardly examples of the intermediate rural village to be found in England or France.

The agricultural community consists of large (200 acres and above), medium (25–100 acres) and small (under twenty-five acres) farmers and those craftsmen and ancillary workers who have a direct involvement in agriculture. To the farmers must be added a fourth group of county council labourers, usually employed in road maintenance, who live mainly in rural council cottages which provide them with about one acre of land – 'the grass of a sheep and a cow'. These distinctions between types of farmer will, of course, vary enormously depending on the characteristics of the land and the type of agriculture which it supports. In dairying areas it may be crudely symbolized by the means of transport used to take the milk churns to the local creamery e.g. lorry, tractor trailer, horse cart and donkey cart.

Of those most directly involved in the agricultural sector apart from the farmers the most significant group, that of agricultural labourers, has sharply declined in numbers in the post-war period. In 1966 they numbered only 46,000 of whom only 5,000 were living on the farms where they worked. There has been a similar decline in the large class of 'relatives assisting' which while not formally employed have traditionally remained a primary labour resource for the small farm unit. Until 1930 when legislation was introduced to fix a scale of agricultural wages the employed agricultural labourer was to a considerable degree part of a peonage class of hired workers exploited by the larger farmers who employed them. McNab in his description of the situation in County Limerick suggests that it was quite usual in that part of the country until the end of the 1930's for annual hiring fairs to be held on St Patrick's Day (17 March). Bargains would be struck between the farmer and the man, or his father in the case of a youth, and he would be bound to work until the end of November. There were no set hours, the labourers were often fed and housed apart from the family, and received a wage of between £20 and £30 at the end of the hiring. The fact that such a situation did not give rise to serious unrest and class consciousness on the part of this agricultural proletariat, must in part be explained by emigration, the 'safety valve', and also by the wide dispersal of the rural population (51–6 per cent of the population living outside settlements of 200 or more persons in 1961).

The Limerick Rural Survey suggests that from the perspective of the farmer it is necessary to take into account a system of stratification based on an assessment of two overlapping dimensions of status estimation and deference relationships. A distinction is made between high and low status conferred either by occupation of a given role in the matrix of the agricultural community or by the possession of certain personal or group characteristics.

Such a paradigm is only indicative of the kind of dual assessment that will usually be made. Occupation and office are entitled to respect but the regard for the office holder is modified by the estimation of his personal qualities. This may apply particularly strongly to those whose major social and occupational orientation lies outside the immediate community. Their reference group so far as the community is concerned is too remote to allow more than a general appreciation of their qualities in comparison with other known examples (often limited to their predecessors). They are therefore judged primarily as men, even though in common-sense terms their technical ability must be shown to be adequate.

	High Status	Low Status
	Priest	
	Creamery manager	
By Virtue	Agricultural Adviser	Labourer
of Occupation	Professional men	Servant
	Shopkeeper	
	Teacher	
	Good Stock	
	Decent men	Malicious people
	Families with members	People who neglect
By Virtue of	in Church	children
Personal or	Families with members	Quarrelsome families
Group Traits	in Professions	Curious people
	Families with members	Strangers, tourists,
	in the Civil Service	foreigners
	Sportsmen	

(Those underlined are my additions to the original list.)[18]

A few of the roles included in the paradigm need further and specific elaboration. The priest is an outsider but one who potentially wields considerable power and judgements will take account of this. The creamery or Co-operative Mart manager has high status because the farmers believe him to hold considerable economic power. He may do so directly in relation to the sales of dairy products or cattle, pigs and sheep but more probably his power will be seen in terms of potential opportunities in the Creamery or market organization for the farmers' children. I have added the post of agricultural adviser to the positions specified by McNab because he too has a limited amount of power over the farmers in terms of sanctions and subsidies and is also viewed as a potential employment broker.

McNab claims that the shopkeeper thinks of himself as belonging to the same class as the farmer but views the farmer as being old-fashioned and less intelligent. My own research in West Cork confirms that this is a point of view held by some shopkeepers though few would readily be so open about it. It was notable that only some 25 per cent of the shop-keepers in Skibbereen wished their daughters to marry a farmer and the prevailing view in the town is that the farm provides a hard life with few comforts compared to the town.[19]

McNab uses the term 'good stock' to refer to those families who have been established members of the community for several generations with an unsullied reputation. Even labourers' families are so distinguished and can thus transcend the occupational distinctions. This kind of assessment of 'moral tone' is a dimension which is frequently invoked at all levels of Irish society to cover a wide variety of conformities to accepted norms of behaviour. He also refers to the 'decent man' whose reputation rests on his proven good judgement, fairness and honesty; he, together with the sportsman who upholds the reputation of the district, can command respect regardless of lack of occupational success or even, in the case of the latter, failings of character.

To those in the low status box of the paradigm included by McNab, I have added a category of outsiders. These are necessarily suspect and not part of the community as such. However, in relation to the significance of tourism to the economy, as well as the settling of outsiders in many rural districts, it is necessary to categorize such people. Their own acceptance may ultimately depend upon their ability to establish a status along one or other of the dimensions we have considered. Such acceptance in terms of the perspective of the local community will always be guarded but will be based on an appreciation of the same kinds of qualitative elements that they would judge in their neighbours. As in other traditional societies the process will be greatly eased if kinship attachment, however remote, can be demonstrated to one of the recognized local and approved families. Remarkably intolerant of cant, the Irish farmer's status estimation has little time for those who put on airs and act above themselves whether they are local people who have struck it rich, or, more probably outsiders, 'Dublin Jackeens', returned Yanks, English tourists and German exiles.

There is not space in this paper to describe in detail the general status system outlined so far. Its main characteristics will be familiar to all who have observed similar communities in France and southern Italy. The catalyst of the system is invariably fear derived from long sustained economic hardship which in turn is expressed by envy, suspicion and secrecy in individual and family affairs.[20]

The stratification system of the small town in Ireland reflects the perspective of the farmer in that it is closely articulated with the rural, 'farmer-based' variables so far considered. The key figure in the small-town system is the shopkeeper whose position is closely defined by the rural basis of his trade and the demands of social obligation on which it rests. Before considering the shopkeepers in more detail it is important to note the various social categories which compose small-town society and the list suggested by Arensberg and Kimball in their description of the town of Ennis in County Clare is a useful typological model with which to begin.

(a) ascendancy families
(b) professional people
(c) large shopkeepers ('big fellows')
(d) small shopkeepers
(e) craftsmen
(f) labourers
(g) tinkers.

Categories (a) and (g) are essentially peripheral while the diminishing category of craftsmen is being replaced by a new group of white-collar workers and government functionaries, which today has far greater significance in provincial towns than it did at the time of their study.[21]

The only true townspeople, they suggest, are the labourers and the artisan. The remaining groups are sustained by heavy migration into the towns from outside. In part, this is the result of a pattern whereby the ranks of the shopkeepers are refurbished from farm families while in turn many of the children of the shopkeepers are likely to move into white-collar and professional occupations often away from the town of their birth. Thus the small town has a significant role in the movement from the land and as part of a wider process of social mobility.

My own research in Skibbereen (population 2,028) confirms this pattern and in the study made there in 1964 it was found that only half of the one in seven sample of the population of the town was born in Skibbereen. Of the remainder 18 per cent came from the surrounding district,

19 per cent from the rest of County Cork, 8 per cent from other parts of Ireland and 3 per cent from outside Ireland altogether. A further 2 per cent failed to indicate their birthplace. Only 46 per cent of the 157 shopkeepers had been born in Skibbereen and rather more than half of them were the first generation in the shop.[22]

Arensberg and Kimball describe in detail the processes whereby a farmer finds employment opportunities in the town for his children. They point out that very few shopkeepers are under thirty years of age and that entry into a shop and entry into marriage are almost simultaneous. As with the case of the farm the possession of a shop provides the security necessary to achieve a desired match and the appropriate recognition by the bride's family in the form of dowry. These new shopkeepers have in the main learned their trade as shop assistants having come into the shop from the country. It is in the interest of the shopkeeper to recruit from the country because he gains from his employees' connections with families in the countryside who will then patronize the shop. From the farm families point of view the shopkeeper who takes in their child, male or female, 'becomes an intermediary through which they make contact with individuals in the town who in other circumstances would not be directly available to them'.[23] This reciprocal relationship is mutually valuable to both town and country and allows both parties an extension of their connections through one of their members. A further significant dimension of this arrangement relates to the status of shopkeeping in the eyes of the farm families. As Arensberg and Kimball remark 'In the eyes of the countryman shopkeeping is a dignified and honourable occupation, and the gentility which it bestows makes of one a gentleman.'[24]

In a brief paper one cannot extend the discussion of this reciprocal pattern which Arensberg and Kimball have elaborated in their classic study. For our purposes, though, one further aspect must be considered since it demonstrates the reason why an intense consciousness of status characterizes the Irish townspeople as much as those in the country. The preliminaries of negotiating for a place in a shop are very comparable to those which occur in marriage negotiations between farm families themselves. When a child is indentured into a shop each side assumes obligations confirmed and institutionalized in legal and social practice. The father of the child pays indenture money, the shopkeeper binds himself to train the boy or girl and to look after his or her welfare. This training will consist of learning, among more specifically technical aspects, the very careful assessment of customers in terms of their status and social and economic position in the community. Thus consciousness of social position, often to the making of very fine distinctions, becomes a component part of successful enterprise in both rural and town relationships. It has clear economic consequences in a situation in which credit relationships serve to consolidate the mutual obligations between shop and customer and where the loss of a single customer can mean, as was suggested by one of my Skibbereen informants, the loss of the trade of a whole kin group with its wide extensions in the rural area to a competitor. As Arensberg and Kimball conclude:

The town's shopkeeping group is constantly being recruited from the rural areas. The channel through which this movement takes place is firmly fixed in both the social system and the legal system of Irish society. Its strength arises from the adaptation of the deeply ingrained patterns of kinship obligation to the economic level, thus transforming that level and converting it into a truly social one.[25]

The fine distinctions in relationships exhibited in the case of farmers and shopkeepers is based on traditional patterns of exchange of family members and resources. Although this pattern has in many ways been loosened in the post-war period it still serves to characterize the basic attitudes of townspeople towards their neighbours. Consequently, the small town demonstrates distributions in the patterns of social life which serve to consolidate and protect these fine distinctions. This is found both in terms of residence, the education of children and in social activities and accounts in part for the very large number of social organizations and clubs to be found in the small town – fifty in Skibbereen, for instance. It also accounts for the much larger number of bars in the town than would be suggested by simple economic considerations. They provide a secluded focus for different groupings and so serve to prevent the invasion of privacy and the embarrassment of those who must necessarily establish and maintain social distance from those of different age, sex and employment, trade, and familial relationships on the proper observation of which the whole structure of the society depends. Within a small community the preservation of these distinctions would otherwise be impossible within the close spatial proximity in which their lives are contained.

Before leaving these considerations of the Irish small town it is necessary to emphasize the role that the town plays in the rural area, a role which underlies the articulation with the rural area which surrounds it. Most small towns in Ireland depend entirely on their marketing function for a wide hinterland. In very few does industry play an important part and even where industries exist their scale is seldom sufficient to produce any group with a permanent status as industrial employees. Those employed in unskilled capacities are either drawn from the labouring group or from the rural areas, often unmarried members of farm families commuting to the town for employment until they get married. Those in skilled work may find factory employment after apprenticeship or training at the technical schools. But even here their education and the consequent life chances it offers as well as their subsequent employment is likely to be responsive to the kinds of forces of social obligation and economic interdependence already characterized by the archetypal pattern of the farmer and the shopkeeper groups. In the case of the professions their practice in a small community is also necessarily responsive to these same forces and they depend for their business principally on recommendation and attachment to particular families in the area who patronize them.

The post-war period has, however, modified the pattern in a number of important ways. The new class of government officials, clerks and public servants employed in local government, the post office, the electricity board and the banks tend increasingly to be recruited on the basis of educational qualifications and to be drawn from outside the immediate area. They characterize, perhaps more accurately than any other group, the changing pattern of Irish social structure most clearly found in the cities where the growth of the tertiary sector is most in evidence. It is this group which by virtue of education is freed from the patterns of dependence which characterize the local community. The new white-collar elite can sustain this freedom more fully even than the professionals in that they are agents of the larger society, but not indigenous members of the complex network of the small community. Others may achieve a break by emigration but often this is only a temporary phenomenon and in any case they may remain tied to the pattern of obligation by their contribution of remittances and the prospect of their eventual return. From the perspective of the small town, however, the key to the new elite positions offered by the wider society as well as to the older professions lies in education and as Arensberg and Kimball note:

'the validation of social position begins early, and the school is not exempt from social distinctions' and 'in Ennis, the girls are sent to the Convent and the boys to the Christian Brothers. There is also a National School with lay teachers, but very few of the shopkeepers send their children there, preferring the more genteel atmosphere of the "Brothers" or the "Convent". The big shop-keepers as well as the more successful professional families are likely to send their children outside the community altogether to fashionable schools in Dublin or Cork from which many can expect to go on to the University. Thus social aspirations for the family are likely to be won or lost in what happens to their children.'[26]

The competitiveness for education in fee-paying schools throughout Ireland indicates the validity of this statement at the present day. The shopkeeper's aspirations for his children reflect both his own ambitions as well as being a mark and index of his own continuing status within the community. Only one child can follow him into the shop, consequently the remainder must be suitably provided for.

One has here, as elsewhere in the society, an example of the tension maintained between particularistic and ascriptive elements in the power conferring functions of the society and those more universalistic demands which have so far made only slight inroads within the society. It is significant that only in 1968 has there been any serious move to apply universalistic standards to higher education. Access to those educational establishments which have been the necessary avenues to the professions and white-collar employment has essentially remained responsive to the monopoly of the middle class and

H

the existence of a bipartite system in which post-primary education was linked inexorably to the ability to pay.

There is, unhappily, very little documentation as yet of the Irish city. What there is leaves a good deal to be desired in terms of the very rapid urbanization and in particular 'suburbanization' that has characterized Dublin in recent years, but also Cork, Limerick and to a much lesser extent Galway. Consequently, in this chapter a particular study will be used to provide a profile which sustains the broad character of the pattern developed in earlier sections in relation to the rural areas and the small town.

Although published in 1966, A. J. Humphrey's study of Dublin families is based on fieldwork completed in 1951.[27] Its emphasis is on those aspects of transition to urban life which affect what he calls the 'New Dubliners', that is those whose urban experience is confined to one or two generations of city life. His general thesis is that though the expected contrasts between rural and urban patterns are found, they are much less marked than might be expected by reference to the United States. Indeed, the general pattern of familial structure and the characteristic demographic consequences with which it is associated are found to be carried into the city and maintained in altered but consistent forms to those already noted in the more rural areas of the country and summarized succinctly by Arensberg and Kimball: 'Townsmen live long. They marry late. They have many children. Country people live longer, marry later and live longer than do the people of the towns.'[28]

This is especially the case where social class is concerned; it is found that the acute sense of social position already observed is equally present among the rather small sample of Dubliners that he observes. Again social status rather than social class is the defining attribute of a system in which attention to relatively minor variations and distinctions of social position serves to inhibit the development of either a distinctive urban elite or a conscious urban proletariat. Humphreys suggests with reference to the prolonged influence of the Anglo-Irish Ascendancy that 'despite this subordination, if not because of it, among Catholics, and even among the lower classes of Catholics, lines of distinction and their corresponding sentiments existed before 1922 whose strength was quite disproportionate to the grounds upon which they were based'.[29] He suggests that far from removing such acute emphasis on class distinctions the intervening period has led to congealing and crystallization of class lines. He further suggests that these rigidities tend to be more apparent in the city where the neighbourhood obligations of rural society do not serve to cut across class lines.

At the same time he notes an ambivalence which is very apparent from general observation in a society which protests volubly of its egalitarian and democratic character, and yet resorts to very rigid selection when it comes to education and marriage. This paradox, he suggests, is due to the unwillingness of the Catholic *nouveaux riches* to be considered as aping the old Ascendancy families while at the same time they are desperate to live up to the image of the style of life which the Ascendancy represented. As he points out,

the basic ambivalence consists in criticizing and even overtly resenting the standards, values and behaviour of people in higher classes and, indeed, of people in their own class and, at the same time, in accepting the same general set of values themselves and in striving to emulate the people criticized.[30]

He suggests that the same kind of dichotomy of feelings is to be found among clerical and artisan families while among the labourers job stability and wage levels, together with protectionist trade union membership serve to heighten relatively slight distinctions in class position and to be reflected in subtle differentiation in residence, spending habits, and age of marriage. Emigration is seen to represent an available escape for both boys and girls of the labouring class from the 'imitations in the range of opportunities available to them, imposed by this strongly competitive status-oriented stratification pattern. One of Humphreys' informants suggests that in the city class consciousness assumes a more rigid form than it does in the country where it is necessarily modified by neighbourhood obligations and he finds a high degree of consistency among not only the families of labourers and artisans but also among the managerial group.[31]

This study of the adjustment of recently urbanized families is particularly revealing in so far as it serves to demonstrate the continuation of many features of social distinction already observed in the small town and in the countryside. Even though the urban environment has the effect of weakening kin links and consequently emphasizes the role of the nuclear family, it replaces these with an intense consciousness of social position. Obligations within the class group cut across those of kin, but the consolidation of support for kin within all class groups serves to make kinship instrumental for the maintenance and achievement of class position. As Humphreys observes 'it is significant that the greatest economic obligation of kinship in the city is not to collaborate in common economic enterprises, but to get a relative a job'.[32] He concludes that for all social classes the effects of urbanization are more at the level of organization than ideology and that the continuity of ideology between the rural and the urban family accounts for the fact that urban families maintain, albeit in modified form, those characteristics of late marriage, familial obligation and intense consciousness of ascribed status position, characteristic of the rural structure. These forces inhibit the formation of urban classes developed as a function of common relation to the work situation and the development of a universalistically defined class ideology. We are thus led back to Eisenstadt's proposition of a monolithic centre which 'will tend to encourage, at least with regard to access to the central position, patterns of "sponsored" mobility'.[33] These are maintained so long as access to all positions directly or through the educational system, remain, as they appear to a large degree to do in Ireland, protected by the ascriptive interests of the centre which is concerned to consolidate its position and absorb the socially mobile by 'sponsored' rather than 'contest' mobility.

Of course, such a characterization of social class in Ireland must be extreme and there is little doubt that the pattern is being rapidly modified within the present generation. Nevertheless, it still characterizes the society to a considerable degree and permeates its institutions at every social level. Both religious and political ideology with an essentially conservative and traditionalist emphasis have acted as a brake on any rapid alteration of the situation. The almost idealized image of the rural family, the small farm and as Lynch puts it 'the myth that farming is in some transcendental sense, not so much an occupation as a way of life on which Providence has placed a special badge of moral approval, whereas other occupations retain a less sanctified character, still survives in Ireland'.[34] It has been a myth that has served the centres of power in Irish society well, particularly when there have also been available in the ideological armoury a number of convenient mythological bogeys such as the Partition issue, the dangers of contaminating secularism in Britain[35] and the fact of emigration to set against the pressures of radical social changes. To a large degree, to take once again Eisenstadt's typification, post-war Ireland has retained 'a centre oriented to "closed" tradition . . . within which primordial qualities are conceived as part of the basic definition of the socio-cultural order [which] will tend to encourage almost all such connections between family and status'.[36]

There is another and important sense in which the stratification system of contemporary Ireland remains that of a 'sponsored' society. This lies in the anachronistic role of the 'old Ascendancy', a Protestant minority in a country in which 96 per cent of the population is Catholic. In spite of the relative decline in its numbers this group retains a quite disproportionate influence in the economic, political and social centres of the society. More important than real power, however, is its influence as a tantalizing mirage of assured, secure and established status, somehow always eluding the successive generations of the new elite. That it should continue to play such a role is remarkable unless we turn back briefly to the position it held in Ireland before the second world war.

In his account of his own youth in an Ascendancy household on the fringes of Dublin, Brian Inglis[37] describes the ways in which this group perpetuated the myth of its own exclusive status. Those within the charmed circle, were by definition, landowners, leading professionals, proprietors and shareholders of businesses. A wholesaler could be included but not a retailer. Normally they had been to a public school (in England) and were Protestant. Even those who were Catholics, who 'dug with the wrong foot' as the saying was, were defined as Protestant, e.g. 'Respectable', Catholics. Such a society and among these families such a view of society, taking little notice of the changes in the social fabric going on about them, has been remarkably persistent and can still be observed, little modified today. Indeed, one of the results of the tourist expansion and the development of investment by mainly English absentee householders in Irish property since the second world war has been to fortify with ex-service and other congenial types the fading remnant of the old Horse-Ascendancy. The Somerville and Ross image, though in part preserved by the aristocracy or near aristocracy, is a shadow of its earlier dominant presence. Today it is sustained by inclusion rather than exclusion and is sustained by the importation of ex-colonials. Ireland provides still an environment and an opportunity where the last glories of the English upper middle-class society can be sustained, in the large houses, among a few of the Church of Ireland families and some of the older Catholic families in the cities. As in India and other vestigial imperial domains the customs and manners of an English past are sustained long after they have disappeared at home. As late as 1964, during our survey of the Skibbereen area the reply of one respondent included in the random sample exhibits the 'dislocated' status enjoyed by such families of Anglo-Irish. The respondent argued that they should not be included because 'it's not meant for people like us' – even though they had been resident in the same house in the district for three generations.

Unlike them, however, we cannot ignore the more tangible and significant Ireland under the faded crust. The Ascendancy still enjoys some power and a good deal of local prestige, a certain amount of sentimental goodwill and pity rather than hatred and envy. An Inglis points out in the near-Dublin society of his time they provided a caste-like barrier to effective social mobility, controlling access to the exclusive clubs and golf courses. Now the aspirant class is no longer held back but it is haunted by its own insecurity of touch – the gaucheries of the *nouveaux riches*.

By the end of the war, especially in Dublin, the change was accelerated by two factors. The first was the consolidation of their position by merchants, distributors and others who had made money out of the war and the second the arrival of a number of wealthy Englishmen 'who fled from England to escape the rigours of a socialist peace'. They in turn added to the wealth of property dealers, auctioneers, solicitors and doctors and brought many of these into their own English Tatler set.

Inglis suggests that, although the exclusiveness of some of the Protestant Ascendancy attitudes remained, there existed the parallel rather than equal development of a Catholic circle, based on those originally termed the 'Castle Catholics' in Dublin because they went along with the then British Administration.

The 'Great Divide' of religion so apparent in any discussion of the Ascendancy and the Catholic elite finds its continued expression in the efforts that are made to ensure that the children of wealthy Protestant families, and some Catholics, can be educated at public schools in England. For the Protestant merchants and the aspiring new elite in the professions and the Civil Service the problems of the divided community remains. Protestant schools are maintained for the exclusive education of their children, receiving support from the State, but developing the social attitudes enjoyed at University level by Trinity College, Dublin. And there remains the North where the Protestant dominance was secure. A number of Protestant children are sent north for their education to schools such as Methodist College or Campbell College in Belfast. In both North and South the religious divide acts as a social demarcation most evident in the elite, but the South shows rather less evidence of the kind of detachment from religious connotation which the terms Protestant and Catholic have acquired in the North.[38]

From the Catholic side the religious issue has raised its own problems. Although the new State was pledged to religious liberty and Protestants have enjoyed considerable freedom, even so during the post-war period the Catholic hierarchy has pressed for the primacy enjoyed by Catholics in other countries such as Spain and Portugal. It found its greatest force in the late 1940s and 1950s in those areas of cultural development, education and morality where the relative insecurity of the secular state could provide little strong opposition.

Although, with one celebrated exception, the Catholic hierarchy has not involved itself directly in politics, there is little doubt that it has been an important force in limiting the development of a politically conscious radicalism. Its tendency to equate socialism with Communism against which it has made a vigorous and sustained attack has been evidence of this. However, the factors we have considered in this necessarily sketchy survey suggest that the laity has itself failed to assert a political consciousness of class interests. Indeed, it is interesting to note that in the contemporary context it is the priests, to whom most Irish communities have traditionally turned for leadership, who are themselves often most receptive to the forces of change. To quote Mr Lynch once more, in conclusion, 'some of the most socially progressive thought in Ireland today is coming from priests who have read Marx and Freud as well as Aquinas'.[39] This, too, is typical of the enigma of social class in contemporary Ireland.

NOTES

1 Although many of the points raised in this paper may have relevance to Northern Ireland, the discussion has been limited to the twenty-six counties of the Irish Republic.
2 A. J. Humphreys, *New Dubliners* (London, 1966), p. 49.
3 P. Lynch, 'The Economic Scene' in C. C. O'Brien, *Introducing Ireland* (London, 1969), p. 72.
4 P. Lynch, 'The Economic Scene', p. 73.
5 T. D. Williams, in *The Spectator*, 20 April 1956.
6 P. Lynch, 'The Economic Scene', p. 76.
7 V. I. Lenin, 'The Irish Rebellion of 1916', *Selected Works*, Vol. 5 (Moscow and London, 1930), pp. 301–6. Lenin was well aware that the 1916 Rebellion lacked class-consciousness. He accepted that social revolution must include the 'revolutionary outbursts of a section of the petty bourgeoisie *with all its prejudices*, the movement of non-class conscious proletarian and semi-proletarian masses against the oppression of the landlords, the church, the monarchy, the foreign nations, etc.', p. 303 (italics in original). He also recognized the failure of the 1916 Rebellion itself: 'The misfortune of the Irish is that they rose prematurely, when the European revolt of the proletariat had not yet matured', p. 306. For a fuller account of the period see D. Macardle, *The Irish Republic* (Dublin, 1950).
8 S. N. Eisenstadt, 'Prestige, Participation and Strata Formation' in J. A. Jackson (ed.), *Social Stratification*, 1968, p. 102.
9 M. Duverger, *Political Parties* (London, 1967).
10 In 1966 at the Party Conference. Two further events may have

significance also. In 1967 the largest of the innumerable trade unions the Irish Transport and General Workers' Union affiliated with the party and in 1968 when it recruited a number of articulate proponents, among them Dr Conor Cruise O'Brien.

11 Census of Population of Ireland 1966, Vol. iv, *Occupation*, 1969, p. xv.

12 For more extensive discussion of this point see W. E. Moore, 'Changes in Occupational Structure' in N. Smelser and S. M. Lipset (eds.), *Social Structure and Mobility in Economic Development* (London, 1966), pp. 194–212.

13 Committee on Industrial Organization, *Synthesis of Reports on 22 Industries* (Dublin, 1965). For a fuller discussion of the implications of small scale in Irish industry see J. A. Jackson, 'Ireland', in *Emigrant Workers Returning to Their Home Country*, supplement to the Final Report (OECD, Paris, 1967), pp. 101–18.

14 The figures from which these percentages have been calculated are derived from Census of Population Ireland 1966, iv, *Occupations* (1969), p. xx.

15 See. C. K. Ward, *Manpower in a Developing Community, a Pilot Survey of Drogheda* (Dublin, 1967), and J. A. Jackson, *Report on the Skibbereen Social Survey* (Dublin, 1967). For a general account of the effects of emigration see A. Schrier, *Ireland and the American Emigration* (Minneapolis, 1958), and J. A. Jackson, *The Irish in Britain* (London, 1963).

16 C. Arensberg and S. J. Kimball, *Family and Community in Ireland* (Cambridge, Mass., 1940 (First Edition), 1969 (Second Edition)).

17 P. McNab, 'Social Structure' in J. Newman (ed.), *The Limerick Rural Survey* (Tipperary, 1964), pp. 201–2.

18 P. McNab, 'Social Structure', p. 197.

19 J. A. Jackson, *Report of the Skibbereen Social Survey*, p. 19.

20 See for instance E. Banfield, *The Moral Basis of Social Development* (New York, 1958). For a much fuller discussion of the structure of the farm family and its articulation within rural Irish society see C. Arensberg and S. T. Kimball, *Family and community in Ireland* (1969 edition).

21 C. Arensberg and S. J. Kimball, *Family and Community . . .*, p. 328.

22 *Report of the Skibbereen Social Survey*, p. 11.

23 C. Arensberg and S. T. Kimball, *Family and Community in Ireland* (1969 edition), p. 344.

24 *Family and Community in Ireland*, p. 345.

25 *Family and Community in Ireland*, p. 360.

26 *Family and Community in Ireland*, p. 377.

27 A. J. Humphreys, *New Dubliners*. A recent and valuable addition to the literature is B. Hutchinson, 'Social Status and Inter-Generational Social Mobility in Dublin', *The Economic and Social Research Institute*, Paper No. 48, October 1969.

28 C. Arensberg and S. T. Kimball, *Family and Community in Ireland*, p. 319.

29 A. J. Humphreys, *New Dubliners*, p. 195.
30 *New Dubliners*, pp. 197–8.
31 *New Dubliners*, p. 199.
32 *New Dubliners*, p. 245.
33 S. N. Eisenstadt, 'Prestige, Participation and Strata Formation', p. 103.
34 P. Lynch, 'The Economic Scene', p. 75.
35 One of the justifications for the long-continued censorship of literature and works of art which is currently being increasingly relaxed.
36 S. N. Eisenstadt, 'Prestige, Participation and Strata Formation', p. 102.
37 B. Inglis, *West Briton* (London, 1962).
38 Note for instance an advertisement a few years ago in a Belfast paper cited in '*Orange and Green*' (Northern Friends Peace Board, 1969), p. 1. 'Wanted – Reliable cook-general, Protestant (Christian preferred)'.
39 P. Lynch, 'The Economic Scene', in *Introducing Ireland*, p. 77.

7 France

Pierre Naville

The evolution of social classes in contemporary France poses too many problems for them to be examined within the scope of this chapter. Discussion is thus restricted to several basic issues which appear to indicate the dominant tendency, while no attempt is made at establishing a comprehensive picture of the present situation in its entirety. However, some preliminary remarks seem a necessary preface to illuminate the data presented below and the conclusions which can be drawn from them.

Firstly, it seems difficult to appreciate the evolution of French social classes in isolation from the form taken by classes in western Europe as a whole and in part of the former 'colonial Empire'. It is becoming increasingly clear that, from the social economic and demographic points of view, the situation prevailing in contemporary France is merely one aspect of the development of classes in western industrial Europe. Hence it is often difficult to differentiate between what is strictly French and what is generally European in the evolution of classes and of other social categories.

Without documenting this point which yet appears to have great importance for the future, the conclusion can be drawn that *national* class structures, particularly in highly industrialized economies and in regions characterized by a high degree of socio-economic homogeneity (especially with a predominance of wages as a form of remuneration) are gradually losing their traditional distinctiveness. Thus a classification based on national differences will need to be replaced by one founded on a *regional* basis which will be employed within each country, and may involve grouping together regions belonging to several countries. This is to say that national structures tend to describe a past state of affairs, while regional structures anticipate the future. There is now an agrarian Europe alongside an industrial Europe, whose internal coherence – despite cross-cutting national conflicts and disparities – is stronger, according to certain criteria, than the internal class structure of a given country.

In addition, it seems important to note that, since the second world war and since the wars of Indochina and Algeria, France has ceased to be a colonial empire and in consequence the class structure of the 'hexagon' can largely be attributed to this new historical situation. For example, over a million of the French from Algeria have been re-integrated into metropolitan France since 1962; such repatriation also occurred for many residents in different Asian countries (Vietnam) and of western and central Africa. Serious consequences have followed upon these migrations, particularly in terms of their repercussions in agriculture and commerce.

Finally, it should be noted that the statistical breakdown by reference to social characteristics remains rudimentary in France, despite post-war efforts to reformulate the methods used. The frequency of demographic censuses is inadequate and their data insufficiently detailed. The most recent figures date from 1968 and are constructed on the basis of a one-twentieth sample; they are not fully published as yet. In spite of the attempts made by the *Comptabilité Nationale* and the *Commissariat au Plan*, economic data (particularly the breakdown of incomes and the structure of employment) remain very inadequate. As a result, serious doubts arise when one needs to make numerical comparisons between phenomena and these become even more grave when one analyses their dynamics and their internal and external contradictions.

Hence this study will be limited to certain phenomena which are so outstanding as to facilitate a characterization of the main features of social class structure in contemporary France and which lead to overall conclusions whose detail cannot be supported by full documentary evidence.

The meaning given here to the term 'class' must first be made explicit. It is employed to indicate social groupings whose situations, behaviour or origins differ sufficiently to permit identification at different levels, e.g. classes based on socio-professional status, on role in production, on educational level, on age, on sex, etc. These factual and analytic groupings have not been rigorously enumerated, but merely referred to, while some aspects of their mutual implications are examined later. Therefore only the elements of a taxonomy, rather than a genuine system, will be employed here. Yet it would be possible right now to define what is meant by a class system, taking into account a ranking of characteristics or properties which can be determined in relation to sets of elements. Thus, 1. on the one hand, the existence of classes can be considered as synonymous with that of sub-sets within sets; 2. every element of a sub-set may belong to others; 3. an ordering can be determined for all sub-sets, albeit incomplete or imperfect; 4. using the same procedures, all these orders could in turn be ordered. In this way a structure would have been described.

Since it is difficult to offer an accurate description at this stage, initial emphasis will be on the *composition* of identifiable classes rather than on their *function*. This approach which appears justified as a first step involves leaving aside the concept of structure, so fashionable at the moment, but still surrounded by much confusion. In dealing with composition, one remains closer to available census data and, in the last analysis, the composition (or morphology) of social sets enables the assessment of their functions to a large extent.

It is first necessary to introduce a distinction, basic to all modern production societies (capitalist and state-socialist alike), between the active and the non-active population, which in itself depends on the age structure of the total population, family size, educational standards, the industrial structure, employment policy and many other factors. In any such societies, the active population taken as a whole (i.e. including all persons remunerated in some way or other for their economic activities) can be considered in our view as a true socio-economic class-set, particularly if one takes into account the polar phenomena of rigidity/fluidity characteristic of industrial societies. The contradictions between the economic fuctions of different categories within this do not seem incompatible with treating the whole set as one class. This is due to the steady extension of wage-earning to the overwhelming majority of the active population, associated with a complementary decline in the peasantry with its 'self-employed' status.

For a total population of about 48 million residents (including French nationals, foreigners and stateless persons) in 1962, the active population slightly exceeded 19 million, or 39 per cent of the population. Yet a significant trend in France is the slow, but regular increase in total resident population, which exceeded 50 millions in 1968, while the active population has remained nearly stable for decades.[1]

Thus, there has been a relative regression in the ratio of active to non-active classes in the total population, which has led certain economists to advocate full employment policies coupled with more dynamic productive investments (particularly in the social and collective sphere) and with a relaxation of regulations governing retirement or even a decelerated policy of raising the school-leaving age.

This stagnation of the active class is characteristic of contemporary France and is often explained by reference to a variety of structural and conjunctural factors. Conjunctural factors include the repatriation of former colonials, constant recourse to foreign manpower accompanied by dependent relatives, the steady increase in the school-leaving age, the under-development of certain western and central regions, the increase in the birth-rate, and also some changes in the statistical definition applied to the active population (for example, the wives of farmers). Structural causes include mainly the decline in the rural and peasant population and the development of capital-intense industries with a low coefficient of wage-earning labour.

This situation, characteristic of contemporary France and indeed of Europe as a whole, means that internal changes in the relationships between classes take place within the context of a quasi-stable social set or even within a contracting one. If this situation continued, it could be said that the optimum population size, estimated by demographers like Sauvy at 70–80 million residents, would not be attained without the active population shrinking to 20 or 25 per cent of this total. From this perspective, France would find itself in a somewhat peculiar position in relation to other European countries, not to mention other parts of the world like Africa and Asia.

In 1962 the composition of the active population by large socio-professional categories was the following:

Table 1. *Active population by socio-professional categories*

	Total number	%	Employers	Employees private	Employees public
Farmers	3,011,600	15·7	3,011,600	—	—
Agricultural Wage earners	829,600	4·3	—	810,540	10,120
Employers in Industry and Commerce	1,996,560	10·4	1,996,560	—	—
Liberal professions and higher managerial	761,040	4·0	127,420	341,540	287,840
Medium-level management	1,490,500	7·8	30,320	811,960	695,780
Clerical employees	2,416,300	12·6	—	1,555,260	817,560
Manual workers	7,024,040	36·7	—	6,005,780	908,380
Service workers	1,042,020	5·4	28,360	858,880	128,760
Others (artists, clergy, army and police)	592,800	3·1	172,300	29,880	387,540
Total (unemployed: 208,080)	19,164,460	100·0	5,366,560	10,413,840	3,175,980

The total represents a slight decrease in relation to the 1954 figures. However small independent farmers still represent a significant proportion of the active population, as do small employers in industry and commerce. Workers, defined in the broadest sense, continue to form the major group and when considered with clerical workers represent nearly 50 per cent of the working population, in which those employed in the public sector already play an important role. The wage-earning group constitutes about 70 per cent of the active population, with considerable differences between industry and agriculture.

If one takes a statistical breakdown slightly different from the one presented above, in order to show the 'tertiary' and skilled categories, the following overall proportions are presented.

This breakdown shows a relative increase in the tertiary sector in relation to 1954, which has grown at the expense of farmers (who have declined from over five million to a little more than three million). Within this tertiary population, commercial and administrative personnel take the lion's

Table 2. Active population by socio-professional categories with special reference to the tertiary sector

	Thousands
Farmers	3,078
Sailors and fishermen	76
Workers and artisans (handicrafts)	7,050
Engine drivers	413
Scientific and technical personnel (other than managerial)	622
Administrative personnel (other than top-level)	1,850
Commercial personnel (other than top-level)	1,627
Top-level management and administrative personnel (in public and private sectors)	378
Health and social services	346
Teachers and writers	506
Trained lawyers	56
Artists	47
Personal services (hairdressers, etc.)	129
Services (including Transport and GPO)	292
Miscellaneous (army, police, firemen, customs officials, clergy)	592
Total	18,944

share, while the categories of scientific workers have increased progressively. Nevertheless, workers and artisans continue to make up the main nucleus around which the other classes crystallize and fluctuate.

This absolute and relative decline in the peasant class, observable throughout western Europe, is particulatly accentuated in France. From 1954 to 1962, the decrease has been —20·8 per cent for men and —30·6 per cent for women (i.e. —24·9 per cent for all).

It is worth observing these movements not only in terms of their subdivision in large classes, but also broken down between different types of classes. It is possible, for example, to examine the structure of certain groups of activities according to their representation in the different sectors of the economy. Figures from the Fifth Plan in 1962 give the following results.

This table shows a subdivision of individual activities (trades and professions) in each group of collective activities (branches of enterprises) and highlights the fact that this

Table 3. Breakdown of the active population by economic sectors and types of jobs (in percentages)

	Fisheries	Agriculture	Extractive Industries	Building and public works	Manufacturing	Transport	Commerce	Services	Administration
Farmers, sailors, fishermen	91·3	98·1	1	0·03	0·5	5	0·8	1·3	0·7
Manual workers	5·8	0·9	89·5	86·4	77	56·7	23·1	9·4	14·0
Engineers and supervisory staff	0·7	0·1	1·8	2·1	3·8	4·6	3·8	4·4	5·3
Technicians, designers	0·4	0·3	1·7	6	3·9	5·3	0·8	1·5	2·2
Medium-level supervision, clerical workers	0·8	0·2	4·1	3·9	7·8	14·5	17·1	9·4	26·3
Shopkeepers, wage-earners in commerce	0·3	0·1	0·1	0·6	3·6	1·5	46·2	1	0·4
Workers in health and social services	—	—	0·2	—	0·3	0·3	0·2	15·4	1·5
Artists, personal services	—	—	—	—	—	—	0·4	7·9	0·4
Service personnel, transport workers	0·3	0·2	1·5	0·9	2·8	11·6	7·5	36·1	10·1
Army, police, customs, fire brigade, clergy	0·4	0·1	—	0·1	—	0·3	—	8·3	20

subdivision is more diverse and less homogeneous, as one moves from primary to tertiary. This confirms the existence of a trend towards the decompartmentalization or the polyvalence of individual activities as a function of the branching structure of modern enterprise.

If the three sectors are regrouped according to individual and collective activities, the following proportions obtained in 1962.

Table 4. Breakdown of collective and individual activities by sectors

Collective activities Individual activities	3 sectors together Absolute numbers	%	Primary	Secondary	Tertiary
Primary	4,396,420	23·26	95·84	3·23	1·57
			91·91	5·75	2·48
Secondary	7,019,880	37·14	2·39	74·57	15·90
			1·43	82·97	15·72
Tertiary	7,539,380	39·60	1·77	22·27	82·64
			0·99	23·06	76·06
3 sectors together %		100	22·27	41·30	36·71
absolute numbers	18,955,680		4,210,420	7,806,420	6,938,920

In each case, 1st figure % per column; 2nd figure % per line.

This table is even more significant than the previous one, because it presents the three classes in their mutual relationships from the point of view of two different criteria. This interpretation, found in all other industrial societies, perhaps appears to be even more outstanding in France than elsewhere. From the table it can be seen that the primary sector is the most homogeneous while each of the other three sectors contains a variable, but often important fraction of the other two; for example, industries in the secondary sector employ a quarter of workers in non-secondary jobs.

Interpenetrations of this type, which may be even more complex, indicate that in relation to 1954 (the data for which is not reproduced here) the decline in the agricultural population has continued until it now represents less than 20 per cent of the active population and that this decline has been to the advantage of workers doing tertiary jobs in the secondary sector, as well as to the advantage of the tertiary sector itself. This process perhaps explains why in France the expansion of the tertiary sector has been a direct product of the decline in agricultural population, although this has not been the case elsewhere.

The 1968 census has provided data still inadequate, but sufficient to confirm that the movement taking place between 1954 and 1962 has continued and accelerated. The following table shows the composition of the principal socio-economic groups in 1968.

Table 5. Active population by socio-economic groups, 1968

Farmers	2,460,000
Agricultural wage-earners	588,000
Employers in industry and commerce	1,962,000
Liberal professions and top-level management	993,000
Medium-level management	2,014,000
Clerical workers	3,030,000
Manual workers	7,698,000
Service personnel (domestic)	656,000
Others (artists, clergy, army and police)	523,000
Total	19,944,000

Thus it appears that the active agricultural population has diminished among farm labourers, as among large and small farmers, while the employers and medium and high-level managers, as well as clerical employees, have increased. Manual workers have increased both proportionately and in terms of absolute numbers. The rate of overall increase in manual workers (from 1962 to 1968) has been by 9 per cent, which is slower than that of clerical workers (32 per cent), medium-level managers (34 per cent) and high-level managers (33 per cent). However, this rate refers to a group which alone accounts for 38 to 40 per cent of the total active population. While it still carries more weight in society than any other group, it exercises its influence in a relationship with other classes which has been seriously modified, since it is confronted above all with the group of small employers rather than that of farmers. This change in alliances and oppositions may be considered as a new form of social equilibrium. This new balance, however, is not exclusive to France and is less striking there than in Japan or in the United States–Canada. This is shown by the following comparison (drawn up by OECD) between increases and decreases in percentages over the ten-year period 1956–67.

Table 6. Variation of active population, in %, between 1956 and 1967

	Agriculture	Industry	Tertiary
France	−12	+11	+23
Japan	−29	+58	+40
USA–Canada	−37	+11	+33

This moderate pace of social evolution in France over the last two centuries is certainly one of the factors explaining the dominance of the *political* over the *economic* in class conflict and in the establishment of a state of equilibrium between classes.

An important variable in accounting for the growth in qualitative fluctuations in employment and in inter-class equilibrium, has been the increase in the rate of school enrolment. The following table shows the increase in the rate of enrolment between 1954 and 1966.

Table 7. Rate of school enrolment at various ages (in percentages)

Ages	1.1.1954		1.1.1966	
	Males	Females	Males	Females
14 years	54·3	57·1	75·7	84·3
15	42·9	47·7	60·2	71·8
16	34·8	37·8	49·1	56·3
18	14·9	14·3	25·2	26·6
20	8·8	5·9	13·6	13·4
22	4·7	2·5	7·0	4·9

This increase in enrolment is more marked in the peasant class and the 'lower middle classes' which are precisely those from which tertiary workers are recruited.

Parallel to these processes, in which social mobility plays an important part, the low rate of geographical mobility must be noted. In other words, changes in social class membership take place 'in situ' rather than involving a change of residence or place of employment. Table 8 presents the following figures on geographical migration in the period 1954–62.

Thus low geographical mobility rates coincide with the stagnation in the active population referred to earlier. One can see the rate of mobility is lower in the active than in the total population.

Table 8. Breakdown of migrations according to residence

	Inter-regional migrations	Inter-departmental migrations
Number of migrants per year:		
In thousands	850	1,300
As a % of the total population	1·8	2·7
Number of migrants among the active population per year:		
In thousands	330	500
As a % of the active population	1·65	2·5

Throughout the country the following rates obtain among the total population:

Change of residence	8 to 10%
Migration between municipalities	6·5%
Migration between departments	2%
Migration between regions	1%

However, special consideration should be given to the role played by foreign residents in stabilizing the active population. Their numbers reached 2,200,000 in 1964 of whom the great majority (1,800,000) were made up of Algerians, Italians, Portuguese and Spaniards. By far the greater part of them belong to the active population as members of the wage-earning working class and hold on average the least well-paid and least-skilled jobs. On the whole they find themselves excluded from jobs reserved to the French, particularly within the public sector and of course in the Civil Service. Their mobility is more marked than that of their French counter-parts and it is often they who respond to conjunctural fluctuations. While the majority belong to distinctive social classes, such as manual workers, small shopkeepers and domestic servants, they constitute in France proletarian pockets without which the economic system could no longer exist.

All these phenomena show that the class composition of the French population tends to coincide with the European trend towards the predominance of a mixture of industrial and managerial population, to the detriment of the agrarian population. This is one of the main sources of the evolution towards an integrated European economy.[2]

In this perspective, the disintegration of the peasant class

is no doubt one of the most curious and original characteristics of France in relation to other industrial countries. The
methods of cultivation and labour could be summarized as
follows in 1954, at a time when the decline had begun to
accelerate.

Table 9. Active population in agriculture, by socio-professional groups and status

	Total	Self-employed		Family help	Wage-earners	
		Independent	Employers		Private sector	Public sector
Farmers, general	145,000	83,000	6,560	55,160		
Owner farmers	2,459,180	984,160	238,100	1,236,920		
Leasehold farmers	1,169,880	377,400	144,700	647,780		
Farmers under 'métayage' contract	209,760	65,280	20,460	124,020		
Wage-earning labourers	1,151,520				1,125,380	11,460

(1954 census, Active Population Tables)

If a breakdown is made on the basis of occupational status,
the following figures obtain for the same date.

Table 10. Types of jobs in Agriculture and Forestry

	Agriculture-Forestry
Unskilled labourers and daily labourers	354,560
Skilled wage-earning agricultural workers	593,660
Specialists in animal husbandry	12,260
Specialists in agricultural machinery	13,880
Supervisory and teaching staff in agriculture	11,240
Breeders	69,560
Cultivators (farmers, wine-growers, rice-growers)	3,877,300
Specialized producers (fruit-tree growers, market gardeners, horticulturalists)	110,000
Total	5,042,460

Wage-earning supervisory staff and manual workers
employed in the agricultural sector can be broken down on
the following lines:

Table 11. Occupational breakdown in agricultural sector

Wage-earners		Agricultur-Forestry	Totals
Higher grades	Engineers	520	
	High administrative personnel	1,460	
	Other top-level personnel	80	2,060
Medium grades	Technicians	700	
	Medium-level administrative personnel	2,200	
	Other medium-level personnel	100	3,000
Clerical workers	in offices	8,000	
	in commerce	1,980	9,980
Manual workers	Foremen	500	
	Skilled workers	11,500	
	Specialized workers	11,280	
	Unskilled workers	8,240	
	Other workers	20	31,540

These data (1954) show that the basic group in the French peasantry whose disintegration announces a general crisis of this class is the sub-group of 'owner farmers', that is the great majority of smallholders. Its gradual disappearance since the beginning of the 1950s which will be accentuating in the years to come, does not mean that other agricultural categories (wage-earners, technicians, machine operators) will replace them. The latter sub-groups have also declined in number since 1954. At the expense of all these there has been an increase in the medium and lower managerial personnel, a mixture of a neo-wage-earning class and of a petty bourgeoisie which in France as in other industrial countries, now represents the new mass which supervises and attempts to control the traditional mass of workers of all categories.

The crisis of the French peasantry is in some ways the trigger releasing all the other elements of class crisis and imbalance. This element is all the more important since its results are felt not only in terms of class relations within the nation, but also within Europe in the context of the Common Market.

From certain points of view, the decline of the traditional peasantry displaces certain forms of power and supremacy enjoyed by the bourgeois classes. Since the eighteenth century, the land-owning bourgeoisie has played an important role in France. Under the Third Republic, the Radical party was largely founded on the medium level peasantry, owing to a form of protectionism which is in the process of disappearing at present, and this party governed France, alone or in coalition, during a fifty-year period. The power of the capitalist and financial classes which grew with industrialization and that of public servants and managers in the public sector finds itself reinforced as a result.

On the other hand, the fact that the vast majority of the active population is now composed of wage-earners, and the gradual incorporation of a growing part of the old peasantry into the wage-earning sector (notably into management) tend to bring about a new equilibrium between classes, such that the traditional antagonism between agricultural and industrial interests (those of employers as well as of employees) are largely shifted into the orbit of the wage-earning population, jointly controlled by the State and big business.

As has already been stated, this situation results in an accentuation of *political* conflict rather than a deepening of purely economic conflict. This phenomenon is perhaps more visible in France than elsewhere, but it is nevertheless present in all industrial countries, including State socialist economies in eastern Europe. The available statistical data on socio-economic class *composition* are not very informative about class functions, changes in function or on the political role played by classes. To undertake such an analysis one would require knowledge of both social evolution and economic and political structures independent from the distribution of individuals in more or less arbitrary statistical categories. It is only by reference to the economic functions of social groups and to political and economic institutions that the evolution of relationships between classes could be determined. Basic figures about the morphology of social groups clearly ought to serve as a basis for this analysis, but in fact only constitute a starting-point. The increase of the wage-earning population and the crisis of the agrarian sector, which are both fundamental features in the evolution of the French socio-economic structure, should be clarified first. Their polar opposites are the increasing weight gained by industry and finance and the ensuing importance of management roles. These trends would then have to be confronted in order to discover the new or modified functions pertaining to classes or groups. It would then become evident that in France, as in other industrial countries, whose pattern she has been following, this evolution leads to a *standardization* of life chances due to the prevalence of wage-earning and State intervention, on the one hand, and, on the other, to the *polymorphy* or multilateralism of specific functions (i.e. the fact that the same individuals or groups discharge diverse or even conflicting functions, as a result of increased social mobility). It is the interplay between these two general situations which should constitute the focus of any study covering the new functions of social classes. While France may not always be the country in which these processes are the most obvious, the very slowness of their unfolding facilitates at times a better understanding of their interrelationships and complexities.

NOTES

1 It is noteworthy that the French public powers are increasingly concerned about the stabilization of the active population, in absolute numbers. Thus at a Press conference on 22 September 1969, President Pompidou made the following statements which can usefully be quoted here. In 1913, in a country of less than 40 million inhabitants there were 20 and a half million actively occupied, i.e. 52 per cent of the total population. In 1969, in a country of more than 50 million inhabitants there are still only 20 and a half million active, i.e. barely 41 per cent of the population. In other words, the active population must now support 11 million more persons. The most plausible forecasts indicate that there will be no more than 21 million active in 1974. With regard to the internal structure of this active population, in 1913 there were seven million farmers; while there are now less than three million. In industry, there are approximately six million workers, as in 1913. It is in construction and public works, and above all in the 'tertiary' sector that the absolute and relative increase has been most pronounced. President Pompidou drew no particular conclusions from this evolution, apart from the fact that it indicated a considerable global development in productivity.

2 Looking back over a century, it can be stated that disparities of development were extremely marked. The following table provides a comparison, on the basis of various indices, between Britain and France. These data were collected around 1820–5 by Villeneuve-Bargemont:

	Britain	*France*
Metropolitan population	24,400,000	32,000,000
External population	115,156,000	602,000
Breakdown of metropolitan population		
Owners	3,400,000	20,000,000
Proletariat	20,000,000	12,000,000
Farmers	9,360,000	25,600,000
Industrialists	14,040,000	6,400,000
Work done by machine and corresponding to the work of approximately	200,000,000	3,000,000
Acreage cultivated	50,000,000	161,013,842
uncultivated	15,000,000	21,363,672
Catholic population	6,200,000	30,620,000
Protestants and other denominations	17,200,000	1,370,000
Number of paupers	3,903,631	1,600,000
Number of beggars	200,000	198,008

(Extracted from a table drawn up from different sources for the years 1820 to 1825 by Villeneuve-Bargemont, *Economie Politique Chrétienne*, Table II, p. 165.)

BIBLIOGRAPHY

Barbichon, G., *Adaptation et formation de la main d'oeuvre des régions rurales au travail industriel* (Paris, OCDE, 1962).

Le passage de la population active de l'agriculture a l'industrie. In *Tendances et volontés de la société française* (Paris, SEDEIS, 1966).

Belleville, P., *Une nouvelle classe ouvriers* (Paris, ed. du Seuil, 1963).

Bloch, G., Praderie, M., *La population active dans les pays développés* (Paris, ed. Cujas, 1966).

Bon, F., Burnier, M-A., *Les Nouveaux intellectuels* (Paris, ed. Cujas, 1966).

Courtheoux, J. P., *Attitudes collectives et croissance économique* (Paris, M. Riviere, 1969).

Essai sur la répartition des activités économiques. Critique experimentale de la theorie des trois secteurs (La Haije, Mouton, 1969).

La structure en classes d'une population active. *Revue économique*, 1965, No. 2.

Frisch, J., *La mobilité des différentes catégories professionnelles selon la formation et la taille de l'établissement d'arrivée, 1959–1964* (Paris, CNRS, Centre d'Études Sociologiques, 1969).

Gervaic, M., Servolin, C., Weil, J., *Une France sans paysans* (Paris, ed. du Seuil, 1965).

Girard, A., Meutey, P., *Développement économique et mobilité des travailleurs*. L'individu, la profession, la région (Paris, INED, 1956).

Goetz-Girey, R., *Le mouvement des grèves en France, 1919–1962* (Paris, ed. Sirey, 1965).

Guelard-Leridon, F., Perspectives sur la population active française par qualification en 1975. *Population* (jan.–mars 1964).

Gurvitch, G., *Études sur les classes sociales* (Paris, ed. Gonthier, 1966).

Krier, H., *Main d'oeuvre rurale et développement industriel*. Adaptation et formation (Paris, OCDE, 1961).

Langlois, F., Les salariés agricoles. *Paysans,* No. 28 (fev.–mars 1961) et No. 29 (avr.–mai 1961).

La mobilité professionnelle en France entre 1959 et 1964. *Études et Conjoncture* (INSEE, dec. 1966).

La population française. Tome I. France métropolitaine. Rapport du Haut Comité de la population (Paris, La Documentation Française, 1955).

L'emploi féminin en France en 1962 et son évolution depuis 1954. *Études et Conjoncture* (INSEE, dec. 1964).

Lengelle, M., *La révolution tertiaire* (Paris, ed. Genin, 1966).

L'espace économique français. Fasc. II. La population active. *Études et Conjoncture* (INSEE, Paris, 1968), 429 pp.

Les nouveaux comportements politiques de la classe ouvrière (sous la direction de L. Hamon), (Paris, Presses Univ. de France, 1962).

Lherbier, P., Les techniciens, catégorie professionnelle ou catégorie socio-professionnelle. *Bulletin du CERP* (1966), No. 2.

Mallet, S., *La nouvelle classe ouvrière* (Paris, ed. du Seuil, 1963).

Mendras, H., *La fin des paysans* (Paris, SEDEIS, 1968).

Mendras, H. Tavernier, Y., *Terre, paysans et politique* (Paris, SEDEIS, 1969).

Naville, P., La théorie des trois secteurs et l'évolution sociale. *Cahiers d'étude des sociétés industrielles et de l'automation* (CNRS, No. 5, 1963).

Eléments pour une étude comparée des trois secteurs de la population active. *Cahiers d'étude des sociétés industrielles et de l'automation* (CNRS, No. 7, 1965).

Perspectives de la population français jusqu'en 1980. Population totale et population active. INSEE, *Etudes statistiques* (avr.–juin 1960).

Population active et population à la recherche d'un emploi. Premiers résultats du recensement de mars 1968. *Études et Conjoncture* (1969), Supp. No. 2.

Praderie, M., *Ni ouvriers, ni paysans: les tertiaires* (Paris, ed. du Seuil, 1968).

Prost, M-A., *La hiérarchie des villes en fonction de leurs activités de commerce et de service* (Paris, Gauthier-Villars, 1965).

Rapport Général de la Commission de la Main d'Oeuvre, Ve Plan, 1966–1970. Commissariat Général du Plan d'Equipement et de la productivité, 1966.

Schmutz, B., *La signification des facteurs de mouvements de la main d'oeuvre dans les transformations de la structure professionnelle.* Un essai d'étude empirique. (Neuchâtel, ed. de la Baconnière, 1965).

Statistiques relatives à la structure de la main d'oeuvre par profession et par niveau d'éducation dans 53 pays (Paris, OCDE, 1969).

Statistiques du Secteur Tertiare. Rapport de G. Levard au Conseil Economique et Social. *Journal Officiel* (14 mars 1968).

Tanguy, L., Fréquentation scolaire et composition de l'emploi. *Cahiers d'étude des sociétés industrielles et de l'automation* (CNRS, No. 8, 1967).

Touraine, A., *La société post-industrielle* (Paris, Denoël. 1969).

Touraine, A. Ragazzi, O., *Ouvriers d'origine agricole* (Paris, ed. du Seuil, 1960).

Vermot-Gauchy, M., *L'éducation nationale dans la France de demain* (Paris, SEDEIS, 1965).

Vinot, C., *La population active* (Paris, Presses Univ. de France, 1960).

Vimont, C., Hughes, P., Peslier, M., La prévision de l'emploi dans le cadre du Ve Plan en France. La répartition de la population active par professions en 1970. *Population* (mai 1966).

8 England

David Martin and Colin Crouch

Social stratification in England hinges on two issues. The first is the question of the right balance in this particular culture between an analysis which leans on the relationship of economic class and one which stresses a plurality of competing status groups. The second is the problem of describing historically and understanding sociologically the relatively unperturbed coexistence of a stable social hierarchy and a capacity for flexibility and reform.

We shall begin with history, describing those social moulds provided by religious and constitutional compromise, by the special character of development in the world's first industrial society, by the peculiar British relation between the aristocracy and entrepreneurial class, as well as by two important experiences – that of being the centre of an empire and of being almost the only European society never to experience defeat in war. We turn then to occupational structure: first its ranking and its variations in freedom and control, second the major processes it exhibits such as the growth of professionalism and managerialism and of routine clerical work, the changing importance of different industries, and the overall movement to the tertiary sector. This occupational structure and its ranking is next related to the concentration of wealth and to the pattern of rewards. We then proceed to the correlates of occupational ranking and differential reward, firstly in the distribution of power, influence and social participation, secondly in the structure of life chances, particularly as mediated by education, and thirdly as evidenced in the pattern of life styles.

These, if you like, have constituted what we will call the 'Weberian' aspects of the subject: power, influence, status, honour, life chances and life styles. At this juncture we turn to what might be called the 'Marxian' problems, i.e., is there a concentration of power in the elite such as may constitute a ruling class, based on industrial concentration and ramified internationally? How far is there countervailing power in the restraining hand of government, in universal suffrage, in the operations of trade unions, in the ethos of expertise and in deeply rooted normative constraints? Is the acerbity of class conflict muted by social welfare and widespread prosperity? Finally, we turn to what are labelled 'Durkheimian' aspects, by which we mean the cultural traditions, the undergirding values and the underlying consensus within which conflict and change are perceived and transmuted. This necessitates a reiteration of the historical basis of stability and institutionalized compromise, which is followed by a study of the complex interrelation between on the one hand a flexible elite, partly resting on a legitimating aura of gentle archaism and deference, and on the other hand a liberal consensus largely excluding the extremes of left and right.

HISTORICAL BACKGROUND

Several important changes have taken place in British social structure since the end of the second world war, but these must be seen against the background of historical features whose influence has proved enduring. These mainly concern Britain's unusual position with regard to the resolution of four major crises in national integration – religion, the constitution, industrialization and the fate of the landed aristocracy.

The British tradition of institutionalized compromise may be seen to reach back to the institutionalization of religious dissent in the middle and late seventeenth century, and even to the establishment of a church settlement which aimed at a fair degree of toleration and comprehensiveness. The set of models provided for Britain were cast in an ecclesiastical mould and comprise a tolerant, flexible, undogmatic establishment confronting a dissent which builds up areas of autonomy and countervailing power without positively taking the commanding heights of elite predominance.[1] These models jointly inform the British political and religious style to such an extent that where religious radicalism did overwhelm the commanding heights in the non-English cultures there eventually appeared a comparable political radicalism, particularly in Wales. That this is not mere historical background is illustrated by the fact that the stratification systems of the non-English cultures are more egalitarian and less deferential in tone.

Second, the English revolution came early, and like childish ailments early revolutions inoculate against more serious disruptions of the body politic at a later date. The later a revolution occurs, the more total its impact, the more all-embracing it is in its claims, and the greater its potential for tyranny riding behind the banners of necessary long-delayed progress. In Britain the parties of change and progress have operated on the basis of reform and have had to compete in reformism with the party of stability and conservation. Parliamentary socialists could not attempt outright revolution nor formulate a total ideology.[2] Changes were forthcoming from the Establishment itself; the rivals of socialism put forward attractive alternatives or eventually acquiesced in many of its achievements; and in any case the debate was suffused with appeals for change based on morality, not class conflict, on universal brotherhood, not proletarian solidarity. No doubt this again relates to the moulds provided by British dissent: its capacity to achieve enough in the way of cultural autonomy not to attempt hegemonic power, its capacity simultaneously to create and restrict the range of criticism within a moral framework, and the sphere it opened up for rational critics to press forward as individuals assured of the inevitability of gradualism.

Thirdly, Britain was the first country in the world to industrialize, and it did so extremely gradually. Neither the promoters of industrialism nor its opponents had any models to follow or expectations of patterns to be developed. The process was for a long time unselfconscious. Gradualness also meant that change disrupted different groups at different times and in a local context. Co-ordinated opposition to industrialization was difficult; even where national organization existed (Chartism), it could not offer a real challenge or develop a coherent ideology. Developing as it did over a long time scale, British industrialization imparted an overall slowness of pace, a length of perspective and a cultural inertia which are even now constituent parts of the British scene. As such they form the substance of lamentation both from a left anxious to impart an immediacy to class consciousness within a theoretical perspective, and from a technical elite concerned to create the conditions of rational efficiency.[3]

Fourthly, there were special features in Britain's transition from a society dominated by land to a society where commercial interests are preponderant. Very early, before the Civil War, the landed aristocracy had turned to commercial farming, thereby gaining a community of interest with the towns. Thus from early on habits and techniques of accommodation, of limited conflict of interests within a framework of consensus, were acquired and practised by British ruling elites. Barrington Moore[4] sees in this development a crucial step in the growth of a pluralist democracy in England, contrasting it in particular with the situation in Germany, where the landed aristocracy, the Junkers, remained isolated from commercial and economic development. In Britain throughout the late eighteenth century most of the great landlords did little to improve their estates, but threw themselves into a hundred non-agricultural pursuits such as iron, coal, canals and the development of London. They became separated from the mere (and to some extent localized) landed gentry, so that their political leaders repealed the Corn Laws against the landed interest and destroyed its political power by electoral reform. As the nineteenth century progressed this mutual integration of bourgeoisie and landed aristocracy was strengthened from the other direction – the permeation of the peerage by leading figures from industry and commerce: the so-called 'beerage'. Later, this was supplemented by the sale of peerages for 'political services' in the time of Lloyd George and by the rise of the newspaper and motor barons. More recently there has been the ennoblement of several figures from the trade union movement and from a new meritocratic elite in professional and academic life. Meanwhile, of course, the power of the Upper House has been gradually attenuated to become a shadow of its former self; increasingly defending itself, not as the spokesman of the traditional landed interest, but as a reservoir of detached and non-partisan expertise and judgement.

An outstanding cause of the great continuity of British social patterns may well be the fact that Britain has never been occupied by a foreign power. Elsewhere, defeat in war or extremely disruptive military action taking place on the home territory tended to produce major upheavals from both left and right of the political spectrum, but in the British Isles war only resulted in significant shifts in a stratification system and a culture which demonstrably retained its continuity. Leaving aside heavy losses, not least among the elite, the worst consequence was the loss of commercial and industrial pre-eminence.

Titmuss[5] has demonstrated how modern warfare has led in Britain to the development of public welfare services. The Boer War revealed the deteriorating physical fitness of a great number of troops, and resulted in elementary measures to establish services that would ensure the maintenance of a physically fit potential fighting force. The first world war, again, aroused concern for the national welfare, leading to such provision as the first instalment of a free national health service. Attention was now directed at the health of the civilian population as well as the military. After the second world war[6] the concept was extended much further to encompass the idea of 'civilian morale', and the need to provide a certain level of guaranteed health and welfare as a badge of citizenship. This idea gave a crucial, if temporary, egalitarian shift to the political consensus at an important time. Further, the first world war occurred at a time when the nation was torn by industrial strife, the suffragette movement, and the challenge to the British Government in Ireland from both the Irish Nationalists and the Unionists. War provided an extremely useful cause for rallying the nation in a common venture and papering over the cracks that had appeared in the old Liberal consensus.[7] Finally, the second world war made it possible to unite the nation, including the Communist Party, in a fight against fascism, neatly providing the consensus with a common enemy on the far right to complement Soviet Communism at the other extreme.

A similar uniting function was performed by the colonial experience. Pride of Empire has increased identification with the nation and also with the monarchy as a focus of national

I

pride. At least part of the popularity of the English crown was gained because it focused a very widespread identification with British imperial power. Moreover, that empire was relinquished with remarkably little tension, when compared with other colonial powers. This rather slow decline in national grandeur was partly masked by a shield of American power which allowed Britain to decline gracefully without too gross reminders from aggressive newcomers of her diminished status. Thus the euphoria of empire was never really complemented by a trauma of decline. Further, the economic gains of colonialism protected the English proletariat, and its stability was further buttressed by a succession of unpoliticized migrants from the Irish to the West Indians who have stepped into the lowest status levels of English society just at the point where Englishmen themselves were becoming increasingly unwilling to fill them.

WEBERIAN ASPECTS: INEQUALITIES OR EQUALIZATION

Occupational structure
Although the concept of class has now been applied to a wide range of societies, it first entered sociology as a means of referring to the divisions of industrializing societies; the traditional societies of Europe were considered to be divided according to estates. This distinction helps to explain the curious fact that most discussions of class have centred round the middle (or bourgeois) and working classes; the upper class has rarely entered the debate. In a sense, the upper class is not regarded as a class at all, but is still an estate. To the extent that members of the upper class have engaged in economic activity and entered the world of classes, they have really adopted middle-class roles. We are thus concerned, in the study of social class, with some kind of occupational ranking of the population. There is an ordering according to the degree of control, supervision and responsibility exercised at work, and also according to the autonomy of action allowed by that work. The hierarchy of supervision within the typical industrial enterprise, from board of directors to unskilled labourer, is reproduced in most statements of the hierarchy of social class. Persons who are not engaged in this industrial chain of command can be positioned according to the degree

of autonomy and personal control exercised in their work; the self-employed professional thus standing 'higher' than the employed professional.

These differences in occupation affect class in two ways. First, the different degrees of control over other men, and personal freedom at work, constitute an important aspect of life chances. Second, the authority of superior rank at work imparts accepted social status over a wider area, although there are of course important elements of status not related to this scale. This occupational structure correlates fairly closely with a similar pattern of inequality in income and other rewards. Together these related structures of inequality constitute the essential base of British social class. The Census[8] gives the following breakdown of the population of England and Wales by 'Social Class':

Table 1

	%
1. Professional, proprietorial	4
2. Intermediate (non-manual)	15
3. Skilled manual and white-collar routine	51
4. Partly skilled (manual)	21
5. Unskilled	9

A more detailed and more useful picture is provided by what the Census calls 'socio-economic groups':

Table 2

	%	%
1. Proprietorial and managerial		12·5
farmers	2	
employers, managers (large)	3·5	
employers, managers (small)	6	
professional (self-employed)	1	
2. Other non-manual		20·5
professional (employees)	3	
intermediate	4	
junior non-manual	12·5	
personal service	1	

	%	%
3. Manual		63·5
foremen and supervisors	3·5	
skilled	31·5	
semi-skilled	15	
unskilled	8	
own account	3·5	
agricultural workers	2	
4. Armed forces		2
5. Indefinite		1·5

Several points in this classification require comment. First, such a table can give no separate attention to that circle of leading industrialists, experts and the new meritocratic elite who play an important part in government advisory bodies and in public decision-making. Second, at the higher levels of industry there has been an inflow of powerful salaried executives alongside the older groups of major shareholders and entrepreneurs. This development has led to a theory of the 'managerial revolution', based on the twin themes of the growing importance of expertise in industry and the increasing diffusion of stock ownership. At the same time there has been a great numerical decline in the ranks of small businessmen and shopkeepers. Third, 'professionalization' has greatly increased as non-manual employees in administrative management, welfare, scientific and technical functions have developed alongside the liberal professions. This search for achieving professional status – on behalf of such diverse occupations as school teacher or estate agent – may be seen as separating this group from both the industrial proletariat and entrepreneurs. In Marshall's view[9] the fortunes of this group are tied to employment. Therefore they look to the administrative professionalism of the social services rather than to the competitive professionalism of lawyers. Paul Halmos[10] suggests that:

professionalism . . . inevitably introduces more and more collectivistic and other-regarding considerations into social functioning, and weakens the *laissez-faire licence* of a free enterprise, the *rapacity* of penal justice, the *harshness* of educational discipline and the *mercenariness* of 'marketable' doctoring.

Fourthly, clerical workers at the lower end of the vast non-manual spectrum have been undergoing change in a reverse direction: increasing routinization of their work, the introduction of office machinery, and the increased size of office establishments, have led to clerical working conditions coming increasingly to resemble the factory situation. Lockwood[11] has studied in detail how these changes are disrupting the class/status barriers that formerly existed between clerks and artisans. An important aspect of this is the growing, though still minor, willingness of some 'white-collar' groups to engage in strike action. This adoption of an essentially collective form of action by groups who formerly prided themselves on their individualism, is in part a reflection of a change that has occurred in their working environment. This important area of change is complemented from a different direction by a fifth factor of importance: the emergence of some occupations in modern technological industries where skilled operatives, who are neither office employees nor manual workers in the accepted sense, operate automated machinery, enjoying considerable autonomy, responsibility and superior working conditions[12] (e.g., chemical processing and the oil industry). This is not, however, a necessary development of mass-production as such; conditions on the assembly line of, say, the motor industry, impose a rhythm on work that deprives the worker of much autonomy.[13] These changes are allied to major trends in the structure of British industry itself.[14] The great industries which formed the basis of Britain's early economic development and provided the mould within which class divisions of occupations were cast, are undergoing a relative decline: mining, railways, ship-building, wool and cotton textiles. The new growth points are in chemicals, metals, engineering, man-made fibres and the public utilities. Sixth, further disruption of earlier class patterns is due to the vast increase in the tertiary sector of employment whose occupations do not always fit easily into the employer/operative dichotomy. Important changes have also occurred within this sector, its growth having concentrated on such fields as transport and communications, professional and financial services, catering and entertainments, public administration and the distributive trades. Meanwhile, domestic service, an occupation which illustrated class distinctions with particular severity, has declined considerably, particularly as the native domestic has been partly replaced by the foreign au pair.

Seventhly, in the last hundred years agriculture has declined from employing 22 per cent of the active population (1851, Agriculture and Fisheries) to accounting now for less than 4 per cent. Simultaneously, agricultural activities have acquired the techniques and methods of industry, so that farmers and their labourers (or, rather, technicians) fit into the occupational classification as any other group of employers or employees. Britain has one of the smallest agricultural populations in the world, and completely lacks a peasant class. This eliminates from the British scene an important point of social division in many societies, including France.

Finally, as the general prosperity of the nation has increased since 1945, some groups have been left behind in the near-universal growth in wealth. The situation of this *nouveaux pauvres* is considerably different from that of the average industrial worker, since it is largely his progress that has left them isolated. It is the existence of this group that leads to talk of Britain's class structure changing from a pyramid to a lozenge. Included in it are workers in declining industries which have not shared in economic growth, workers in medium-income service industries in large cities where living costs are high, people in areas of continuing high unemployment, the old and the chronically sick.[15] One might also add the majority of coloured people, who suffer from particular disadvantages and discrimination.

Income and reward

Occupation and income must be considered jointly in order to appreciate their interrelationship. Unfortunately, this has only been done by Routh[16] and, valuable as his work is, it gives very little detailed information on differences within the major categories of occupation. Nevertheless, useful data are provided on the continuance of inter-occupational income differences over half a century (see Table 3).[17]

Routh says that his most impressive finding was the rigidity of inter-class and inter-occupational differences over the years.[18] There were some striking changes, including the general reduction in the relative pay of professional workers

Table 3. Occupational class averages as percentages of the average for all occupational classes: (men only)

Group	1913/14	1922/4	1935/6	1955/6	1960
1. Professional					
A Higher	410	372	392	290	298
B Lower	194	204	190	115	124
2. Managerial					
A Employers and entrepreneurs: no information*					
B Managers, etc.	250	307	272	279	271
3. Clerks	124	116	119	98	100
4. Foremen	141	171	169	148	149
Manual					
5. Skilled	124	115	121	117	117
6. Semi-skilled	86	80	83	88	85
7. Unskilled	79	82	80	82	79

* The absence of information for this crucial group is particularly unfortunate.

and of male clerical employees, as well as a reduction in the relative position of skilled manual workers. However, he stresses that changes do not come about gradually, but suddenly within short periods and as a result of special factors. In the intervening period the egalitarian tendencies have disappeared or have even been reversed. The structure of reward and shifts within it have therefore tended not to correspond to the doctrines of marginal productivity or the balance of supply and demand, but to a set of broadly accepted views on the appropriateness of certain differentials between occupational groups; in other words, an accepted class structure.

It is in the extent to which these differences of income correspond to the scale of control and autonomy at work that the main basis of the class structure is to be found. The importance of this hierarchy of occupation and income is heightened by its stability over time, as Routh suggests. Thus the pattern is not one of a shifting set of occupational groups whose life chances vary with the market, but one of consistency. Closely related to income is the question of fringe benefits and working conditions. In some cases these may be held to 'compensate' for relatively low incomes, but despite some such examples, fringe benefits on the whole tend to follow the same pattern as the income differentials.[19] They reinforce this pattern and provide important points of class segregation and status differentiation.

Of greater importance are the differences in private welfare schemes provided by firms for their employees. Tony Lynes[20] has identified a distinction among pension schemes between (i) very high-value schemes, with a high degree of tax-avoidance, for directors and top executives; (ii) pensions worth between one-third and half salary, related to past income and often transferable, for salaried employees; and (iii) modest pensions based on service and not income, for manual workers. Several firms have schemes for assisting senior staff with the cost of private education for their children; or for private health insurance. Inequalities of this kind buttress further still the income hierarchy. An indication of the size of these benefits and their effect on income distribution was given in *The Economist*[21] as follows:

Table 4. Fringe benefits as a percentage of salary

£1,000 per year	11%
£1,600 ,, ,,	15%
£3,500 ,, ,,	19%
£4,200 ,, ,,	21%
£7,000+ ,, ,,	31%

Finally, the impact of taxation has to be considered. Although Britain has a progressive income-tax system, the effect of this is weakened by (a) the existence of a wide number of possibilities for tax-avoidance, the great majority of which are available only to the upper-income groups; these practices have been studied in detail by Titmuss[22]; and (b) the impact of rates and indirect taxation, which are generally regressive in their impact.

The regressiveness of the rating system has recently been studied by an official committee[23], while its operation in indirect taxation has been estimated by Peston,[24] who stresses the enormous complexity of trying to reach definite conclusions in this field. An attempt has been made by Hughes[25] to give some idea of the combined net impact on households with different incomes of income tax, rates and indirect taxes. While his work covers the lower and middle ranges only of family income, and makes no allowance for avoidance, it provides useful evidence of movement in recent years:

Table 5. Total taxes as proportion of original income, 1961 and 1966 (household of two adults and one child). Households ranged by size of original income (£p.a.)

1961 Income £	559	676	816	988	1,196	1,448	1,752–2,122
1966 Income £	676	816	988	1,196	1,448	1,752	2,122–2,566
% taxed							
1961		29	29	28	29	29	29	29
1966		38	38	35	34	33	31	28

Education and wealth

These two factors both *determine* and are *determined by* position in the control/reward ladder. They thus have a rigidifying effect on the position of individual families in the class structure. Many of the steps upward in the occupational ladder involve successively higher levels of education and training, while the higher income and superior life style made possible by the higher position increase ability to provide a good education for one's children.

Wealth operates in similar fashion. The very highest positions in the control and ownership of industry are obtained through wealth and property ownership. Meanwhile, the large income derived from these high positions results in an accumulation of wealth to be inherited by the next generation. Revell[26] has estimated that in 1960 the wealthiest 1 per cent of the population held 42 per cent of the total dutiable wealth, while the wealthiest 5 per cent held 75 per cent of the total. Since death duties are subject to so many loopholes, private wealth continues to provide an extremely important element in the British economy, restricted to the hands of a small number of families. It was private wealth that initially made it possible for the landed class to transfer its attention to, and remain at the helm of, British industrialization. Wealth continues as a source of rigidity and inequality in the modern economy, as suggested by the following table[27] showing the spread of investment income through different income groups in the total population.

Table 6. Spread of investment income

Net income range (all income) £	Net investment income £000	%	Running Total	Number of cases per 000	%	Running Total	£ per case
Up to 499	67,560	3·8	3·8	598	14·7	14·7	113
500–999	195,100	10·8	14·6	1,428	35·2	49·9	137
1,000–1,499	161,090	8·9	23·5	908	22·4	73·3	177
1,500–1,999	129,840	7·2	30·7	427	10·6	82·9	304
2,000–2,499	106,940	5·9	36·6	200	4·9	87·8	535
2,500–2,999	102,300	5·7	42·3	120	3·0	90·8	851
3,000–3,999	164,040	9·1	51·4	137	3·3	94·1	1,195
4,000–4,999	125,770	6·9	58·3	77	1·9	96·0	1,630
5,000–5,999	104,690	5·8	64·1	49	1·2	97·2	2,152
6,000–7,999	152,300	8·4	72·5	50	1·3	98·5	3,037
8,000–9,999	102,250	5·7	78·2	25	0·6	99·1	4,165
10,000 and up	392,790	21·8	100	37	0·9	100	10,477

Source: 'Inland Revenue Statistics', 1965–66.

That the privileged position of earnings from wealth as opposed to earned income is not declining in its effect in modern Britain is suggested by data on the rate of change in the increase of both in recent years:[28]

Table 7. Personal income and earned income 1955–65

	1955 (£m)	1960 (£m)	1965 (£m)
Personal property income	1,534	2,372	3,595
Earned income	12,905	17,168	23,736
INDICES (1955 = 100)			
Personal property income	100	155	234
Earned income	100	133	184

Social class and life chances

Social class, and in particular the non-manual/manual dividing line, is one of the best predictors of variance within the population on a host of different scales. In a study of the factors accounting for the differences in social characteristics between a wide sample of English towns, Moser and Scott[29] found that 30 per cent of the variance could be accounted for by social class, the largest single component. Such indices of health as infant mortality continually show a social-class differential.[30] Despite the long-term absolute decline in infant mortality this century it is only in comparatively recent years that there has been a decline in the relative differential between the classes.

Perhaps the single most important of these differences in life chances is education. One of the more significant and enduring effects of social class on education is found in the public schools, where an elite still purchases for its children access to segregated, privileged instruction, with a strong probability of it leading to high-status positions. The extent to which politics, industry, the civil service, the Church and the armed forces are dominated by the progeny of these schools, which at present contain less than three per cent of all boys aged fourteen, and $16\frac{1}{2}$ per cent of all boys in sixth forms, can be seen from the following,[31] which has been compiled from a variety of original sources:

Table 8. Percentage of posts filled by those with a public school education

	%
Conservative Cabinet (1964)	87
Judges	76
Conservative MPs (1964)	76
Ambassadors (1953)	70
Lieutenants-General and above (1953)*	70
Governors of the Bank of England (1958)†	67
Bishops (1953)	66
Chief Executives in 100 largest companies (1963)	64
Air Marshals (1953)	60
Civil Servants above Assistant Secretary (1950)	59
Directors of leading firms (1956)	58
Chairmen of Government Committees of Inquiry (1944–60)	55
Members of Royal Commissions (1960)	51
Civil Servants above and including Assistant Secretary (1950)	48
All City Directors†	47
BBC Governors (1949–59)	44
Members of Arts and British Councils (1950–9)	41
Labour Cabinet (1964)	35
Top managers of 65 largest firms (1953)	33
Members of Government Research Councils (1950–5)	31
Labour MPs (1964)	15

* Boarding schools only.

† Only six of the leading schools.

However, the influence of social class can be traced throughout the educational system, though at the same time egalitarian policies have recently been applied to reduce this effect.

At primary level, research[32, 33] has indicated how parental interest and encouragement, superior home conditions and values conducive to educational success have assisted children from non-manual backgrounds in performing better at the eleven-plus examination. Nevertheless, the designation of educational priority areas by the Plowden Report represented an attempt to counteract this tendency. Similarly, at secondary level the widespread abolition of the eleven-plus and the accelerated development of comprehensive schools were intended to equalize opportunity, although in some cases the lowest streams (or sets) are neglected in order to imitate the traditional grammar schools. There has been much debate about the extent to which equality can be achieved by such organizational means, since the influence of disadvantageous home conditions, economic pressures for early-leaving or the persuasive example of peers who have achieved an enviable economic independence[34, 35, 36] – well documented by the Crowther, Newsom and Plowden Reports – may still exert their influence in a changed educational structure.

These inequalities are partly a by-product of the continued existence of a traditional, but flexible, elite. Social mobility through education in Britain has been described[37] as a sponsored (as opposed to contest) system, whereby the existing elite co-opts members of other classes who manage to acquire *its* social norms and life styles. This is reinforced by the belief of many working-class parents that education, particularly its higher levels[38] is the preserve of other classes. Little and Westergaard[39] report that at each successive stage of education progressively smaller numbers of children survive to enter the next stage. As this process of elimination goes on, so the relative prospects of survival as between children of different social origin becomes steadily less equal. At age eleven to thirteen, a professional or managerial family's child has nine times as much chance of entering a grammar school as a manual worker's. At seventeen he would have thirty times as high a chance of being still at school. Among non-manual middle-class families, one in four of their children who go to grammar school go on to university; whereas only one in fifteen or twenty of unskilled workers' children who achieved grammar school do so. A far higher proportion of working-class children receive further education at non-university institutions, but these have long been characterized by the inferiority of their facilities in comparison with universities, just as secondary modern schools have worse facilities than grammar schools.[40]

It is the existence of these steep inequalities of effective educational opportunity that is one of the most important causes of rigidity in the structure of social mobility. This rigidity is, however, far from absolute, as it would seem that roughly one-third of the population is likely to stay in the same socio-economic grouping as their parents, a third to rise and a third to fall. The main study so far carried out on social mobility in Britain[41] found that of men born 1900 to 1909, 46 per cent of those with fathers in the upper occupational groups fell in social status, while 53 per cent of sons of semi-skilled and unskilled manual workers rose. However, long-range movement up and down the scale was more limited, most mobility taking place at the manual/lower non-manual level. Although over 60 per cent of sons of fathers in the top classification fell in status, their chances of staying in that group were thirteen times greater than random.

Social class and life styles
Differences in life styles, while strongly influenced by class differentials, cannot always be attributed to class inequalities, but reflect also variations in habits, culture and way of life. Whereas in the past differences in family size between the classes corresponded to unequal access to information on birth control, and therefore pertained to life chances, increasingly with the development of family-planning facilities this factor becomes an aspect of life style. The following quotation summarized the present situation according to the 1961 census:[42]

For those married for between ten and 14 years the mean family size of the unskilled manual group is 2·30 compared with 2·02 for the semi-skilled manual group, and there are progressively lower means through the skilled manual, foreman and service worker groups until that of 1·68, recorded for the lowest non-manual workers. Then the curve swings upward, reaching its high point on the other side with the professional self-employed groups. Professional employees have slightly lower means.

The other more qualitative elements in life style might be summarized under housing and domestic environment, pattern of communal interaction, speech and social control, the use of leisure, and differential receptivity to high culture. The lower working class is characteristically housed in rented accommodation or in subsidized council housing, whereas the middle class aspires to owner-occupation (preferably detached and at a distance from industrial locations) or the more expensive type of flat. The difference between the lower middle-class semi-detached house on a mortgage and the council house is very marginal; indeed, as in everything else, differences are minutely graded (and regionally varied) rather than grossly contrasted.

In the more crowded older urban centres working-class life achieves a density of communal interaction based on kin and neighbourhood which contrasts with the more tangential middle-class relations of the suburb, even though such communal elements are attenuated (privatized) by moves to housing estates or high tower blocks.[43, 44] To the extent that the middle class consists of 'the migratory elite', its pattern of relationships is professional and inter-area, and this contrasts with the older professions (doctors, lawyers, clergy) and minor businessmen who put down local roots and took up local responsibilities, particularly in the smaller towns.[45] Whereas the working class depends more for assistance and support on neighbours and kin, the middle class tends to employ paid help.

The clearest and most enduring mark of class consists in accent, regional and proletarian speech contrasting with the haughtily swallowed or exquisitely vowelled Establishment speech.[46] Middle-class vocabulary is naturally more wide-ranging and abstract, characteristics which ease passage through the educational system where its norms tend to predominate. Similarly, despite the increased availability of cultural pursuits due to the mass media, the use of leisure by the different social classes is connected with a differential receptivity to high culture. However, the working-class preference for the commercial television channel[47] should not allow one to forget about the existence of an uncultured section within the middle class, often found among the new professions. Sport, too, tends to be minutely graded, partly in terms of expense involved and partly as a result of class-bound customs: the upper class still shoots grouse and the lower class fancies pigeons.[48] Institutionalized religion and indeed the whole range of interests in voluntary associations are also frequently defined as belonging to 'them' rather than 'us'. The principal exceptions are Pentecostal religion among West Indians and Catholicism among the Irish. Belief in and identification with the Church of England – as distinct from practice – are fairly evenly spread through the status hierarchy. Quakerism, Unitarianism, Humanism are largely confined to upper-status groups; the Free Churches (Methodist, Baptist, Congregational) are strongest in the groups of medium status. These churches have been the source of a semi-autonomous life style, now under pressure, but still diffused widely beyond their institutional borders and based on respect for education, self-help and independence, voluntary association for singing, thrift and mutual aid, all of which characteristics are of prime importance in understanding the resistance of the English (and Celtic) cultures to 'mass society'.

In sum, and allowing for all the minute gradations and immense variety in regions, occupations and milieux, the working class remains more localized, communal, more contiguous both at home and leisure, more concrete and emphatic in its verbal and decorative style, and above all more inclined to view the social world within the perspective of 'us' and 'them', conceived in terms precisely of these differences of style rather than in terms of political opposition. The problem of equality, even in a society where the overall standard of living has been raised considerably during this century, is that superior status groups can always attempt to utilize non-monetary differentials like speech to maintain social distance, and that as soon as a lower status group acquires the leisure opportunities, household amenities and sartorial appearance which were once exclusive, new areas of exclusiveness are marked off, such as holiday patterns.

Social class and power

Class membership is associated with differential decision-making power in a variety of spheres, in spite of the existence of constraints on its exercise. First, positions of high authority within industry provide their incumbents with wide powers of control, despite the relative decision-making deprivation sometimes experienced among the highly placed, and particularly technical, personnel. Large-scale industries can shape their own markets, determine the course of technological development, and significantly affect the country's pattern of investment. Further, industrial interests are in a strong position to put pressure on Government. It is not, however, always easy to identify the class interest pursued by lobbying. Sometimes it may be the interest of owners and shareholders, at other times those of the leading executives, and occasionally the whole cross-class group of people whose fortunes are bound up with a particular enterprise, industry or region. A restriction of the power and scope of private enterprise derives jointly from nationalization, the civil service, government legislation, various state boards and the countervailing power of trade unions. The latter is particularly important in that it is evidence of power derived from a different class base. It is thus not possible to argue simply that large-scale property ownership brings with it unbounded power in modern Britain.

Participation in decision-making and control activities outside the occupational sphere varies also with socio-economic background. For many years participation in government and politics was restricted to the landed and entrepreneurial classes, with a fair sprinkling of lawyers and other professionals.[49] The rise of the Labour Party saw a great influx of manual workers, particularly miners, and trade union officers, although in more recent years there has been a swing towards a new group of professionals – journalists, teachers and university lecturers.

At lower levels of participation in political activity, pressure groups and voluntary groups of various kinds tend to have membership drawn from the more articulate middle classes,[50, 51] with, of course, the great exception of the trade-union movement. Finally, at the minimal level of participation implied by voting in elections, the proportion of abstentions among poorer manual workers tends to be greater than among other classes.[52]

*　　*　　*

The inequalities thus established between social classes extend in their influence throughout life, leading to the existence of distinctive class life styles, and affecting every sphere in which differences of power and wealth operate. It remains to be seen how far differences of power and wealth *can* operate, what checks exist on their operation, and what is the nature of these checks. It is to these problems that the next section is devoted.

MARXIAN PROBLEMS: CONCENTRATION OR PLURALISM?

For a Marxian model of class structure to apply to modern Britain, it would be necessary to identify a ruling class made up of the elite from industry and government. It is certainly possible to identify the small group of powerful men whose positions of leadership and/or influence are perpetuated by inherited wealth. The high degree of internal cohesion in this group has been evidenced by research on interlocking directorships[53] and studies showing its disproportionate representation among leading politicians and in other elite positions. Further, the power of the industrial interest has grown with increasing industrial concentration. This recent trend is very different from the movement of cartelization, monopoly and massification that took place between the wars as part of a defensive 'rationalization' in the face of economic adversity.[54] Now the prime mover of concentration is the growth of the giant corporation based on modern automated methods. Galbraith[55] has suggested six main consequences of this development: first, an increasing span of time separates the beginning from the completion of the productive task; second, there is an increase in the capital that is committed to production; third, the commitment of time and money tends to be made even more inflexibly to the performance of a particular task; fourth, technology demands heavy concentrations of skilled manpower; fifth, there is an increasingly large and specialized organizational structure; sixth, these investments of time, money, skill and organization being so great, there is a need for careful planning to ensure that the smooth progress of the production and subsequent marketing are unimpeded.

Galbraith is mainly writing of the American economy,

where these developments have gone furthest; but they are by no means without application to Britain. Enterprises in Britain are growing in size and declining in number, and an Industrial Reorganization Corporation has been established to facilitate the process. The Government is, as suggested by Galbraith, increasingly called upon to underwrite major technological investments and share the enormous risk-bearing, leading to an increasing identification of interest between government and industry. There has been a great increase, through the National Economic Development Council and its associated industrial committees, of inter-firm and inter-industrial planning and co-ordination. Industry has begun to stake a greater claim in the activities of the educational system. And there has been an attempt at achieving more industrial stability through an incomes policy.

In addition to this development within the borders of individual countries, the increasing scale of industrial enterprise has led to the emergence of the international corporation; richer than several nation states, these firms are able to choose between the countries in which they carry on their activities – an important lever on government policies.

It is clear that these trends must have an important effect on the balance of power within a society, but what are the implications of this shift for social class? Miliband,[56] who is mainly concerned about the role of privately owned industry, sees an intensification of existing cleavages. Galbraith,[57] however, who acknowledges little difference between the changes taking place in capitalist economies and in socialist ones, contends that power is moving into the 'technostructure' of industrial enterprise, and that this power is so institutionalized that it cannot be attributed to any group of individual persons. This whole area remains one of the most unexplored, though possibly most important, aspects of modern social structure.

The difficulty of dubbing industrial power 'class' power is not limited to the field of modern technology. Throughout the economy the interests of many people in a firm, an industry or a whole region may be bound up in the decisions of the directorate of individual companies. An example is the campaign for regional development waged by industrialists and trade unions alike in the relatively depressed areas of Britain.

It is also extremely important, in assessing the power of those in superior positions in industry, to analyse the crucial checks which may be imposed on this power by trade unions and by the existence of a Labour Party as one of the two dominant political parties in Britain. There may be some doubt about the direction in which this potential countervailing power is exercised, and it has been suggested[58] that the Labour Party has now become the party of technology, leaving the working class without Parliamentary representation. It is only possible in the scope of this chapter to point out that governments still exercise some powers of restraint and control over industry and must at least on occasions be responsive to the electorate. Unsurprisingly this affects the policies of all parties who seek public office and the much-observed similarity between parties is not the result of one-sided compromise by the forces of the Left. Thus, although the existence of an industrial elite conforms to the image of a class society, there are constraints upon this elite. Corporations have to exercise their power within a tight network of laws and regulations. The geographical location of industry is controlled by a more elaborate system of regional policies than in virtually any other country of Europe. Workers' safety, consumer protection, amenity legislation, taxation, government-planning organizations – all these create the restrictive context within which the corporations, great and small, must take their decisions. Of course, an international company may sometimes be strong enough to insist on expanding in an area formally banned to industrial development; damage to amenity is by no means checked in every case; the consumer is by no means always sovereign; but the network of controls is important enough to render the image of the completely class-ruled society a caricature.

The Marxist image can always be rescued by simply redefining all these controls as steps that the ruling class has had to take in order to continue its rule. But even if such an interpretation is accepted, it entirely misses the point and misunderstands what is meant by pluralism. If an industry's interests demand, for example, that it take care of the safety of its workers, then this is in some limited way a reflection of the power of those workers, although, of course, it cannot be assumed that this coincidence of interests will necessarily extend over a wide area. It may be a very different sort of power from that exercised by the company, but that is precisely what pluralism is about: a system of checks and balances brought about by the coexistence of different kinds of power.

The theory of the managerial revolution, mentioned above, is often put forward as further evidence that class structure in the classic mould is fragmenting and that ownership is becoming progressively divorced from control. But stock ownership remains highly concentrated. The few still own large holdings and the many own smallholdings, even if there has been some diffusion. The top executives themselves are usually large stockholders, though not necessarily in their own company. The partial division of function cannot realistically be viewed as a sharp break with profit maximization as the main motive of business enterprise. However, the theory does retain its point in indicating a degree of general devolution and delegation of authority within industry. Although ultimately and formally all power in an enterprise resides at the top, delegation nearly always implies a certain shift in direction and autonomy. The problems of implementing at ground-level policies decided at the top are notorious, and possibly modern technology is intensifying this process.

This autonomy may extend to the manual worker. Although managers will retain, and no doubt often use, a vast battery of pricks and goads ranging from incentive schemes to dismissal, the worker in a large factory may be protected against this by the unofficial norms of the work-group, by unions, and by the wider supports often available from the work-force as a whole. Structurally he is semi-dependent; but in terms of the psychology of the work-place surprisingly autonomous. Indeed, management may find itself able to *decide* within only the most restricted and delicately demarcated areas. Take the role of a bus conductor, in itself a fairly lowly status based on service, but also affording the constant use of authority against every other status position, with the added protection of the work-group norms preventing any too-frequent exercise of restraining power by the inspectorate.

The drive to professionalization similarly creates new areas of autonomy for different groups. The changes in an opposite direction taking place in the lower levels of clerical employment, parallel with increased responsibility in certain 'manual' tasks in advanced industries, indicate other areas of change. It becomes increasingly difficult to mark a clear break between employers-controllers-wealthy on the one hand and employees-powerless-poor on the other. Just as responsibility and autonomy at work are delegated and spread, so the structure of income differentials becomes more confused. Finally, the emergence of the new poor as a group set apart even from other manual workers is relevant to a study of class relations, since any measures designed to improve their position, such as subsidies and income transfers or the operation of an incomes policy, must involve a charge on the mass of better-paid workers as well as on the wealthy.

Private consumption and the welfare state
Turning to patterns of consumption, life chances and life styles, two great changes since 1945 have made a distinctive impact on the pattern of class relations in the 1960s. These are the general increase in prosperity and the strengthening of the Welfare State. Both developments have raised the position of nearly everybody, while leaving the *relative* distribution of resources untouched. The inequality between more and less, the Have Mores versus the Haves, has replaced that between the possessors and the dispossessed, the Haves versus the Have Nots. This does not simply mean that the earlier pattern has been reproduced at a higher level. Inequality has been shifted to areas where its operation is less harsh, less fundamental, less invidious, less provocative. In any case, workers (and professionals for that matter) assess their relative deprivation within a restricted frame of social reference such as occupations which traditionally have been more or less comparable. More manual workers have cars, fridges and washing machines; more wealthy families have two cars and better appliances. There are now publicly provided health services, social security benefits, free education and grants towards further education, subsidized local authority housing: but these measures are partly diverted from their egalitarian aims by the continued existence of

private provision and by inadequate investment in the public sector.

Britain has moved away from the classic image of a class society, but although it has moved in the direction of a pluralistic, fairly egalitarian society, the move has been partial, halting, possibly on occasions reversed. We cannot assume that the movement must necessarily continue in the direction of further equality: some indicators, such as income from private property, suggest a reverse trend. British class structure may best be described as a pluralistic one, but it is a heavily skewed and weighted pluralism. And by and large the skewing and weighting conforms to the classical model of class inequalities. A more comprehensive summary of the balance of this weighted pluralism is provided by the following table:

Table 9

Area	Factors favouring continuing influence of Class	Factors reducing the influence of Class
Politics	Class bias of membership of Governments, Parliament, Civil Service and other authorities.	Power of Labour Party and Trade Union movement. Need, with universal suffrage, for all Governments to make some appeal to mass element.
	Power of industry to influence Government, through attempted identification of its interests with those of national prosperity, and through economic power.	Network of legislation designed to make private industry in some ways compatible with 'national interest' (e.g., regional development policies.
	Greater ability of middle class to organize and lobby through pressure groups.	
	* Traditional working-class isolation from Government and authority (them/us relationship); 'deference' vote among working classes.	

* These aspects are discussed in the following section.

Area	Factors favouring continuing influence of Class	Factors reducing the influence of Class
Economic/ Industrial	Tendency to concentration in industry; rise of the international corporation. Importance of wealth in ownership and control of industry. 'Prerogative' of management within enterprise. Differentials in rewards and conditions of work.	Delegation of management functions. Rise of professionalism. Routinization of clerical work coinciding with increased skill and autonomy of some technical tasks. Power of unions, and power of worker through full employment. Cross-cutting nature of conflicts (e.g., inter-industry conflicts; workers and employers *versus* consumers). Lack of clear dichotomy between interests of workers and employers
Elite Cohesion	Public schools as common background of elites in professions, industry, politics, military. Interlocking directorships. Continuance of distinctive upper-class life style. Role of inherited wealth and of class differentials in education.	Social mobility. Emergence of element of meritocracy. Flexibility and reforming impulses of elite; 'liberal' elements in elite ideology.
Life Chances	Effect of inequality of wealth and income on: education housing health diet possessions	Change in wealth/income structure from pyramid to lozenge mainly through emergence of *'nouveau pauvre'*.

Area	Factors favouring continuing influence of Class	Factors reducing the influence of Class
	General differential access to the good things in life through differences in wealth, status and knowledge.	Welfare State as provider of basic minimum. Shift in area of operation of inequalities as result of general prosperity (i.e., TV, cars, home aids, holidays abroad)
Life Style	Continued existence of certain class cultures.	Emergence of elements of cultural homogeneity through mass media.

DURKHEIMIAN ASPECTS: VALUES AND LEGITIMACY

As Montesquieu observed in his distinction between monarchy and despotism, it is insufficient to note the formal position of a ruler without examining the network of constraints and prohibitions on him resulting from the values and traditions of the wider society. Similarly, an analysis of the broad values that guide and inhibit action fills out our characterization and suggests an answer to the second of our two major problems: the need to account for the combined conservatism and flexibility of British society.

Institutionalized compromise

Several extremely important trends in British history produced its distinctive style of institutionalized compromise, observed by and imposed upon both establishment and dissent. In Alasdair McIntyre's[59] view the crucial institutionalization of compromise occurred in the latter years of Britain's period of prosperity 1850–75, that is, in 1865–75. These were the years of legislation for unionism and of the appearance of the working-class Conservative under Disraeli's auspices. The important point about these years, however, is that they crystallized a set of attitudes which precluded from the start a Marxist movement of any importance whereas, say, in Germany, a substantial Marxist movement had to wait for ameliorating influences, including affluence, within capitalist society to experience any substantial erosion. In McIntyre's view certain secondary virtues of pragmatism, co-operation, tolerance, fair play and compromise took first place to the exclusion of any totalizing perspective, whether political or religious. Religious dogmatism weakened into moralism or amorphous generalities held outside any ecclesiastical format, and no political dogmatism was able to take its place.[60] All this is as true of Britain today as it was then, but the intervening crises and changes are worth indicating.

Although the first world war assisted the resolution of several crises, the onset of depression, particularly in the mining areas, again built up to industrial crisis and the General Strike of 1926. This was the period when a substantial leftward movement could have occurred in Britain, but on the whole it did not succeed in breaking the pragmatic, reformist and liberal traditions of the Labour Party. Even in 1927, the Mond-Turner conversations symbolized an attempt to reinstitute compromise. Moreover, the crisis of 1929 occurred while Labour was in office and the Labour Party was regarded as responsible. The National Government of 1931 had the biggest majority ever, and the leftward turn of both the Labour Party and sections of the intelligentsia took place in the context of electoral rejection. Nevertheless the period of Labour Government 1945–51 was one in which social democratic policies were implemented at least in part: substantial nationalization and planned economy, socialized medicine, the extension of welfare, the dismantling of empire, the narrowing of income differentials. The Welfare State, in particular, took its place in the political consensus. By the late 1950s, however, there was a discernible shift of political debate away from these concerns to those of technical efficiency, rationalization, productivity and solvency. Just as the social democracy of the immediate post-war period characterized both Labour and Conservative parties alike, so have the technocratic concerns of recent years been similarly characteristic of both parties. The essentially competitive nature of British politics leads to reforming impulses inaugurated from the Conservative side and to rationalizing impulses from the Labour side, and in so far as the latter disturb the deeply rooted conservatism of British society, the Labour Party again receives disproportionate blame. Fundamentally, however, the problem of Labour as the party of the English working class is that it operates within a profoundly conservative society, and this is well symbolized in the fact that the oldest 'proletariat' in the world in industrial Lancashire is a conservative one. But this conservatism – most convincingly documented in McKenzie and Silver's *Angels in Marble*[61] – is of a very special kind and must not be confused with authoritarian reaction. It rests on the twin pillars of a flexible elite and a more or less politically integrated working class.

The flexible elite

At the centre of English political culture is an absorbent and flexible elite, usually ready in the long run to concede whatever is necessary to its continued existence, and only resorting to repression on a small and local scale and when confident of its success in doing so. The more it has conceded, the more continuous has been its dominance; and the more habitual its dominance, the more it can afford to concede. Each 'leap in the dark', the urban, rural and female franchise for example, has assisted the survival of the elite. Thus it has been able to live in the aura of a tradition barely broken, and on cultural symbols the more powerful because the more covered with the patina of time. It may allow economic parity and intermarriage to a rising bourgeoisie, but will gentle them with elite education; it may admit parity of political and economic power with trades unions, but will infiltrate the working class with appropriate deference. Indeed, members of the elite may even 'earn' that deference by ideals of service exercised within a paternalistic framework. Not universally so, of course: those responsible for the enclosure movement or the depopulation of the Scottish Highlands earned nobody's deference, but paternalistic care and concern has been a frequent enough *motif* in the English upper class for the epithet, 'he's a real gentleman' to be used without irony by older people to this day. The psychology of deference among those in loyal, personal dependent relations with the elite, particularly domestics, is still operative. Certainly the royal family is the clearest exemplar of the motif of service: through it they have graduated from disputed power to undisputed influence, and have become simultaneously the keystone of a status group and the symbol of a nation. By the same token the English Church, so closely knitted historically to the gentry style, manages to be both a remote and barely comprehended repository of a cultural ethos and also the symbol and focus of a nation's traditions.

Paradoxes of this kind remain central to English life. They are the essence of a genius for the kind of gentle archaism which maintains continuity of symbol and thus psychological security while modernizing the substance, and which has prevented any rising group acting out the logic of its position to the point where it could establish new systems of legitimation.

Legitimacy is central to stratification, and in Britain it operates by accumulation and assimilation, and not by revolution. A revolution is normally the work of a new social force claiming a rational legitimacy superior to tradition, and therefore demanding a more absolute because more seemingly justified loyalty from 'the people'. Gentle archaism has been strong enough to prevent any tyranny in the supposed name of 'the people' (or the proletariat) and not strong enough to avoid continuous compromise. It is on this loom that the complicated, inconsistent tapestry of English liberties has been woven. This has enabled an Englishman to identify not so much with 'the people' or 'the masses' but with his individual rights as a citizen which, rightly or wrongly, he attributes to that complex of forces called the Constitution. If he is subject to injustice he is outraged primarily as an Englishman, less so as a member of a class, and this is central to any understanding of class-consciousness in Britain.

The integrated working class
The elite's flexibility is paralleled within the mass of the population by three different but complementary attitudes to the political system: (i) that of overall satisfaction with its operation in the mass interest; (ii) that of deference to the elite: and (iii) that of restricted selection of reference groups.

It is quite wrong to suggest[62] that English socialism derives from a betrayal of proletarian revolution by its leadership: that leadership is the direct expression of a cultural tradition compounded of liberalism, religious dissent, and a pragmatic temper that rejects all total ideologies and utopian changes for whatever localized gains are to be had. A Conservative Party armed with deference and a Labour Party armed with a sense of working-class identity must both ultimately compete for the vote of an uncommitted centre under liberal Queensberry rules, within the legitimacy accorded by the ballot, and in terms of the pragmatic gains they can offer and deliver. Working-class consciousness is there of course, but it is a consciousness of kind, not a unity of doctrine, and it is by no means universal: the working-class conservative comprises nearly a third of the electorate. Activists on either side may be the life blood of party organization, but the party which appeals to the nation in terms of the motives and ideals activating its party workers is doomed. Yet the British Liberal Party cannot revive, partly indeed because its social base is eroded and because the system favours the alternation of only two parties, but more importantly because it historically provided just that middle ground of personal liberty, welfare and moderate reform which neither of the other two dares repudiate.

Because the constitution is viewed as the source of individual liberty and because there is this agreed liberal and pragmatic centre to English life, the institutions of law and law enforcement are rarely called into fundamental question on the ground that they are creatures of a class, and can employ a relaxed style which actually renders challenge even more unlikely. The law is accorded an objectivity even greater than it deserves. The widespread respect for a policeman, who significantly remains unarmed, contrasts sharply with the situation obtaining in France or indeed in the majority of continental countries. This respect needs to be linked with the more diffuse influence of the English school, especially the primary school; both the policeman[63] and the primary school teacher[64] are drawn from the 'respectable' working class, and represent forces of immense stability within the society. Put shortly, English people are more prone to queues than barricades. This stability of political consensus is complemented by values of orderliness and of what constitutes a respectable decent way of life which are very widely diffused in working-class culture. Politics rests on and complements culture in the widest sense.

The idea of deference is closely related to this acceptance of the existing political structure. Nordlinger,[65] in a study ostensibly concerned with working-class Conservatism, ends by discussing the contribution made towards a stable political system by the attitudes of many supporters of the Labour Party as well. Parkin,[66] writing on a similar theme considers that Conservative values are so well entrenched in Britain that it is Labour voters who should be regarded as the 'deviant' group, even within the working class, rather than the working-class Tories on whom Runciman[67] and McKenzie and Silver[68] concentrate much of their attention. Nevertheless, this latter study provides us with a valuable profile indicating precisely what constitutes the attitude of deference. It is the acceptance of the superior ability to govern of the traditional elite rooted in belief in the symbols of that superiority: public-school education, inherited wealth, and so forth. It also involves trust in the ability of this elite to work unselfishly and impartially for a 'national interest' that is shared by all classes.

Finally, Runciman[69] found a great lack of awareness in the British working class of its relatively deprived condition within British society, or at any rate the lack of any great concern about it. This was mainly a function of a restricted choice of reference group: when asked to name a group doing better than themselves, manual workers were likely to choose another group of manual workers. They tended to be unaware of other groups doing better than themselves and in any case believed it just that non-manual workers do better than they. Even when an authority relationship becomes a problem, it is conceived in personalized terms rather than the impersonal form of class exploitation. Or it may be seen in terms of 'Them' and 'Us', in which all kinds of different entities play the roles of 'Them' and 'Us'. In any case, conflicts in which 'They' are the *local* management increasingly centre on such instrumental matters as more pay.[70] Alternatively, attention centres on the way particular persons play particular authority relations within one's own perceptual vicinity. In the vague distance there remains a generalized 'Them', as unspecific as the High God of Anglican theology, who is the scapegoat of current misfortunes, and this 'Them' notably includes all politicians of whatever persuasion and most bureaucrats.

Indeed, the Generalized Them is almost equivalent to large-scale organization, of which the state is the largest and most blameworthy. So much for nationalization. Where a Britisher cheers the person of the monarch he impugns the organization of the state – a subtle and happy division of function and loyalty. But apart from this Generalized Bureaucratic Other is the whole series of 'others' who *vary* from time to time, but are quite frequently strikers in unions other than one's own, even within the same plant. One's own aspirations as a status group or profession for the good life are endorsed, but these are seen as in competition with other status groups who constitute the blameworthy 'Them'.

CONCLUSION

Like the Sovereign, the British elite reigns, ensconced as the apex of a hierarchy of wealth and status, but it rules only by the grace of a liberal consensus and by virtue of the pragmatic test. Its authority retains the aura of legitimacy provided that authority appears as no more than influence. The deference it still evokes depends on the observance of normative constraints which are rooted in the ordinary man's sense of fair play. We have shown that the inequalities it represents are cumulative, not only in terms of the concentration of wealth and privilege in the small upper middle class but also at each point in a minutely graded hierarchy of status articulated throughout the broader bands of class, including the working class itself. Yet such inequalities are perceived only within a restricted range of local and immediate comparisons, and the conflicts based on them express a continuous jockeying for place rather than the major oppositions of class warfare operative over a wide front. The sense of class gives rise to no more than a pervasive awareness of 'us' and 'them' symbolized most clearly in differences of cultural style.

We have argued that the liberal consensus constrains both major political parties to the point where the Liberal Party itself has a diminished *raison d'être* and must submit to the persistent theft of its clothes because its rivals realize that there is no other acceptable political dress. Thus, while Britain is a conservative society in its attitudes and in its deferential bearing it is also a society without a genuine right wing. By the same paradox, it is a social democracy with well-developed social services and an apparatus of governmental restraint, yet these rest on appeals to decency, to minimum standards for all, and to brotherly solicitude which have little to do with the traditional dogmas of left-wing parties elsewhere. British politics, like British religion, consists of ways of acting, of a nice sensibility to the safe range of variation on hallowed precedent, of modern innovations allowed to prove themselves by competition with traditional models. In such a situation the Right represents a cultural manner but it cannot define the political matter. With the Right confined to manners and a Left reduced to brotherhood and morality in a society where widespread comfort, however modest, renders unlikely any fundamental change, liberalism may pursue liberty unhampered by fear of totalitarianism, or by anticipation that conflicts between Haves and Have Mores will disrupt the pattern. It has done so now for over a hundred years.

We conclude that pluralism in Britain is not based primarily on competition between groups equal in power and prestige, but on an elite which gives enough to prevent its having to give more to groups which have enough power to make it give more if it does not give enough. This elite sponsors those whom it co-opts through social mobility, and in spite of the lacerations and drop-outs involved throughout that process its worst acerbities are muted in so far as what sponsorship asks is a style and an attitude which mere intelligence can easily acquire. Mere wealth, by contrast, may conspicuously consume itself in incongruous display when it would be more gainfully employed acquiring the style. This is, of course, one rationale of expensive public schooling. Part of the contemporary problem of mobility and of sponsorship is that so many mobile persons are required, and an increasing proportion of them by the needs of a technology to which style is not particularly relevant. Rising expectations are in any case not compatible with rising numbers of aspirants who cannot be absorbed by the elite culture; meanwhile, the elite culture, by attempting to absorb them, can only experience a dilution of its distinctive quality, to which mass communication no doubt contributes. Thus cultural identification cannot be fully achieved nor rising expectations fully met. Those who do acquire the style often feel excluded from its appurtenances, whereas the mobile technologist feels excluded from the style. The conflict reinforces the resentments of a deviant section of the 'progressive' professional class,[71] thus providing a nice complement to that other and more fundamental paradox of British society – the working-class conservative.

NOTES

1 Cf. D. Thomson, *The Democratic Ideal* (1944), Chapter 1.
2 Cf. R. Miliband, *Parliamentary Socialism* (1961).
3 E. Hobsbawm, *Industry and Empire* (1968).
4 Barrington Moore, Jnr., *Social Origins of Dictatorship and Democracy* (1966), pp. 417–27.
5 R. M. Titmuss, 'War and Social Policy', in *Essays on the Welfare State* (1958).
6 R. M. Titmuss, *Problems of Social Policy* (1950), pp. 506 *et seq.*
7 G. Dangerfield, *The Strange Death of Liberal England* (1935).
8 The Census, England and Wales (1961).
9 T. H. Marshall, 'The recent history of professionalism in relation to social structure and social policy', in *Class, Citizenship and Social Development* (1963), pp. 160–3.
10 P. Halmos, 'The personal service society', *British Journal of Sociology*, 1967, p. 27.
11 D. Lockwood, *The Black-coated Worker*, 1958.
12 R. Blauner, *Alienation and Freedom* (1964), Chapters 6, 7.
13 R. Blauner, Chapter 5.
14 G. C. Allen, *The Structure of Industry in Britain* (1961), Chapter 1.
15 P. Townsend, 'Poverty, Socialism and Labour in power', in *Socialism and Affluence, Four Fabian Essays* (1967).
16 G. G. C. Routh, *Occupation and Pay in Great Britain, 1906–1960* (1965).
17 Routh, p. 107.
18 Routh, pp. 147–54.
19 J. H. Goldthorpe and D. Lockwood, 'Affluence and British class structure', *Sociological Review* (1963).
20 T. Lynes, *Pension Rights and Pension Wrongs*, Fabian Tract No. 348 (1963).
21 'Executive Salaries', *The Economist* (27 August 1966), p. 829.
22 R. M. Titmuss, *Income Distribution and Social Change* (1962).
23 Report of Committee of Inquiry into the Impact of Rates on Households (Allen Committee), Cmd. 2582 (1965), Table 221.

24 M. H. Peston, 'Equality and the fiscal system', *New Society* (1 April 1965), p. 7.

25 J. Hughes, 'The increase in inequality', *New Statesman* (8 November 1968), p. 622.

26 J. Revell, 'Changes in the Social Distribution of Property in Britain during the Twentieth Century', *International Economic History Conference* (1965).

27 O. Stutchbury, 'The Case for Capital Taxes', Fabian Tract No. 188 (1968).

28 J. Hughes, 'The increase in inequality', p. 620.

29 C. A. Moser and W. Scott, *British Towns* (1961), p. 14.

30 J. N. Morris and J. A. Heady, 'Social and biological factors in infant mortality', in *The Lancet* (1955, 26 February, 5 March, 12 March).

31 H. Glennerster and Richard Pryke, 'The Public Schools', *Young Fabian Pamphlet*, No. 7 (1964).

32 J. W. B. Douglas, *The Home and the School* (1964).

33 Children and their Primary Schools (Plowden Report) Central Advisory Council for Education (England), Vol. I, Part 3 (1967).

34 J. W. B. Douglas, *et al.*, *All Our Future* (1968), Chapters III, IV, VI, VII, XII, XXIV.

35 R. R. Dale and S. Griffith, *Down Stream* (1965), pp. 14–30.

36 B. Jackson and D. Marsden, *Education and the Working Class* (1962).

37 R. Turner, 'Modes of social ascent through education', in A. H. Halsey, *et al.* (ed.), *Education, Economy and Society* (1965).

38 Report of the Committee on Higher Education (Robbins Report), Cmnd. 2154 (1964), pp. 49–54.

39 A. Little and J. Westergaard, 'The trend of class differentials in educational opportunity in England and Wales', *British Journal of Sociology* (1964), p. 301.

40 *Half our Future* (Newsom Report), Central Advisory Council for Education (England), (1963), Chapters 2, 3, 25.

41 D. V. Glass and J. R. Hall, 'Social mobility in Britain: a study of inter-generation changes in status', in D. V. Glass (ed.), *Social Mobility in Britain* (1954).

42 G. Hawthorne and J. Busfield, 'A sociological approach to British fertility', in J. Gould (ed.), *Penguin Social Sciences Survey* (1968), p. 205.

43 M. Young and P. Willmott, *Family and Kinship in East London* (1957).

44 M. Stacey, *Tradition and Change* (1960), Chapters 6, 7.

45 Stacey, Chapter 3.

46 B. Bernstein, 'Language and social class', *British Journal of Sociology* (1960), p. 271.

47 J. Halloran, *The Effects of Television* (1970).

48 G. R. Lavers and B. S. Rowntree, *English Life and Leisure* (1951).

49 W. L. Guttsman, *The British Political Elite* (1963), pp. 38, 41, 82, 84, 102, 103, 105, 107.

K

278 *Contemporary Europe*

50 M. Stacey, *Tradition and Change* (1960), Chapter 5.
51 T. B. Bottomore, 'Social stratification in voluntary organisations' in D. Glass (ed.) *Social Mobility in Britain.*
52 J. Blondel, *Voters, Parties and Leaders* (1963), p. 55.
53 S. Aaronovitch, *The Ruling Class* (1961).
54 G. C. Allen, *The Structure of Industry in Britain*, Chapter 4.
55 J. K. Galbraith, *The New Industrial State* (1967), Chapter 2.
56 R. Miliband, *The State in Capitalist Society* (1969).
57 J. K. Galbraith, *The New Industrial State*, Chapter 9.
58 A. McIntyre, 'The strange death of social democratic England', *The Listener* (4 July 1968).
59 A. McIntyre, *Secularisation and Moral Change* (1967), pp. 24 *et seq.*
60 D. Martin, *A Sociology of English Religion* (1967), p. 67.
61 R. T. McKenzie and A. Silver, *Angels in Marble* (1969).
62 R. Miliband, *Parliamentary Socialism* (1961).
63 T. A. Critchley, *A History of Police in England and Wales, 1900–1966* (1967), pp. 145, 304.
64 A. Tropp, *The School Teachers* (1957), Chapter III *passim*, p. 262.
65 E. A. Nordlinger, *The Working Class Tories* (1967).
66 F. Parkin, 'Working class Conservatives', *British Journal of Sociology* (1967).
67 W. G. Runciman, *Relative Deprivation and Social Justice* (1966), pp. 142 *et seq*, and Chapter 9.
68 R. T. McKenzie and A. Silver, *Angels in Marble* (1969).
69 W. G. Runciman, *Relative Deprivation and Social Justice*, Chapter 10.
70 J. H. Goldthorpe, D. Lockwood, *et al.*, *The Affluent Worker: Industrial Attitudes and Behaviour* (1968), pp. 175 *et seq.*
71 Cf. F. Parkin, *Middle Class Radicalism* (1968).

9 West Germany

René König

To understand the structure of a given society it is inadequate to restrict analysis to a presentation of its contemporary situation because of the risk that the deeper trends in the structural development of this society would be missed. For this reason historical references have to be made to point to the origins of present structural trends.

In other words, attempts to study the structural changes of the German post-war society since 1945 cannot by any means be limited to an analysis of these twenty-five years without looking further back – to the early 1930s and the 1920s, to the period before 1914 or even to the beginning of the century and, in one case, as far back as 1882. Such a strategy is particularly useful when rapid changes are occurring, the trend of which cannot be caught by a snapshot of the present situation. Otherwise there would be a danger of confusing short-term events with the long-range trend.

As for Germany, 1945 seems too recent to be regarded as the starting-point for the contemporary social structure. Nevertheless, for many German historians it is still the 'year zero', and many outside observers have been inclined to accept this year as the beginning of a new phase of German history, including the origin of a new system of stratification. Sociologists, however, are accustomed to distrust what is all too obvious because the obvious is not always true, particularly when social structures and models of stratification are at stake. Both have an inherent durability and it is likely that their origins escape the contemporary observer. This is of the greatest importance when dealing with a developed industrial society with its inherent high degree of bureaucratization; Max Weber reminds us that, once established, a bureaucracy is practically indestructible. This fact in itself forces us to link the present situation to the immediate (pre-war) era and sometimes to an even more remote past.

It is easy to show that this is a practical approach, as can be seen by using an example from another field of research. In post-war Germany we can observe, as in many other countries, an enormous increase of divorces in the years from 1945 to 1948. In fact, divorces per 100,000 population more than doubled between 1939 and 1948. This gave rise to a long discussion, the essence of which was once again the prediction of the imminent end of marriage as an institution. But if a wider perspective is taken it is easy to see that the enormous rise in divorce was nothing but a temporary event, limited in time, without any effect on the secular trend. A glimpse at the following table will make that clear.

Table 1. Divorce in Western Germany
(divorces on 100,000 pop.)

1914	26
1939	89 ←———
1948	187
1950	158
1952	105
1954	90 ←———
1963	88

The arrows indicate the general trend, while the figures enclosed between them require a separate explanation as a limited occurrence due to special causes. Similar developments are to be found in other countries as well (e.g., in England or in the Netherlands) after the first world war. Therefore, they can be said to be a limited short-term event within a long-range trend.

Taking the year 1945 as a starting-point, one might come to the conclusion that Germany, then, had ceased to be an industrial society. With its network of communications seriously injured, with one part of its industry destroyed by the effects of bombing and another part by dismantling, the Germany of the 'year zero' had in fact lost an impressive part of its industrial infrastructure. Does this, however, lead to the conclusion that Germany, in 1945, was no longer an industrial society?

The exact meaning of such a question requires clarification.

Does a society cease to be an industrial society when its factories have been destroyed by the effect of war? This approach appears too crude. An industrial society is not merely a complex of material goods, of factories equipped for the production of goods. It is, in addition to that, something different and something less trivial. An industrial society, properly speaking, is above all a system capable of self-reproduction. It is an organization comprising many institutions of training and higher learning which represent its real industrial potential by teaching how industrial plants can be constructed, equipped, organized and maintained, and this potential is far more important than the simple material presence of certain material goods. In other words, it is not the goods in themselves that are crucial, but rather the faculty to produce them. This is the most important difference between an industrial society and what has been called an economically underdeveloped society. The faculty to produce had not been destroyed in 1945; notwithstanding the enormous wartime destruction, Germany was still an industrial society.

This accounts for a series of facts which otherwise could not be explained. Among them the most important is that the population in rural occupations which had been declining throughout the nineteenth and twentieth centuries, still continued to shrink after 1945. This is contrary to what could have been expected and to what had actually been forecast by some German and foreign observers, that Germany would return to a more agrarian economic system. However, even during the worst period of need and want, such has never been the case. Thus, the percentage of population in agricultural occupations which, in 1939, had been 14·9 per cent of the active population had diminished to about 10 per cent in 1965, although it had stood at 22 per cent at the beginning of the century. The trend in the twentieth century is as follows:

Table 2. *Population in agriculture*

1900	1939	1955	1965
22%	14·9%	12%	10·87%

All the circumstances which seemed to indicate a decrease in the industrial potential of Germany after 1945 have proved ineffective in view of this development. This shows again that the observer of a complex society cannot limit himself to the contemporary situation if he wants to gain genuine insight into structural changes.

The same holds true for a strange prophecy of some German conservatives who really believed, between 1929 and 1933, that Germany had already reached the end of industrialization and that she would from now on return to a 'folk'-culture as opposed to industrial civilization (Hans Freyer, Werner Sombart). This prophecy corresponds in some way to the pessimistic outlook of the post-war observers, both German and from abroad. The rapid recovery of Germany in the post-war period can be explained by making reference to the secular trends and by neglecting the immediate post-war situation. With the monetary reform of June 1948 and with the help of the Marshall Plan and the European Recovery Plan (1947), the Federal Republic was able to recover very rapidly. Taking steel production as one index of economic productivity, Germany was back to pre-war standards as early as 1953.

Another point indirectly connected with the former and which recurred in post-war discussions was whether the structure of German society had become less differentiated under the impact of war and post-war developments. As a matter of fact, Professor Helmut Schelsky has coined the term of a 'levelled middle-class society' (*nivellierte Mittel-klassengesellschaft*) corresponding to a less differentiated German society. However, here too, it was easy to show that he had taken a passing state of crisis for structural change. On the contrary, if anything can be taken for granted in German post-war development, it is its growing differentiation, i.e., the opposite of what Schelsky had assumed. Again, it would be easy to show that this development is in conformity with pre-war trends originating from the period of economic reform during the 1920's.

This leads immediately to another assumption which seems to be more in line with the facts than the theory previously described. Far from being levelled, our contemporary industrial societies are much more differentiated than any society before. Incidentally, Raymond Aron emphasized this point immediately after the second world war, as did the author of this chapter. This furthered a new conception of the advanced industrial societies as 'pluralistic societies', a term which was first used in the immediate post-war period by Georges Gurvitch and which appears particularly apt. In fact, this pluralism seems to have reached such proportions today that social integration has become a problem in its own right. As opposed to most of the older types of society, the advanced industrial societies are so complex that it becomes questionable if the integration of such a system is still possible. Perhaps integration cannot be achieved any more in real life, but rather through the help of intervening symbols, maybe only with the aid of the social sciences. This particular situation may account for the fact that, as can easily be demonstrated, German post-war sociologists seemed more interested in a conflictual social system than in an integrative one. The controversy between Ralf Dahrendorf and Talcott Parsons seems to point in this direction.

The growing complexity of contemporary German society, begun already at the turn of the century, became more and more accentuated after the first world war and the second world war. The old Marxist prophecy, first developed in the Communist Manifesto, whereby simplification of the class system would be the main trend of development in industrial societies, simply did not come true. This prophecy can be refuted by several arguments of which we enumerate only the four most important. Firstly, the old middle classes did not disappear; secondly, many new professions developed and considerably broadened the old system of the capitalist bourgeoisie; thirdly, a 'new' middle class came into being, first from among employees in the field of industrial production, then with the inflation of 'services' in contemporary 'affluent' society; fourthly, a new class of industrial enterpreneurs originated as a consequence of new technological developments, part of them joining the old upper classes, another building up a new elite of technocrats, organization men and managers. This development was clearly outlined in *Grundriss der Sozialökonomie*, the large encyclopedia of the social sciences launched and edited by Max Weber and others before and after the first world war.

This growing complexity can be shown in all parts of

contemporary societies, in Germany as in other countries. Perhaps there is still a relatively homogeneous upper upper class although its role in public life seems to have become less and less important. While its power is still considerable its standing and its social prestige have declined. Today the very wealthy people cannot flaunt their fortune unashamedly. This is indeed an important difference between German society in contemporary times and at the beginning of the century. In imperial Germany, the upper upper class of the '*Junker*' displayed features of a new upper class adjusted to the new values of industrialism. In general, the class of the '*nouveaux riches*' in German industry, the '*Grunder*' who started the extraordinary boom of the late 1880's, the European and colonial businessmen, like the '*Junker*', loved ostentation in public life. Such an attitude furthered bad taste in German cultural life before 1914. This style of life corresponded exactly to what Thorstein Veblen called 'conspicuous consumption' at the turn of the century. The architectural and artistic horrors of the Bismarck and the late Hohenzollern era are a good testimony to this exhibitionistic capitalist feudalism and its incapacity to create a satisfactory cultural atmosphere of its own. However, this upper class was conscious of its importance and tried to impose this evaluation on the rest of society with the help of artistic symbols and through many other channels.

In contrast, the contemporary upper classes are by no means anxious to be over-conspicuous. On the contrary, they practise a special form of mimicry to pass for members of the middle classes. This seems to be a more or less general feature of all advanced industrial societies. Today, ostentatious feudalism only survives in underdeveloped societies where it has even become a means of national integration, partly even in underdeveloped societies with socialist governments. On the other hand, the *nouveaux riches* of the Federal Republic have not been able to develop a style of life of their own. They borrow cultural fragments from a variety of sources, by preference from the international jet-set, without having been able to create a new coherent life style. In other words: they are rich, even fabulously rich; however, they did not develop a value system of their own. It also seems that the rate of mobility of these new upper classes is so high that continuous turnover prevents family continuity. In this connection Professor Dahrendorf spoke of a complete capitulation of the German elites and upper classes in 1945. He also stressed the necessity for Germany to create *ex nihilo* a new upper class in the immediate post-war period.

However, it is felt – contrary to Dahrendorf's thesis – that the values of advanced industrial societies are not oriented towards the upper upper classes, but rather towards the middle classes. Therefore, the cultural role of the upper classes can be neglected in such societies, at least on a national level where they have become a very small minority. This does not exclude the possibility that the upper upper classes still play an important role on an international level, but this is outside the scope of the present contribution.

It is necessary to differentiate between two aspects of the problem discussed here before proceeding further. The first is closely connected with the Marxist prophecy discussed earlier and refers to the redistribution of percentages of the different social classes during the development of capitalist industrial societies into what has been termed advanced industrial societies. The second point is connected with the problem of whether or not a new value system has developed already in the new stratification system. As to the first aspect, it is easy to develop different structural models of the class systems in the Middle Ages, in capitalist industrial society and in the advanced industrial societies. These models show the dramatic decrease of the lower classes from a maximum of more than 90 per cent to approximately 20 per cent in the last third of the twentieth century.

Without going into details, it is apparent that (a) the system has become more and more complex and (b) that the lower classes have diminished so much that many societies need a continuous importation of unskilled labour from abroad. Each country solves this problem in her own way. West Germany received millions of refugees from Eastern Germany and other eastern countries; in addition, she has a foreign labour power of about one and a half million, mostly from Turkey, Yugoslavia, Greece, Italy and Spain. Among the refugee population many elderly people still live under very primitive conditions, although the younger ones have fully shared in the post-war boom.

Table 3

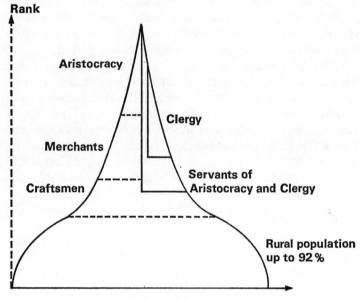

A. Middle Ages

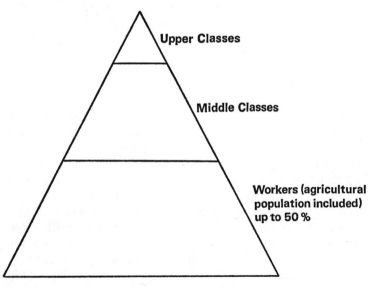

B. Capitalist Society

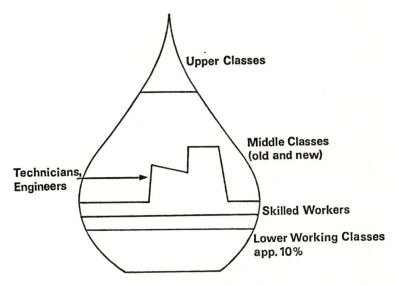

C. Advanced Industrial Societies

The essential point seems, however, to be the second namely, the restructuration of the value system of the new middle classes after the upper classes declined in social standing. This is also the main reason why the structural development of the middle classes has become a major problem today. In contemporary mass democracies value perspectives have to be restructured. This has become a major problem especially for Germany, because the middle classes achieved this historical role with a considerable time lag in relation to other advanced industrial societies in the world.

Since the process of differentiation of the German middle classes is still in full development, and since destructuration and restructuration are still occurring, value systems are still vague and fluid. Thus the contemporary German middle classes are undergoing a transformation which accounts for many hesitations and ambiguous decisions. Other advanced industrial societies have experienced the same development, with the essential difference that this occurred during the late 1920s and the beginning of the 1930s. The major problem for the future of the German middle classes will surely be the structuration of the contemporary plurality of value systems into a consistent middle-class ideology.

It is for this reason that so much attention has been paid to the middle classes. This by no means implies a neglect of the old lower classes, and in particular of the working class. But it is essential to understand that the working class is undergoing the same process of differentiation as the middle classes. One part of the working class has experienced an enormous rise in income which has completely changed its standards of living. This development has brought some of its sections nearer to the middle classes than ever before. This holds particularly true for highly skilled workers, technicians and engineers. An important indicator of this development is the replacement of a weekly by a fortnightly wage or even by a monthly salary with a year's contract. Therefore, the contemporary skilled worker cannot be compared any more to the old labourer with a low level of skills, with little hope for the future, i.e., for his children, and with generally low aspirations. In fact, one part of the former lower classes, the skilled workers, have changed completely. This implies that the whole of the contemporary lower classes have gone through a considerable process of change. As in the United States and in other advanced industrial societies with the chances they offer for training and learning, the unskilled labourers have become numerically less and less important. Skilled labour has become increasingly differentiated from unskilled labour, with a strong tendency to be absorbed into the ranks of technicians and engineers. On the other hand, it can easily be shown that the percentage of unskilled labour which is approximately 20 per cent of all the workers corresponding to approximately 10 per cent of the total gainfully employed population, has declined continuously since the beginning of the century. This also means that the national or native resources of unskilled labour are exhausted or nearly so and therefore it has to be imported from abroad. Everything seems to indicate that the class of unskilled labour is becoming smaller and smaller with the improvement of schools and opportunities for occupational training. The same holds true for the unskilled agricultural workers who had decreased to 3·8 per cent of the total active population by 1955. So much for the remainder of the underprivileged proletarians of the nineteenth century. This, incidentally, is particularly true of Western Germany since before the war the rural populations were mostly concentrated in the eastern parts of Germany, where the large estates of the '*Junker*' employed large numbers of rural proletarians, mostly of Polish origin.

This is not to deny that there are today underprivileged strata, but their composition has changed. Although many refugees from Eastern Germany and from other eastern European countries have had their full share in the economic boom from 1950 to 1970, many elderly persons are still economically deprived. Pauperism in advanced industrial societies mainly hits elderly people from sixty years of age onwards, and people with a low level of training, either because they did not have the opportunity to acquire skills, or because they were unable to live up to the requirements of industrial civilization.

The composition of the new lower class in Germany is therefore different from in the pre-war period. A significant section of skilled workers does not belong to it any more but is joining the middle classes both in terms of actual standards of living and of expectations. This development is the same as in the United States and in other European countries between 1925 and 1935. However, some obstacles have made it more difficult in Germany than in other countries. Again these are to be found mostly on the level of value formation.

This development is seriously hampered in Germany by the survival of the specific value orientations of the old German bourgeoisie. This inhibits the aspirations and lowers the self-esteem of the highly skilled workers because bourgeois values seem strange to them; therefore, they still do not dare to aspire to the same levels as the rest of society. Furthermore, these ideas contribute seriously to a separation of the highly skilled workers from other parts of the middle classes because the latter are mainly composed of non-manual workers and because non-manual work – according to bourgeois ideas – enjoys a higher esteem than manual. In complete opposition to this view, the truth seems to be that, under the impact of technological change, the limits between manual and non-manual work have considerably shifted. Thus, it could be stated that many of the purely manual activities of skilled workers are gradually disappearing and being replaced by intellectual and moral skills like, e.g., punctuality, concentration, responsibility, precision, comprehension of complex technological processes, and also a keen comprehension of the necessities and needs of complex organizations, etc. By contrast, some groups of employees seem to follow a downward trend in so far as the required skills become less and less important under the impact of both office mechanization and office automation. On the other hand, many categories of workers need a training that is on average much superior to that of many employees, with the result that a group of highly paid technicians has developed from among the skilled workers. While it was certainly true that skilled labour and employees could be distinguished until a generation ago by the distinction between manual and non-manual work, this differentiation does not apply any more today. New styles of work have appeared in the meantime which have changed these categories. What we need most today is a new classification of skills. In addition, it should be acknowledged that decision-making processes have become more and more integrated with a wider range of skills, or even taken over from some skills to a certain extent, which again forces us to reorganize our value schemes. It is true that, in Germany as elsewhere, this development has been observed several times already in the past, but it has been explained so far with the help of the old value standards alone. This is exactly how Schelsky's concept of the 'levelled middle-class society' originated. Admittedly, German society in 1945 and immediately after was certainly less differentiated than before the war, but this was only a transitional phase due to an acute state of crisis. On the other hand, the trend towards growing differentiation started again immediately after the economic recovery of the late 1940s and the early 1950s.

If it is true that certain great inequalities in the class systems of advanced industrial societies have disappeared due to a general trend towards democratization, it is also true that within this new system of mass democracy new forms of differentiation have appeared. It was Alexis de Tocqueville who hinted that in the new mass societies minor differentiations and nuances would become more prominent than the incisive class differences of the past. In our contemporary societies, slight shades become more significant, and have also more meaning for both the actors and the observers, than the more irreconcilable contrasts of yesterday. If on the one hand it seems that a more or less generalized style of life and of consumer behaviour has developed, one must admit on the other hand that at the same time innumerable fine distinctions and innuendoes of behaviour have emerged within this system.

These forms of differentiation have become a general feature of our occupational system. But, in addition and more specifically, they also hold true for single professions. Let us look, e.g., at the medical profession: once upon a time the medical profession was more or less represented by the medical practitioner, at best it was possible to differentiate the specialist from the general practitioner. Of course, these two types still exist, as can be seen from the curricula of most of our medical faculties. Besides this, however, a great variety of new medical professions have originated meanwhile, among them the medical experts in governmental health services, the medical doctors employed by the big industrial plants which often run health services of their own, the assistant doctors in the big hospitals, the clinic directors and administrators, etc., etc. But it is not only the medical profession as such which has become more and more differentiated; a whole range of new occupations with a medical character have come into being, auxiliary occupations of a more technical kind like the X-ray specialists, the anaesthetists, and also occupations with a more therapeutic nature from trained nurses to the different representatives of physical therapy, rehabilitation, etc. Finally, all these occupations are subject to considerable regional variation. It is in the urban centres that specialists and the complex bunch of auxiliary services are encountered, while in the countryside the general practitioner is still the rule and therapy properly speaking is still mostly exercised in the family. In the villages or even in the middle-sized towns, the general practitioner still belongs to the local dignitaries. Therefore, the village doctor still plays an important political role and enjoys a high esteem, while the city doctor does not, despite the fabulous prestige of the great and fashionable specialists.

However, apart from regional variations, there are also

important differences according to economic sector. If we accept for a moment Colin Clark's division into a primary, a secondary and a tertiary sector within the economic system, it is easily understood that an employee in the primary sector (e.g., the inspector of a big agricultural enterprise) differs from an employee in the secondary sector (e.g., a technical designer in a construction office), and finally that both are different from an employee in the service sector. As a matter of fact, the three of them engage upon three completely different types of work, although their representatives appear in government statistics under a common heading as 'employees'. Finally, these three categories all should be distinguished from the representatives of the cultural services, leisure-time services, recreational services, etc. Their essential skill is to mediate between services and people; most of the time they are concentrated in the greater urban centres, and have in general a highly urban character.

There are, however, other types of differentiation. In considering the workers alone there is a tendency to cling to the old concepts of the nineteenth century with its classical scheme of differentiation between unskilled, semi-skilled and skilled workers which only repeats a rank order from a completely different world, namely that of handicrafts. In this scheme it is especially the concept of the semi-skilled worker which has changed considerably. In the nineteenth century, he was a man who, most of the time, got an on-the-job-training of a few hours, a few days, a few weeks. In the twentieth century there are some traces of this old system, but there exists also a new type of semi-skilled worker who is not trained for a limited number of well-defined tasks, but who can be employed in a great variety of jobs. He can be characterized as a very intelligent, adaptable and versatile all-round worker. It is interesting to remark that this kind of worker comes from many different social backgrounds. He represents an entirely new category of workers, with a new style of life and a keen sense of self-confidence.

A similar situation prevails among the group of employees. It can be shown that, since they first appeared, they have been growing not only in absolute number but also diversifying in terms of occupations. In Germany, their numerical growth made a rapid start between 1882 and 1895 and has been developing at a high rate ever since, as can be seen from the following table:

Table 4. Relation of employees to workers

1882	1895	1907	1925	1939	1960
1 employee 2 workers	1 employee 13 workers	1 employee 9 workers	1 employee 4 workers	1 employee 4 workers	1 employee 2·5 workers

It is, furthermore, typical of this category of white-collar workers that they already started at a higher level of differentiation when compared with manual workers. They range from very small jobs like office and sales clerks, secretaries, typists, etc., to highly skilled occupations requiring a long and complicated training. The best way of classifying these different occupations is perhaps an order following the decision-making power corresponding to their respective activities. In the highest ranks of top industrial management, power of decision may be as big or even bigger than that of political leaders, and the strains are correspondingly great. At the other end of the scale are the incumbents of very subordinate occupations in the mechanized offices and administrative bureaux who do not, however, experience the effects of proletarization as did the unskilled in the nineteenth century.

All these occupations develop a variety of value systems and life styles. They are not only differentiated by their occupational activities, but also – and mainly – by their leisure-time activities which become more and more important. Reading of books, newspapers, magazines, illustrated weekly or monthly journals, consumption of broadcasting and television, preferences for movies, theatre, concerts, visits to museums and other exhibitions, and also participation in sports and similar activities – everything varies and differentiates group from group. Equally differentiated are the uses made of free time during week-ends, the ways vacations are spent, friends, neighbours or colleagues entertained, and eating-out or drinking-out patterns.

Here again one is confronted with new forms of differentiation in approaches to everyday life which are completely opposed to any kind of levelling. Even if it is true that all are dependent on the economic market, they are none the less at the same time independent in the choice of how they want to live. This eventually leads to a distinct polarization between work and leisure. If it is true that the pressure undergone in daily occupations becomes heavier and heavier, new escapes have been created in our leisure-time activities. This has even produced a label for contemporary post-industrial societies emphasizing that leisure plays a more important role than it has ever done in the past.

While all these problems are well known in contemporary Germany, the difficulties begin with their evaluation. It seems, in fact, that the old value systems still prevent a neutral assessment of all these factors when considering their function for human happiness. Therefore, the real problem of social stratification in post-war Germany is not so much the acceptance in practice of a new model of stratification, but rather the development of a new moral system. Therefore, new trends in the formation of images, values, ideas of the modern life situations may be more important than the material facts. It is the author's firm belief that we are witnessing today the advent of a new secular morality in Germany which corresponds to the self-awareness of this new society. It would be extremely interesting to follow up this new trend of ideas in more detail, but this is outside the scope of the present chapter.

BIBLIOGRAPHY

Baumanns, H. L., Grossmann, H., *Deformierte Gesellschaft?* Soziologie der BRD (Reinbek b. Hamburg, Rowohlt, 1969).

Bolte, K.-M. Typen sozialer Schichtung in der Bundesrepublik Deutschland. *Hamburger Jahrbuch für Wirtschaftsund Gesellschaftspolitik* (1963), Vol. 8.

Bolte, K.-M., Kappe, D., *Struktur und Entwicklung der Bevölkerung*, 4th ed. (Opladen, Leske Verlag, 1967).

Bolte, K.-M., Vertikale Mobilität. *Handbuch der empirischen Sozialforschung*, König, R. (ed.), Vol. 2 (Stuttgart, Enke, 1969), pp. 1–42.

Bolte, K.-M., Kappe, D., Neidhardt, F., *Soziale Schichtung* (Opladen, Leske Verlag, 1966).

Bolte, K.-M., Einige Anmerkungen zur Problematik der Analyse von 'Schichtungen' in sozialen Systemen. *Soziale Schichtung und soziale Mobilität. Sonderheft 5 der Kölner Zeitschrift für Soziologie und Sozialpsychologie.* Glass, D. V., König, R. (eds.), 3rd ed. (Köln–Opladen, Westd. Verlag, 1968).

Daheim, H. Neuere deutsche Veröffentlichungen zum Problem der sozialen Schichtung. *Soziale Schichtung und soziale Mobilität. Sonderheft 5 der Kölner Zeitschrift für Soziologie und Sozialpsychologie.* Glass, D. V., König, R. (ed.), 3rd ed. (Köln–Opladen, Westd. Verlag, 1968).

Dahrendorf, R., *Gesellschaft und Demokratie in Deutschland* (München, Piper, 2nd ed. 1968).

Eisermann, G., Die Struktur der sozialen Klassen in Deutschland. *Kölner Zeitschrift für Soziologie und Sozialpsychologie* (1965), Vol. 17, pp. 568–83.

Fröhlich, K.-H., *Die sozialen Schichtungen und Umschichtungen in Deutschland in der Zeit der Hochindustrialisierung* (Diss. Köln, 1959).

Fürstenberg, F., *Die Sozialstruktur der Bundesrepublik Deutschland* (Köln–Opladen, Westd. Verlag, 1967).

Geiger, Th., *Die Klassengesellschaft im Schmelztiegel* (Köln–Hagen, Verlag Gustav Kiepenheuer, 1949).

Geiger, Th., *Die soziale Schichtung des deutschen Volkes* (Stuttgart, Enke, 2nd ed. 1967).

Glass, D. V., König, R. (eds.), *Soziale Schichtung und soziale Mobilität. Sonderheft 5 der Kölner Zeitschrift für Soziologie und Sozialpsychologie,* 3rd ed. (Köln–Opladen, Westd. Verlag, 1968).

Hamilton, R. F. Einkommen und Klassenstruktur. Der Fall der Bundesrepublik. *Kölner Zeitschrift für Soziologie und Sozialpsychologie* (1968), Vol. 20, pp. 250–87.

Hofbauer, H., *Zur sozialen Gliederung der Arbeiterschaft.* Arbeiter und Angestellte in der Gesellschaftshierarchie (Köln–Opladen, Westd. Verlag, 1965).

Huffschmid, J., *Die Politik des Kapitals.* Konzentration und Wirtschaftspolitik in der BRD (Frankfurt/M., Suhrkamp, 1969).

Jaeggi, U., *Macht und Herrschaft in der Bundesrepublik* (Frankfurt/M., Fischer Verlag, 1969).

Janowitz, M., Soziale Schichtung und Mobilität in Westdeutschland. *Kölner Zeitschrift für Soziologie und Sozialpsychologie* (1958), Vol. 10, pp. 1–38.

Kätsch, S., *Teilstrukturen sozialer Differenzierung und Nivellierung in einer westdeutschen Mittelstadt* (Köln–Opladen, Westd. Verlag, 1965).

Kleining, G., Moore, H., Soziale Selbsteinstufung (SSE). Ein Instrument zur Messung sozialer Schichten. *Kölner Zeitschrift für Soziologie und Sozialpsychologie* (1968), Vol. 20, pp. 502–52.

Kluth, H., *Sozialprestige und sozialer Status* (Stuttgart, Enke, 1957).

Kruk, M., *Die oberen 30,000. Industrielle, Bankiers, Adlige* (Wiesbaden, Betriebswirtschaftl. Verlag Th. Gabler, 1967).

Mayntz, R., *Sozialer Wandel und soziale Schichtung in einer Industriegemeinde* (Stuttgart, Enke, 1958).

Münke, St., *Die mobile Gesellschaft*. Einführung in die Sozial-struktur der BRD (Stuttgart, Kohlhammer, 1967).

Nellessen, W., Nold, K., *Unterlagen der deutschen amtlichen Statistik für eine quantitative Abgrenzung der Mittelschichten* (Köln–Opladen, Westd. Verlag, 1963).

Scheuch, E. K., Daheim, H., Sozialprestige und soziale Schichtung. *Soziale Schichtung und soziale Mobilität. Sonderheft 5 der Kölner Zeitschrift für Soziologie und Sozialpsychologie*. Glass, D. V., König, R. (eds.), 3rd ed. (Köln–Opladen, Westd. Verlag, 1968).

Steiner, H., *Soziale Strukturveränderungen im modernen Kapital-ismus*. Zur Klassenanalyse der Angestellten in Westdeutschland (Berlin (Ost), Dietz Verlag, 1967).

Zapf, W., *Beiträge zur Analyse der deutschen Oberschicht* (2nd ed., München, Piper, 1965).

Zapf, W., *Wandlungen der deutschen Elite* (2nd ed., München, Piper, 1966).

10 Yugoslavia

Frank Parkin

The stratification system of contemporary Yugoslavia has been largely fashioned by a combination of modern industrialism and a somewhat novel interpretation of Marxian socialism. Ideology appears to have played a more formative role in Yugoslavia than in neighbouring Socialist states, and has given rise to a social and economic order which varies in important respects from the standard eastern European model. These variations came about as a direct result of government legislation introduced after the break with the Soviet Union in 1948. Until that time, and for a short while after, the class structure of Yugoslavia followed the pattern common to the People's Democracies. This period immediately following the revolution, and generally referred to as the period of 'socialist reconstruction', was marked by a series of sweeping social changes, many of them of an egalitarian nature. Their total effect was to strip away the social and material power of the pre-war bourgeoisie and rentier class and to distribute a greater share of rewards to the peasantry and the proletariat. Thus, about four million acres of land, much of it belonging to the Catholic Church, the banks, and the *Volksdeutsche*, were expropriated by the State; about half of it was redistributed to the peasants.[1] At the same time it was made illegal to hire labour and to rent or sell land. Similarly, industrial and commercial enterprises were nationalized, although small shops and handicrafts were mostly left in private ownership. Free health and welfare facilities were introduced on a far-more generous scale than ever before, as well as subsidized housing and travel for industrial workers. Villas belonging to the old bourgeoisie were confiscated for use as sanatoria, workers' holiday resorts, student centres, and the like. Food was rationed in accordance with the physical demands of an individual's occupation, favouring manual workers as against sedentary white-collar employees.

Income distribution showed a highly egalitarian trend. In 1938, according to Vinski's calculations, the professional, entrepreneurial and rentier classes comprised 5·3 per cent of the population, but absorbed 25·6 per cent of the national income. Industrial and agricultural workers, and the small peasantry, comprised 34·6 per cent of the population, but absorbed only 18·2 per cent of the national income.[2] In the post-revolutionary period, white-collar real incomes dropped considerably, while the blue-collar share increased. In 1951 the average earnings of highly qualified white-collar personnel were only 25 per cent more than the average earnings of manual labourers. Skilled workers earned on average only about 20 per cent more than the unskilled.

Far-reaching reforms were introduced in the system of education, designed to improve the opportunity structure of previously underprivileged groups. Among the most important of these were changes in the field of higher education. In the pre-war years access to university was confined largely to the children of the upper middle class and wealthy landowners. After the revolution, the abolition of fees and the introduction of a system of stipends, and subsidized student hostels, opened up the universities and technical institutes to a broader section of society. By 1951, 35 per cent of undergraduates were of peasant and manual working-class origin; by 1957 the figure had increased to 44 per cent.[3] The entry to university of young men and women from families without an established tradition of education shows no sign of abating at the present time. A 1965 study of students at the universities of Zagreb, Belgrade and Sarajevo, found that just over 60 per cent had parents whose own education did not go beyond the eighth grade of elementary school.[4]

Changes in the political structure also brought about rapid social promotion for certain categories of the population who formerly had menial status. Peasants and workers who served as Partisans in the resistance, or who were members of the clandestine Communist Party in the pre-war years, were drafted to fill managerial and administrative posts which could not be trusted to the old middle class. Partly as a result of these political appointments, and partly as a result of the social and economic reforms, Yugoslav society showed a considerable degree of fluidity and mobility. For example, Milić's analysis of the 1960 census has shown that about 30 per cent of those in white-collar positions in 1960 were either manual workers or peasants in 1946.[5] The extent of inter-generational mobility is no less marked than that of intra-generational mobility. Of men and women in non-manual occupations in 1960, 40·4 per cent were of peasant origin and 29·6 were of working-class origin.[6] Furthermore, it is important to note that much of this upward social movement consisted of 'elite' rather than 'mass' mobility. Thus, 48·9 per cent of highly qualified white-collar personnel were of manual and peasant background, as were 61·8 per cent of those in 'managerial' posts.[7] Clearly, this indicates a scale of change in the stratification system which is altogether unusual by Western standards. Taken together, the data summarized above offer little support to those who deny any causal relationship between ideology and the reward structure of industrial society.

As previously mentioned, many of the features of the Yugoslav social system during the phase of socialist reconstruction, were to be found in other eastern European states.[8] But from the early 1950's onwards a series of additional reforms were set in train which gave the stratification system a somewhat different character. The most important reforms were those which greatly reduced the extent of centralized control over the economy in favour of more reliance on market forces; and those which accorded the manual workforce an influential voice in the management of industrial undertakings. There is now an impressive volume of literature describing and assessing these innovations, and it would be out of place to discuss them at any length here.[9] Rather, it will be sufficient to confine ourselves to those aspects of workers' self-management and the operation of the 'socialist market' which have a direct bearing on the stratification system. It should at this point be emphasized that, notwithstanding these reforms, the stratification system is still best understood as a variant of the ideal-typical eastern European state. There can be no doubt that the class structure and the overall distribution of rewards in Yugoslavia are more similar to those of eastern than of western Europe.

Perhaps the best way of illustrating the contrast with Western capitalism is by reference to the fact that in Yugoslavia the main 'break' in the stratification system occurs not between manual and non-manual workers. The class structure of Britain and other Western societies is commonly presented in terms of a dichotomous model, expressing the material and social division between blue-collar and white-collar positions. Although it is well recognized that such a two-fold division is a fairly crude representation of the class structure, this has nevertheless proved quite serviceable in the analysis of many types of social behaviour. Crucial to this particular model is the recognition that skilled or craft workers, while enjoying certain market advantages over semi- and un-skilled workers, still have sufficient in common with the latter to place them all in a roughly similar 'class position'. Equally, it is held that lower white-collar groups enjoy the kind of status and long-term material advantages which warrant their inclusion with the middle-class proper, rather than with the upper ranks of the manual working class.

The conditions which justify this manual/non-manual division are not present to anything like the same extent in Yugoslavia. The most obvious cut-off point in the reward hierarchy occurs *within* the proletariat. Furthermore, lower white-collar groups do not comprise the tail end of a more prosperous professional middle class endowed with greater prestige; they are, in fact, in a decidedly inferior social and economic position to the skilled manual workers. Thus, if we wished to portray the overall reward structure in terms of broad occupational categories, the hierarchy of positions would run from high to low as follows:

1. Qualified white-collar employees (i.e. managerial, professional and technical personnel).
2. Skilled manual workers.
3. Lower white-collar employees.
4. Unskilled manual workers.

The fact that skilled workers occupy a more favourable position than those in routine non-manual occupations means that we cannot usefully speak of middle class and working class as separate and inclusive categories, with competing or conflicting interests, as we can for Western capitalist society. This can be well illustrated by an examination of the data relative to present social and economic inequalities in Yugoslavia.

One of the consequences of the economic reforms carried out over the past two decades has been the gradual erosion of the egalitarian incomes structure introduced after the revolution. The release of market forces has produced a steady drift towards increasing income differentials, favouring in particular the highly qualified and skilled occupational groups. Paul Landy, reviewing economic developments in the early 1960s noted that, 'The most recent statistics substantiate earlier worries that "the rich will become richer and the poor will be poorer".'[10] He pointed out that in 1960 wages in some enterprises ranged from about 8,000 to 70,000 dinars a month; by the following year the highest salaries had increased by more than 50 per cent, while the lowest had risen by only 25 per cent. The figures quoted by Landy refer to *individual* incomes, and it is certainly not the case that differentials of this magnitude reflect the movement of *average* earnings for different occupational groups. Nevertheless, if we examine the long-run trend of average earnings we find a clearly discernible pattern of increasing inequality.

Table 1. Income differentials in industry
(Wages of unskilled workers = 100)

	1951	1954	1957	1959	1961
White-collar					
Highly qualified ⎫		238	290	316	333
⎬	125				
Qualified ⎭		155	170	186	190
Unqualified	101	123	119	132	135
Blue-collar					
Highly skilled ⎫		205	223	243	249
⎬	120				
Skilled ⎭		146	149	159	160
Semi-skilled	105	118	117	125	124
Unskilled	100	100	100	100	100

Source: UN Economic Survey of Europe in 1965, Pt. II, Ch. 12, Table 12.8.

Table 1 shows the average income of different skill categories as multiples of the average earnings of unskilled manual workers. Thus, whereas in 1951 highly qualified white-collar personnel were earning only a quarter as much again as unskilled labourers, by 1961 they were earning three and a third times as much. Highly skilled manual workers also made rapid gains, consolidating their advantages over all white-collar groups except the most qualified. It is apparent that the most skilled manual workers are, by Western standards, privileged in relation not only to white-collar groups, but to unskilled workers also. In Britain, France, West Germany and the United States, skilled workers earn on average only about 25 per cent more than unskilled labourers. It could in fact be said that skilled workers in Yugoslavia comprise what might be called a 'labour aristocracy', a term which could not be applied to their counterparts in the West.[11] The division between this aristocracy of labour and the unskilled work-force is reflected in another crucial aspect of their general market situation – the incidence of unemployment. Un-employment rates have risen continuously over the past fifteen years, parallel with the growing emphasis on enterprise autonomy and market rationality. In most eastern European states unemployment tends to be of the 'concealed' variety; that is, enterprises hire labour over and above the level strictly required for productive efficiency. Clearly, this type of strategy is more feasible in a command economy than in one based more firmly on the market. Yugoslav enterprises are discouraged from taking on labour surplus to requirements, since this would mean an increase in the number of workers staking a claim on the firm's income, without a corresponding increase in the size of the income pool resulting from higher productivity. Consequently, the threat of unemployment is now a serious negative attribute of the market position of the manual worker. In 1952, there were 45,000 registered un-employed, or 2·6 per cent of the non-agricultural workforce; by 1963 the figure had reached 230,000, or 6·8 per cent, and it has continued to rise since then.[12] The situation of the unemployed is made more critical by the relatively meagre provisions for unemployment relief. This is perhaps partly due to official reluctance to acknowledge, until quite recently, that unemployment could occur on a large scale in a socialist society. However this may be, the fact remains that the conditions attached to the payment of unemployment benefits are extremely stringent by the standards of welfare capitalism, so that only a small minority of those seeking work prove eligible for relief.[13]

As might be expected, unemployment does not threaten all sectors of the workforce to the same degree; it is much more likely to hit the unskilled worker than anyone else. Table 2 shows the occupational structure of the unemployed in 1965, and, for comparative purposes, the occupational structure of the total workforce.

Table 2. Unemployed by occupational skill category (1965)

	%	(N)	Total workforce* %
Unskilled manual	78·2	185,285	41
Skilled manual	11·7	27,704	31
Lower white-collar	5·6	13,255	14
Higher white-collar	4·5	10,727	14
	100·0	236,971	100·0

* 1960 census.

Source: Vaska Duganova, 'Neki ekonomski i socijalno-politički aspekti zapošljavanja', *Naše Teme* (4) April 1967.

This demonstrates clearly enough the disadvantaged position of the unskilled manual workers, when compared with other groups. Again, it should be noted that the position of the skilled worker is much more similar to that of white-collar employees, including the best qualified, than to that of the ordinary labourer. This, then, is further evidence that the main 'break' in the reward hierarchy is not between manual and non-manual groups, but within the manual category itself. Further contrasts with the Western class system can be elaborated by reference to differences in the status position of skilled workers and lower white-collar groups. It was suggested above that the rewards accruing to the former gave them a status comparable to that of the 'labour aristocracy' in nineteenth-century England. However, one important difference is that the labour aristocracy of Victorian capitalism held a privileged position within the industrial proletariat, but not really within society at large. The lower middle class of white-collar employees and small shopkeepers tended to rank above the skilled workers in social status and gentility. In contemporary Yugoslav society this is certainly not the case; the lower white-collar *salariat* enjoys very few status or material privileges. As we have already seen, the income of the latter is generally less than that of the skilled man; furthermore, unlike his Western counterpart, the Yugoslav employee cannot look forward to automatic annual increases as part of a rising salary scale. Decisions on incomes, for manual and non-manual workers alike, are taken by workers' councils, the members of which are unlikely to single out office employees for favourable treatment. Again, most enterprises do not have separate entrances, canteens, lavatories, and other facilities for 'works' and 'staff', on the Western pattern. Nor are there differences in the treatment of blue-collar and white-collar employees with regard to social benefits such as sick pay, pension rights, paid holidays, hours of work, notice of dismissal, and the like, which are built in to the British system of industrial relations.[14] In line with all this, the overall social standing of the lower white-collar employee is rather low. Studies of occupational prestige have shown that routine non-manual occupations are rated lower in rank order than skilled manual occupations, though higher than unskilled manual jobs.[15] This is undoubtedly a reversal of the pre-revolutionary situation when clerical employment, particularly in banks and government offices, carried considerable social esteem. It would be tempting to explain this as an outcome of the official glorification of productive labour and socialist ideology in general, but other more prosaic factors are probably more important. Firstly, the rapid increase in literacy and mass education has made clerical skills more widely available than ever before, thereby undercutting their market value. Secondly, office employment is attracting more women than in the pre-revolutionary era, a development which generally seems to lead to a decline in the status of an occupation.

In Western countries, one of the chief advantages of lower white-collar employment over skilled manual work is the pattern of career mobility. Male clerical positions are often regarded as the bottom rungs of the managerial ladder, whereas there is no comparable career structure for manual workers, including the skilled. In Yugoslavia there does not appear to be a very-well worn path from the general office to the managerial or executive desk. As the figures in Table 3 demonstrate, the great majority of those in higher white-collar posts received their qualifications through full-time education.

Table 3. *Qualifications, and the means of attaining them*

	Formal education	On-job and vocational training	Not known	Total
White-collar				
Highly qualified	89·5	9·6	0·9	(100·0)
Qualified	74·2	25·4	0·4	(100·0)
Blue-collar				
Highly skilled	12·9	86·4	0·7	(100·0)
Skilled	17·9	81·5	0·6	(100·0)

Source: Milić, *General Trends in Social Mobility in Yugoslavia*, Table 9.

That is, they tend to be men recruited direct from university, not men who have worked their way up from the lower echelons of the white-collar hierarchy. It is not at all surprising that so many of those in top positions should have used the springboard of higher education. Entry to university is relatively easy by Western standards, and all higher education is organized along 'mass' rather than 'elite' lines. Given the large annual output of graduates, it is inevitable that the promotion prospects of unqualified white-collar employees will be fairly slender. Interestingly enough, the chances of career mobility within the working class appear to be much better. As Table 3 shows, the great majority of skilled and highly skilled workers have gained their qualifications at the workplace, by passing trade examinations while in full-time employment. Comparatively few enter skilled jobs direct from trade school. More difficult to gauge is the extent to which workers are able to rise from the shop floor to managerial white-collar positions. Blumberg suggests this is likely to be a common occurrence as a result of the administrative experience gained by workers elected to serve on workers' councils.[16] However, he presents no evidence in support of this view, and it must be as difficult for manual workers as for lower white-collar employees to compete with qualified university graduates. In any case, the rewards of highly skilled manual work are quite attractive, and the attainment of trade qualifications would provide a smooth route to social promotion for the ambitious worker.

Even though the Yugoslav system of workers' management may not offer especially great opportunities for promotion from the shop floor, it does in many other ways create a work situation highly favourable to the industrial worker. A series of laws enacted over the past two decades have accorded increasingly greater powers to workers' councils, the effect of which has been to alter the traditional patterns of authority in industry, and in particular the line between blue-collar and white-collar employees. Yugoslav workers now enjoy a degree of control over the job situation much greater than that available to their peers in other societies, capitalist or communist. The workers' councils are responsible for the hiring of all labour, including white-collar employees and technical staff. They also have ultimate authority over the dismissal of workers, arising either from breaches of discipline or redundancy. Again, the councils play an important role in the allocation of jobs within the plant, in setting production norms and wage rates for piece work, the distribution of bonuses, and the like.[17] The ideological bias in favour of the industrial worker is reflected in the legal stipulation that manual employees must occupy at least 75 per cent of the seats on workers' councils. The authority now vested in the workers' councils, particularly since the mid-1960s, means that the organizational division between shop-floor and white-collar personnel operates with much less force in Yugoslavia than it does elsewhere. It would, of course, be unrealistic to assume that the director and his white-collar experts do not exercise considerable influence in the day-to-day management of the enterprise. Many of the decisions to be taken are of a highly technical nature and do not readily lend themselves to lay control. Again, where the workforce is made up largely of rural migrants unused to industrial routines, real power is almost bound to lie with the director and his white-collar aides. The large corpus of empirical work now available on the management of Yugoslav enterprises suggests there is a good deal of variation in patterns of authority. It is this fact which has encouraged disagreement between observers as to who 'really' runs industry, since so much depends on the choice of cases. In so far as any general trend is observable, it seems that workers' councils are more likely to enjoy real as well as formal authority in enterprises where the workforce is urbanized, fully proletarianized, and well endowed with skills. Faced with a sophisticated urban workforce, the director of an enterprise is less likely to be able to act in an authoritarian manner than one operating in a backward rural area, whose workers are ignorant or careless of their legal rights over management.

In view of the importance attached to the distinction drawn above between the labour aristocracy and the unskilled workers, it is not surprising to learn that it also makes itself felt in the sphere of self-management. The study by Brekić and his colleagues of forty-four enterprises in the commune of Varadžin found that semi- and un-skilled workers were poorly represented on the councils; all other occupational groups were over-represented in terms of their relative numbers in the total workforce.[18]

Table 4. Representation on workers' councils, by occupational skill category (Varadžin commune)

	Total workforce %	Workers' councils %
Highly skilled manual	6·5	16·2
Skilled manual	33·7	40·6
Semi-skilled manual	25·7	11·3
Unskilled manual	20·8	9·3
Higher white-collar	4·8	11·4
Lower white-collar	8·5	11·2
	100·0	100·0

Source: Jovan Brekić, *Organi Radničkog Samoupravljanja*, Zagreb, 1960, p. 15.

As Table 4 shows, the highly skilled manual workers were represented in greater proportion on the councils than any other group, followed closely by the qualified white-collar staff. Election to workers' councils does not generally bring in its wake many tangible material rewards or privileges. But the possession of authority does perhaps carry certain status rewards, and satisfactions of an intrinsic kind, all of which serve to supplement the advantages of the skilled men over the unskilled. Interestingly enough, the social and material division within the proletariat appears to have given rise to certain normative differences concerning the authority structure in industry. Thus Matić discovered that the unskilled workers in his survey showed a definite preference for an extension of the *director's* authority in the enterprise. Skilled workers, on the other hand, were far more likely to be opposed to any increase in the director's power.[19] Matić suggests that the unskilled workers' preference for the director over the workers' council is due in part to their under-representation on elected bodies. If the councils are dominated by skilled men, and represent the interests of the labour aristocracy, then the labouring poor may come to think of the workers' councils, or skilled men in general, as 'them'. In this case, the director would be cast in the role of a mediating agent, countering the influence of the labour aristocracy and their elected representatives. At any rate, it is certainly unusual, by Western standards, to find lower paid manual groups favouring the extension of white-collar authority over the work situation. As workers themselves have become increasingly involved in managerial functions, the material division within the proletariat has become overlaid by a division of authority. The latter line may not be as sharply drawn as the other, but even so it reinforces the main cleavage in the stratification system and blurs still further the line between manual and non-manual groups.

One further characteristic of the labour aristocracy which might contribute to a 'them' and 'us' outlook on the part of the unskilled, is the former's involvement with the Communist Party. In the Varadžin commune, only 14·2 per cent of the total workforce were Party members; but 45·7 per cent of those elected to workers' councils were Party members.[20] The great majority of communists serving on the councils were skilled manual workers, and less than 12 per cent were semi- or un-skilled. There is thus a strong association between the labour aristocracy, the Communist Party and the workers' councils, sufficient at least to support a generalized image of 'them' in the eyes of the unskilled labourers.

The over-representation of Communist Party members on the workers' councils inevitably raises doubts about the genuineness of industrial democracy in Yugoslavia. It has been suggested that despite the formal powers vested in workers' management bodies the Party effectively controls the decision-making process through the influence of its members on these bodies. The reasoning is that since the director himself is almost always a Party member, he would be able to control the workers' council by relying on the support of the elected communists. This view, however, appears to exaggerate the degree of consensus between white-collar experts and shop-floor representatives. There is a good deal of evidence that conflicts frequently occur between the two groups, and that they are by no means always resolved in the director's favour. The surest way for the Party to maintain close control over the decision-making process in industry would be by strengthening the authority of the director; this is the approach common throughout the rest of eastern Europe.[21] The most recent legislation in Yugoslavia, however, has been designed if anything to produce the opposite effect. The ILO investigation team noted the degree of control exercised by the workers' councils over the directors.

> The system of workers' management has . . . had rather far-reaching effects on the working conditions, and especially the remuneration of directors. The workers' management bodies now settle these in the same way as they settle the remuneration of everybody else in the undertaking. . . . Despite the lack of any accurate comparative data, there can be little doubt that workers' management in practice has led to a strong egalitarian attitude towards the remuneration of directors, and of executives in general. The same appears to be true of the other perquisites and emoluments such as per diem allowances, fares while travelling on business, entertainment, etc., which are regulated with growing strictness and often require the approval (sometimes beforehand) of the workers' management bodies.
>
> Thus directorship of an undertaking has lost some of the material and political attractions and prestige it once had.[22]

The fact that many members of the workers' councils are also likely to be Party members does not necessarily strengthen the director's hand. It is quite clear from Party literature that shop-floor communists are expected to mobilize support for workers' councils among the apathetic, and to resist the encroachment of white-collar managerialism. (This would be in line with Brekić's finding, reported above, that it tends to be the labour aristocracy who are most opposed to any extension of the director's powers.) The argument that the heavy representation of communists on elected bodies must weaken their authority rests on the assumption that the Party is not genuinely in favour of industrial democracy. In this view, the Party is 'really' committed to authoritarian control while adopting the rhetoric of workers' management. However, rhetoric is one thing, legislation another. The evolution of laws relating to self-management point to a strong *ideological* commitment to this principle on the part of the Communist Party leadership. As Blumberg has pointed out, the ideology of workers' participation has permeated throughout the society and has taken on a moral as well as legal embodiment. Since it is the Party itself which has created this moral and institutional framework, it does not really follow that the communist presence must undermine it.

More to the point, perhaps, is the problem of whether the workers' councils are able to conduct affairs in the interest of blue-collar workers as a whole, given the present cleavage within the working class. In other words, the division between the skilled and the unskilled may be more salient than the division between Party and non-Party personnel. As we have seen, managerial control by a privileged aristocracy of labour may be perceived by the unprivileged as no less irksome than control by white-collar executives. With time, the social and material differentiation of the proletariat is likely to become much less pronounced than it is at present. As in the case of England and other industrial societies, the spread of literacy, and vocational training, and the readier access to skills throughout the workforce should gradually narrow the gap between skilled and unskilled. With a fully proletarianized and more homogeneous working class, we might expect self-management bodies to be more representative than they are at present; if this occurs blue-collar men in general should enjoy the degree of control over their work environment which is now largely the prerogative of the labour aristocracy. This is always assuming, of course, that the government does not reverse its present policies on workers' management.

So far this discussion has been mainly concerned with the location in the stratification system of manual and lower white-collar groups. As was previously noted, however, the occupational group ranking highest in material and status terms was the white-collar intelligentsia. Those in the most important technical, creative, administrative and professional positions in society enjoy certain kinds of privileges and advantages which give them a more favourable status *vis-à-vis* other groups than that indicated by income differentials. Thus, the intelligentsia generally has greater access than other groups to high-quality accommodation, official cars and other state property, foreign currency for trips abroad – whether privately financed or, more commonly, as members of a sponsored delegation, and so on. The privileges of this stratum could be said to derive directly from their occupational position, so that they share a functionally similar status to that of white-collar professionals in Western capitalist society. At the same time, however, it should be noted that the intelligentsia tends to become increasingly fused with the Communist Party, and that membership of the Party is often a source of privileges which are not directly contingent upon occupational position. It could thus be said that the greater an occupational group's involvement with the Party, the greater its share of benefits is likely to be – independently of those benefits resulting from the division of labour. The following table shows the changing social composition of the Communist Party, and with it changes in the distribution of advantages which membership brings.

Avakumović's figures do not go beyond 1957, but recently published official statistics of Party membership show that the

Table 5. Social composition of the communist party

	Blue-collar Workers %	Peasants %	White-collar Workers %
1948	29·53	49·41	21·06
1952	32·14	42·39	25·47
1954	28·30	22·65	49·05
1956	31·36	17·66	50·98
1957	32·29	17·32	50·39

Source: Ivan Avakumović, 'The Communist League of Yugoslavia in Figures', *Journal of Central European Affairs*, (19) July 1959.

trend towards 'embourgeoisement' has not been halted.[23] This close identification of the white-collar intelligentsia with the Party means that it becomes increasingly doubtful whether one can draw a sharp distinction between this group and the so-called 'new class' of political functionaries and bureaucrats. Djilas defined the 'new class' as '. . . those who have special privileges and economic preference because of the administrative monopoly they hold'.[24] That is, it was the men who occupied political or Party office on a full-time basis who were the main beneficiaries of the system, rather than those in professional white-collar positions who were simply Party members. Other writers, however, tend to incorporate both the white-collar intelligentsia and the Party bureaucrats in the same privileged class.[25] This is plausible enough in so far as there do not now appear to be such sharp differences in life style, social background, and education between the two groups as there were in the early post-revolutionary years. As the veteran ex-Partisan functionaries go into retirement their places are taken by those who have gone through the same system of higher education as the intelligentsia. Indeed, there is a certain amount of two-way traffic between the two groups, as men change career in mid-stream. For all his emphasis on the importance of *political* office, Djilas himself recognized that the new class extended beyond the boundaries of the Party apparatus. As he put it, 'The party makes the class, but the class grows as a result and uses the party as a basis. The class grows stronger, while the party grows weaker.'[26]

Djilas was concerned to point up the parallels between the new class and the property-owning class in capitalist society. He argued that the class based on the Communist Party enjoyed virtually the same rights over property as the bourgeoisie. If ownership is defined in terms of the use and consumption of social goods, and not simply legal title, then the new class can be conceived of as a propertied class in the usual sense. However, one serious objection to this comparison is that in the absence of legal title to property, there can be no inheritance within the family. The privileges of the new class rest upon their Party positions, and these are not transferable from father to son. What gives the bourgeoisie of capitalist society its distinctive class character is its high degree of social self-recruitment from one generation to the next; and this is made possible precisely through the legal ownership and transfer of wealth. Under these conditions the propertied class takes on a definite *cultural* distinctiveness which tends to reinforce its social exclusiveness. This is hardly true of the new class in Yugoslavia. There is little evidence that the Party bureaucracy and white-collar intelligentsia are becoming a closed social group with a distinct culture, accent, mode of dress, and the like, in the manner of the English upper class or the French *haute bourgeoisie*. Indeed, an important feature of the stratification system is the extent to which recruitment to the new class is open to those from lower social strata. Djilas noted that 'The new class is actually being created from the lowest and broadest strata of the people, and is in constant motion. Although it is sociologically possible to describe who belongs to the new class, it is difficult to do so; for the new class melts into and spills over into the people, into other lower classes, and is constantly changing.'[27]

The fact that the new class is not predominantly self-recruiting has an important effect on the stratification system as a whole. In societies where the upper class shows a high degree of social exclusiveness, normative patterns of a 'defensive' kind tend to emerge among lower status groups. That is, where the latter perceive the opportunity structure to be weighted against them, they will tend to generate a normative system in which the values associated with achievement and ambition are strongly de-emphasized. Thus in England, for example, patterns of 'working-class culture' give little support to the norms of educational and occupational advancement. This arises from collective experience of the opportunity structure, and the social knowledge that few of those born in the working class can expect to achieve high social status. This is not a feature of the Yugoslav stratification system. On the contrary, there is a great deal of normative support for upward mobility among the working class. A national study conducted by the Belgrade Institute of Social Sciences found that manual and non-manual respondents alike had high educational and occupational ambitions for their children. Table 6 summarizes the main findings.

Taken collectively, white-collar parents show slightly higher aspirations for their children than do blue-collar

Table 6. *Parents' occupational aspirations for their children*

Desired occupa- tion for child	Respondent's own occupational category				
	Peasant %	Unskilled/ Semi- skilled worker %	Skilled/ Highly skilled worker %	Lower White- collar employee %	Higher White- collar employee %
Agricultural worker	6·8	0·4	0·3	—	—
Manual worker/ craftsman	18·3	27·2	14·4	10·5	6·1
Clerk	10·7	6·6	3·9	5·7	1·8
Technician	3·8	3·7	6·6	5·7	5·7
School teacher	13·6	11·5	8·1	9·5	7·0
Doctor	8·9	9·9	12·2	18·1	15·7
Engineer	12·4	15·6	24·1	13·4	24·9
Other 'higher professions'	18·3	17·7	20·2	26·6	28·6
Other/Don't know	7·2	7·4	10·2	10·5	10·2
	100·0	100·0	100·0	100·0	100·0

Source: Institut Društvenih Nauka, *Jugoslovensko javno mnenje o aktuelnim političkim i društvenim pitanjima*, Belgrade, 1965, Table III.

parents. Nevertheless, as Albert Meister has pointed out,[28] the latter are remarkably ambitious by the standards of the working class in western Europe. The Yugoslav workers' expectations for their children are no doubt somewhat over-optimistic when judged against the actual possibilities of their entering the white-collar intelligentsia. Nevertheless, the point is that opportunities for social promotion into the new class *are* sufficiently favourable to generate normative support for achievement principles. This is not to say of course that working-class families are themselves the agencies which transmit aspirational values to their offspring. Even in a socialist society the working class is likely to be much less adept than the middle class in preparing the young for success. What is important, however, is that the working class does not set up a normative system which *negates* aspirational values, and which socializes the young into prior acceptance of low status. In the absence of such a defensive, anti-achieve-ment value system, the formal socializing agencies, and especially the educational system, are likely to be more effective in the motivation of working-class youth. The nature of the value system of the working class, and the general perception of the opportunity structure, will depend very largely on the *factual* distribution of opportunities. In other words, Yugoslav workers' hopes regarding their children's entry into the new class is in itself a useful index of the openness of the stratification system. It is unlikely that workers in capitalist society would be as optimistic about their children's chances of entering the ranks of the propertied bourgeoisie or of the white-collar professions; and with equally good reason. To overlook this difference in the nature of class formation is to miss one of the most fundamental of all contrasts in the stratification systems of European communist and capitalist societies.

NOTES

1 Doreen Warriner, *Revolution in Eastern Europe* (London, 1950), p. 136.
2 Ivo Vinski, 'The Distribution of Yugoslavia's National Income by Social Classes in 1938', *Rev. of Income and Wealth* (13) September 1967; and UN, *Economic Survey of Europe in 1965*, Pt. II, Table 12.8.
3 Vojin Milić, 'General Trends in Social Mobility in Yugoslavia', *Acta Sociologica*, (9) No. 1/2, 1965, p. 133.
4 Rudi Supek, 'Sveučilišna politička obrazovanja, socijalno porijeklo studentata i uspjeh u studiranju' (Zagreb, 1966), (mimeo).
5 Milić, 'Social Mobility . . .', p. 129.
6 Milić, p. 120.
7 Milić, p. 125.
8 See Frank Parkin, 'Class Stratification in Socialist Societies', *British Journal of Sociology*, December 1969.
9 For an account of the economic reforms see Svetozar Pejovich, *The Market Planned Economy of Yugoslavia* (Minnesota, 1966). On workers' councils see International Labour office, Studies and Reports (New Series) No. 64, *Workers' Management in Yugoslavia* (Geneva, 1962); also, Paul Blumberg, *Industrial Democracy* (London, 1968), Chapters 8 and 9.
10 Paul Landy, 'Reforms in Yugoslavia', *Problems of Communism*, Nov.–Dec. 1961, p. 26.
11 The term was of course commonly used in Victorian England to distinguish skilled craftsmen from the 'labouring poor'. See

E. J. Hobsbawm, 'The Labour Aristocracy in Nineteenth-century Britain', Chapter 15 of *Labouring Men* (London, 1964).

12 Robert G. Livingston, 'Yugoslavia Unemployment Trends', *Monthly Labour Review* (87) July 1964.

13 Livingston calculates that only about 13 per cent of the unemployed were receiving benefits in 1963. Men seeking work for the first time, and those employed for less than a year do not qualify for relief. See the official trade-union publication, *Employment and Material Position of Temporarily Unemployed Workers* (Belgrade, 1965).

14 For an excellent account of the different treatment accorded to blue-collar and white-collar workers in British industry, see Dorothy Wedderburn and Christine Craig, *Relative Deprivation in Work*, paper presented to the British Association for the Advancement of Science, Exeter, September 1969.

15 Joze Goričar, 'Vrednovanje nekih zanimanje', in M. Janićijević (ed.), *Promena Klasne Strukture Savremenog Jugoslovenskog Društva* (Belgrade, 1967).

16 Blumberg, *Industrial Democracy* (London, 1968). He argues that workers' management 'tends to connect the severed link between office and factory and allow exceptionally able workers to move up into the office, into the managerial staff, occasionally even as director', p. 221.

17 ILO, *Workers' Management in Yugoslavia* (Geneva, 1962). Workers' councils have also been given considerable influence in the appointment and removal of enterprise directors. Hoffman and Neal report that in 1956 workers' councils initiated the dismissal of 168 directors. G. Hoffman and F. W. Neal, *Yugoslavia and the New Communism* (New York, 1962), p. 242.

18 Jovan Brekić, *Organi Radničkog Samoupravljanja* (Zagreb, 1960).

19 S. Matić, *et al.*, *Aktivnost Radnih Ljudi u Samoupravljanju Radnom Organizacijom* (Zagreb, 1962), pp. 138/9.

20 Brekić, *Organi Radničkog . . .* , p. 67.

21 Compare, for example, the case of Poland. Jiri Kolaja, *A Polish Factory* (Lexington, 1960).

22 ILO Report, *Workers' Management in Yugoslavia*, p. 115.

23 The Party newspaper, *Komunist*, reported that in 1966 the number of engineers and technicians entering the Party increased by more than 4,400 over the previous year's entry; the number of medical and teaching staff by more than 3,700; and the number of economists and lawyers by more than 3,600 over the 1965 intake. In the same twelve-month period the recruitment of manual workers, except the highly skilled, declined. Furthermore, 52·1 per cent of those expelled from the Party were manual workers, as were 53·6 per cent of members who resigned voluntarily. *Komunist*, 6 April 1967.

24 Milovan Djilas, *The New Class* (London, 1957), p. 39.

25 Albert Parry, *The New Class Divided* (New York, 1966); also, Z. Bauman, *The Second Generation's Socialism* (mimeo, 1969).

Bauman argues that white-collar experts and Party bureaucrats cannot really be 'separated into two classes with different and conflicting interests. On the contrary, many intrinsic attributes of their respective social positions and roles testify to their basic sociological unity', p. 12.

26 Djilas, *The New Class*, p. 40.
27 Djilas, *The New Class*, p. 61.
28 Albert Meister, *Socialisme et autogestion: l'experience yougoslave* (Paris, 1964), pp. 117–18.

11 Poland

Michalina Vaughan

Poland shares with popular democracies other than Czechoslovakia and East Germany and with developing countries in
general the problems arising out of a rapid transition from a
predominantly agrarian to an industrial economy and the
accompanying disruption of traditional social hierarchies.
However, a major difference between popular democracies
and other developing countries is that in the former social
change is never seen as an unintended consequence or as a
mere price to be paid for economic advantages. Thus change
is always State-initiated and this is in sharp contrast with the
pattern of western European industrialization in the
nineteenth century. Some aspects of this change can be
related to the transition from agricultural to industrial and
from rural to urban, while others correspond to the implementation of ideological tenets. Neither can be assessed
without a preliminary understanding of the pre-war social
structure.

1 PRE-WAR SOCIAL STRATIFICATION

Prior to the second world war, the population of Poland was
not ethnically homogeneous[1] and was still predominantly
rural (72·3 per cent in 1931). Approximately 60 per cent of
this population derived their livelihood from agriculture[2],
10 per cent being landless agricultural labourers, mainly
employed on a seasonal basis on large privately owned
estates. Modern industry, geographically concentrated in the
regions better endowed in raw materials, particularly in
Silesia, depended on western European investments for
much of its capital[3] and employed only a small proportion of
the labour force. The total number of manual workers–
excluding the agricultural sector – was assessed at approximately 1,318,000[4] in 1931 and 1,970,000[5] in 1936; however,

about 45 per cent of the working class were engaged in small, scale production, in cottage industries, handicrafts and seasonal employment.[6] Due to the relatively low level of economic development, opportunities for clerical employment in industry, trade and transport were scarce and the State remained the main employer of white-collar workers. Thus in 1938–9, 50 to 60 per cent of the 800,000 so-called 'intellectual workers' received their wages from the State.[7] During the economic crisis of the early 1930s, such a situation led to unemployment and a threat of 'proletarization' for members of this intermediary strata. While this category of wage-earners was particularly vulnerable to fluctuations on the labour market and although its activities were semi-manual in some cases,[8] it was not considered akin to the working class. Its members were usually included in the 'intelligentsia', in spite of the great occupational, educational and economic differences between them and 'intellectuals' *sensu stricto.*

The Intelligentsia. The existence of the intelligentsia as a group distinct from the urban bourgeoisie, sufficiently heterogeneous to be closely related both to the aristocratic upper class (through the high echelons of the civil service) and to the industrial proletariat (through clerical workers), and yet considered as one stratum in spite of its internal differentiation – is the most original characteristic of pre-war Polish society. Its formation – in the late eighteenth and mainly in the nineteenth century – can be explained by the decay of a feudal society resulting in rapid urbanization, but slow industrialization. 'In its structure Polish intelligentsia is linked with the underdevelopment of Polish civilization from the technical-economic point of view, with the fact that, as someone put it, Poland had no nineteenth century.'[9] Of predominantly aristocratic origin[10] the intelligentsia found a refuge in the professions and the civil service after the disintegration of the 'aristocratic courts' (manors) which followed partition. It was neither equipped nor inclined to pioneer industrial development, and assumed a responsibility for preserving Polish national culture, threatened by the occupying powers, rather than for initiating economic progress. Its decisive influence in maintaining Polish not only as spoken, but as a literary language (particularly in the

Russian part of the country, where the official policy was most repressive) increased its prestige as a group embodying national consciousness. Genetic links with the former ruling class and similarities in life style were additional sources of prestige. After 1918 the intelligentsia found new occupational outlets as a State machinery and an educational system appeared. This led to a numerical increase of this stratum – access to which represented the main avenue of social mobility. Social promotion thus took place through educational channels and the composition of the intelligentsia was gradually, albeit slowly, modified by intakes from the peasantry and the petty bourgeoisie. By pre-war estimates, about two-thirds of the intelligentsia members were of upper class or intelligentsia background, while between one-fifth and one-quarter were of peasant or working-class origin.[11] Apart from this slight widening of the social basis from which the intelligentsia was recruited, occupational diversification occurred and a process of vertical stratification within this stratum ensued. Thus, while before independence (1918) the intelligentsia had been a numerically small group, characterized by similar educational attainments and patriotic commitments, but with dissimilar levels and sources of income (earned or unearned), between the two World Wars it was construed as a general category including all non-manual workers other than small shopkeepers. Therefore it ranged from the high civil servants, officers, clergy and members of the professions to office workers and technical and supervisory staff in the tertiary and secondary sectors. It cut across the class structure (defined by relations to means of production) and should not be considered as one stratum (since its members had extremely different styles of life, varying degrees of educational qualifications[12] and correspondingly graded occupational prestige). While it is generally maintained that the pre-war intelligentsia was gradually downgrading the 'lower intellectual workers' (semi-manual and lower clerical) into the proletariat, this would not have sufficed to turn it into a homogeneous group – either economically or culturally. For example, school teachers were differentiated in both respects from the 'bourgeois intelligentsia' (civil service and professions).[13] In 1939 the intelligentsia as an occupational category represented about 5·7 per cent of the active population, i.e. approximately 2 per cent had functions of 'leadership and expertise' in the civil service, the professions, cultural and scientific life and the high levels of economic management, while the remaining 3·7 per cent were 'intellectual workers' with some educational qualifications.[14]

In spite of the socio-economic heterogeneity of this category, it is often considered as a class and the structure of pre-war Polish society is currently described by contemporary sociologists as including six classes: the 'szlachta' (landed gentry), the capitalist bourgeoisie, the intelligentsia, the petty bourgeoisie, the working class and the peasantry.[15] The first two, numerically very small, corresponded to the remains of rural feudalism and the embryo of urban capitalism. Although the aristocracy was alleged to be losing some of its wealth, as the agrarian reform was slowly and tentatively implemented between the wars, and the bourgeoisie to derive added strength from industrialization, the conservatism of official agrarian policies and the share of foreign capital in industry resulted in a fairly static situation. Although one of these classes was rural and the other urban, they shared a commitment to political nationalism and economic conservatism. While they are now described as 'ruling classes' of pre-war Poland, many key posts in the government and the administration were occupied by members of the intelligentsia, the top layers of which were thus part of the ruling elite. Therefore, the demarcation line drawn between the two 'privileged classes' and the intelligentsia is somewhat artificial, as is the distinction between 'capitalist' and petty bourgeoisie, since the latter two categories both imply the ownership of means of production, with differences of scale rather than of kind. The multiplicity of small industrial and commercial enterprises in an underdeveloped economy resulted in the petty bourgeois being relatively numerous both in towns and in the country, but the traditional assumption that the intelligentsia was better fitted for functions of leadership deprived them of the possibility of playing a political role.[16]

2 THE PEOPLE'S REPUBLIC

The second world war destroyed the institutions of the Polish State and transformed the structure of Polish society. The fact that 22 per cent of the inhabitants of Poland in 1939 were killed as a result of military operations, of mass persecutions or of forced labour[17] modified not only the ethnic composition of the population by virtually eliminating the Jewish minority,[18] but also its social composition, since during the occupation repressive policies were specifically aimed at the intelligentsia. Thus, 35 per cent of the educated population (including secondary school graduates) perished in the war. These biological losses facilitated the advent of a new political regime at the end of the war; while the depletion of the former ruling elite made it possible, the exigencies of international politics made it unavoidable. A neighbour of the Soviet Union, Poland was not only bound to become a popular democracy, but also to accept the territorial exchange whereby it lost its eastern provinces[19] and acquired a new western frontier by incorporating the formerly German regions delineated by the Oder-Neisse line.[20] Transfers of population brought about by this exchange affected approximately 1·5 million Poles (moving westward out of Soviet territories), two million Germans (moving westward out of Poland) and 0·5 million members of various Soviet ethnic groups (moving eastward out of Poland). The first post-war census in 1946 took place while these migrations were occurring and its data (a total population of 23·9 million) cannot be considered as fully reliable. However, it provides an indication of the extent of war-time losses and its analysis highlights the increased ethnic homogeneity of the post-war population.[21]

Economic reform. Two major reforms accompanied the proclamation of a popular democracy and radically altered the social structure of post-war Poland – the expropriation of 9,327 large rural estates (covering approximately six million hectares in toto)[22] and the nationalization of 10,662 industrial and 2,252 commercial enterprises each employing more than fifty workers.[23] The agrarian reform, implemented between 1944 and 1946, and the colonization of the western territories during the same period gave land to more than a million peasant families, 76 per cent of whom had previously been landless and 24 per cent of whom were smallholders.[24] The disappearance of the landed aristocracy as a class and the considerable reduction in the number of agricultural labourers transformed social relationships in the country. The basic unit of production became the small privately owned farm. Subsequent attempts to introduce collective farming met with so little success that the policy of collectivization was gradually relinquished in the 1950s, while State farms were increasingly considered as experimental and currently account for a mere 9·5 per cent of gross agricultural output.[25]

The policy of nationalization resulted in eliminating foreign capital and in abolishing the pre-war capitalist bourgeoisie as a class by depriving it of the ownership of means of industrial production, as the aristocracy had been deprived of the means of agricultural production. Members of the two former privileged classes found various forms of employment either in managerial capacities, in teaching and in other 'intellectual' occupations (in which case they were considered as members of the intelligentsia) or started small businesses in the remaining private sector (and were then considered as petty bourgeois).[26] After the initial period of reconstruction and nationalization, the six-year plan (1949–55) corresponded to an acceleration in the process of economic development and of social change. Industrialization, facilitated by the resources of the western territories, was assigned an overriding priority, while the socialist organization of cultural production ceased to be regarded as an immediate target. Industrial growth rapidly exceeded the level of pre-war production in the main sectors.

Table 1. Growth of industrial production (1938 level = 100), 1963

Electricity	929
Coal	297
Iron Ore	613
Steel	555
Nitrogenous Fertilizers	717
Sulphuric Acid	470
Cement	446
Raw Sugar	247

Source: D. Gataj, 'Problems of Research in Poland's Regions Under Industrialisation', see note 27.

Urbanization. Industrialization was accompanied by rapid urbanization, the rural population declining by 0·9 per cent per year on average between 1950 and 1960[27] and the number of towns and cities of over 100,000 inhabitants reaching twenty-one (as against eleven in 1939). Industrial employment attracted a steady inflow of migrants from the country, approximately three million in eighteen years, 65·5 per cent of whom were young men aged between fifteen and twenty-nine. Housing difficulties acted as a brake on the rural exodus but a new category of 'peasant workers', commuting to work in industry sometimes on a seasonal basis – without leaving the land – provided an additional source of cheap industrial labour.[28] In 1960, this category accounted for 5·8 per cent of the active population;[29] its existence helped solve the problems raised by the concentration of industry in overcrowded towns and particularly in the Silesian conurbations. Peasant workers are a highly differentiated group, since about 20 per cent have very small plots of under 0·5 ha. and derive their main income from their factory job, about 40 per cent are smallholders with farms of 2 to 3 ha. which would be uneconomical without an additional income, and the remaining 40 per cent were predominantly farmers whose employment in industry was seasonal or temporary.[30] Their common characteristic is that they are unskilled and imperfectly adapted to working conditions in industry, that they seldom have received a complete primary education and have little incentive to receive additional training or instruction, and that they are not fully integrated with the working class. In spite of these social handicaps, they have been considered as economically privileged, although the difference between their prosperity and that of urban workers can be accounted for by the work of women on the land (without remuneration). The existence of this group will probably be limited to a period of transition, during which their low-cost labour favours industrial growth and their influence in the countryside is viewed as progressive, since they spread urban mores and contribute to raising living standards.[31]

Industrialization has led not only to a considerable growth in the number of urban manual workers, assessed at 3·7 million in 1961, an increase of approximately one million in ten years,[32] and representing 35·7 per cent of the population in 1964,[33] but also to a complete change in type of employment. The pre-war cottage industries and small workshops have dropped to a statistically insignificant level, to be replaced by large-and medium-size State-owned factories. The ties between the 'new' working class and the peasantry are particularly strong, since approximately 50 per cent of factory workers and 60 per cent of workers on building sites have been brought up in the country until the age of fourteen and 25 per cent in both sectors are peasant workers.[34] In 1960, there were four 'new' workers who had recently entered industrial employment for each 'old' worker.[35] Hence the need for accelerated training in order to increase the level of qualification of newcomers and their adaptation to factory conditions and to urban surroundings, while developing their feeling of solidarity with the working class. Approximately one industrial worker in three received complete primary schooling, therefore the development of adult education is a major prerequisite not only for a socialist society, but for the operation of a modern economy. With the reduction of wage differentials between non-manual and manual labour and the attribution of higher wages to skilled industrial than to clerical workers, it is mainly the level of educational attainment which differentiates the working class from the 'intellectual workers'.

A growth in tertiary employment had been the corollary of post-war industrialization. New opportunities arose for managerial and clerical workers in mining and industry (which now account for 27·3 per cent of all 'intellectual workers' as against 16 per cent in 1931).[36] In nationalized industry, there are nineteen engineers, technicians and administrative or clerical workers per 100 manual workers.[37] The development of welfare services, of education at all levels and of cultural organizations has also resulted in an increase in non-manual employment, still considered as a criterion of belonging to the intelligentsia. In a series of studies of the composition and the functions of the intelligentsia in a context of social change,[38] the number of 'intellectual workers' at the end of the 1950s was assessed at 1·5 million, while the professions and the higher civil service accounted for approximately 600,000. The so-called 'creative intelligentsia' (writers, scientists and research workers), while counting no more than 50,000 members, continued after the war to be considered as an elite whose prestige remained great and favourably influenced that of the intelligentsia as a whole,[39] which corresponded to 17·8 per cent of the population in 1964.

3 EDUCATION AND SOCIAL CHANGE

However, the social origins of the members of the intelligentsia have been modified by the development of educational facilities, considered both as a corollary of economic growth[40] and as an instrument of workers' and peasants' promotion to new social and political responsibilities. The need for such a change in composition was emphasized from the beginning of the People's Republic by government and party officials, both with reference to the rights which the children of manual workers had previously been denied and to the unreliability of the surviving section of pre-war intelligentsia. 'Regardless of opinions and activity during the twenty years between the wars, almost every intellectual had the stigma of being "alien" because of his connections – no matter how indirect – with the pre-war ruling classes.'[41] Therefore the priority given to educational investments corresponding to about 4·8 per cent of national investments in the 1950s[42] was justified not only by the requirements of an expanding economy deprived of trained cadres, but also by the necessity to recruit them from among the new ruling class, so that they would not share the values of the 'defeated classes'.[43] To these ends the re-organization of the educational system has been guided by an overriding concern for the growth of technical education both at post-primary and at higher level. Indeed, technical education alone could serve the two goals of party policy: economic growth and promotion of the manual classes without recreating an 'alien' intelligentsia from among their most able children. The principle of 'polytechnicization', borrowed from the Soviet Union, was intended to pervade the whole educational system and could be defined as a predominance of the scientific subjects over literary ones,[44] of practical over theoretical knowledge[45] and of 'committed' over disinterested scholarship.[46] Its main sphere of application in the Soviet Union is at post-primary level, in the so-called general secondary schools parallel with technical secondary establishments, but less narrowly specialized and intended to provide a general scientific and technical background. It is from these schools that the overwhelming majority of university entrants are drawn, rather than from vocational secondary schools. In

Poland, as in other popular democracies, the Soviet pattern has not been fully applied in this respect. The coexistence of 'general' and 'professional' secondary schools (lyceum and technicum) has not been accompanied by a genuine 'polytechnicization' of the former, whose curricula still attempt to balance humanistic and scientific subjects and include no technical skills.[47] It is almost exclusively from this general secondary sector, devoid of vocational content,[48] that higher education recruits its entrants.[49] Therefore the elite of the new intelligentsia is drawn from a group selected at fourteen years of age on grounds among which family background (urban rather than rural, non-manual rather than working class) is influential. Thus entry into higher education corresponds to a bottleneck in a system designed for ideological reasons as not only open, but favourable to the 'manual' classes. To reverse the trend towards a self-perpetuation of the intelligentsia, a policy of social selection of university applicants has been enforced with a view to giving the student body a predetermined 'moral and political physiognomy'.[50] Thus, the selection procedure takes into account social origin, defined by parental occupation,[51] intellectual aptitude, exemplified by previous educational attainments and ascertained by an entrance examination and social utility, since the number of places available for various courses is fixed annually by the Ministry of Higher Education in accordance with the needs of the economy defined by the Plan.[52] The emphasis on 'useful' studies, with the resulting increase in the intake of higher technical schools, has altered the respective shares of the various disciplines and increased the technical section in relation to the pre-war pattern.

Table 2. Percentages of students of various disciplines

Discipline studied	1937–8	1950–1	1955–6	1963–4
Technical studies	15·3	28·4	44	38
Agriculture	6·6	7·5	9·2	9·4
Law and Economics	36	19·5	11·6	11·1
Arts	17·3	12·4	6·4	13·2
Sciences	9	9·2	7	9·7
Medicine	11·6	19·9	18·9	15·7
Plastic Arts, Music	4·5	3·1	2·9	2·9

Source: Rocznik Statystyczny, 1964.

While these proportions correspond to a modified definition of culture, and even reflect a 'softened' attitude to generalists and theoreticians after the thaw of 'the Polish October' (1957), they also show the growth of those specialities which are most sought after by applicants of working-class and peasant origin. It is precisely to higher technical schools, directly related to planned economic growth, that these applicants are mostly attracted:

Table 3. Social background of applicants and type of educational Institution

Type of Institution	Working class origin	Peasant	Intelligentsia (inc. managerial)	Artisan et al.
Universities	25·7	14·9	52·3	8·1
Higher techn. schools	38·1	17·4	40·9	3·6
Higher agric. schools	19·9	34·8	39·7	5·5
Higher econ. schools	36·7	19·4	39·6	4·3
Teacher Training	39·1	23·6	31·8	5·5
Medical Academies	23·1	14·2	57·1	5·6
Higher art schools	21·2	9·6	62·4	6·8
Acad. of Theology	25·2	50·2	19·2	5·4

Source: Rocznik Statystyczny, Warsaw, 1965, p. 421.

The concentration of applicants with a non-manual background in traditional institutions of higher learning and in sectors corresponding to the pre-war definition of culture (centred on the arts and the professions rather than on applied techniques) confirms the trend towards an ideologically undesirable differentiation within the graduate population. The survival of pre-war attitudes is not only illustrated by the attempted entrenchment of the intelligentsia, but also by the attachment of peasant families to theological studies, access to the Catholic clergy being the traditional avenue of mobility for the rural population.

During the first post-war years it became increasingly obvious that university selection boards, by attempting to maintain intellectual standards (both for the sake of the disciplines and in the national interest), tended to favour the applicants whose home environment had been stimulating rather than those belonging to the less favoured social classes.

Therefore, a quota of 60 per cent of students with a working-class or peasant background was imposed as a minimum by a ministerial decree in 1950. However, during the following ten years there was a steady downward trend in the admission of such candidates, accelerated by the events of October 1957 which reduced official control over educational institutions.

Table 4. Candidates admitted in higher educational institutions (1951–2 to 1961–2)

Year	Working-class origin	Peasant origin	Both origins
1951–2	39·1	24·9	64
1952–3	35·9	25·1	61
1953–4	33·9	25·9	59·8
1954–5	34·6	24·4	59·0
1955–6	32·2	24	56·2
1956–7	30·7	22	52·7
1957–8	25	21·1	46·1
1958–9	27·8	21·3	49·1
1959–60	28·2	20·1	48·3
1960–1	27	19·3	46·3
1961–2	27·9	19·4	47·3

Source: J. Szczepański, *'Socjologiczne problemy wyzszego wyksztaɫcenia'* (Sociological problems of higher education), Warsaw, 1963, p. 123.

As a remedial measure, additional marks for applicants of working-class and peasant origin were introduced in 1964.[53] This reform, attacked on grounds of educational efficiency and defended by reference to equality of opportunity,[54] does not seem to have appreciably altered the composition of the student body[55] or to have stimulated the expected wave of applications from the appropriate groups. Thus, while 300,000 graduates were produced in the first twenty years of the People's Republic, their social origins do not fulfil initial expectations. Future educational policies intended to grant special privileges to the children of manual workers would presumably meet with strong opposition from this new intelligentsia, increasingly less willing to become a mere occupational category of intellectual workers and to be classified by reference to social origin rather than to educational qualifications. It is significant in this respect that among graduates of a textile technicum of working-class background, only those who were over forty years of age identified with this class, while all those who had completed their primary schooling after the war considered themselves as members of the intelligentsia. These attitudes tend to be reinforced by inter-marriage among graduates and by wide differences in life style. 'Even though there is no contradiction of interests between the working class and the various categories of the intelligentsia, there is no common language, or at least understanding is difficult.'[56] The major difference in relation to the pre-war period seems to be a greater integration of all the intellectual workers with the intelligentsia rather than its rapprochement to the manual classes.

4 MAJOR FEATURES OF SOCIAL STRATIFICATION

The rural/urban and the intellectual/manual dichotomies, derived from the division of labour, have been inherited from the previous semi-feudal capitalist structure of society, but transformed by the agrarian reform and the nationalization of means of production – equated with the abolition of class exploitation. However, the private ownership of means of production has not been fully abolished and therefore remains of the former capitalist classes exist in trade, industry and agriculture.[57] The survival of such classes is construed as transitory and limited to a period of adaptation to socialist production. In agriculture, private property remains the rule, as State farms cover only 12·6 per cent of cultivated lands and co-operatives 1·1 per cent.[58] The redeeming feature of peasant ownership appears to be its small scale, since nearly half of the individual farms cover less than four ha. and approximately a quarter – less than two ha. while only 5 per cent exceed 20.[59] Hence there is no opportunity for employing hired labourers and therefore no scope for exploitation, reinterpreted to cover employment rather than property relationships as such. The smallest farms which are not the exclusive or even the main source of income for their owners are considered as a short-term characteristic of the transition period. Larger ones are unlikely to grow to 'capitalist proportions' because of the lack of manpower absorbed by industry. This objective factor is allegedly reinforced by the 'subjective acceptance (conscious or not) of socialist values'[60] and undoubtedly complemented by the insertion of individual production units in a collective framework, by the allocation of government credit, the loan of collectively owned heavy machinery and the gradual development of co-operative institutions. Agrarian policies, while directed against 'kulaks', are therefore not intended to eradicate the small individually owned farms, adapted to the amount of family labour available and producing nearly 90 per cent of agricultural marketable products.

Private ownership in towns is limited to a small sphere of artisanal production and retail trade. At the end of the war, because of acute shortages and considerable regional differences of supply, the private sector flourished and this 'black market' resulted in a proliferation of shops and workshops. Assessed at 400,000 in the late 1940s, these firms gradually shrank as the economic life of the country became more settled; there were still some 100,000 left in 1953.[61] Their owners are considered as petty-bourgeois and, unlike farmers, are not 'redeemed' by the small scale of their undertakings from the original sin of capitalist property. In fact, they are presented as hostile to socialist planning and, in most cases, as potential enemies of the regime, if not actual conspirators against it. These accusations seem to be derived from the assumption that most members of the former ruling classes found a refuge in private enterprise after the expropriations of 1944–6 – although many of them actually joined the intelligentsia and although the pre-war petty bourgeoise must account for a high proportion of the artisan and entrepreneurial property. However, in assessments of this heterogeneous group whose livelihood is derived from the urban private sector, Polish sociologists clearly consider it as a capitalist survival, extraneous to and parasitic on the planned economy.[62] Therefore the petty bourgeoisie is condemned because it is not economically productive and because it is not politically reliable. Of the four distinct categories identified in contemporary Polish society, it is the only one whose existence cannot be justified on grounds of social utility – unlike that of the working class, the peasantry and the intelligentsia.

While these four categories are clear when used descriptively, they are sociologically ambiguous. Two of them correspond to social classes which existed in pre-war Poland, i.e. the working class and the peasantry, while the other two, the intelligentsia and the petty bourgeoisie, would have been more accurately described as strata. According to Hochfeld's terminology, the latter two were 'non basic classes' or groupings whose existence results from the 'mixed' character of social relationships irreducible to the bi-polar Marxist model of domination of one basic class over another.[63] This model, purely theoretical since it can never be embodied in any actual society, describes the objective basic conflict rooted in a mode of production and posits the exploitation of one class by another who appropriates the fruit of its labour. However, in any society several modes of production coexist – thus feudalism and capitalism did in pre-war Poland – and the bi-polar model merely points to the development of one predominant mode. It 'defines the dynamic of development',[64] without accounting for the existence of other divisions in society, such as the manual/intellectual dichotomy, made possible by the existence of surplus value and necessary by the organization of production. Hence the difficulty in locating intellectuals in the social structure of pre-war Poland, since they are linked with capitalists by their role in management and in producing conservative ideologies and with workers by the fact that they hired their labour and that they also produced progressive ideologies. The intelligentsia is thus viewed as ambivalent,[65] whereas the petty bourgeoisie, whether considered as a class or as a status group within the bourgeoisie,[66] belonged to the capitalist classes, though – in the former interpretation – not to the ruling classes. Conversely the intelligentsia, while not a capitalist class (though including some capitalists, e.g. in the liberal professions), can be construed as part of the pre-war ruling class.[67] The position of the peasantry – since its members were not all propertyless and since some even employed hired labourers – cannot be interpreted as the exact equivalent of that held by the working class. The bi-polar model which expresses the exploitation of industrial workers by bourgeois capitalists cannot be applied without reservations to relationships of agricultural production. It had a counterpart in the dichotomy between landed aristocracy and landless agricultural labourers, but only a scheme of 'gradation'[68] which replaces the qualitative approach to social class by a quantitative one and emphasizes differences of degree rather than of kind – could account for the complicated pattern of property relationships in the country. The basic postulate of post-war sociologists that a fundamental solidarity exists between the peasantry (excluding 'kulaks' characterized by reference to the subjective criterion of 'anti-social attitudes', while the objective criterion of 'large property' remains relative and generally unspecified) is founded on their solidarity as 'manual' classes and as 'oppressed' classes. Therefore it refers to an exclusion from power, to economic and cultural deprivation and to lack of 'social honour' rather than to a similar relationship to modes of production.

According to Polish Marxist sociologists, the monopolization of means of production by exploiting classes has been abolished in contemporary Poland, since structural conflict between oppressor and oppressed no longer exists, and therefore all social relations are radically transformed. Having posited this basic superiority over capitalism, they do not maintain that other forms of conflict have simultaneously disappeared or that the contradictions inherited from pre-war society will be easy to eradicate. It would be a 'naïve, eschatological view of socialism'[69] to equate its advent with the abolition of social conflicts. Since resources are not unlimited, there will unavoidably be competition between groups and between individuals to secure a larger share of material goods and cultural advantages, and to influence social and economic policies with a view to acquiring or perpetuating privileges in these respects.[70] Group interests may be contradictory in the short term, although the basic contradiction deriving from capitalist ownership no longer exists. Its suppression constitutes merely a necessary, not a sufficient condition for the elimination of alienation in the economic, the political and the cultural spheres. Increases in freedom on all these dimensions can only be achieved over the long term, while the transition period is necessarily characterized by competing claims from groups whose share in income, education or power can only be increased by reducing that of others. There are two possible approaches to such claims: either to attempt an equalization of all shares, or to retain differences provided that they are justified by differential contributions to the general welfare. This is a traditional debate among socialists, some of whom are content to give individuals chances for promotion to positions of greater responsibility, carrying greater rewards, while others seek to impose egalitarianism as an ethical principle. 'While the former attack the hereditary character of privileges in the class system, the latter attack the privileges themselves.'[71] It is the 'realistic' rather than the 'radical' view which has prevailed in post-war Poland, where the ascetic implications of egalitarianism have been considered detrimental to the interests of the proletariat. Indeed, the working class and the peasantry require a rise in living standards more than any other section of the population, and are therefore most interested in economic growth – which cannot be achieved without the retention of economic incentives. Inequalities of treatment during the transition period are thus justified as ultimately conducive to social promotion for all, provided privileges correspond to relevant differences in contributions to the general welfare.

As a fact, stratification is thus founded on interests or rather on the necessary existence of individual interests. However as a structure it is regulated by the general interest; in other words, for society to remain socialistic, i.e. so that conflicts within it do not degenerate into a class struggle choices must be harmonized, regulated and ordered according to the good of the collectivity as a whole. . . . For equality to be possible one day, there must be socialist stratification at present.[72]

5 SOCIAL CLASS IN POLISH SOCIOLOGY

Polish sociologists have consistently acknowledged that stratification exists in a socialist society, even while the 'belief that society is divided in social strata' was rejected in the Soviet Union as 'arbitrary and unscientific' and when 'the notion of social mobility' was branded as 'an invention of bourgeois sociology'.[73] They have admitted the survival of 'residual classes', rooted in the past structure of property relationships and preserved during the transition period by the existence of the private sector (petty bourgeoisie) and of individually owned farms (peasantry). However, they are

aware that these correspond to a small enclave within the
socialized economy and that both the economic functions
performed by property owners and their relations to other
producers have been radically transformed by central
planning.[74] Therefore, the existence of private property
implies that of classes as logical categories, but not as sociological ones, in the Marxist-Leninist sense, since they cannot
be linked by relationships of exploitation. Lenin's definition:
'Classes are groups such that some can appropriate the
labour of others'[75] could not be applied to any groups in a
socialist society and the concept of 'class' either has to be
reserved for the study of capitalism or has to be redefined to
fit changed relationships to production. The same dilemma
has arisen in the Soviet Union and has not received any
unequivocal solution. Denial of the logical possibility for
class divisions to outlive class oppressions have been followed
by statements about the stable coexistence of 'non-antagonistic' classes corresponding to different sectors of the
economy.[76]

Obviously these are not classes in the old sense of the word, its
general sense. The concept of class was historically created to
describe social relations in societies polarized by ownership and
non-ownership. There are no relations of this kind in a socialist
system, in which classes draw closer and closer to each other.
Inter-class relationships are no longer comparable with those of
masters and servants, they are relationships between equals, based
on collaboration in efforts to produce and on a fair allocation of
material and intellectual goods.[77]

This definition of non-antagonistic classes by the Soviet
sociologist Glezerman exemplifies the revision undergone by
the concept of class to adapt it to the existence of State
ownership in industry and collective ownership in agriculture.
Therefore it emphasizes 'relations to various means of
production rather than various relations to means of production'.[78] A related attempt has been made by the Polish
sociologist Minć who distinguishes two classes of socialist
producers corresponding to the State sector and the co-
operative sector and posits a schema of stratification remotely
connected with St Simon's theory of social organization
centred on productivity. The occupational hierarchy of the
enterprise, reflecting the different shares of responsibility

assumed in the productive process by the managers (function of leadership), the specialists (function of expertise), and the skilled and unskilled workers, is the basis on which society is stratified. This approach overlooks the differences existing within each of these occupational categories (for instance, the differential prestige of leaders) and does not in fact take into account any objective or subjective criteria unrelated to production in industry but relevant to stratification in society. The classes it posits have not generally been accepted as discrete homogeneous groupings in Polish society, whereas the 'residual classes' identified by reference to property relationships are not covered by it at all.

With the exception of Minc,[79] Polish sociologists have not attempted to apply the concept of non-antagonistic classes and have either assumed that classlessness would eventually result from the nationalization of all means of production, or equated it with the elimination of class exploitation. The latter interpretation, adopted by Ossowski, has enabled him to use the terms 'unegalitarian classlessness' – pointing to the existence of stratification in socialist societies and to the lasting inequalities unaffected by the transformation of property relationships. In this perspective differences between the social structure of socialist and capitalist societies are blurred, since economic privileges and a status hierarchy exit in both. 'The liquidation of levels in the socialist structure does not necessarily involve the destruction of the social ladder.'[80] While maintaining that the existence of private property – albeit in a small sphere on a small scale as in Poland – is incompatible with classlessness and that Ossowski's use of this concept is incorrect, Wiatr acknowledges the growing irrelevance of class divisions to an understanding of socialist societies and the possibility of analysing Polish society as a system of stratification.

Although the notion of strata . . . of prestige or income is not explicit in Marx, it may be used to analyse capitalism. However while capitalist countries are divided in classes, these strata will be subordinated to them in the analysis. The situation changes under a socialist regime. Even before the complete liquidation of exploiting classes, as is for instance the case now in Poland, the elimination of classes from the main activities and the anihilation of their social significance outline a structure which is less and less amenable to a division in classes and more and more amenable to stratification.[81]

Thus, while there is disagreement on the definition of classlessness, there is virtual unanimity on the irrelevance of class divisions to an understanding of Polish society under socialism and the unimportance of 'residual classes' arising from the vestigial character of private ownership. 'Although in socialist societies classes have disappeared, there remains a social differentiation which we may call stratification.'[82] Some would alter the first statement to 'classes are disappearing' – but the second seems non controversial.

There is a major difficulty involved for Marxist sociologists in analysing classes in Poland as residual and intrinsically impermanent, whereas stratification is conceived as a stable consequence of the division of labour, influenced by class divisions in capitalism, but capable of outlasting them and giving no signs of withering away in socialist societies.[83]

> The fact which does not facilitate the work of post-revolutionary sociologists . . . is that Marx, in his critique of capitalism, develops the reverse scheme: for him, it is the division into classes which is the major fact . . . which orientates the fate of society, stratification being only its transitory aspect.[84]

While the concept of class is retained for analysing the social structure of capitalist countries, an alternative approach has had to be devised for the societies in which the private ownership of means of production is either abolished or residual and devoid of major significance. Since this approach must be compatible with a Marxist frame of reference, it has been based on a concept which Marx himself used when he posited conflicts of interest as the objective source of class struggle. *Interest* has been redefined as a 'sociological category'[85] to provide a general criterion of social differentiation. The existence of stratification is derived from the scarcity of available resources which does not allow for the satisfaction of all objective needs; thus, a hierarchy of interests must be introduced until an economy of plenty has been achieved. 'I realize that divergent interests exist wherever goods are scarce; these goods are necessarily shared in such a way that if some have more, others have less. The socialist regime cannot avoid contradictions between interests because of the simple fact that abundance does not prevail'.[86] However, such a regime must solve existing contradictions by imposing priorities defined by reference to the needs of society as a whole. This leads to a quasi-functionalist theory of stratification.

> In a market economy, the aspiration of everyone is to increase his share of goods; from this aspiration springs the urgent need to grant privileges to those whose position – occupational or other (e.g. political) – maximizes the chances of fulfilling these aspirations. The person whose specialization is rare may have exorbitant privileges far beyond the simple reward of his qualification by reference to the principle 'to each according to his work'.[87]

The justification of inequalities by the social utility of tasks performed and the scarcity of individuals capable of performing them is not unlike Davis and Moore's theory.[88] Wiatr, in his analysis of Polish stratification, underlines the relevance of *qualifications* to social differentiation. This is reminiscent of the criteria of individual talents and training by reference to which social roles are assessed according to Davis and Moore. However, there is a double difference between the American and the eastern European approach. Firstly, functionalism aims at formulating world-wide principles, whereas a basic distinction between capitalist and socialist societies underpins the approach of Polish sociologists. Secondly, the acceptance of genetic inequalities between individuals is easier for the functionalist than for the Marxist sociologist. However this difference is merely programmatic, as development of latent aptitudes is largely deferred and as equality is subordinated to efficiency during the transition period.

6 STUDIES OF STRATIFICATION IN POLAND

These studies are therefore undertaken with the two preliminary qualifying statements that they are more relevant to an understanding of socialist than of capitalist societies and that they may become irrelevant after the transition period, in a more egalitarian society. For the present, differences between strata largely supersede the former class division, but have been partly shaped by it before the advent of the

People's Republic, and are thus rooted in the social differentiation of the capitalist period. Hence the coexistence of
criteria which are a legacy of the past and are gradually being
eliminated by planning policies with others which are
rationally adapted to the construction of socialism. Thus
stratification along some dimensions is a regrettable perpetua-
tion of the past, while along other dimensions it is a legitimate
structure of the transition period. Of the four main criteria of
differentiation in contemporary Poland – as listed by Wiatr –
three can be assigned to the latter category, whereas the
urban/rural dichotomy is clearly less acceptable.

A Although Poland is no longer a predominantly agrarian
country the urban/rural distinction remains basic. The
economic and cultural disparities between the towns – centres
of industrial production in nationalized large-scale enterprises – and the countryside, where agricultural production
remains predominantly based on privately owned small
farms, have proved more lasting than class differences. After
the virtual disappearance of landless agricultural labourers
and the emergence of peasant-workers, after considerable
official efforts for the modernization of farming and for
popular education, the 'residual class' of peasants, remains
strikingly different in its living and working conditions from
the urban manual workers. This is a problem common to all
eastern European countries. To merge the urban and rural
masses into one has been the constant concern of Soviet
leaders ever since the revolution paradoxically occurred in a
largely unindustrialized country; industrialization has transformed the economy, but has not sufficed to solve this
difficulty. The contradictions implicit in the existence of two
entirely different forms of production and environments could
only be eliminated by an urbanization of the rural habitat (an
experiment which has been attempted in vain in 'agrovilles')
and on industrialization of farming (attempted in the
kolkhozes). On a smaller scale and with smaller resources, the
Polish political leadership could not endeavour to radically
transform the countryside and has had to retain the structure
of private ownership. However, the main aspect of the urban/
rural dichotomy is not the differential rate of collectivization
in industry and agriculture or the survival of the peasantry as
a residual class. It is the contrast between levels of income,

degree of occupational mobility, consumption patterns, degree of education and 'cultural consumption' between town and country dwellers. While the fact that life styles differ may be explained as unavoidable in the early stages of the transition period, the existence of differences in life chances is likely to perpetuate an undesirable differentiation. For instance, the educational opportunities of rural children are much less than those of town dwellers: in 1959–60, 83·8 per cent of applicants for entry into higher educational institutions came from secondary schools located in the main cities.[89] Objective difficulties, such as distance to school and lack of information about the educational system, are increased by expectations centred on early gainful employment rather than on training for a qualification. Thus, while to the working-class child social promotion is equated with education, the peasant child would define it as working in industry for a fixed wage and in an urban setting.[90] The ideologically undesirable distinction between two modes of production is therefore linked with a differentiation between producers which technical progress is expected to eliminate over time but which temporarily perpetuates the exploitation of rural producers by urban consumers.

B Occupational differentiation being due to the division of labour, the manual/intellectual dichotomy reflects an objective fact in the organization of the economy (though not necessarily a permanent one, since the advent of automation may be expected to render this differentiation ultimately redundant). However, it does not imply that the demarcation line between manual and non-manual employment is the main divider and that crossing it represents 'a decisive index of social mobility'.[91] This was undoubtedly the case in pre-war Poland, when manual work was on average less well paid, required less instruction and carried less prestige than clerical. The legal recognition of the 'manual classes' as ruling classes, while it was merely a formal statement in itself, was accompanied by gradual changes of the economic and social context which altered the scales of remuneration and the hierarchies of prestige.

As a result, next to the *individual promotion* of the worker, i.e. the mobility typical of the capitalist system, which consists in *leaving the working class*, we are witnessing in our country a mass promotion of the working class, consisting in a change in its position and its role in society, without a change in social membership.[92]

This promotion of the working class is linked with the industrialization which made employment plentiful and stable and created a greater demand for skilled operatives; it is a product of the interrelated facts of economic and political change. As a result,

changes in prestige are universal and great, and undermine the thesis according to which occupational prestige is comparatively stable. Apart from traditional individual mobility, a specific *group* mobility . . . witnesses to considerable *structural* change and represents a basic element of the pattern of a socialist society.[93]

Studies on the prestige ratings and the attractiveness of various occupations[94] indicate that the ranking of manual jobs, both skilled and unskilled, has improved since the pre-war period. They are located higher on a Polish hierarchy of prestige than on the corresponding hierarchies elaborated in the United States and in West Germany.[95] Nevertheless, the passage from 'manual' to 'intellectual' employment is still generally considered as a form of individual social promotion, even when it corresponds to a 'socio-economic demotion',[96] according to Szczepanski. This could be explained as a survival of traditional attitudes and is related to the ambiguous interpretation of the intelligentsia's role. In the early days of the People's Republic it was the social origin of most intellectuals and their connections with the previous ruling classes which were condemned, the appointments of the most politically active and most-enterprising members of the working class to non-manual posts were construed both as a necessary renewal of the composition of the pre-war intelligentsia and as an individual reward for militants. They were certainly perceived as upward mobility by those who were thus given executive posts.[97] Although some of these promotions proved unwise and had to be cancelled, there was nevertheless a fairly considerable inflow of manual workers into the intelligentsia as a result of political appointments to managerial positions.[98]

After about ten years of this process, the mass of workers initially selected (for such positions) was divided into those who

M

having failed at their task, joined again the ranks of manual labourers and those who, by acquiring qualifications, secured their non-manual position and amalgamated with the survivers of the old intelligentsia and with the young *cadres* freshly qualified from the new universities. Because of this new intelligentsia, heterogeneous in its origins but made culturally homogeneous by the very persistence of the concept of intelligentsia (with the prestige traditionally attached to it), the high value openly and officially given to manual work was contradicted by facts. . . .[99]

The contradiction between assessing manual work as the most socially useful and promoting the most valuable workers to non-manual posts corresponds to an ideological uncertainty. On the one hand, the promotion of the working class to ruling class is understood as an attempt to abolish traditional hierarchies of prestige. On the other, it is construed as merely giving workers maximum chances of reaching high echelons in these hierarchies. The two policies appear to have been applied simultaneously.

C Although ideally unacceptable in a socialist regime, income differentials have been retained since planned development requires the preservation of economic incentives for individuals to seek additional qualifications and to maximize their productivity. Thus inequalities of remuneration are justified by reference to individual contributions to the economy, but the assessment of these contributions is necessarily changeable. It must take into account temporary and regional shortages of specialists and skilled workers. However, the operation of the law of supply and demand on the manpower market is impeded by the understandable tendency of privileged groups to perpetuate their advantages. Therefore the problem of fair remuneration essential in a socialist economy, is increased by the contradiction between proportionality to qualifications and efforts, risks and responsibilities, on the one hand, and, on the other, the concern for minimum needs of the less productive groups and individuals. The occupational strata whose rewards are highest by virtue of the first principle, appear to be least concerned with the application of the second, which embodies the communist principle limited to the possibilities of the intermediary phase. Thus, according to Malewski's investigation on the psychological implications of unequal wages,[100] engineers – who are among the economically privileged – are less egalitarian and more meritocratic in their outlook on fair remuneration than their less qualified co-workers. Since the best-paid posts are those involving the greatest decision-making power, the economic hierarchy appears likely to prove self-perpetuating.

Only remuneration in the private sector is therefore comparatively high. Thus a ranking of occupations by material rewards would give precedence to the owners of private industrial and commercial firms over the intelligentsia, followed by skilled manual workers, clerical workers and the unskilled, in that order. However, the rating of persons associated with the private sector on a subjective hierarchy of utility has been found lower than that of either members of the intelligentsia or skilled workers.[101] Economic privilege does not coincide with subjective utility in the case of non-wage earners, because their position in the economy is marginal and unstable. For wage-earners the coefficient of similarity between remuneration and utility oscillates between 0·38 and 0·66, according to Sarapata's investigations.

The discrepancy between actual wages and what would be considered as fair remuneration for the main occupations by a sample of 1,400 persons representing a variety of occupational categories indicates that while a hierarchy of retributions is generally considered compatible with the principles of socialism, the existing income stratification is not viewed as founded on perceived contributions to the economy. The coefficient of similarity between the hierarchy of fair remuneration and of subjective utility is 0·915 – a degree of concordance due to the fact that both are ranked with reference to education, training and responsibility. However, existing incomes do not coincide to this extent with either educational and occupational qualifications or with the responsibilities involved. Hence the existence of stratification by income cannot be justified by relevant differences in qualifications for or responsibilities in the job, as public opinion would wish. **D** While inequalities resulting from the division of labour and the structure of remuneration have been the object of many sociological investigations in contemporary Poland, the power structure has not been analysed as thoroughly or as often. The existence of a rulers/ruled dichotomy has been accepted as a necessary implication of the survival of the State machinery in the intermediary phase. However, in the long term the State is to wither away according to the basic tenets of Leninist theory and therefore this dichotomy is as temporary as the urban/rural without being as undesirable. Indeed, it is through central planning that the evolution towards more advanced modes of socialist control is to be hastened. The forms of collective management which are deemed ultimately to replace democratic centralism will be the outcome of decisions made by present-day rulers. Therefore the State structure is legitimated by the political leaders' commitment to its disappearance. This commitment in turn is guaranteed by the fact that they emanate from the workers' party which crystallizes the aspirations of the ruling class/the working class/and its political ally/the peasantry. The contradiction implied by the non-manual character of Party work and by the role thus assigned to a bureaucracy shaping, interpreting and executing collective decisions has been insufficiently investigated. It has been stated that the dichotomy is replaced by a continuum, a rising scale of power, and that the concepts of rulers and ruled interpenetrate each other, as the Party bridges the chasm between ordinary citizens and the political elite. However – unlike an incomes scale – this ranking of political influence has not been attempted[102] and investigations of Party membership have been discouraged. There has also been a widespread reluctance to investigate conflicts betwen groups competing for power. Since the role of the State is to solve potential conflicts between occupational and economic interests in accordance with the official ideology, political leaders tend to be presented as embodying the general interest and arbitrating disputes accordingly rather than as representing pressure groups and contending for power. An additional reason for neglecting the investigation of the interlocking Party and State hierarchies and the socio-economic background of the political elite – assuming that such studies would not be prevented – is the doubt about the degree of autonomy of the Polish power structure within the Eastern bloc. It is undoubtedly misgivings in this respect which contribute to the low rating of politics as a career in public opinion polls. The hierarchy of power appears to be little known, but it is clearly dissociated from the hierarchy of subjective utility to an extent which confirms the existence of two parallel value systems.[103] While rapid changes have occurred simultaneously in the power structure and the economic structure since the advent of the People's Republic, the former appear to have been associated with a decrease in the subjective utility attached to official positions – e.g. those of civil servant or of career officer – and the latter with a lessening of the correlation between social utility and remuneration.

Thus the main criteria of social differentiation in a socialist regime are either temporarily acceptable, but ultimately intended to disappear as a result of planned change (e.g. the urban/rural dichotomy, inequalities of remuneration and of power) or are resented even in the intermediary phase since they are not ideologically justifiable (e.g. inequalities of wealth due to the survival of the private sector). On the other hand, the lasting effects of the division of labour – which are the main source of inequalities – are legitimated by the concept of qualifications. These, by guaranteeing competence, make the occupational stratification functional and by linking social promotion to education increase equality of opportunity. Provided the educational system is open, a differentiation based on formal qualifications is in accordance with the meritocratic tenets of the official ideology without contradicting its interpretation of egalitarianism. 'It can be substituted for the criterion of property like the "talents" of French revolutionaries were substituted for birth.'[104] It is on this basis that a new social hierarchy has been constructed by contemporary Polish sociologists describing the present system of stratification. The unskilled manual workers constituting a mobile labour force are located at the bottom – as indeed they are on the scales of remuneration and of subjective utility. They are followed by the rural workers – whether or not these are self-employed and regardless of the size of their farm. Then intellectual workers possessing only elementary qualifications and employed in the civil service or in tertiary posts are located beneath skilled manual workers. Thus neither intellectual nor manual occupations are seen as corresponding to distinct strata, but both are subdivided by reference to qualifications possessed. Skilled manual workers are both rated more highly on a scale of prestige and remunerated more generously than in capitalism. The next level corresponds to the medium qualified intellectual workers and the top of hierarchies of remuneration and of prestige is occupied by the highly qualified 'creative, technical and leading intelligentsia'.[105] This social hierarchy in terms of educational and vocational qualifications is thus claimed to be highly correlated with both the hierarchy of prestige and the scale of remuneration. However, this statement disregards the widespread discontent about a system of remuneration which does not reward qualifications.[106] Moreover, it leaves aside the self-employed petty bourgeoisie whose material benefits are high, but whose prestige rating is low and whose formal qualifications are negligible. Thus it is not through education that the highest rewards are obtained. Nor is there a complete coincidence between the hierarchies of social position as indicated by occupation and of prestige.[107]

CONCLUSION

In a socialist regime, the existence of stratification can only be considered as legitimate – i.e. as a feature of the new society rather than a survival of the past – if the main criteria on which it is based do not contradict the fundamental tenets of official ideology. Educational qualifications constitute such a variable, since they contribute to the economic ends of State policy without necessarily contradicting the egalitarian legacy of Marxism. They have been claimed by Polish sociologists to provide the key to the system of stratification which is allegedly comprised only of levels and types of knowledge and skills. It has been maintained that material rewards and social prestige are attributed proportionally to qualifications. In this view, there would be a perfect concordance between the rates of remuneration, the hierarchy of prestige and the scales of qualifications. Any discrepancies could be explained as temporary distortions due to lingering social prejudice or occasional maladjustments in the planning of the economy. Thus stratification is presented as unidimensional – with only minor deviations.

However, empirical investigations show that such an approach – ideologically correct and politically reassuring –

does not result in an accurate description of contemporary society. They disprove the existence of the alleged correlation between the qualifications gained by individuals and the remuneration obtained. Far from being incidental, discrepancies in this respect are a major source of discontent and cause fairly widespread negative attitudes to educational promotion, particularly among manual workers. Thus working-class children who prefer immediate earnings to spending additional years in the educational system, support this choice by stating that the possession of formal qualifications does not secure appropriate material rewards. By a logical corollary prestige is withheld from qualifications which often do not result in occupational promotion and in increased earnings. The 'devaluation' of some diplomas, whose holders are seen to be unrewarded or insufficiently rewarded, e.g. the secondary school-leaving certificate, illustrate the lack of connection between educational attainments and promotion on both the scales of remuneration and the hierarchy of prestige. Lastly, it is not through acquiring qualifications that a larger share in political decision-making can be obtained. The Party hierarchy is not regulated by reference to educational criteria, or to any formalized scale of proficiency. Political promotions – which are not confined to the Party, but occur in the State bureaucracy and the nationalized industries as well – are prompted by considerations of orthodoxy and expediency. This may well be in accordance with the imperatives of class rule at any given moment and may therefore be doctrinally justified. Nevertheless, there is a distinct contradiction between this autonomy of politics and the uni-dimensional view of stratification. There appears to be at least one dimension – that of power – on which formal qualifications are irrelevant, while on others, their relevance cannot be uniformly assumed.

In his study of social stratification, Wesołowski concludes that an analytical approach to the subject shows the need for applying several criteria to take account of rapid changes in the economic and the political structure. The three dimensions he posits for a study of Polish society appear to be possible and necessary spheres of investigation. They are possible in so far as they correspond to genuine forms of social differentiation in relation to real criteria as distinguished from 'desirable or 'legitimate' variables, such as qualifications. They are necessary since they appear to be uncorrelated and therefore to make any unilateral approach to stratification incomplete. The lack of correlation between political *power* and social *prestige* is corroborated by the low rating given to politicians on the scale of desirable careers and by the comparatively low rank awarded to civil and military officials in the evaluation of occupations by the Sarapata-Wesołowski sample. The fact that university professors were ranked above Cabinet ministers in a hierarchy of prestige although their political influence is small and their power – even that to admit or reject students in their own departments – is limited by political considerations, shows the dissociation of the two hierarchies. The same example illustrates also the existence of an imperfect correlation between *prestige* and *remuneration*. Indeed the whole of the teaching profession is notoriously underpaid and yet its prestige rating does not reflect this economic handicap. The reverse applies to the group engaging in private enterprise whose members have high earnings, but gain little respect in a society in which this sector is discredited. The third attempted correlation – between *power* and *remuneration* – may be considered as unexplored or unproven. The remuneration of the highest political posts appears to indicate that power brings material rewards on a rather more generous scale than the initial austerity of Leninism would warrant. There are various economic advantages and privileges for members of the Party hierarchy. Such non-monetary forms of remuneration are a subject for diffuse criticism rather than for study and the lack of adequate information precludes one from positing anything other than an imperfect but unpopular correlation between these two dimensions.

This multi-dimensional view of contemporary stratification can be contrasted with the uni-dimensional approach which adequately described the pre-war system. Until 1939 the correlated factors of birth and wealth characterized the ruling class – comprising the aristocracy, the bourgeoisie and the upper strata of the intelligentsia. This privileged group cumulated political power, social prestige and economic wealth (still predominantly agrarian). On all these dimensions the deprivation of other groups was correspondingly great. That of manual workers, both rural and urban, was virtually complete, whereas intellectual workers benefited from some of the prestige attached to the intelligentsia – in so far as it could be defined as a non-manual category. However, their scales of remuneration were low and their employment stability decreased after the crisis of the early 1930s. In spite of the slight prestige derived from 'intellectual' rather than manual occupations, they were economically handicapped and politically insignificant. The petty bourgeoisie in crafts and trade had some material advantages in being self-employed, although it was vulnerable to economic fluctuations. This group enjoyed little social esteem and had little say in the politics of the country. Thus, in spite of some discontinuities – mainly connected with the traditional position of the intelligentsia – a uni-dimensional view of stratification could be adopted.

In the post-war period, the policy of planned social change was not intended to create an unstratified, egalitarian society, but to replace the ideologically illegitimate criteria of stratification, birth and wealth, by a legitimate variable. In the early phase of the Popular Republic, it appeared that social origin – i.e. a manual background – might constitute this variable. According to Leninist doctrine, the working class and its political ally, the peasantry, were meant to be the new ruling class. They were to accede to the highest political responsibilities, to reach the top of the hierarchy of prestige and to receive material rewards reflecting the importance of their contributions to the economy. Therefore the degree of correlation between the dimensions of power, prestige and remuneration which existed before 1939 was intended to endure; only the ruling class was replaced. The criterion of tested merit, embodied by formal qualifications, was gradually substituted for that of social origin, since it was better adapted to the requirements of productivity and, in the long run, less inegalitarian than birth. Moreover, it was expected to transcend the manual/intellectual dichotomy – whose existence was unavoidable in the present system of production, yet difficult to reconcile with the rule of the 'manual classes'. It did not result, however, in the uni-dimensional system of stratification which it was meant to ensure. Indeed, three main dimensions remained imperfectly correlated with qualifications – and with each other. The traditional prestige of the intelligentsia survived the modification of its social composition. No longer linked with the aristocracy, but originating to a great extent from the working class, the intelligentsia has retained its sense of special responsibility for and identification with the culture of the country. From this is derived the widespread awareness that this social group has a national role to play, particularly in times of political stress such as the 'Polish October'. Hence a prestige rating which perpetuates the manual/intellectual division in spite of official policy and of economic incentives for skilled manual workers. The scale of remuneration does not follow this division, thus confirming the dissociation between the hierarchy of prestige – still influenced by a tradition dating back to the period of Partition – and the hierarchy of remuneration, dictated by the requirements of industrialization. Finally, while prestige and remuneration are partially independent dimensions, the power structure is less known, but is presumably independent from the other two. In spite of statements about the 'manual ruling classes' and of the 'intellectual character' of political and administrative work, the possession of power is unrelated to the manual/intellectual dichotomy. Although ideological attempts have been made to isolate a single variable to which the three dimensions could be reduced, empirical studies show hierarchies of power, prestige and remuneration to be separate in contemporary Polish society.

NOTES

1   According to the census of 1931, 31 per cent of a total population of 32·1 million were not of Polish mother tongue.
2   About 64 per cent of farms were under 5 ha. in area. Cf. *International Social Science Bulletin*, UNESCO, Vol. 4, No. 2, 1957, p. 185.
3   Cf. Z. Bauman, *Zarys Marksistowskiej Teorii Społeczenstwa* (Outline of a Marxist Theory of Society), (Warsaw, 1964), pp. 198 f.
4   Cf. J. Piekałkiewicz, *Sprawozdanie z badań składu ludności robotniczej w Polsce metoda representacyjna* (Account of research on the composition of the working class by the representative method), (Warsaw, 1934), p. 91.

5 Cf. L. Landau, *Płace w Polsce w związku z rozwojem gospodarczym* (Remunerations in Poland in connection with economic development), (Warsaw, 1938), p. 87.

6 Cf. W. Wesołowski, 'Przemiany struktury klasowo-warstowowej w Polsce Ludowej' (Changes in the class and strata structure of Popular Poland) in *Nowe Drogi*, Warsaw, i(231), August 1968.

7 Cf. J. Zarnowski, *Struktura społeczna inteligencji w Polsce w latach 1918–1939* (The social structure of the intelligentsia in Poland in the years 1918–1939), (Warsaw, 1964), p. 146.

8 Idem, p. 341. According to Zarnowski, about 60 per cent of 'intellectual workers' belonged to the lower (clerical and semi-manual category).

9 J. Chałasiński, *Przeszłość i Przyszłość Inteligencji Polskiej* (The Past and the Future of the Polish Intelligentsia), (Warsaw, 1958), p. 64.

10 Chałasiński, 'Intelligentsia' and J. Szczepański, 'Materialy do ogolnej charakterystyki ludzi polskiego swiata naukowego w 19 i poczatkach 20go wieku' (Materials for a general characterization of members of the Polish scientific world in the nineteenth and the early twentieth centuries) in *Kultura i Społeczenstwo*, Vol. vi, No. 2, July–September 1962 (a study of the social background of Polish scientists confirming the thesis of the intelligentsia's predominantly aristocratic origins).

11 Cf. M. Falski, '*Srodowisko społeczne młodzieży i jej wykształcenie* (The social origin of the young and their education), (Warsaw, 1937).

12 According to J. Zarnowski (*Social Structure* . . . , p. 331) only one-third of the 'Higher Intelligentsia' members (Functions of leadership and expertise) had higher educational qualifications, while only 30 per cent of 'intellectual workers' had completed a full secondary course.

13 Cf. J. Zarnowski, *Social Structure*, p. 331, on the low prestige and remuneration of primary teachers.

14 Collated from J. Zarnowski.

15 Cf. Polska Akademia Nauk (Polish Academy of Science), *Wykształcenie a Pozycja Społeczna Inteligencji* (The education and the social position of the intelligentsia), J. Szczepański (ed.), Part 1 (Lodz, 1959), p. 9.

16 Cf. J. Chałasiński, *Past and Future of Polish Intelligentsia*, p. 97.

17 Cf. S. Szulc, 'The Demographic Problem' in *International Social Science Bulletin*, Vol. ix, No. 2, p. 177.

18 According to S. Szulc, 'The Demographic Problem', there were 3·2 million Jewish war victims in Poland out of a total of over 6 million Polish nationals killed in 1939–44.

19 These territories covered about 181,000 km² and had a total population of 12 million (33 per cent of which had Polish as their mother tongue) according to the census of 1931.

20 The subject of the western territories is among the best docu-
    mented in contemporary Polish literature. See in particular
    W. Markiewicz and P. Rybicki (eds.), *Przemiany społeczne na
    Ziemiach Zachodnich* (Social Change in the Western Territories),
    (Poznan, 1967), (bibliography) and on problems of sovereignty,
    M. Lachs, 'The Polish–German Frontier' in *Social and Political
    Transformation in Poland* (S. Ehrlich, (ed.)), (Warsaw, 1964),
    pp. 115 f.
21 Ethnic minorities are assessed to under 500,000 (on the basis of
    incomplete census data).
22 Cf. J. Tepicht, 'Problems of the Development of Polish Agri-
    culture' in *Social and Political Transformations in Poland*, pp. 71 f.
23 Cf. J. Szczepański's Conclusion, in Polska Akademia Nauk,
    Education, etc., pp. 459–60.
24 Approximately 460,000 families acquired land in the pre-war
    territory of Poland (expropriated land) while about 600,000
    were settled in the western territories (on former German land).
    Cf. J. Tepicht, Introduction, *International Social Science
    Bulletin*, Vol. IX, No. 2.
25 Cf. B. Gatłęski, 'Sociological Research on Social Changes in
    Poland's Rural Areas', in *Empirical Sociology in Poland*
    (J. Szczepański, (ed.)), (Warsaw, 1966), pp. 79 f.
26 Cf. J. Szczepański, *Zagadnienia Socjologii Współczesnej*
    (Problems of Contemporary Sociology), (Warsaw, 1965), p. 67.
27 D. Gałaj, 'Problems of Research in Poland's Regions under
    Industrialization', in *Empirical Sociology*, pp. 53 f.
28 Cf. M. Jarosińska, *Adaptacja Młodzieży Wiejskiej do Klasy
    Robotniczej* (Adaptation of Rural Youth to the Working Class),
    (Wroclaw – Warsaw, 1964), p. 12.
29 Cf. R. Turski, 'Chłopi-Robotnicy' (The Peasant Workers) in
    Socjologiczne Problemy Przedsiębiorstwa Przemysłowego (The
    Sociological Problems of the Industrial Enterprise) (A. Sarapata,
    (ed.)), (Warsaw, 1965), pp. 107 f.
30 Cf. W. Wesołowski, *Changes in Class and Strata . . .* , p. 232.
31 Cf. R. Turski, 'The Peasant Workers', and Z. Bauman, *Outline
    of a Marxist Theory . . .* , p. 206.
32 Cf. M. Dziewicka, 'A New Social Group in Poland: the Peasant
    Workers', in *International Social Science Bulletin*, Vol. IX, No. 2,
    pp. 184 f.
33 Cf. Z. Bauman, *Outline of a Marxist Theory . . .* , p. 198.
34 *Rocznik statystyczny* (Statistical Yearbook), (Warsaw, 1964).
35 Cf. A. Sarapata, *Studia nad uwarstwieniem i ruchliwością
    społeczna w Polsce* (Studies of social stratification and social
    mobility in Poland), (Warsaw, 1965), p. 67.
36 Cf. M. Jarosińska, *Adaptation of Rural Youth . . .* , p. 21.
37 Cf. W. Wesołowski, *Changes in Class and Strata . . .*, pp. 228 f.
    During the same period there was a reduction in tertiary
    employment in the administration and the judiciary (from 25·4
    per cent of intellectual workers in 1931 to 9·1 per cent in 1960).

38 Cf. Z. Bauman, *Outline of a Marxist Theory...*, p. 199.
39 Polska Akademia Nauk, *Education*, etc., p. 8.
40 Cf. A. Borucki, *Kariery zawodowe i Postawy Społeczne Inteligencji w PRL (1945–1959)* (Professional careers and Social Attitudes of the Intelligentsia in the Polish People's Republic) (Wroclaw – Warsaw, 1967).
41 A. Borucki, *Professional Careers, etc.*, p. 17.
42 Cf. UNESCO, *Facts and Figures* (Paris, 1961), p. 78.
43 Cf. Chałasiński, . . . *Polish Intelligentsia*, p. 97 about the aristocratic tradition of the intelligentsia in Poland 'separating thought from work, theory from practice, the charms of life from its duties and burdens, amateurism from profession, honour from the necessity to do productive work, "mind" from "matter" '. This is in complete contradistinction with the cult of technique and production, the professionalism and the materialism expected from the new intelligentsia.
44 Cf. B. Suchodolski, 'Poland – a statement of aims and achievement', in E. J. King, *Communist Education* (London, 1963), p. 247: 'Polytechnicization of training is based on the teaching of mathematics, physics, chemistry, biology.'
45 Cf. B. Simon, *Education in the New Poland* (1954), p. 19: 'Linking almost all school subjects with economic, social and technical problems, . . . giving the schoolboy or schoolgirl a practical knowledge of the technical side of modern civilization.'
46 Cf. B. Suchodolski, 'Poland . . .', p. 248: 'We do not deny the political character of our schools in the sense that we want them to bring up people with an understanding of the present historical situation, with an awareness of the historical paths of capitalist developments, and with a grasp of the laws governing socialist construction. We do not conceal our desire to infuse our young people with a conviction, based upon scientific knowledge, that the capitalist system is entering the stage of its final decay.'
47 The curriculum of the four-year course in general secondary schools is roughly divided into one-third languages, one-third mathematics and sciences, one-sixth physical education and military training, whereas the 'technicum' course reduces the share of theoretical (particularly non-scientific) subjects to include 6–8 hours of practical work per week. Cf. B. Simon, *Education in the New Poland*. On the non-vocationalism of the lyceum, cf. a study of the employment problems of a sample of graduates not proceeding to higher education by A. Borucki and S. Dzięcielska, in PAN, *Education . . .*, pp. 22 f.
48 The importance of post-primary vocational education is reflected by the development of two-year vocational schools in which three days a week are spent in the classroom and three in a workshop or factory. In 1963–4, 5·18 million pupils attended

primary schools, 1·37 million received vocational post-primary education, and only 378,500 attended general secondary schools. Cf. *Rocznik statystyczny* (1964).

49 Higher education accounted for 212,558 students in 1963-4 (idem), i.e. 6·99 per cent of the whole pupil and student population in Poland. 10 per cent of primary school entrants apply for entry to higher institutions, 6 per cent are admitted. Cf. J. Szczepański, 'Sociological aspects of higher education in Poland', in S. Ehrlich, *Social and Political Transformation*, p. 255.

50 Cf. M. Jaroszyński, J. Litwin and W. Togroski, *Prawo szkół wyzszych* (The law of higher educational institutions), (Warsaw, 1965), Vol. 1, pp. 199 f.

51 This formal definition, centred on the manual/non-manual and the wage-earner/self-employed distinctions, has been severely criticized as artificial and often detrimental to deserving candidates (e.g. children of workers promoted to managerial posts for services rendered to the party). Cf. K. Grzybowski, 'Pochodzenie społeczne' (Social Origin) in *Zycie literackie* (7 August 1966).

52 In spite of the rapid growth of higher education (from six universities and thirty-two higher educational institutions in pre-war Poland to eight universities and seventy-three degree-granting institutions), the number of places is insufficient to meet the demand.

53 Entry exams include three papers, for which additional marks can be granted as a 'bonus for social origin' up to 10 per cent of the maximum mark; this bonus is inversely proportional to the percentage of applicants of working and peasant origin. Bonus marks are also granted to those applicants who achieved the best results at secondary level.

54 Cf. E. Polański, 'W. sprawie doboru kandydatów na studia wyższe' (About the choice of candidates for higher education) in *Zycie szkoły wyższej*, No. 5 (1966).

55 Cf. J. Zieliński and Wierzyński, 'Punkty zawisły w próżni' (Points hanging in mid-air) in *Polityka*, (28 August 1965,) according to whom candidates to the Warsaw Polytechnique who qualified for the 'bonus for social origin' did not need it and were only 5·5 per cent of all applicants.

56 J. Szczepański, *Inteligencja i Społeczeństwo* (Intelligentsia and Society), (Warsaw, 1957), p. 13.

57 Cf. W. Wesołowski, 'Changes in the Social Structure of Poland' in *Empirical Sociology in Poland*, p. 225.

58 Cf. B. Gałęski, *Sociological Research* . . .

59 Cf. Z. Bauman, *Outline of a Marxist Theory* . . . , p. 206.

60 B. Gałęski, *Sociological Research* . . .

61 Cf. J. Szczepański in *Polska Akademia Nauk, Education* etc., pp. 460–1.

62 Cf. J. Wiatr, *Społeczeństwo. Wstęp do Socjologii systematycznej*

(Society. An Introduction to Systematic Sociology), (Warsaw, 1964), p. 244 and Z. Bauman, *Outline of a Marxist Theory* . . . , p. 190.

63 Cf. J. Hochfeld, *Studia o marksistowskiej teorii społeczeństwa* (Studies on a Marxist theory of society) (Warsaw, 1963), pp. 171 f.

64 Z. Bauman, *Outline of a Marxist Theory* . . . , p. 50.

65 Cf. J. Szczepański, *Zagadnienia Socjologii Współczesnej*, pp. 50 f.

66 In pre-war Polish sociological literature the petty bourgoisie is considered as one of the six classes in society (the term 'class' being used in a non-Marxist sense and not being clearly distinguished from strata). In post-war literature, there is some uncertainty arising from the various interpretations of class structure in Marx's works (cf. S. Ossowski, *Class Structure in the Class Consciousness* (London, 1963), pp. 75 f.), but the 'multi-divisional' view tends to prevail and the pre-war petty bourgeoisie to be termed a class.

67 Cf. J. Szczepański, 'Inteligencja i Społeczeństwo', in P.A.N. *Education* . . . , p. 26: 'The intelligentsia ruled over the minds . . . though the ideas fermenting in it had a class content drawn from the classes which were its support.'

68 Cf. S. Ossowski, *Class Structure* . . . , p. 78.

69 O. Lange, *Ekonomia polityczna* (Political economy), Vol. 1, (Warsaw, 1959), p. 81.

70 Cf. W. Wesołowski, *Klasy, warstwy i władza* (Classes, strata and power), (Warsaw, 1966), p. 22.

71 Cf. J. Wiatr, 'Uwarstwienie Społeczne a Tendencje Egalitarne' in *Kultura i Społeczenstwo*, Vol. VI, No. 2, 1962, p. 35.

72 J. Lagneau, 'Stratification et Egalitarisme. Théorie et pratique de la différentiation sociale en pays socialistes' (Doctorate Thesis, Paris University), unpublished (Paris, 1968), p. 54 f.

73 *Sociologia v SSSR* (Sociology in the Soviet Union), Vol. 1 (Moscow, 1965), p. 410.

74 Cf. J. Szczepański, '*Zagadnienia Socjologii Współczesnej*', p. 63.

75 V. I. Lenin, *Dzieła* (Works), Vol. 29 (Warsaw, 1951), p. 415.

76 The concept of non-antagonistic classes was used by Stalin in 1935. While he denied the existence of classes in the Soviet Union in 1945, this concept has been sporadically used by Soviet sociologists.

77 G. E. Glezerman, 'Ob Klassovoj diferenciacii i socilonoj odinorodnosti' (On class differentiation and social levelling) in *Voprosy filosofii*, No. 2, 1963.

78 S. Ossowski, *Class Structure* . . . , p. 81.

79 Cf. B. Minć, 'Klasy i warstwy w społeczeństwie socjalistycznym' (Classes and strata in socialist society) in *Polityka*, Nos. 39, 42 and 46 (1961).

80 S. Ossowski, *Class Structure* . . . , p. 97.

81 J. Wiatr, *Uwarstwienie społeczne* . . . , p. 37.

82 W. Wesołowski, *Klasy warstwy i władza*, p. 186.
83 This withering away, predicted by Bukharin in his *Theory of historic materialism* (*Teoria Materializmu Historycznego* (Warsaw, 1936), Chapter 8), was rejected as an impossibility by Kautsky (*Materialistyczne pojmowanie dziejów* (The materialist conception of history), Vol. 2, Part 1 (Warsaw, 1963).
84 J. Lagneau, *Stratification et Egalitarisme* . . . , p. 52.
85 Cf. Y. E. Glezerman, 'Interes kak sociologiceskaja kategorija' (Interest as a sociological category) in *Voprosy filosofii*, No. 10 (1966), pp. 15 f.
86 W. Wesołowski, *Klasy, warstwy i władza*, p. 22.
87 J. Wiatr, *Uwarstwienie społeczne* . . . , pp. 42–3.
88 Cf. Davis and Moore, 'Some principles of stratification' in ASR, No. 2 (1945).
89 *Przegląd Socjologiczny* (1958), Vol. 12.
90 Cf. R. Turski, *Dynamika Przemian Społecznych w Polsce* (The Dynamics of Social Change in Poland), (Warsaw, 1961), pp. 28 f.
91 Cf. Lipset and Bendix, *Social Mobility in Industrial Society*, pp. 14.
92 A. Sarapata, *Studia nad uwarstwieniem i ruchliwoscią społeczną* (Studies on stratification and social mobility), (Warsaw, 1965), p. 44.
93 A. Sarapata, *Studies on Stratification* . . . , p. 41.
94 Cf. W. Wesołowski and A. Sarapata, 'Hierarchia zawodów i stanowisk' (The hierarchy of professions and occupations) in *Studia socjologiczne*, No. 2 (1961).
95 Cf. W. Wesołowski and A. Sarapata, 'The Evaluation of Occupations by Warsaw inhabitants', in AJS, Vol. 66 (May 1961).
96 J. Szczepański, *Inteligencja i Społeczenstwo*, p. 10.
97 Cf. K. Lutyńska, *Pozycja społeczna urzędników w Polsce ludowej* (The social position of civil servants in Popular Poland), (Warsaw, 1965), p. 269, who quotes memoirs written by workers promoted to non-manual jobs (e.g. 'In 1948 I was appointed to a non-manual post: I considered this appointment as a promotion').
98 There were approximately 60,000 promotions of this type among Party members between 1945 and 1956 (cf. J. Janicki, 'Kariery zawodowe urzędników administracyjnych i biurowych' (The careers of administrative and clerical employees) in *Studia socjologiczne*, No. 1 (1965).
99 J. Lagneau, *Stratification et Egalitarisme*, p. 74.
100 A. Malewski, 'Psychologiczne następswa nierówności dochodów niektórych warszawskich przedsiębiorstw i instytucji' (The psychological consequences of inequalities of workers' incomes in some enterprises and institutions in Warsaw), unpublished (Warsaw, 1958).
101 Cf. A. Sarapata, *Studies on Stratification*, pp. 117 f.
102 Cf. J. Wiatr, *Uwarstwienie społeczne*, p. 37.

103 Cf. Wesołowski, *Studia z socjologii klas i warstw społecznych* (Warsaw, 1962), p. 168.
104 J. Lagneau, *Stratification et Egalitarisme* . . . , p. 210.
105 J. Wiatr, *Społeczenstwo* . . . , p. 247.
106 Cf. A. Sarapata, p. 406.
107 Cf. S. Wanderszpil and J. Janicki, 'Do jakiej klasy należysz? (To what class do you belong?) in *Zycie Gospodarskie*, No. 25. (1959).

12 Scandinavia*

Kaare Svalastoga and Gøsta Carlsson

INTRODUCTION

Our task is a new one. No previous attempt has been made to consider the Scandinavian (here including Finnish) contributions to stratification and mobility research together. However, for most of the region the relevant literature has been assembled in easily accessible bibliographies[1] and in this paper we shall draw upon works listed in these bibliographies, as well as upon Norwegian studies not yet appearing in reference works. In particular we shall try to take into account research performed after 1945 for the whole region.

It may be asked whether Scandinavia, as here defined, really forms a region which is set apart from the rest of western Europe by common social characteristics. No doubt we usually think of ourselves as forming a small family of nations strongly resembling each other. If sociological studies cast some doubt on this assumption it is not so much because they reveal striking internal differences, but because we cannot be sure that the Scandinavian countries are in all respects closer to each other than they are to the rest of western Europe. The case for Scandinavia as a social region is stronger if we define the term as including Denmark, Norway and Sweden, excluding Finland. These three countries share some important attributes which do not occur in this combination in any other part of the world. They are all industrialized nations with a very high degree of ethnic, religious and linguistic homogeneity within and between each country, with a fairly long tradition of political unity and independence, and with the absence of power politics and war experience typical of most small nations. Finland differs

* This contribution first appeared as an article, under the title 'Social Stratification and Social Mobility in Scandinavia', in *Sociological Inquiry*, Vol. XXXI (Winter 1961), No. 1.

in several of these attributes. In Finland's comparatively short history of political independence, the civil war of 1918 left deep scars. There is evidence of much more acute class conflict than in the other three countries and only 8 per cent of the Finnish population belongs to the Scandinavian linguistic group. Thus Finland seems internally more heterogeneous and differs sharply from the Scandinavian mode.

STRATIFICATION VARIABLES

Since stratification research deals with attributes that are both desired and scarce, it may be proper to raise the question as to whether these are the same in Scandinavia as elsewhere or whether it is possible to achieve high social rank in Scandinavia, or in part of that region, by possessing attributes that would not give such high rank elsewhere?

It seems clear that most groups are somewhat ethnocentric in these respects. Thus the reward for conforming to certain norms of language, tact, loyalty and societal insight will vary from place to place.

More dubious is the problem of whether some major stratification variable, e.g., occupational prestige, power, wealth, or education, tends to mean more in Scandinavia than elsewhere. Tentatively we would suggest that three attributes carry more prestige in Scandinavia than in the United States: (a) to pursue a non-manual occupation,[2] (b) to be a public employee, and (c) to possess a scholarly degree. With the relative and absolute numerical increase of all these attributes in recent times, the differential gain in rank may, however, be declining.

One aspect of Scandinavian life seems to be connected with these distinctions: in most of Scandinavia a person's *occupation* is considered an important part of his identity. Occupational and scholastic titles are used frequently in addressing people and most public records will not only identify people by name, time and place of birth, but also by occupation and, frequently, by one's parental occupation. Thus the Danish *Who is Who* typically gives a minimum of three occupational entries for married persons (own occupation, father's occupation, and occupation of father-in-law).

Since fairly long series of public records are available it follows that mobility research can be executed either by documentary analysis or by conventional survey methods. In fact, Carlsson[3] has used the former method and Svalastoga[4] the latter. Carlsson obtained a person's own occupation from a sample of the Swedish census which is kept up to date. Because this source also contains information on time and place of birth, it is practically always possible to locate birth certificates where the father's occupation is entered. Svalastoga obtained these two pieces of information from an interview with the person.

Considering the numerous biographical sources (books on physicians, ministers, schoolteachers etc.) which contain information on the parent occupation, it may appear surprising that comparatively few modern studies of this material are available. This is partly due to sheer lack of sociological labour force, but although the data on parental occupation is presented, they are frequently so imprecise that refined mobility estimates are not possible. Danish occupational titles like *landmand* (agrarian), or *håndværker* (artisan), exemplify this deficit. To the degree that occupational prestige rather than occupational activity is of primary interest, it is important to secure supplementary information such as the social responsibility associated with the occupation and the skills or education needed for performing the job.

The contribution of animal studies of *rank-order* has been highly informative in an approach to these sociological studies. They clearly reveal the negative relationship between the presence of rank-order and in incidence of social conflict. The pioneer in this field was the Norwegian Schjelderup-Ebbe,[5] whose interest began with his patient, meticulous observation of the behaviour of his mother's chickens, and formed the basis of his doctoral dissertation. The search for animal rank-orders thus initiated has established the widespread incidence of such rank-orders within birds and mammals. In a more recent publication, Schjelderup-Ebbe even asserts the presence of rank-order among certain species of insects. Among humans the most comparable hierarchies, because they are so closely associated with relative fighting ability, may be the rank-orders among boys of school age. Segerstedt and Lundquist[6] have shown how a formal rank-order, as found in a factory, limits the communication load of persons in supervisory or managerial positions. The percentage among male manual workers in one of the towns investigated who had never or only more than a year ago spoken to a boss one, two or three steps removed from his immediate supervisor was, respectively, 36, 68 and 87 per cent.

Although common sense as well as sociological theory includes *social power* as a major stratification variable, little effort has been devoted to the measurement of inequality along this dimension among human groups. Social power seems to be quite unevenly distributed in Scandinavia, as probably is true everywhere. Such power will most of the time appear in the form of authority vested in an office and hence is partly taken into account in prestige ratings of occupation. With the increasing predominance of large-scale organizations (the expanding government, employers' unions, and employees' unions, larger productive units, etc.), it seems that the power gap between the top and the bottom may be widening.

Although, as will be documented later, *education* is not the only nor even the most frequently used avenue towards the achievement of higher status, it does enjoy a position of high and growing importance in the mobility process. Furthermore, as pointed out by Boalt,[7] the educational escalator seems to carry a person upward with more public approval than other escalators. Persons who are lifted up by successful capital accumulation or by organizational efficiency may perhaps be rejected or classed as egoistic manipulators. It seems that the educational gap, like the power gap between the top and the bottom, may become wider rather than narrower, with the rapid increase of scientific knowledge. This contention is not necessarily contradicted by the well-established fact that a larger percentage of young Scandinavians than ever before now attain the student examination (gymnasium graduation examination and entry ticket to most institutions of higher learning). In Sweden, male graduates constituted only 3 per cent of their age group in 1910, but 6 per cent[8] in 1950 and the change for females was from ·4 per cent in 1910 to 4 per cent in 1950.[9]

In Norway the proportion of an age group who passed the matriculation examination increased only slowly and with many vacillations conditioned by the business cycles during the nineteenth century. From about 1910 a more rapid increase set in.

The empirical figures are:

Year	Per cent
1910	1·8
1920	3·0
1930	4·1
1940	6·2
1950	9·9
1955	9·7

Wealth is, for at least three reasons, an important stratification variable: (a) it enables the one who possesses wealth to exercise social power; (b) it affords an opportunity of publicly stressing or making conspicuous the possession of high status; and (c) it is transmissible from generation to generation, contrasting strikingly with organizational power and scholastic achievements. Because of the transmission to coming generations, it is eminently suited to act as a kind of brake on the mobility process, increasing the probability that sons will inherit the status of their fathers and decreasing the chances of social ascent and descent. Wealth or accumulated capital seems to be a more important criterion of economic status than annual income, because annual income, even if high, does not necessarily imply capital accumulation and hence generational transmissibility. Inequality as measured by the Gini index is in Denmark ·80 (Pareto exponent 1·12) for wealth, but only ·34 (Pareto exponent 1·99) for income after tax deductions, indicating that wealth is much more unevenly distributed than income. No value judgements are implied here; it may well be that present income differentials are too small in Scandinavia to ensure maximum incentives to productivity. It is suggestive that Soviet Russia operates with considerably higher income differentials.

Research in *occupational prestige* is a post-war phenomenon in Scandinavia. So far prestige ratings based on national samples are available for Sweden and Denmark, while student ratings are available for Norway, and ratings from a small village for Finland.

In co-operation with the Swedish Institute of Public Opinion, Carlsson[10] obtained ratings on a five-point scale of twenty-six occupations in a Swedish national sample of 1,700 adults. Carlsson showed that the rank-order obtained correlated with r = ·88 with Danish data and American data. Svalastoga (Danish data) reported a correlation of ·91 with American and Dutch data and a correlation of ·88 with English data. Slightly lower correlation was reported by Carlsson between Sweden and West Germany (·80 rank-order), and between Sweden and Japan (·83). All correlations are product moment when nothing else is indicated.

Svalastoga[11] had a nationwide sample (N = 1000 males and 200 females) rate seventy-five occupations in terms of social standing in five categories. The male responses were analysed in terms of respondents' occupation and the mean rating of each of the seventy-five occupations was correlated in an 11 by 11 matrix. A high level of consensus was evidenced by the fact that no correlation coefficient lower than ·96 appeared in the matrix. Also high was the correlation between the sexes (r = ·99) and between communities (lowest entry, r = ·986) of different size while the correlation between age groups (21–49, 50 and over) was considerably lower (·88).

The approximate invariance of the rank-order did not prevent numerous occupations from being ranked significantly higher or lower, depending upon the characteristics of the respondent. The results of prestige ratings may tentatively be accounted in terms of four sets of factors: (1) the scale of values of the rater; (2) the informedness of the rater; (3) the social importance of the occupation rated, and (4) the level of skill or education required for the execution of the occupation rated.

In Svalastoga's study a deliberate attempt was made to minimize the influence of the second set of factors by including only the better-known occupations, and by associating each occupational title with a given number of subordinates and a given educational level. Correlating the latter two pieces of information with the outcome of the prestige ratings gave a multiple correlation of ·91. To the extent that number of subordinates may be taken as one possible operational definition of the Davis-More concept 'social importance', we have here a demonstration of the dominant importance of factors 3 and 4 and, by inference, of the minor importance of differences in value scales between respondents.

Validity of rank-ordering was measured in terms of per cent of respondents who turned an existing official hierarchy upside down, e.g., by placing mailman higher than postmaster, etc. The available Norwegian[12] and Finnish[13] prestige ratings support the generalization that the occupational prestige hierarchy is virtually invariant within Scandinavia and that little error will be involved in basing estimates for one country on research findings from another.

A twelve-nation metropolitan poll[14] conducted by local Gallup Institutes in 1959 revealed that two occupations far outranked all others in popularity as prospective employment for a son of sufficient ability.[15] These two were those of physician and engineer.

The figures for the Nordic countries are as follows:

	Engineer %	*Physician* %
Copenhagen	29	18
Oslo	17	30
Stockholm	11	19
Finland (national sample)	15	21

In all four samples 'engineer' and 'physician' were the most frequently mentioned jobs.

SOCIAL CLASS AND CLASS DISTINCTIONS

In this section we shall devote a few words to the historical background of present-day social stratification. We shall then report research dealing with class identification and class conflict, and finally we shall consider a sample of the numerous studies dealing with differential class behaviour.

Medieval Scandinavian society as mirrored in ancient poetic literature (Rigsthula[16]) sharply differentiated social classes: the class of the *chieftains* (the nobility), the *farmers*, and the *slaves*.

The slaves are described as having a darker and uglier appearance than the others, while the noblemen are described as lighter and more attractive than the rest. The slaves did the heavy manual work or work of a routine character, the farmers were the managers of the economy, and the noblemen are pictured as a well-to-do leisure class devoted to war and play while at the same time retaining a monopoly on the art of writing. Swine and goats were the animal associates of the slaves, oxen those of the farmers, while the noble earls appeared with hounds and horses.

The slaves have long since disappeared. The nobility has lost all formal prerogatives, but is still in existence in all Scandinavian countries, except Norway. Its numerical strength is about two persons per thousand in Sweden, and about one person per thousand in Denmark and in Finland. Homogamy is, according to Willebrand,[17] the principal technique whereby a noble class can maintain itself. Hence, it is the decline of the homogamic tendency which reveals the falling status of the group. As of 1930, 74 per cent of all marriages contracted by Swedish noble persons were heterogamous, whereas the corresponding percentage for 1954 was 50 per cent. However, considering the small size of the nobility, the homogamic tendency is still quite strong. Although nobility in Scandinavia does not confer privileges other than the right for males to use certain titles and for all to be entered in a separate nobility yearbook, it still is a fact that noble origin adds to a person's status. Boalt[18] investigated the relationship between family name and social class in Sweden. He reported on the basis of a register of Stockholm citizens that the most common names were those ending in '-son'. Among the holders of the thirteen most frequent names (1,073 columns in the register), only 3 per cent belonged to the upper class. The group of fifty-four names coming next in frequency (539 columns) had 7 per cent in the upper class. In comparison, 63 per cent of noble-names belonged to the upper class. A sample of the whole Stockholm register gave 9 per cent upper-class names.

To the extent that the rest of Scandinavia resembles Denmark, there will be a tendency to conceive of modern society as composed of hierarchical social classes: the *upper*, *middle*, and the *working* class. In fact, these labels were those most frequently found in Denmark, while the label *lower class* was very rarely used. Also rare were all designations of specifically Marxian flavour (proletariat, capitalists, etc.). A more or less militant class identification was found only among 5 per cent of the respondents. When Danish respondents were confronted with a list showing nine hierarchically

arranged classes (upper-upper to lower-lower) nearly everyone was able to and willing to identify himself with one of
these but, when a comparable sample was given an open-end
question on social class identification two major changes
occurred: (a) a much higher tendency to reject identification
with any class, and (b) a much higher tendency to choose a
middle-class title.

In interpreting these findings, the author drew upon the
theory of cross pressures. The higher levels of the working
class (as classified by others) will have the working class as a
membership group, but may have the middle class as a
reference group. The latter relationship will tend to weaken or
change their working-class identification, particularly when
fewer cues are given to ease working-class identification.
Results obtained in Swedish studies, however, do not
corroborate these findings. Rather there seems to be a
tendency among Swedish workers to identify solidly with the
working class regardless of method of questioning, and a
tendency among middle class (middle-middle and lower-
middle) to identify with the working class, again regardless of
method of questioning.[19]

One may perhaps say that there are three partly overlapping foci of potential social conflict in modern Scandinavia: the manual/non-manual split; the rural/urban split;
and the employee/non-employee split.

In all three areas it seems that technological changes will
gradually make these distinctions less important. The manual
worker increasingly acquires the typical privileges of the
non/manual worker. Farming as an occupation is declining
and the farmers that remain tend increasingly to resemble
urban businessmen, although the economic interests of the
former may not be identical with those of the latter. Entrepreneurial activity (non-employee occupations) is gradually
declining in relative numerical importance and, providing no
new foci of dissension develop, the outlook for the achievement of national consensus should be better in the near future
than it was in the past.

The importance of the manual/non-manual split may
probably best be measured in terms of the percentage of
persons voting Communist in a free election. Thus measured,
class antagonism is low in modern Scandinavia proper

(Communist-vote about 5 per cent), but high in Finland (Communist-vote 23 per cent). Generally speaking, ideological class differences reveal themselves in the relationship between social class and political party preference. The percentage voting the Social Democratic ticket in Denmark is largest in the lowest strata and declines rather sharply with increasing status. Adherence to the Conservative party reveals exactly the opposite relationship to social status, while all other parties in Denmark, except the Communist, have their maximum popularity in the middle strata. The Communist party may be curvilinearly related to status with maximum adherence at or near both ends of the social ladder.

Tingsten[20] documented, on the basis of election statistics from many countries, including Sweden and Denmark and ranging in time from about 1890 to about 1935, that participation in an election tends to increase with increasing social status. This generalization still holds, at least for Sweden.

Segerstedt and Lundquist, who studied five Swedish industrial plants, found a small, but positive, correlation between employee attitudes toward the greater society, and attitudes toward his own company. Thus, persons who felt that the police could be trusted were also more likely to feel that management in their factory was taking employee interests and abilities into account. Furthermore, the view of Swedish society, as one putting a premium on talent and initiative, was associated with a positive evaluation of the chances of social advancement inside the plant where respondents were working.

While the distinction between discrete classes seems likely to be declining, the same does not necessarily hold for distinctions of social status or rank and for the sensitivity to such distinctions. In fact, such distinctions and sensitivity may gain in importance as society moves from a state dominated by the small and independent entrepreneur to a state dominated by functionaries in large-scale organizations.

A study of Danish school children executed by Ingrid Koch[21] revealed a rather regular and steep increase of status sensitivity with increasing age. Svalastoga[22] showed that such sensitivity was more frequent the higher the social status of the respondent.

It is a common experience that small local communities governed by one or two major industrial plants tend to be considerably more sensitized to status distinctions than larger communities with a more varied industrial equipment.[23] Dahlstrøm, however, found no reason to assume that Swedish communities of the former type either possessed, or were felt by inhabitants to possess, greater communication barriers between various occupational groups. Nor did he discover consistent differences in social-class attitudes between the two types of communities. Dahlstrøm's study is based on 2,170 questionnaires collected in 1952 at seventy-nine Swedish factories.

While efforts to establish the extent and intensity of social attraction and repulsion within and between social classes have been few, there have been numerous analyses of differential class-behaviour, where class has been arbitrarily taken to mean more or less hierarchically ordered occupational groups. It is beyond the scope of this chapter to review all studies under this heading. We shall limit ourselves to a few problem areas.

Of particular importance is the problem of *differential net-production*, because of its direct implication for social mobility. The fertility pattern in Stockholm, as established by Edin and Hutchinson,[24] revealed for the period 1917–30 a positive correlation between fertility and income and between fertility and level of education. Both these relations were obtained even if the third variable was controlled. For families married for 5–14 years, the Swedish census in 1945 established a curvilinear relationship between family income and mean number of children, the very high and the very low income categories being more fertile than the middle-income categories. Recent Norwegian research shows that farmers are more prolific than agricultural workers, and that officers in the merchant marine beget more children than able-bodied seamen, and that factory-workers have only slightly larger families than factory-owners (1946). In the first two instances the relationship sixteen years earlier was completely opposite. These findings, from a paper by Jahn,[25] refer to marriages of eighteen or more years' duration and in which the wife was aged twenty-four or twenty-five years at marriage. Collapsing Jahn's occupational categories into strata based on occupational prestige one would, however, probably still find the conventional negative relationship between fertility and social class, although differences would be considerably smaller than sixteen years earlier.

For Denmark it has been established that fertility is negatively related to social class: higher class, lower fertility. At the same time infant mortality is also negatively related to social class. However, the latter difference does not seem to be large enough to neutralize the influence of the former variable, so it seems likely that Denmark has a lower net-reproduction in the upper social classes than in the lower ones.

Lindhardt[26] investigated the relationship between morbidity and social class, partly by large-scale samples of the Danish adult population, partly by a special survey of hospitals. Limiting the analysis to males and controlling for age, she found that manual workers were slightly more likely than others to report ailments, and much more likely to become hospitalized (p. 57). Although reports of ailments showed no consistent differences between functionaries and owner-operators, the functionaries were clearly the group most protected against disease leading to hospitalization. The only major category revealing a consistent manual/non-manual difference was accidents. Accident proneness was about 50 per cent higher among young workers than among young nonworkers (age: 20–44 years), and the risk-difference increased to about 300 per cent in the case of older people (age: 45–64 years). In other disease categories, functionaries seemed particularly protected while workers and owner-operators were both more exposed. These categories were ulcer and other diseases of the digestive system, plus goitre and muscular diseases.

Class distinctions may also be seen in studies of visiting patterns. This research has tended to support two conclusions: (1) that mutual visiting patterns are sensitive to social distance and hence occur with greatest frequency among class equals; (2) that one-sided visits or friendship choices under certain conditions may reveal a status jump, i.e., a higher social class being more frequently chosen than one's own, relative to the maximum number of choices.

A study by Honkala[27] gave results which suggested that the last conclusion may be limited to communities which are both small in size and relatively homogeneous.

SOCIAL MOBILITY

Most Scandinavian research on social mobility centres on the comparison of parental and filial occupation. Interest centres on intergenerational mobility.[28] Since the study of mobility from generation to generation usually aims at unravelling not only the frequency and distance of given status-moves, but also the conditions and consequences of such moves, longitudinal methods seem the superior research tools. However, because of the heavy demands on research personnel, time, and money implied by such methods once they get beyond the use of public records, no womb-to-tomb study of social mobility has so far been undertaken in Scandinavia.

The predominant procedure has been retrospective. Starting with a sample of adults, social origins are investigated. Three sub-types of the retrospective procedure may be distinguished, depending upon the universe which the sample aims to reflect. The universe may be (a) the nation, (b) a local community, or it may be (c) an occupational or otherwise socially distinct subpart of some population. Studies of all three types are available in Scandinavia, although types (a) and (b) are much more rare than type (c).

National mobility tables are now available for all the Scandinavian countries. Because of the classification differences between various Scandinavian mobility-researchers, it is necessary to limit comparisons to special groups or to apply a highly simplified scheme of classification. By the latter method, which will be illustrated, it is important to strive for such simplifications as will tend to give marginal similarity between mobility tables to be compared. The significance of this criterion is related to the decisive effect of social distance on relative mobility-rates (see below).

It is possible to arrive at a set of three 2-by-2 tables with roughly similar marginal percentages for each of the countries Sweden, Norway, Denmark (Table 1).

The tables for Sweden, Norway and Denmark reveal several similar features:

(a) The percentages of sons having upper-class status varies only between 42 per cent and 43 per cent.

(b) The percentage of fathers having upper-class status varies only between 42 per cent and 45 per cent.

(c) Hence there is in each case a high degree of approach to marginal identity for rows and columns.

(d) Finally, the correlation between parental and filial status may be approximated by means of a single parameter, e.g., percentage ascending from parental lower-class to filial upper- or middle-class. The ascending percentage for Denmark is 24 per cent, Norway 27 per cent, and for Sweden 32 per cent.

Table 1. Social mobility in Scandinavia

		Sweden (Carlsson)[29] Fathers			
		Lower Class %	*Upper Class* %	*Total* *No.*	%
Sons	Upper	32	58	5,423	43
	Lower	68	42	7,080	57
	Total %	100	100		100
	Total N	7,190	5,313	12,503	

		Norway (Rokkan)[30] Fathers			
		Lower Class %	*Upper Class* %	*Total* *No.*	%
Sons	Upper	27	61	313	42
(Respondents)	Lower	73	39	428	58
	Total %	100	100		100
	Total N	417	324	741	

		Denmark (Svalastoga)[31] Fathers			
		Lower Class %	*Upper Class* %	*Total* *No.*	%
Sons	Upper	24	63	1,000	42
(Respondents)	Lower	76	37	1,391	58
	Total %	100	100		100
	Total N	1,308	1,083	2,391	

Finland (Hellevuo)[32]
Fathers

		Lower Class %	Upper Class %	Total No.	%
Sons and					
daughters	Upper	11	78	581	19
(Respondents)	Lower	89	22	2,426	81
	Total %	100	100		100
	Total N	2,638	369	3,007	

The Finnish data do not permit direct comparison with the others because of the large difference in marginals. However, a comparison with another breakdown of the Danish data[33] is possible and this leads to the tentative conclusion that Finland must be deemed less mobile than Denmark. The upward mobility index for the Finnish table shown is ·57, which may be compared to a Danish upward mobility index of ·62. The Danish index value is derived from a dichotomy, which gives a slightly smaller parental lower class: Denmark 84 per cent, Finland 88 per cent and a filial upper class which also is smaller (Denmark 14 per cent, Finland 19 per cent). The Finnish study comprises males and females aged twenty years and over. It is here compared with the Danish study of males aged twenty-one years and over.[34] However, a separate analysis of female mobility in Denmark gave no basis for assuming a sex difference in mobility.

The findings suggest, but do not prove, that Sweden slightly outranks the other Scandinavian countries in social mobility between generations. In the case of Sweden, independent craftsmen, regardless of number of employees, were classified together with employed craftsmen and hence it was necessary to subsume them all under the heading *Lower Class* in Table 1. A further difficulty is presented by the group of independent farmers. Since the Swedish study does not differentiate according to size of farm, all farmers had to be placed in one category. With some hesitation we assigned upper-class status to this group. It is true that this was done with Danish and Norwegian farmers, too (but not with Danish and Norwegian smallholders), but although the distribution by size of farm is not markedly different between

Norway and Sweden, Danish farms are on the average considerably larger.

We will have to conclude, then, that for Scandinavia as a whole the per cent who ascend from lower- to upper- and middle-class status is about 25 per cent, corresponding to a correlation coefficient of about $+ \cdot 4$ between parental and filial status (approaching $\cdot 5$ with more refined measurement).

Carlsson[35] compared urban mobility in Sweden and England and concluded that there may be 'some difference in the supply-demand relation with respect to occupational positions but hardly any considerable difference in the manner available positions, or opportunities are distributed'.

Svalastoga compared mobility in Denmark and England, and found that most criteria revealed English mobility to be slightly higher. One important exception was the incidence of *long-distance mobility*, such as from the twentieth percentile or lower to the ninety-seventh percentile or higher on a percentile index of status. Such mobility was in England so rare as to be unobserved in a sample of about eight hundred respondents of low-status origin. The same degree of mobility was rare in Denmark too, but did materialize for six sons of unskilled workers (N = 530).

The hypothesis of a somewhat higher chance of long-distance upward mobility in Scandinavia than England was further substantiated by Carlsson, whose data suggest a long-distance mobility rate of about 1 per cent for the bottom 20 per cent in terms of parental status – about the same order as observed in Denmark.

Carlsson compared his own Swedish data with Janowitz's data for Germany, and concluded with some reservations that Sweden has a considerably higher rate of mobility.

Studies of the recruitment to specific achievement categories are too numerous to allow specific mentioning of each contribution. It must suffice to mention some of the major studies.

Geiger[36] analysed the changes in social recruitment over time characterizing the Danish intelligentsia on the basis of *Dansk Biografisk Leksikon* (Danish Biographical Dictionary). His sample included nearly 9,000 persons born between 1501 and 1900. He showed that, regardless of time, the road to eminence was easier with an urban than with a rural birth

N

certificate. Furthermore, he documented the extremely narrow social recruitment basis of the intelligentsia. Recruitment from the lower or working class does not reveal any increase over time. It is difficult to use Geiger's study for detailed assessment of the fluctuations in long-distance mobility over time. There is no assurance that eminence is equally narrowly defined at different times nor are statistics available for most of the period that permit an exact assessment of the size of the social recruitment basis.

Geiger also initiated a study of the *Who is Who* population. After his death, Ulv and Carlsen[37] have continued his work. Recently they published some findings with *Who is Who* entries of 1910 and 1946, limiting the analysis to persons of rural origin. Classifying the fathers of this group into three wealth categories (wealthy [gentlemen] farmers, average farmers, smallholders and agricultural workers) they found the following relationship:

Social origin	Per cent entered in Who is Who		Per cent with these occupations in Census 1921
	1910	*1946*	
Wealthy farmers	56	34	·5
Average farmers	31	50	20·4
Smallholders and agricultural workers	13	16	79·1
Total rural males	100	100	100·0

The major change in mobility pattern affected only the upper 20 per cent of the rural population. This is particularly illuminating because it suggests that considerable mobility changes may be covered up in conventional mobility tables, due to crudeness of grouping. It will be seen that in order to establish the above mobility difference, a thin stratum numbering only $\frac{1}{200}$ of total rural male society was analysed.

One of the most carefully executed studies of occupational recruitment was done by Mannsåker,[38] who deals with the social origin of Norwegian (state church) ministers in the nineteenth century. He classified the fathers of ministers into four strata:

(1) Upper class: elite group consisting of top civil service, leading businessmen and landowners (1st percentile).
(2) Upper middle: average civil service and equals (clergy included here) big farmers (2–5th percentile).
(3) Lower middle: other nonworkers class, small farmers (6–50th percentile).
(4) Working class: workers, urban-rural (51–100 percentile).

His data reveal that the clergy, although during the entire period nearly inaccessible to working-class people, still did become accessible to a larger group of society in the course of the nineteenth century. Before 1850, access to the clergy was predominantly reserved to status equals or superiors so that only 27 per cent of the ministers were upwardly mobile. The corresponding percentage for the years 1851–1900 was 48 per cent. Such change of relative accessibility may be, but is not necessarily, associated with change in occupational prestige. Indications suggest that in the case of the clergy there has been a correlation between increased accessibility and status decline.

Linders[39] documented increasing working-class recruitment of Swedish ministers between 1600 and 1800. After 1800 (Linders has figures up to 1920) no marked change has occurred. In contrast, upper-class recruitment falls rather regularly from 66 per cent for 1601–40 to 26 per cent for 1881–1900, and 35 per cent for 1901–20. The typical recruitment base of the Swedish clergy, which up to 1800 was predominantly upper- or upper-middle-class, thus became, in the course of the nineteenth century, accessible to a larger group. In particular, the self-recruitment of the clergy declined from 59 per cent (1601–40) to 25 per cent (1901–20). The percentage base is the total number of ministers for which relevant information was available.

Suolahti's[40] non-quantitative historical study tends to stress the narrow social recruitment of the Finnish clergy 1600–1800, and the immense difficulties facing the gifted young man of humble social origin who was destined for a clerical career. Suolahti suggested the rule that upward mobility, even to a minor clerical position, tended to be followed by downward mobility in the next generation unless the ascending minister had settled on the Russian side of the border where, according to Suolahti, the mobility conditions were more favourable.

A group of political scientists at the University of Uppsala have made a study of recruitment to some branches of the civil service system of Sweden during the period 1917–47[41] covering positions normally requiring university education or its equivalent. The sample was divided into three strata by origin (taken from the official election statistics). Stratum I is an upper- and upper-middle-class stratum comprising about 5 per cent of the adult population. Stratum II is a middle-class stratum including farmers, white-collar workers and small-scale entrepreneurs (about 42 per cent). Stratum III is a working-class stratum including agricultural workers (about 53 per cent of the adult population).

In Table 2, three main sections are distinguished: departments, semi-autonomous administrative governmental agencies (a far bigger group than the departments), and the state country officials appointed by the government. The table shows the distribution according to father's stratum during different time periods. Stability rather than change is the dominant result. There are somewhat more working-class children now than earlier, but the development has neither been rapid nor uniform.

Laaksonen investigated the social origin of the Finnish business elite and found that 21 per cent were from working-class homes, and 17 per cent from the category of farmer (all size categories of farms included), while the rest, 62 per cent, were recruited from the urban middle and upper strata, which as of 1920 comprised only 11 per cent of the male labour force.

Table 2. *Civil servants according to father's stratum: Percentage distribution*[42]

	1917				1927				1937				1947			
	I	II	III	Total	I	II	III	Total	I	II	III	Total	I	II	III	Total
Departments	77	21	2	100	77	20	3	100	75	22	4	101	80	19	1	100
Central boards	64	32	3	99	60	36	4	100	56	39	5	100	48	43	9	100
County administrations	49	49	3	101	43	49	7	99	45	46	8	99	47	46	7	100
All branches studied[43]	65	32	3	100	61	35	4	100	58	37	5	100	52	40	7	99

The relative increase in positions requiring education beyond the legal minimum makes it important to evaluate the accessibility of higher education.

Most Scandinavian research on educational groups has centred around two categories of persons: those who have passed the 'student examination' (twelve years of schooling) and those who have in addition obtained a university degree (about six years additional schooling).

Ramsøy[44] investigated the relationship between level of education and several demographic factors using a 2 per cent sample of the Norwegian 1950 census and including only persons born between 1 Dec. 1929 and 30 Nov. 1935. In this group 20 per cent had either passed the student examination or were preparing for it (senior secondary school-group or sss). Nineteen per cent had completed or were in the process of completing other schools, while 61 per cent possessed only a grade-school education. The sss percentage was the same for boys and girls, while level of urban development showed a sizeable difference in favour of the cities (34 per cent for cities, 11 per cent for 'scattered settlements').

Ramsøy reports the following sss percentage for certain paternal occupational categories:

Workers:
Forest and agricultural workers   3
Fishermen   6
Other workers   17

Functionaries and professionals:
Superordinates and professionals   58
Others   52

Non-employees:
Rural   11
Urban   34

He was able to show further that with occupational category constant, an important difference appears between communities having high school and communities without. Another important variable for constant occupation was paternal level of education. A most surprising negation of a commonly held hypothesis appeared when the sss percentage was computed by occupation for boys and girls separately. It appeared that workers, who are underprivileged in terms of filial education, reveal no sex differences in sss percentage, while such a difference in favour of boys appears most sharply in the privileged category of higher functionaries and professionals.

Similar findings are reported for Sweden by Moberg,[45] who also reveals that the dominant tendency in terms of student recruitment from 1910 or 1920 to 1943 was one of approximate invariance. If one knew the 1910 or 1920 percentage of all students coming from a certain occupational or educational environment as measured by parental occupation, one could with a modal error of three percentage points predict the 1943 percentage of nine categories. Thus Moberg reports that 8 per cent of all students, as of 1920, stemmed from the category of skilled, semi-skilled, and unskilled urban workers. The corresponding percentages 1930, 1937 and 1943 were respectively 10, 6 and 8. A major increase seemed to be limited to certain lower middle-class categories. Moberg made an attempt to relate the number of male students for certain parental employment categories to the total number of males aged twenty in these categories. He was then able to show that in 1937 about 2 per cent of working-class sons obtained the student examination, and that about 4 per cent did in 1950. In comparison, as of 1950, 45 per cent of grade school teachers' sons, and 70 per cent of the sons of ministers passed the same examination.

The handicap of working-class origin continues to make itself felt even after passing the student examination. While about three-quarters of all males who pass this examination, and who have a university-educated father, take up university study, the corresponding proportion for males similarly qualified, but of working-class background, is about one-half. These proportions change somewhat over time, but no consistent trend seems discernible.

In Scandinavia, university study is taken up by many more than those who complete it. Moberg shows an overall drop-out rate of 24 per cent for the 1930 generation of students (those who started university study in 1930 at about twenty years of age). Low student examination grades and low social origin both tended to be associated with failure to graduate.

For Norway, Palmstrøm[46] showed a rather consistent trend towards increasing middle and lower strata recruitment of students passing the student examination over the period 1813 to 1933. Thus while business men, the professions, and the higher civil service accounted for 80 per cent of all students from 1813 to 1825, the corresponding percentage for 1931–3 was 39 per cent. However, around 1930 no occupational group was more likely to recruit students than that of the clergy.

Waris[47] studied the career of Finnish university students from the period from 1810 to 1867. He concluded that the universities at that time provided chiefly a social mechanism whereby a son could retain the (high) social status of his father. A tiny upper stratum of society recruited 90 per cent of all university students. Only 8–10 per cent of the students were farmer-sons, and these experienced upward mobility mostly through the clergy. A comparative analysis of the period 1760–90 revealed 15–20 per cent farmer-sons among the students. This was a rate of upward mobility which was not attained again until the 1870s.

Over the last one hundred years the Finnish institutions of higher learning have gradually changed into important vehicles for upward social mobility. This process was associated with a bitter linguistic conflict ending with the gradual replacement of Swedish-speaking people with Finnish-speaking people. According to Ehrstrøm,[48] Swedish-speaking students who become university teachers or physicians are mainly recruited from a small upper stratum now as before, whereas social ascent has been continually increasing among Finnish-speaking students. The proportion of Finnish-speaking students who experienced upward mobility is estimated at one-third as of 1900 and about four-fifths as of 1950.

Anderson[49] analysed the recruitment of students at Helsingfors University from 1885 to 1914 by class, sex and language. Eleven per cent of Helsingfors University students in 1951 stemmed from working-class homes.[50] The corresponding percentage for Denmark in 1959 was 10.[51]

By means of documentary material, Boalt followed a cohort of about 5,000 Stockholm children who were born in 1925. He established the following percentages for completion of specified schooling:[52]

	Per cent
Seven years of grade school	52
Some junior high school (realskole)	15
Junior high school completed (minimum 9 years)	16
Some gymnasium	6
Gymnasium completed (12 years) (student examination achieved)	11
	100

Corresponding figures for the birth cohort 1926 are available for larger subdivisions and reveal that no place of residence in Sweden is as favourable for the obtainment of student examination as Stockholm.

Boalt documented that the most important socially conditioned selection among these children occurred when they were about eleven years old. He showed that, holding grades constant, there was a correlation of ·6 between social class and chance of being admitted to secondary schools. Slightly lower (·5) was the partial correlation (grades constant) between social class and chance of being admitted to the gymnasium (at about fifteen years of age). Boalt followed up the group of boys in his study to 1949 in a more recent publication.[53] He reported on the trivariate relationship: parental social class, 1936; filial social status, 1949 (modal age twenty-four years) and test intelligence. He was able to document that, IQ constant, sons of high-status parents were more likely to attain high status than sons of low status, and that one major explanatory factor was the higher tendency of high-status parents to give their children advanced education.

Since the major stratification variables tend to resemble a log-normal distribution when logarithmically transformed, an approximate model of social mobility may be constructed in the form of a bivariate log-normal distribution.

FACTORS AFFECTING SOCIAL MOBILITY

Research on conditions and consequences of mobility has so far been limited to comparisons between persons characterized by similar social origin and dissimilar mobility-experience.[54]

The interesting problem of the determinants and consequences of national differences in mobility rates has so far not been studied. One hypothesis would be that nations characterized by more extreme vertical or horizontal distances between people should reveal lower mobility rates than those characterized by less extreme distances. Since Finland may be characterized as dominated by more class conflict than Scandinavia proper, we should expect a lower mobility rate. This, it will be remembered, is also suggested by our data.

Regarding individual differences in mobility experience, Danish research has established that women are as mobile as men. Women, although suffering from some handicaps on the labour market, possess access to the status elevator of marriage which by definition is not available to the male. At marriage a woman is considered the status-equal of her husband, his status by definition determining that of the whole nuclear family.

Age is also related to mobility. A Danish male seems on the average to climb to the top of his career around his fiftieth birthday. Furthermore, no age-decade seems as favourable to mobility as that between the twentieth and thirtieth birthday.

Informal evidence supports the hypothesis that social selection of persons to offices tends to be structured to give preference not to the brightest person but to the one who seems most likely to become a loyal and congenial collaborator.[55] However, data available at the present time do not enable us to say this with certainty. What we do find in Svalastoga's study is that upwardly mobile people tend to conform to the norms of the stratum to which they move.[56]

It may probably be said that a person of low social origin can only become socially mobile by accumulating skills[57] or by accumulating capital, or by doing both.

Cases of conspicuous capital accumulation, converting a man in a few years from penniless job-hunter to a millionaire are on record, but Philip's[58] study of the career of fifty-year-old persons lacking higher education revealed that whereas one-third of the sample of those who at some time in their life had a business of their own, only one-sixth did so at the age of fifty. The failure rate was thus about one-half. The arduous passage from poverty to wealth is also indirectly documented by the large proportion of adults who are classified by tax authorities as propertyless (in Denmark about 40 per cent). In the same sample the top 1 per cent owned no less than one-third of the total wealth.

The acquisition of skills as a factor in the mobility process can best be studied where such acquisition has been formalized and made autonomous as in the school-system.

Warner in the United States and Floud in England have both voiced the hypothesis that, in their respective societies, *education* has become the principal means of an upward move in status. Both of the present authors have tested this hypothesis in Scandinavia, but the educational factor is somewhat de-emphasized in their conclusions. It is true that in Scandinavia, too, educational achievement is a major mobility escalator, but since higher education among the present adults is a comparatively rare achievement, and upward mobility relatively common, upward mobility is not usually the result of superior education.

The importance of the family in the mobility process is generally granted, but there have been few deliberate attempts to unravel the family conditions under which social mobility is likely. Some information will be found in a publication by one of the authors.[59]

More will be learned about the relevance of family conditions from studies now under way in Norway (Rogoff) and Denmark (Andresen). Both these researchers work with large-scale samples of military recruits, Andresen with about 20,000 questionnaires.

A group of Scandinavian research workers in social stratification are presently tentatively considering a new approach to the study of social mobility, the sequential (longitudinal) approach applied to metropolitan communities. The advantages and the difficulties of the sequential method are well known and shall not be discussed here. The advantages of limiting such studies to metropolitan (meaning urban population concentrations in the 10^5 to 10^7 size categories) are primarily three: (1) research economy, since Scandinavian universities are located in or near such cities; (2) metropolitan centres are commonly characterized by low rates of out-migration. (Boalt was able to show that over 90 per cent of his Stockholm grade school sample had not left the city between the ages of 11 and 24.); and (3) predictive power, since the conditions of the metropolitan population in many respects may be considered equal to the condition that the rest of the nation will attain with some time lag.

STRUCTURAL CHANGES

The society of Scandinavia around 1800–50 differed from modern Scandinavian society, in regard to both the amount of mobility and to the (vertical) social distance between the high and the low.

Myrdal[60] remarks, in regard to the latter problem: 'It is indeed a regular occurrence endowed almost with the dignity of an economic law that the poorer the country, the greater the difference between poor and rich.' It is likely that this invariance holds for Scandinavia, too. Thus Steen[61] reports for Norway that the income of a supreme-court judge around the year 1800 was sixty times larger than the income of an unskilled worker.[62] The corresponding difference today is probably reduced from sixty to six or maybe less. The changes in the vertical income distribution in Sweden during the period 1935–49 have been studied by Bentzel,[63] who concludes that there was a significant shift in the direction of more equality. He estimates that about one-fourth of this shift was due to taxation, and three-fourths to the 'automatic factor', meaning such influences as the migration from the farms to urban occupations, the increase in farm incomes, government and trade union policies, and many other less-known mechanisms.

Published research invariably suggests a negative relationship between vertical social distance and social mobility. Long-distance mobility is, even relative to chance expectations, more rare than short-distance mobility, so one might infer lower mobility rates in pre-industrial Scandinavia than in present-day Scandinavia. At any rate this inference is corroborated by a comparison between marital heterogamy rates, as established by Sundt[64] for Norway about 1850, and modern research findings.

In contrast, neither of the present authors has been able to establish any major mobility difference between generations of sons and generations of fathers or between various filial birth-cohorts; hence over the last seventy years or so, no major change in mobility rates seems indicated.

NOTES

1 Sweden: G. Boalt, and C. Janson, 'A selected bibliography of the literature on social stratification and social mobility in Sweden, *Current Sociology* (1953–4), *2*, pp. 306–27. Norway: The authors are indebted to Ø. Øyen for supplying references to Norwegian research. The Finnish and the Swedish bibliographies are amply annotated. Denmark: K. Svalastoga, *Prestige, Class and Mobility* (Copenhagen, 1959), pp. 432–4. Finland: S. Åstrøm, 'Literature on Social Mobility and Social Stratification in Finland', *Transactions of the Westermarck Society* (1953), *2*, pp. 221–7. Erik Allardt kindly supplied detailed information on recent Finnish research in the field. Eva Karsten Carlsson translated Hellevuo's paper.

2 Although prestige ratings as obtained by Carlsson did not definitely support this hypothesis.

3 *Social Mobility and Class Structure* (Lund, 1958).

4 *Prestige, Class and Mobility*.

5 *Beiträge zur Sozial- und Individualpsychologie bei Gallus Domesticus* (Greepwald, 1921); 'Social Behaviour of Birds' in *A Handbook of Social Psychology*, C. Murchison, ed. (Worcester, 1935); *Liv, reaktjoner og sociologi hos en flerhet insekter* (Oslo, 1953).

6 *Människan i Industrisamhället* (Stockholm, 1952).

7 *Skolutbildning och skolresultat* (Stockholm, 1947).

8 For reasons of comparability with the rest of Scandinavia, graduates from commercial and technical schools were not included.

9 S. Moberg, *Vem blev student och vad blev studenten?* (Lund, 1951); H. Palmstrøm, 'Om en befolkningsgruppes utvikling gjennem de siste 100 år', *Statsökonomisk Tidsskrift* (Oslo, 1935), *49*, pp. 161–370.

For later Norwegian figures see *Forskningsrådenes fellesudvalg: Om tilgangen på og behovet for akademisk arbeidskraft* (Oslo, 1957). Palmstrøm's denominator is the mean of the 18–21 years old. Later figures use mean of 19–20 years old.

10 *Social Mobility and Class Structure*.

11 *Prestige, Class and Mobility*.

12 W. Simenson and G. Geis, 'Comparison of prestige rating of Norwegian and American students', *Journal of Higher Education* (1955), *26*, pp. 21–5.

13 R. Korpela, 'Yhteiskuntaluokat maalaiskirkonkylässä (Social Stratification in a Church Village). Unpublished M.A. thesis (Helsingfors, 1956).

14 Danish Gallup Institute, 20 February 1959.

15 See also: R. McDonagh, S. Wermlund, J. Growther, 'Relative Professional Status as Perceived by American and Swedish University Students', *Social Forces* (1959), *38*, pp. 65–9.

16 On the Lay of Rig, cp. Svalastoga, *Prestige, Class and Mobility*.
17 *Den svenska adeln* (Stockholm, 1932).
18 'Family-name and social class', *Theoria* (Lund, 1951), 17, pp. 1–12. The presence of class conflict indicates that the traditional rank-order of social classes is no longer readily and universally accepted. Sariola (*Defining Social Class*. Transactions of the Westermark Society (1953) 2, pp. 134–57) investigated two Finnish communities with a communist voting strength of about one-third. He found that under these conditions several of the judges, who were given the task of rank-ordering people, tended to grade people according to their political ideology, thus reducing consensus.
19 E. Dahlstrøm, *Tjänstemännen, Näringslivet och Samhället*. With an English summary (Stockholm, 1954).
20 H. Tingsten, *Political Behaviour* (London, 1937). Cp. also: *Riksdagsmannavalen, 1949–1952* (Stockholm, 1953), pp. 236–9.
21 'En undersøgelse af 430 danske skolebørns syn på klassesamfundet', *Soc. Medd.* (1955), 2, pp. 55–63.
22 A study of social stratification in a concentration camp written by a participant observer is available in: K. Svalastoga, *Sosial ulikhet i en fangeleir* (Griniboken, Oslo, 1947), 2, pp. 320–54. In this camp such basic desiderata as food, rest and social contact (with the outside world) were scarce. This scarcity had mainly been handled according to the rule *share, and share alike* when the camp was small and the prisoners were few in each room. As the camp grew, the dominant criterion for distributing scarce and desired goods became prisoner seniority.
23 Mathiesen collected 73 interviews with persons in a rapidly growing Norwegian industrial town. The data tended to confirm the hypothesis that such change is associated with a sense of decreasing social distance. The very rate of change may be the most important factor. T. Mathiesen, 'Aspects of Social Stratification in a Changing Community', *Acta Sociologica* (1959), 4, pp. 42–54.
24 'Studies of Differential Fertility in Sweden' (London, 1935). *Sveriges officielle Statistik* (Folkräkningen, 1945, Stockholm, 1949), vii, 2.
25 'Befolkningsspørgsmål og familierstørrelse', *Statistiske Meldinger* (Oslo, 1952), 70, pp. 165–207.
26 *Sygdomsundersøgelsen i Danmark, 1951–1954* (Copenhagen, 1960).
27 'Social Class and Visiting Patterns in Two Finnish Villages', *Acta Sociologica* (1960), 5, p. 1.
28 Information on intragenerational mobility is available in: C. Anderson, 'Lifetime Inter-Occupational Mobility Patterns in Sweden', *Acta Sociologica* (1956), 1, pp. 168–204; and in G. Carlsson, 'Samhällsklasser och social rörlighet', *Svensk Samhällsstruktur*, E. Dahlstrøm. ed. (Stockholm, 1959).
29 *Social Mobility and Class Structure*.

30   S. Rokkan, *Estimates of Father-Son Mobility* (1960).
31   K. Svalastoga, *Prestige, Class and Mobility* (Copenhagen, 1959).
32   T. Hellevuo, *Poimintatutkimus säätykierrosta* (Sample Study of Social Mobility), (Suomalainen Suomi, 1952), *20*, pp. 93–6.
33   Svalastoga, *Prestige*, p. 347.
34   S. Lipset, and H. A. Zetterberg, 'Theory of Social Mobility', *Transactions 3*. World Congress of Sociology (London, 1956), *3*, pp. 155–77.
     Lipset and Zetterberg used the same data as those in the present paper for Denmark and for Finland. In the study reported by Hellevuo, respondents' fathers were classified in the same way as respondents themselves, but for the parental generation the respondent acted as classifier, and for the present generation the investigator was the classifier. Lipset and Zetterberg used the results of two studies antedating Carlsson's for Sweden and they were unable to obtain comparable data for Norway because such data were simply nonexistent at the time.
35   *Social Mobility and Class Structure.*
36   T. Geiger, *Den danske intelligens fra reformationen til nutiden* (Copenhagen, 1949).
37   M. Ulv and P. Carlsen, 'The Social Rise of Farmer-Sons in Denmark, *European Society for rural Sociology* (1958): Rural migration papers and discussions (Bonn, 1959), pp. 116–30.
38   D. Mannsåker, *Det norske presteskabet i det 19. hundreåret* (Oslo, 1954).
39   F. Linders, *Demografiska studier rörande svenska kyrkans präster skap* (Uppsala, 1925).
40   G. Suolahti, 'Prästerskapets sociala struktur i Finland', *Nordisk Tidsskrift* (1926), *2*, pp. 422–33.
41   S. S. Landstrøm, *Svenska ämbetsmäns sociala ursprung* (Skrifter utgivna av Statsvetenskapliga föreningen i Uppsala genom C. A. Hessler, xxxiv, Uppsala and Stockholm, 1954). 'The Social Origin of Swedish Civil Servants.' Summary in English.
42   *Ibid.*, p. 93.
43   Including some branches not here detailed.
44   O. Ramsøy, *Samfunnsbygning og skolesökning* (Oslo, 1957).
45   Moberg, *op. cit.*
46   'Om en befolkningsgruppes utviking gjennem de siste 100 år'.
47   H. Waris, 'Yliopisto sociaalism', *Historialinen Arkisto* (1940), *47*, pp. 199–272. With German summary.
48   R. Ehrstrøm, *Universitätslärar- och läkarkårens sociale struktur i Finland'*, *Nordisk Tidsskrift* (1950), *26*, pp. 85–94.
49   C. Anderson 'Social Class as a Factor in the Assimilation of Women into Higher Education', *Acta Sociologica*, 4, *3*, pp. 27–32.
50   P. Koli, *Hensingin Yliopistossa syyslukukandella 1951* (Helsingfors, 1951).
51   T. Agersnap, *Studenterundersøgelsen 1959* (Copenhagen, 1960), p. 29.
52   Boalt, *Skolutbildning och skolresultat* (Stockholm, 1947).

53 G. Boalt, 'Social Mobility in Stockholm', *Transactions 2*, World Congress of Sociology (London, 1954), *2*, pp. 67–73.
54 Svalastoga, *Prestige, Class and Mobility*.
55 Cp. J. Kahl, *The American Class Structure* (New York, 1957), p. 196; see also J. Scott and R. Lynton, *The Community Factor in Modern Technology* (Paris, 1952), p. 49.
56 Although informal evidence may point to a preference for nonconformers in the case of the rare long-distance mobility.
57 The conformity factor mentioned above may perhaps be identified with what is loosely called social skills.
58 G. Philip, 'Hvad 3000 mænd uden skoleeksamen blev til', *Socialt Tidsskrift* (Copenhagen, 1955), *31*, pp. 1–74.
59 K. Svalastoga, 'The Family in the Mobility Process', *Recherches sur la Famille* (Gøttingen, 1958), *3*, pp. 287–306.
60 G. Myrdal, *An International Economy* (New York, 1956), p. 133. Here cited after S. Lipset and R. Bendix, *Social Mobility in Industrial Society* (Berkeley, 1959).
61 S. Steen, *Det gamle samfunn* (Oslo, 1957).
62 The felt disparity in status is revealed in the remarks of Ole Nielsen, a Norwegian who emigrated to Iowa 1866, wrote home as follows: 'You do not have to bow and scrape, either to the minister or to the sexton. . . .' Blegen, ed., *Land of their Choice* (St Paul, 1955), p. 413.
63 R. Bentzel, *Inkomstfördelningen i Sverige* (Stockholm Industrins Utredningsinstitut, 1952). 'The Distribution of Income in Sweden', in Swedish. English Summary, pp. 211–18.
64 E. Sundt, *Fortsatte Bidrag* (Chra., 1868), pp. 28, 29. Some early Swedish mobility figures are presented in S. Carlsson, *Svensk Ståndscirculation* (Uppsala, 1950).

13 The Class Structure in western Europe

T. B. Bottomore

During the 1950s many sociologists came to accept the view that the class structure in western European countries was undergoing a profound transformation, and that the direction of change was towards a form of society in which class differences would be much less marked, the barriers between classes less formidable, the opposition and conflict between them less acute, and the consciousness of class membership itself less vivid and intense. An extreme version of this view maintained that classes had almost, if not quite, disappeared as significant social groups in the most industrially advanced countries. The principal factors bringing about this new situation were generally considered to be the rapid and continued rise in levels of living; the advance of technology and the associated changes in the organization of production; a redistribution of wealth and income resulting in part from the extension of social services financed out of progressive taxation; a higher rate of social mobility, due in large measure to the expansion of educational opportunities; and finally, in the ideological sphere, the overshadowing of earlier social problems by the post-war concern with economic growth in the industrial countries, industrialization in the developing countries, the population explosion, and the threat of nuclear war.

These changes were described and interpreted in diverse, but largely complementary ways, in the writings of some of the most widely read social scientists of the 1950s and early 1960s. J. K. Galbraith, in *The Affluent Society* – a book which epitomizes, in many respects, the social thought of that time – argued that there had occurred a 'decline of interest in inequality as an economic issue', and that the progressive increase of aggregate output was now seen as an alternative to redistribution. In line with this argument Galbraith redefined the 'social problem' as being no longer class inequalities, but the contrast between private opulence and public squalor.

Ideas of this kind did not merely reflect American experience in the post-war period. M. M. Postan, in his *Economic History of Western Europe, 1945–64*, has observed that the ascent of the European economy after 1945 was steeper and smoother than in any other period of modern history. Between 1918–38, he calculates, productivity in western Europe increased at a rate of 1·7 per cent per annum, whereas between 1945–63 it increased at more than twice that rate, 3·5 per cent per annum. The aggregate GNP of western Europe (at constant prices) was two and a half times greater in 1963 than in 1938. At the same time this post-war boom was much less interrupted by recurrent crises than was the case in any earlier period. The causes of this vigorous and more or less continuous growth are not entirely clear, but two important factors, according to Postan, were the very high rate of investment (much of which was government or government-sponsored investment), and the rapid and widespread advances in technology. Postan also suggests how an 'ideology of growth' emerged, not simply as a reflection of actual growth, but also arising out of earlier preoccupations with full employment which had their source in the controversies of the 1930s. 'Full employment', he writes, 'eventually developed into a policy and an economic philosophy much wider in its implications . . . into a policy of economic growth'.

It is this process of growth, and the concomitant changes in the organization of production and in government policy, with which Galbraith has been largely concerned, without considering in any detail its effects upon social stratification.[1] Two other influential social scientists, Raymond Aron and S. M. Lipset, have examined more directly the changes in class structure, in the context of economic growth and political action. Aron's view, which is expounded most fully in *La lutte de classes* (1964) and *Progress and Disillusion* (1968), may be summarized in the following way: as a result of economic development the system of stratification in industrial societies has become much more complex and the polarization of society between two antagonistic classes has not occurred; the proportion of industrial or manual workers in the population has not increased, and in the most-advanced societies it has begun to decrease; working hours have been reduced and real incomes have increased; the rate of social mobility has increased or is now increasing. These changes mean, according to Aron, that the essential conditions for the formation and maintenance of a class system – the cohesiveness of each class, its continuity from generation to generation, the individual's awareness of belonging to a class, and the self-consciousness of the class itself – have been greatly weakened, if not destroyed. More broadly, Aron, like Galbraith, has redefined the 'social question' in the second half of the twentieth century, by substituting for the contrast between capitalism and socialism a contrast between industrial and non-industrial societies; and by singling out as the vital and determining fact in modern societies the application of science to production irrespective of the character of the economic regime in which it occurs.

Lipset has treated the changing class structure in much the same way, though placing a stronger emphasis upon the 'end of ideology' and expressing with fewer qualifications the conviction that the old class structure of capitalist society has largely withered away. In *Political Man* (1959) he reached the conclusion that the conjunction of affluence and political democracy had already established the 'good society' (initially in the USA), with the result that no fundamental social and political changes can be expected, or for that matter desired, in this type of society. In a later essay on the western European countries,[2] he argues that '. . . instead of European class and political relationships holding up a model of the United States' future, the social organization of the United States has presented the image of the European future' – that is to say, of a relatively 'classless' society from which there would be absent any profound ideological oppositions or political conflicts about the basic structure of the society.

Both Lipset and Aron arrived at the conclusion that class conflict and ideological politics had diminished greatly in the advanced industrial countries and would certainly continue to decline. Lipset asserted the existence of a constant trend towards greater equality of income and the transformation of the class struggle into a process of limited bargaining between interest groups; while Aron observed, with some reservations, that '. . . experience in most of the developed countries suggests that semi-peaceful competition among social groupings is gradually taking the place of the so-called deadly struggle in which one class was assumed to eliminate the other'.[3] However, the reappearance of flux, uncertainty and more intense conflict in political life since the mid-1960s has cast doubt upon some of these interpretations and is leading to reappraisals of the ideas about class structure which were current a decade ago. Aron's remarks on the class struggle, for example, were written before the events of May 1968 in France; and that upheaval, although it was initiated by a student revolt, seemed to some observers to assume the character of a massive confrontation between classes, of a kind unknown since the 1930s. The same events, in the context of a general resurgence of radical movements, prompted Lipset to intimate a revision of his earlier ideas; in the preface to a collection of papers on comparative political sociology[4] he writes:

The year 1968 marks a watershed in the history of democratic mass politics: the quiet years of accommodation, integration and domestication were finally over, new waves of mobilization and counter-mobilization brought a number of Western democracies out of equilibrium, a new generation challenged the assumptions and the rhetoric of the old. The year 1968 also marks a watershed in the history of the international discipline of political sociology: the violent eruption of new forces did not only challenge the models and the theories of the fifties and sixties, but also forced a revaluation of data-gathering techniques and analysis strategies.

In what way do the political events of the late 1960s oblige us to reconsider the kind of analysis of class structure which was commonly made in the previous decade? Let us consider first the contrast between the effects of economic growth and redistribution. There can be no argument about the reality of increasing affluence in the western European countries, or about some of its consequences. A much larger proportion of the population than ever before has a level of living which, in material terms, is equivalent to that which was regarded as characterizing the middle class a generation or so ago. Moreover, the continuance of economic growth at present rates will ensure that increasing numbers attain this level. In this sense, at least, we may speak of the emergence of 'middle-class societies'. It is also plausible to argue that a few years of economic growth at post-war rates makes a greater difference to working-class levels of living than any redistribution of wealth and income could achieve.

But these facts may be regarded in a different way. It is undoubtedly the case that working-class levels of living have improved largely as a result of economic growth, because there has been little or no redistribution of wealth or income. In Britain, several recent studies suggest that while there may have been some redistribution of income in favour of the poorest sections of the working class over the whole period since the beginning of this century, there was no substantial change between the 1930s and 1950s, and after 1959 there was increasing inequality.[5] Similarly, although the concentration of wealth in the hands of the top 1 per cent of the population declined between 1911 and 1960, there was still no significant redistribution, since 75 per cent of all personal wealth remained in the hands of the top 5 per cent of the population (as against 87 per cent in 1911–13) and these property owners received 92 per cent of all income from personal property.[6] So far as the evidence is available there seems to have been no greater redistribution in other western European countries.

Thus, although the general level of living has risen considerably, the *relative* positions of the various classes have changed little, if at all, since before the war; and the economic bases of class differentiation – the ownership or non-ownership of property – remain much as they were. The question we have to consider is whether these class differences have the same social and political significance at the present time, in conditions of general prosperity, as they had in the earlier history of the western European societies. One thing is clear: we can no longer contrast working class and upper class (or *bourgeoisie*) simply in terms of poverty and wealth. There is a great deal of poverty in the affluent societies, but it is not the poverty of a whole class, or of a majority of the population. It is the poverty of particular social groups – old people, ethnic

groups, immigrant workers, or workers in declining industries – and its abolition involves specific social policies, not
necessarily a transformation of the class system; although it
may be the case that such policies would be more actively
promoted by working-class or left-wing parties than by right-
wing parties.

More generally it may be argued that increasing prosperity
changes the character of the relations between classes even
though their relative positions in the hierarchy of income and
wealth remain unchanged. Aron, for instance, suggests that
'. . . even if relative inequality has not been changed appreciably, the general increase in wealth has narrowed the gap
between different modes of living. If the basic needs . . . are
provided in an approximately similar way, what real difference is made by great fortunes or huge incomes. . . ?'[7] This
view took a more specific form in the idea of the *embourgeoisement* of the working class; that is to say, the assimilation of
the affluent working class into the middle class in terms of
economic situation, style of life, cultural values and political
outlook. It was partly a misleading analogy with the social
situation in the USA (which has a historically unique class
system), partly the social peace of the 1950s in the western
European countries, which gave credibility to this conception
of a 'new working class'; but subsequent research, as well as
the revival of radical politics, have cast doubt upon the
existence of a general trend towards *embourgeoisement* in the
cultural and political sense. The most thorough investigation
yet made of affluent workers, by Lockwood, Goldthorpe and
their colleagues, shows that there has been no change in the
political allegiance of these workers, and concludes that
'. . . the understanding of contemporary working-class
politics is to be found, first and foremost, in the structure of
the worker's group attachments and not, as many have
suggested, in the extent of his income and possessions'.[8] In
France and Italy the political loyalty of a large part of the
working class to the Communist Party is undiminished, as is
the attachment of workers to the Social Democratic Party in
West Germany, or to socialist parties in other western
European countries. In the Scandinavian countries, as Erik
Allardt has pointed out, class membership has become
increasingly important in voting; as traditional class barriers

have been reduced working-class voters have been more apt to vote for workers' parties than before.

Nevertheless, it may be that a change in the political outlook and aims of the working class has come about as a result of increasing prosperity and can be discerned in the changing objectives of the traditional working-class parties themselves, which no longer seek a fundamental transformation of capitalist society, but only the enactment of reforms within it. This notion, however, also seemed more plausible in the 1950s than it does in the late 1960s, when there is a marked, though still limited, revival of radicalism in working-class politics. In my view, the future development of the class system, and hence of some important aspects of political life, will be more strongly affected by changes in the situation of the working class in the process of production than by increasing prosperity. Among the most significant changes in the economic systems of the industrial societies is the movement of labour from the agricultural and extractive industries sector to the manufacturing sector, and then from the manufacturing sector to the services sector;[9] and within manufacturing industry itself the shift of labour from manual to clerical and professional occupations. This process has gone furthest in the USA, where clerical and professional workers already form a larger proportion of the labour force than do manual workers, but it is continuing rapidly in the western European countries. Postan notes that in the UK employment in manufacturing industries increased between 1948 and 1962 by 1·1 million workers, but that 745,000 of these were 'salaried workers', mainly clerical and technical personnel.[10] Similar changes have occurred in the other industrial countries, and they are likely to be accelerated with the advance of automation. Thus, it may be expected that the working class – the traditional class of manual, industrial workers, which is the subject of Marxist theory and of many sociological interpretations – will continue to contract as a proportion of the population, and this will necessarily have important social and political consequences. The working class can no longer figure, in quite the same way, as the rising and expanding class which Marx, for instance, depicted. It should be noted, moreover, that certain occupations, such as coal mining, whose members played a major role in the labour movement because they formed particularly class-conscious and radical communities, have experienced an exceptionally rapid decline in numbers.

There is another important influence upon the situation of the working class in some of the developed industrial countries of western Europe; namely, the influx of immigrant workers either from former colonial territories or from the poorer countries of Europe. These immigrants go, for the most part, into the least attractive and worst paid manual jobs, and they form a distinct section of the working class. In Switzerland their numbers (about one-third of the total labour force) are such that they are coming to constitute almost the whole of the manual working class, and Swiss citizens can look forward to a situation in which they themselves do not need to enter manual occupations at all. This is an exceptional case, but the proportion of immigrant workers is also quite considerable in France and Germany. The fact that these workers are citizens of another country, speak another language, and participate in a different culture, largely excludes them from political life in the countries where they work, with some important consequences for working-class political movements in those countries. The most significant features are the growing heterogeneity of the working class as a result of ethnic diversity, and the creation of a distinct, socially isolated sub-proletariat. In these respects there is some resemblance to the conditions in the USA at an earlier time when ethnic differences and the distinctive position of the Negroes impeded the development of a radical labour movement.

One of the most striking features of the changing class structure is, therefore, the onset of a decline in the size of the traditional working class. This contraction of the working class implies the expansion of the middle classes. In terms of the occupational structure, as well as in terms of levels of living, the advanced industrial countries of western Europe may be seen as being already, or as very close to becoming, predominantly 'middle-class' societies. The question we have now to consider is whether this new, expanding middle class does, in fact, continue to have the economic, cultural and political characteristics of the middle class as it existed earlier in the present century. This is a tangled issue, not least because the European middle class of the first third of the twentieth century was itself 'new', in the sense that it was composed increasingly of clerical workers and professional employees, rather than independent professional people and small businessmen, and for that reason was becoming less homogeneous. Nevertheless, the middle class as a whole was still a relatively small and privileged section of the population, more or less clearly marked off from the working class. The new middle class of post-war Europe is a much larger, more diverse, and expanding group, whose members may be less conscious of occupying a distinctive class position.

The question as to whether there is a historical continuity between this new middle class and its predecessors, or whether its economic and social situation, and its political outlook, are now profoundly different, has been answered in three different ways. The first answer, which was most prevalent in the 1950s, emphasizes the elements of continuity and foresees the advent of middle-class societies in which political conflict arising from opposed class interests will have ceased, and will have been replaced by a broad consensus of opinion about general matters of economic and social policy, disturbed only by minor and transitory disagreements between more 'conservative' and more 'progressive' groups. This view includes the idea of the assimilation of the working class into middle-class society, but it is not entirely clear whether it implies the disappearance of an upper class. Some sociologists and political scientists have argued that there is no longer an upper class in the USA, at least in the sense of a class which rules society, and that upper classes in the European countries are in process of dissolution. These writers see the industrial societies as becoming wholly middle class, with many different social groups having power or influence in particular areas or on particular occasions, even if it is no more than a veto power. Other social scientists, however, while accepting the thesis that the working class is being incorporated into middle-class society visualize the new society as remaining divided between the mass of the population and an upper class, an elite, or a coalition of elites. Thus, C. Wright Mills counterposed the ruling elites and the masses in American society; and Herbert Marcuse, in *One-Dimensional Man*, describes the advanced industrial societies as societies of 'total mobilization' in which the mass of the population sacrifice liberty to comfort under the rule of the large business corporations and the political elite, cajoled and persuaded by the mass media which these groups control. There is collusion and alliance between business and organized labour; dissent and opposition no longer have a social base; but the distinction between the rulers and the ruled still remains.

The second interpretation of these changes conceives the new middle class (or at least large sections of it) as a new dominant class, which differs, however, from previous ruling groups in including a relatively large part of the population, and in being much more committed to the general welfare through its commitment to economic growth. Galbraith refers to this new class, in *The New Industrial State*, using the term 'technostructure' to describe the organization of the 'very large group of people', ranging from the most senior officials of the corporation down to those who are just above the level of routine clerical workers and manual workers, who now participate in the management of industry and more generally in the determination of social policies; and he attributes a particular importance to the rapidly growing part of this class which he calls the 'educational and scientific estate'. Dahrendorf, in an essay on changes in European class structure,[11] expounds similar ideas, though with a number of qualifications. He suggests that the ruling groups or elites (which he regards as being still quite small in numbers, but recruited increasingly from the middle class) plus what he calls the 'service class' (the bureaucrats and managers) may constitute a new ruling class in the European societies. In his view, however, these groups together form a relatively small part of the population (not more than 15 per cent of the whole); and their importance lies not in their numbers, but in the fact that their values, especially that of individual competition, have spread to all other groups. To some extent Dahrendorf's thesis supports the idea of historical continuity; the values of the new 'service class', as he presents them, do not seem very different from the values of the old 'middle class'. Nevertheless, the gradual increase in the numbers of those in the 'service class', and their infiltration of the former ruling class (as Dahrendorf sees it), may produce in the

European countries a new dominant class of the kind which Galbraith describes as already existing in the USA. It is possible, however, to interpret the same phenomena in another way, as the rise to power of a new minority, comprising the technocrats and bureaucrats. This conception, which goes back at least to Veblen, and revives the idea of the managerial revolution, has been put forward especially in France in recent years; first by Georges Gurvitch,[12] and lately by Alain Touraine.[13] The theme of Touraine's argument is that the major social struggles in the advanced industrial countries are no longer centred upon the ownership of property; thus, they are no longer struggles between the old social classes of capitalist society. Social conflict now takes the form of a 'directly political struggle and a rejection of alienation, a revolt against a system of integration and manipulation'; it opposes various social groups, and above all the students, to the bureaucratic and technocratic controllers of society.

The third interpretation diverges radically from those which I have so far discussed in regarding the new middle class primarily as a variant form of the working class which is now emerging in the advanced industrial countries. It has been expounded from one aspect by Serge Mallet,[14] and from another by some of the groups in the student movement. Mallet claims that it is the technically and professionally qualified workers in the most modern industries who have been most opposed in recent years to the capitalist organization of industry, and who have taken up most vigorously the traditional working-class struggle to transform the ownership and management of economic enterprises. Within the radical student movement the idea has been formulated that students are apprentices being trained to take their place in the technically qualified working class of the future, and it is suggested that students are coming to see themselves increasingly in this light, as potential workers rather than professional and middle-class people. This is still, in fact, the outlook of a small minority, but it has had a wider influence in the radical movements of the 1960s and it may presage a significant change in the social consciousness of the 'educational and scientific estate' in the next generation. Already there are some indications of the kind of change which Mallet discusses, in the growth of white-collar and professional trade unions, and in their increasing militancy and even radicalism. During the events of May 1968 in France a number of professional groups became very radical in outlook and developed a collective orientation quite opposed to the traditional middle-class individualism, and even to the 'instrumental collectivism' which Goldthorpe and Lockwood have ascribed to the new middle class.[14]

These diverse interpretations describe tendencies, all of which are present, none of which is clearly predominant, in the western European societies. The working class has not yet withered away, nor has it been absorbed fully into a traditional middle class; there is not yet an established technocratic-bureaucratic ruling class; the 'new middle class' does not yet conceive itself as a working class, and it remains to be seen whether the students of the 1960s will actually bring about or sustain a new social awareness in their eventual professional occupations. Before these tendencies can be more adequately assessed we have to consider another aspect of the class structure – the situation of the upper class – which is evoked, directly or indirectly, in the theories about the new working class and the new middle class. Is there any longer an identifiable upper class in the Western European societies? Is it still the capitalist class of Marxist theory; a class which exercises political rule because it owns the essential instruments of production? Or has the old upper class disintegrated, and has its political power been dispersed among numerous pressure groups or taken over by a new elite?

As I indicated earlier the upper class is far from having lost its superiority in the possession of wealth or in the share of the national income which it receives. But is it the same upper class as it was half a century ago, and does its wealth still give it a preponderant influence in determining the course of economic and social life? So far as economic affairs are concerned, those who consider that important changes have taken place refer generally to two phenomena: the growth of public ownership of industry, and the separation between ownership and management in private business. However, publicly owned industry does not account for more than about 15 per cent of the total employment of wage and salary earners in Britain, and less than this in most other western European countries. M. M. Postan concludes his survey of the effects of nationalization by saying that nationalized industry has been 'a powerful but not predominant ingredient in "mixed economies" '.[16] Alongside the gradual extension of public ownership there has occurred an increase in governmental regulation of the economy as a whole, closely associated with planning for economic growth, and this too, it has been argued, diminishes the power of the private owners of wealth. But the association between business corporations and government can be interpreted in different ways; as the growing control of private interests by an elected political authority, or as the growing control of government by private interests. It is by no means easy to unravel these lines of influence and power running in opposite directions, but it may be attempted by looking at the extent to which representatives of the large corporations occupy important political posts, and by examining the character of particular policy decisions or of general economic and social policy over a longer period. The fact that there has been no substantial redistribution of wealth and income over the past half century is one indication that the upper class has maintained its preponderant influence upon the course of events, while another indication of the same kind is provided by the tenacious and largely successful resistance to the extension of welfare services, as a result of which there are vast inequalities in the provision of housing and education, and very few attempts to increase the range and variety of goods and services provided free of charge to the whole population.

The second question which I have raised, concerning the separation between ownership and management of industry, is important in so far as those who emphasize this separation go on to argue that it has eliminated or drastically reduced the control which the owners of wealth have over the economy, and at the same time has changed the social character of the large business corporation. There is indeed a formal separation between ownership and control (between share-ownership and management functions) in modern business firms, even though many predominantly family businesses (some of them large) survive;[17] but the existence of a real social distinction between owners and managers is much more doubtful. Mills noted, in *The Power Elite*, that the categories of the 'very rich' and the 'top executives' overlap considerably in the USA, and there is little doubt that the same is true in European countries, although the European upper class has been much less thoroughly studied than the American. Postan observes, for example, that in the western European countries the *grande bourgeoisie* has adapted itself to the demands of the managerial age by ensuring that its members acquire the requisite education for careers as business executives. In France, this process began in the late nineteenth century when the École Libre des Sciences Politiques provided members of the upper class with the skills necessary to maintain their dominant position in business and in the higher administration; and in other European countries certain kinds of university education have been directed towards the same end.

The general development towards managerial and technocratic control of business enterprises would only have a significant effect upon the social situation of the upper class of property owners if there were very considerable mobility through the educational system. In fact, however, access to higher education in the western European countries has changed very little over the past thirty years; in Britain, the proportion of university undergraduates from working-class homes was 23 per cent in the period 1928–47, and 25 per cent in 1961, while in Germany the proportion of working-class students has risen only from 5 per cent before the war to 6 per cent today, and in France there has been a similarly modest increase from 6 per cent before the war to about 8 per cent today.[18] It is not surprising, therefore, that the elite groups – business leaders, higher civil servants, a large part of the political leadership – continue to be recruited largely from the upper class and the upper levels of the middle class in these societies.[19] The upper class still perpetuates itself by passing on wealth, educational privileges, and occupational chances, and these things ensure the continuing concentration of property ownership, prestige and power in a few hands. Of course, there is some circulation of individuals and families between the upper class and other social classes, but there is no evidence to suggest that this circulation is now more extensive or more rapid than it was at any earlier time during the last hundred years.

The upper classes in the western European countries thus remain relatively closed groups, in which the continuity of membership from generation to generation is still strongly marked. In the rest of society social mobility may have increased over the past few decades, largely as a result of the changing occupational structure,[20] but it is clear that most mobility occurs *within* classes rather than between them. A study of intra-generational occupational mobility in France, based upon an inquiry conducted by the Institut National de la Statistique et des Études Economiques, shows that between 1959 and 1964 about 14 per cent of manual workers changed their occupations, but two-thirds of them remained in manual jobs, while one-third went into non-manual jobs; among non-manual workers some 12 per cent changed their occupations, again with two-thirds remaining in non-manual jobs while one-third went into manual jobs.[21] Where there is movement (either intra-generational or inter-generational) between classes it takes place usually over short distances; for example, from the skilled working class to the lower levels of the middle class. In no Western industrial society is there any considerable amount of long-range mobility, from the working class directly into the upper class or elites.

Nevertheless, the relatively high rates of *occupational* mobility which most studies reveal may have a strong influence upon class structure, and particularly upon the character of the working class, in so far as such mobility tends to inhibit the formation of occupational communities which have a continuing membership over several generations, and which may constitute focal points around which a more general class consciousness is able to crystallize. I drew attention earlier to the possible importance of this factor in the case of coal miners, but it may well be that occupational mobility, when it rises above a certain level, has consequences similar to those which flow from the decline of an occupation in terms of its size and economic importance. If this is so, the outcome might be a general decline in the class consciousness of workers; and many observers have reached the conclusion, though often upon quite different grounds, that this has been happening.[22] Their results are contradicted, however, as I have noted, by recent studies of working-class political allegiance.

The most important implication of the preceding discussion of the major social classes is that the extent and nature of changes in class structure have to be assessed in large measure by an examination of the political movements and political conflicts which take place in a society. Few social scientists would dissent from the view that class interests and class consciousness have been pre-eminent elements in the political life of all the western European countries over the past hundred years, although they have assumed diverse forms of expression and have been more or less strongly affected by other social divisions – of religion, language or culture – in the different countries. The question of a changing class structure in these societies then resolves itself into a question as to whether class-based political struggles have retained their importance, or whether new forms of political activity and new political aims have emerged, and in the latter case, how these new forms and objectives are related to the undoubted changes in the occupational structure and the system of production.

In the first place we should note the extent to which class is still a major force in politics, not only because the upper class retains its character as a group of large property owners, in spite of the development of new technological and professional elites, but also because the working class still adheres strongly to its own long-established organizations, the trade unions and working-class political parties, and has its social outlook largely shaped by the historical traditions of the labour movement. The decline of union membership in the USA, which Galbraith cites in the course of his argument about the emergence of a new industrial system, has no counterpart in western Europe, where trade union membership has generally increased since the war, and the growth of white-collar unionism has been closely correlated with the expansion of manual workers' unions.[23] Similarly, working-class support for labour and socialist parties has tended to grow rather than decline, and in the later 1960s a more radical outlook seemed to be spreading in some sections of the labour movement, as evidenced, for example, by the revival of interest in the concept and practices of workers' control.

Nevertheless, it may be said that the present time marks a turning point, when the established class parties have attained a peak in their development, while new political forces are beginning to challenge their dominance. There are four main directions, it seems to me, in which a new style of politics has become apparent. The first style is that associated with the rise of new elites, committed above all to rationality and efficiency in production and administration, and subscribing to the doctrines of technological progress and economic growth, who may be able to establish themselves and become accepted as the controllers of society for the sake of the economic benefits which they can assure. The second style is directly opposed to this; it is the radical movement, mainly among students at present, which attacks the technocratic and bureaucratic character of modern industrial society, and proposes 'participation' and 'community' as alternatives to the 'authority' and 'elitism' implied in the conception of a society directed by experts. Alone, the student movement is unlikely to accomplish very much, but its influence may grow if it finds a sympathetic response either in the working-class movement (from which, after all, its radical ideas derive), or in those middle-class groups from which the students largely come by virtue of their family origins and which they subsequently enter on their own account as professionally qualified workers.

The other two styles of politics, though differing widely in some respects, are alike in having as their basis a community which is quite distinct from social classes. At one extreme are the regional or nationalist movements which have sprung up in recent years (for example, in Scotland and Wales, among the Flemish-speaking people of Belgium); at the other extreme is the movement for a European community. In both types of movement there is a strong emphasis upon a cultural identity which is seen as transcending the divisions within the community, and this cultural quality, along with considerations of economic development, becomes the focus of political thought and action. These two styles largely exclude the distinctions based upon class differences, and the political issues which are of vital importance to the traditional parties in so far as they represent particular classes; thus, in the discussions of a European Community, the question as to whether the new Europe will be capitalist or socialist is scarcely ever raised.

The future development of these styles of politics in relation to the established parties and movements can only be discussed at present in a speculative manner. Nevertheless, there are certain conditions and processes of change which can be determined more exactly and which are likely to have an important influence. The decline of the manual working class as a proportion of the population will continue, but it is unlikely to be so rapid as to undermine the militancy and radicalism of a considerable part of the trade union and labour movement. It may be that trade union militancy will become increasingly defensive, particularly in those occupations most affected by technological advance, and will play a smaller part in animating movements for radical change in society at large, but there is, as yet, little indication that such a state of affairs is coming about. On the other hand, radicalism may receive an accession of strength as the expansion of higher education continues at a rapid pace, if we assume that the ideological orientation of the student movement continues to be that of the late 1960s; and experience so far, in Europe, suggests that student radicalism is something more than a passing mood.

There is another circumstance of vital importance for the future development of classes and political movements which is extremely difficult to evaluate; namely, the probability that economic growth will continue in the same rapid and uninterrupted fashion as during the past two decades. The difficulty arises from the lack of an adequate theory of a 'mixed', but predominantly capitalist and market economy. The Marxist theory of capitalist crisis is obviously no longer satisfactory; but on the other side the expectation of continued prosperity and growth seems to rest upon purely empirical and short-term observations, without any theory which would explain what changes have occurred in the capitalist economy which now eliminate the possibility of crises. There is no certainty, therefore, about the future development of the economy, and thus about some important aspects of the class structure – the radicalism of the working class, the expansion of the middle class, and the rise of new elites.

o

In spite of the imponderable elements, and the diversity of interpretations, to which I have drawn attention throughout this essay, I think a tentative conclusion is possible, at least in a negative form. There is, as yet, no sign that in the western European countries the egalitarian impulse which came to life with the rise of the labour movement has lost its force. Indeed, the struggle for equality, arising out of the relationship between social classes in a capitalist society, may have been reinforced by the more directly political conflicts which now take place in various spheres over questions of authority and participation in decision making.[24] In so far as classes have been, and largely remain, the principal embodiment of inequality in modern societies their political significance is undiminished.

NOTES

1 In his recent writings, especially *The New Industrial State*, Galbraith has discussed some aspects of stratification, and I shall refer to these later.
2 S. M. Lipset 'The Changing Class Structure and Contemporary European Politics' in S. R. Graubard, *A New Europe?* (1964).
3 *Progress and Disillusion*, p. 15.
4 S. M. Lipset and S. Rokkan, Preface to *Party Systems, Party Organizations, and the Politics of New Masses* (Papers of the 3rd International Conference on Comparative Political Sociology, Berlin, 1968).
5 See, for a summary of the data, S. Pollard and D. W. Crossley, *The Wealth of Britain*, Chapter 9.
6 See Pollard and Crossley, op. cit.; J. E. Meade, *Efficiency, Equality and the Ownership of Property*.
7 Aron, *Progress and Disillusion*, p. 11.
8 J. H. Goldthorpe, D. Lockwood, F. Bechhofer and J. Platt, *The Affluent Worker: Political Attitudes and Behaviour*, p. 82.
9 In Colin Clark's terminology, from the primary to the secondary and then to the tertiary sector.
10 M. M. Postan, *Economic History of Western Europe 1945–64*.
11 Ralf Dahrendorf, 'Recent Changes in the Class Structure of European Societies', in S. R. Graubard, *A New Europe?*
12 European Societies', in S. R. Graubard, *A New Europe?*
13 Georges Gurvitch (ed.), *Industrialisation et technocratie* (1949). Alain Touraine, *La société post-industrielle: naissance d'une société* (1969).

14 Serge Mallet, *La nouvelle class ouvrière* (1963), and 'La nouvelle classe ouvrière en France', *Cahiers internationaux de sociologie*, XXXVIII (1965).
15 John H. Goldthorpe and David Lockwood, 'Affluence and the British Class Structure', *Sociological Review*, XI (2), July 1963.
16 Postan, *Economic History of Western Europe*.
17 See Jean Meynaud, *La technocratie*, Chapter III.
18 See P. Bourdieu and J. C. Passeron, *Les héritiers*.
19 See the discussion in my *Elites and Society*, Chapter IV; and on Germany, Wolfgang Zapf (ed.), *Beiträge zur Analyse der Deutschen Oberschicht*.
20 The most thorough discussion of the problems involved in making historical comparisons of rates of social mobility will be found in Peter M. Blau and Otis D. Duncan, *The American Occupational Structure* (1967), Chapter 3. In order to obtain strictly comparable data it would be necessary to repeat studies of mobility (designed for comparability) at regular intervals. The first attempt along these lines, so far as I know, is the mobility study being carried out at Nuffield College, Oxford; this is intended to make possible comparisons with the data of the 1949 study reported in D. V. Glass (ed.), *Social Mobility in Britain* (1954).
21 Michel Praderie, 'La mobilité professionelle en France entre 1959 et 1964', *Etudes et Conjonctures* (10), October 1966.
22 See especially A. Andrieux and J. Lignon, *L'ouvrier d'aujourd'hui* (1960); H. Popitz, H. P. Bahrdt, E. A. Jüres, and H. Kesting, *Das Gesellschaftsbild des Arbeiters* (1957); K. Bednarik, *Der junge Arbeiter von heute: ein neuer Typ* (1953).
23 See Adolf Sturmthal (ed.), *White Collar Trade Unions* (1966).
24 See especially the discussion in Touraine, *La Société post-industrielle* . . . , p. 68 et seq.

Appendix

Section I

Active Population

(1) Czechoslovakia (1950)

Age Group	% Active Male	% Active Female	% Active Total	
−15	0·1	0·1	0·1	
15–19	76·2	70·1	73·2	
20–24				
25–29				
30–49	88·2	48·9	67·9	
50–54				
55–59				
60–64				
65+	24·7	11·8	17·3	
?	60·8	35·7	46·5	
Total	59·5	35·4	47·1	Total Population 5,811,724
Total 1963	51·9	38·9	45·3	6,338,042

(2) Federal Republic (1961)

Age Group	% Active Male	% Active Female	% Active Total	
−15	2·6	2·4	2·5	
15–19	81·5	78·6	80·1	
20–24	91·4	71·7	81·8	
25–29	96·4	50·1	73·9	
30–49	97·4	44·1	68·1	
50–54	93·8	37·5	62·4	
55–59	88·7	32·3	58·4	
60–64	72·5	21·0	43·5	
65+	22·8	8·4	14·2	
?	75·7	42·0	57·6	
Total	64·0	33·2	47·7	Total Population 25,763,084
Total 1966	61·3	31·4	45·6	27,161,000

(3) *France (1962)*

Age Group	% Active Male	% Active Female	% Active Total
-15	—	—	—
15–19	49·1	35·7	42·5
20–24	87·7	61·8	75·2
25–29	96·0	45·6	71·4
30–49	96·8	41·2	69·1
50–54	93·0	45·6	68·8
55–59	85·3	42·8	63·3
60–64	71·1	34·2	51·4
65+	77·8	11·3	17·5
Total	58·4	27·9	42·7
Total 1967	56·8	25·5	40·8

Total Population 19,829,165

20,269,000

(4) *Greece (1961)*

Age Group	% Active Male	% Active Female	% Active Total
-15	6·6	5·3	6·0
15–19	66·0	46·8	56·4
20–24	55·7	52·3	53·9
25–29	95·0	43·6	68·4
30–49	96·1	37·4	65·7
50–54	91·9	32·5	61·7
55–59	86·7	27·3	56·5
60–64	74·7	21·0	45·1
65+	43·7	9·9	24·5
Total	59·7	27·8	43·4

Total Population 3,638,601

ILO Year Book of Labour Statistics, 1967.

(5) Ireland (1961)

Age Group	% Active Male	% Active Female	% Active Total
–15	1·5	1·1	1·3
15–19	64·3	53·8	59·2
20–24	90·0	67·2	78·8
25–29	96·3	38·7	67·3
30–54	97·0	20·8	59·1
55–64	88·9	23·0	55·8
65+	51·5	14·7	32·1
Total	58·0	20·4	39·3
Total 1966			38·3

Total Population 1,108,108
1,106,000

(6) Italy (1961)

Age Group	% Active Male	% Active Female	% Active Total
–15	4·2	2·6	3·4
15–19	68·9	39·3	54·3
20–24	88·8	40·6	65·0
25–29	95·8	30·1	63·0
30–44	95·8	26·5	60·4
45–54	90·8	22·7	56·0
55–59	83·7	16·8	48·8
60–64	53·6	12·8	31·4
65+	23·6	5·1	12·9
Total	61·1	19·5	39·8
Total 1966	56·8	19·8	37·8

Total Population 20,172,902
19,653,000

(7) *Poland (1960)*

Age Group	% Active Male	% Active Female	% Active Total
–15	0·3	0·4	0·3
15–19	46·5	41·2	43·9
20–24	88·1	67·8	76·8
25–29	96·4	62·8	79·5
30–49	96·9	66·6	80·8
50–54	94·8	65·6	79·3
55–59	91·4	60·2	74·5
60–64	81·9	48·9	62·9
65+	55·5	30·1	39·7
?	65·0	51·9	58·1
Total	55·1	40·1	47·3

Total Population 13,907,442

(8) *Portugal (1960)*

Age Group	% Active Male	% Active Female	% Active Total
–15	11·1	2·8	7·0
15–19	86·5	27·3	56·3
20–24	95·0	26·5	59·2
25–29	98·0	19·8	57·5
30–49	97·5	15·3	54·7
50–54	93·5	13·6	50·8
55–59	89·4	13·3	47·6
60–64	81·8	12·1	42·5
65+	62·6	7·8	29·5
Total	66·2	13·1	38·5

Total Population 3,423,515

(9) *Spain (1960)*

Age Group	% Active Male	% Active Female	% Active Total	
-15	3·3	1·4	2·4	
15–19	74·0	27·1	50·1	
20–24	90·4	28·2	59·8	
25–34	96·8	16·6	56·2	
35–44	97·7	15·1	54·4	
45–54	96·7	17·1	54·5	
55–64	91·9	15·9	51·3	
65+	55·5	10·2	29·0	Total Population
Total	64·2	13·5	38·1	11,634,214
Total 1966	59·7	17·5	39·9	12,201,800

ILO Year Book of Labour Statistics, 1967, p. 31.

(10) *United Kingdom (1961)*

Age Group	% Active Male	% Active Female	% Active Total	
-15	—	—	—	
15–19	75·4	71·5	73·5	
20–64	98·2	41·5	69·2	
65+	24·7	5·4	12·8	Total Population
Total	65·3	29·3	46·7	25,480,791

ILO Year Book of Labour Statistics, 1967, p. 37.

(11) *Yugoslavia (1961)*

Age Group	% Active Male	% Active Female	% Active Total	Total Population
−15	2·4	3·7	3·1	
15–19	65·8	57·6	61·7	
20–24	90·4	62·0	76·3	
25–29	96·3	53·2	74·8	
30–49	97·0	44·3	69·0	
50–54	94·0	33·0	62·5	
55–59	85·5	27·4	55·3	
60–64	74·4	22·2	46·4	
65+	56·3	14·3	31·6	
?	81·2	51·5	66·2	
Total	59·6	31·1	45·0	

ILO Year Book of Labour Statistics, 1967.

Section II

Structure of economically active population: Distribution by Branch of Economic Activity.

Branch of economic activity	Fed. Rep. (1950)	Greece (1951)	Ireland (1951)	Italy (1951)	Poland (1950)	Portugal (1950)	Spain (1950)	France (1954)	UK (1951)	Yugoslavia (1953)
Agriculture 0. Agriculture, forestry, hunting and fishing	5,113,732	1,367,271	503,836	8,261,160	7,089,624	1,590,112	5,271,037	5,212,760	1,142,438	5,240,463
1. Mining and quarrying	700,299	13,623	10,440 ⎫	4,720,195 ⎫	2,327,940	25,751	173,808	411,580	860,507	112,277
Industry 2.3. Manufacturing	6,806,372	450,424	192,793 ⎬	⎭	inc. manufact.	619,680	1,904,016	4,936,960	8,446,686	839,596
4. Construction	1,811,137	74,959	96,335	1,472,749	519,095	165,920	574,279	1,357,180	1,430,475	240,794
5. Electricity, gas, water and sanitary services	150,222	11,212	10,747	96,789		10,470	56,512	134,960	360,523	—
6. Commerce	2,121,385	219,903	155,670	2,571,418	643,656	239,623	697,674	2,640,040	3,160,351	240,431
Services 7. Transport, storage and communication	1,150,291	138,025	59,769	785,275	468,882	113,608	421,305	1,005,420	1,733,817	167,955
8. Services	3,736,734	387,622	228,549	1,669,694	1,264,339 inc. some banks & transport	514,831	1,522,475	3,227,980	5,366,044	548,699
9. Activities not adequately described	483,835	176,442	13,899	1,094,497	90,641	8,457	171,951	567,500	109,205	20,057
Total	22,076,007	2,839,481	1,272,038	20,671,777	12,404,177	3,288,452	10,793,057	19,494,380	22,610,046	7,410,272

* ILO Yearbook of Labour Statistics, 1960, Table 4. (Many of these countries have not used the International nomenclature for classification.)

Structure of the economically active population: distribution by occupational group.

	France (1962) %	Fed. Rep. (1961) %	Greece (1961) %	Ireland (1961) %	Italy (1961) %	Portugal (1960) %	Spain (1960) %	UK (1961) %	Yugoslavia (1961) %
0. Professional, technical and related workers	9·1	7·6	3·4	7·1	5·2	2·7	4·1	8·6	5·6
1. Administrative, executive and managerial workers	3·1	3·1	0·7	1·2	1·2	1·3	1·0	2·6	1·1
2. Clerical workers	8·0	11·9	4·0	7·0	7·0	4·4	5·8	12·8	3·8
3. Sales workers	8·6	7·5	6·1	8·9	7·3	6·2	6·1	9·5	2·7
4. Farmers, fishermen, hunters, loggers and related workers	19·9	13·5	53·7	35·7	27·9	42·0	39·8	4·3	56·7
5. Miners, quarrymen and related workers	1·1	1·4	0·5	0·6	0·6	0·6	1·6	2·1	1·3
6. Workers in transport and communication occupations	3·1	4·7	3·0	5·1	3·6	3·0	4·1	6·1	2·5
7. 8. Craftsmen, prod. process workers and labourers not elsewhere classified	34·3	38·5	18·7	25·0	35·4	27·2	26·4	40·6	19·5

	7·5	7·6	6·8 inc. armed forces	8·5	7·8	8·9	8·3	10·4	5·9 inc. armed forces
9. Service, sport and recreation workers	7·5	7·6	6·8 inc. armed forces	8·5	7·8	8·9	8·3	10·4	5·9 inc. armed forces
X. Workers not classifiable by occupation	1·1	4·2	0·5	0·1	0·6	0·7	1·5	1·6	0·9
Members of armed forces	1·3	—	—	0·8	0·5	1·3	1·3	1·4	—
Those on military service	2·9	—	—	—	—	—	—	—	—
those seeking work for the first time	—	—	2·6	—	2·9	1·7	—	—	—
	100%	100%	100%	100%	100%	100%	100%	100%	100%
	19,829,165	26,821,100	3,638,601	1,108,108	20,172,902	3,423,551	11,634,214	24,616,620	8,340,400

From Table 2B. ILO Yearbook of Labour Statistics 1968 and 1966.

Structure of economically active population:

	Branch of economic activity	Spain (1960) % employed	Spain (1960) % employed in each sector	France (1962) % employed	France (1962) % employed in each sector	Fed. Rep. (1961) % employed	Fed. Rep. (1961) % employed in each sector	Greece (1961) % employed	% employed
Agri-culture	0. Agriculture, forestry, hunting and fishing	41·3	41·3	19·8	19·8	13·4	13·4	53·9	
Industry	1. Mining and quarrying	1·7		1·6		2·8		0·6	
	2. Manufacturing	21·9		26·9		36·4		13·4	1
			30·7		36·7		47·8		
	4. Construction	7·1		8·2		8·6		4·6	
Services	5. Electricity, gas, water and sanitary services	0·7		0·9		0·8		0·5	
	6. Commerce	7·8		13·2		13·4		7·3	
			27·0		39·6		38·7		2
	7. Transport, storage and communication	4·6		5·4		5·6		4·3	
	8. Services	13·9		20·1		18·9		12·1	
	9. Activities not adequately described	1·0	1·0	3·9	3·9	0·1	0·1	3·4	
		100%	100%	100%	100%	100%	100%	100%	10
	Total size of Active population including both sexes	11,634,214		19,711,500		26,821,112		3,638,	

* ILO Yearbook of Labour Statistics 1968, Table 2A.

tribution by Branch of *Economic activity**

	Ireland (1961)		*Italy* (1961)		*Poland* (1960)		*Portugal* (1960)		*UK* (1961)		*Yugoslavia*	
% employed	*% employed*	*% employed in each sector*	*% employed*	*% employed in each sector*	*% employed*	*% employed in each sector*	*% employed*	*% employed in each sector*	*% employed*	*% employed in each sector*	*% employed*	*% employed in each sector*
·2	35·2		28·3	28·3	47·7	47·7	42·3	42·3	3·8	3·8	57·0	57·0
·9			0·7				0·8		2·9			
·0		24·5	26·5	38·8		29·0	20·3	27·8	34·8	44·4		22·0
·6			11·6				6·7		6·7			
·1			0·6				0·4		1·6			
·8		39·8	11·1	30·0		10·6	8·0	26·6	15·6	48·5		14·9
·2			4·8				3·6		6·9			
·8			13·5				14·6		24·4			
5	0·5		2·9	2·9	12·7	12·7	3·3	3·3	3·3	3·3		6·1
%	100%	100%	100%	100%	100%	100%	100%	100%	100%	100%	100%	100%
108,108			20,172,902		13,907,442		3,423,551		24,616,620		8,340,400	

and classification of economic sectors differs somewhat, probably to inflate 2nd
or at expense of tertiary in relation to occ. grouping in other countries. S. Baum (Int.
. Rev.) indicates size of tertiary 24% (rest of figures agree for other sectors).

Section III

Sectorial changes in the economy of several European countries.

I. Years 1950–1 to 1960–1

I. Years 1950–1951 to 1960–1961

Branch of Economic Activity	Fed. Rep.	Greece	Ireland	Italy	Poland	Portugal	Spain	U.K.
				Percentages of change				
Primary	−9·7	+5·8	−4·4	−11·6	−9·4	−6·0	−7·5	−1·2
Secondary	+5·5	−0·4	+0·9	+8·9	+6·1	+3·1	+6·1	−3·3
Tertiary	+6·3	−2·6	+4·1	+5·2	+8·6	−0·1	+2·0	+1·6

II. Years 1954–1964

Branch of Economic Activity	U.K.	Spain	Ireland	France	Italy	Fed. Rep.
			Percentages of change			
Primary	−1·2	−8·3	−5·7	−8·9	−7·7	−7·8
Secondary	−1·1	+5·7	+3·5	+3·7	+10·7	+3·7
Tertiary	+2·3	+2·6	+2·2	+5·2	+6·8	+3·5

Source: OECD.

Section IV

Educational Trends

All tables abstracted from UNESCO, *World Survey of Education, Vol. IV Higher Education*, 1966.

Table 1. Estimated school enrolment (all levels)

	1957/8	1961/2
North and West Europe	18·2	19·2
Central Europe	16·0	17·1
Southern Europe	13·9	15·2

Page 16.

Table 2. Percentage of estimated school enrolment at each level

	1957/8			1961/2		
	First	Second	Third	First	Second	Third
North and West Europe	64·4	33·0	2·6	58·6	38·4	3·0
Central Europe	68·8	30·4	2·8	68·7	28·0	3·3
Southern Europe	79·9	17·6	2·5	76·0	21·0	3·0

Page 48.

Table 3. School enrolment ratio for different levels of education

Country	Academic year beginning	Unadjusted school enrolment ratio by level			Adjusted school enrolment ratio first and second levels	
		First	Second	First and Second	Ratio	Average annual rate of increase of the ratio
France	1957	80	55	73	84	
	1961	70	87	74	85	0·3
Fed. Rep.	1957	64	92	74	85	
	1961	71	77	73	84	−0·3
Greece	1957	67	39	58	73	
	1960	62	44	56	70	−1·4
Ireland	1957	94	41	78	98	
	1961	88	45	75	94	−1·4
Italy	1957	55	41	50	58	
	1961	48	56	50	58	—
Poland	1957	71	26	58	79	
	1961	77	47	70	95	4·7
Spain	1957	68	22	53	66	
	1960	73	24	56	70	2·0
Portugal	1957	51	20	41	56	
	1960	53	30	46	62	3·5
England	1957	70	95*	78	84	
and Wales	1961	61	105*	75	80	−1·2

* Excluding vocation ed.

Note: Enrolment ratio obtained by relating total enrolment at one level of education to the population aged between 5 and 14 (1st level) 15 and 19 (2nd level), 3rd level to 100,000 pop. (as age limits of higher education so varied). The adjusted enrolment ratio is useful for comparing progress between countries – it calculates the geometric rate of change. Page 25.

Table 4. Total number of graduates at 3rd level of education per 100,000 population

Country	Academic year beginning	Number of graduates per 100,000 population
France	1957	43
	1960	55
Fed. Rep.	1957	73*
	1960	78*
Greece	1957	62
	1960	65
Ireland	1957	82
	1960	93
Italy	1957	42
	1960	44
Poland	1957	56
	1960	54
Portugal	1957	26
	1960	25
Spain	—	—
England and Wales	1957	110
	1960	133

* Excluding Fine Arts.
Figures not strictly comparable for graduates.
Page 37.

The progress of higher education since 1930

Table 5. Average number of students per 100,000 inhabitants, 1930–59

Country	1930–4	1945–9	1955–9
Poland	—	380	571
Germany	130	152	411
France	201	319	409
Ireland	209	282	368
Italy	130	383	321
UK	169	265	284
Greece	152	—	255
Spain	157	182	241
Portugal	—	175	229

Note: Data from questionnaires sent to member states
3 types of higher education distinguished
(A) Universities and equivalent degree granting institutions;
(B) Teacher education at non-university institutions;
(C) Other education (general and professional) at non-university institutions.
Page 67.

*Table 6. Increase in enrolment per 100,000 inhabitants, 1930–59 (as %
of 1930–4 average)*

Percentage	Countries	Percentage
0–4	Greece, Spain	2
	Ireland, United Kingdom	3
	France	4
5–9	Italy	6
10–14	Czechoslovakia	7
	Germany	11

Page 68.

*Increase in enrolment per 100,000 inhabitants, 1945–59 (as % of 1945–
9 average)*

Percentage	Countries	Percentage
Negative	Italy	−2
0–4	United Kingdom	1
	Czechoslovakia, France, Ireland	3
	Portugal, Spain	
5–9	Poland	5
10	Germany	17

Page 69.

Table 7. Enrolment of women students 1930–59

Country	Average 1930–4 %	Average 1945–9 %	Average 1955–9 %
France	26·6	33·0	37·1
Germany	15·5	13·9	22·7
Greece	9·6	—	26·8
Ireland	32·2	30·4	29·8
Italy	11·1	25·4	27·6
Poland	38·2	36·0	33·9
Spain	6·1	10·1	17·6
UK	32·0	30·7	33·3

Note: Measures the changing proportion of female to total
enrolments.

Page 69.

*Table 8. Percentage increase in annual enrolment of women students,
1930–59*
(Expansion is expressed as an annual % of the average starting
enrolment for the period considered)

Percentage	Countries	Percentage
0–4	Ireland	2
	United Kingdom	4
5–9	France	8
10–19	Germany	10
	Poland	12
	Greece	19
20	Italy	20

Percentage increase in annual enrolment of women students, 1945–59

Percentage	Countries	Percentage
0–4	Italy	0
	Ireland, United Kingdom	2
5–9	France	6
	Poland	7
9 and over	Germany	36

Page 70.

Section V

Social mobility in several European nations compared

1959

Intergenerational mobility

	From manual to non-manual 1.	*From non-manual to manual* 2.	*Col. 1* ——— *Col. 2*
Switzerland	42	10	·2
England	35	35	1·0
Norway	31	22	·7
France	30	18	·6
USSR	30	14	·4
Sweden	25	28	1·1
Denmark	24	37	1·5
W. Germany	19	29	1·5
Holland	18	24	1·3
Finland	11	24	2·2
Italy	8	35	4·5

From K. Svalastoga, *Social Differentiation*, New York: David MacKay, 1965, p. 121, after Miller 'Comparative Social Mobility', *Current Sociology*, 1960, 9, pp. 1072.

Rates of occupational mobility from non-manual into manual work, and from manual into non-manual, in several European countries.

(Percentages)

Countries	*(1)* Non-manual into manual	*(2)* Manual into non-manual
Denmark	+36·8	+24·1
Finland	−24·0	−11·0
France I	−20·5	+30·1
France II	+26·6	+29·6
Great Britain	+42·1	+24·8
Hungary	+27·5	−14·5
Italy	+34·4	−8·5
Netherlands	+43·2	−19·6
Norway	+28·6	−23·2
Sweden	+27·7	+25·5
West Germany	+29·0	−20·0

Miller, 'Comparative Social Mobility', *Current Sociology 1960/9*, p. 34.

Bibliography

A Chronological Bibliography of some important works on the stratification of European Societies

The following list of sociological sources on the stratification of European societies may be of some help in elucidating the shifting interests and the growing awareness of social scientists about most of the problems dealt with in this volume. The list is plainly selective and does not pretend to be exhaustive; it only intends to be a minor indicator of certain trends in the history of sociology. For this reason, and for the sake of greater clarity, complete bibliographical details have been omitted.

1771 John Millar, *The Origin of the Distinction of Ranks; or, an Inquiry into the Circumstances which give rise to Influence in the Different Members of Society.*

1798 T. R. Malthus, *An Essay on Population.*

1822 A. Comte, *Plan des travaux scientifiques nécessaires pour réorganiser la société.*

1840 E. Buret, *La misère des classes laborieuses en Anglaterre et en France.*

1845 F. Engels, *Die Lage der arbeitenden Klassen in England.*

1850 K. Marx, articles on French class conflicts in *Neue Rheinische Zeitung* (later known as *Les luttes des classes en France*, 1895, F. Engels, ed.).

1851 A. Comte, *Système de politique positive, ou Traité de Sociologie, instituant la religion de l'Humanité* (1851–5).

1854 K. Marx, *Die deutsche Ideologie.*

1855 Le Play, *Les ouvriers européens, Étude sur les travaux, la vie economique et la condition morale des populations ouvrières de l'Europe, précédé d'un exposé de la Méthode d'observation.*

1867 K. Marx, *Das Kapital.*

1884 *F. Engels, Der Ursprung der Familie, des Privateigentums und des Staates.*

1890 G. Schmoller, 'Wesen der Arbeitsteilung und der sozialen Klassenbildung' in *Jahrbuch für Gesetzgebung*, 1890.

1893 K. Bücher, 'Arbeitsteilung und soziale Klassenbildung' in *Die Entstehung der Volkswirtschaft*, Tübingen.

E. Durkeim, *De la division du travail social.*
1901 J. Costa, *Oligarquía y caciquismo.*
1902 A. Bauer, *Les classes sociales.*
1905 E. Bernstein, *Klasse und Klassenkampf.*
M. Weber, *Die protestantische Ethik und der 'Geist' des Kapitalismus.*
1912 F. Toennies, *Gemeinschaft und Gesellschaft.*
1913 M. Halbwachs, 'La classe ouvrière et les niveaux de vie' in *Année sociologique.*
1916 V. Pareto, *Trattato di sociologia generale.*
1920 M. Weber, *Wirtschaft und Gesellschaft.*
1922 R. Michels, 'Beitrag zur Lehre von der Klassenbildung' in *Archiv für Socialwissenschaft und Sozialpolitik.*
1923 G. Lukács, *Histoire et conscience de classe.*
1927 J. A. Schumpeter, 'Imperialismus und soziale Klasse' in *Archiv für Sozialwissenschaft und Sozialpolitik,* Vol. 57.
1929 J. Díaz del Moral, *Historia de las agitaciones campesinas andaluzas.*
K. Mannheim, *Ideologie und Utopie.*
1930 E. Goblot, *La barrière et le niveau.*
1932 T. Geiger, *Die soziale Schichtung des Deutschen Volkes.*
1933 M. Halbwachs, *L'évolution des besoins dans les classes ouvrières.*
1937 M. Halbwachs, *Les classes sociales* (cours de Sorbonne, ed.).
T. H. Marshall, ed., *Class Conflict and Social Stratification* (including article on 'Nature of Class Conflict').
1938 M. Halbwachs, *Morphologie sociale.*
M. Halbwachs, *Esquisse d'une psychologie des classes sociales.*
J. Lhomme, *Le problème des classes.*
1939 L. Robbins, *The Economic Basis of Class Conflict.*
Inventaires III, *Les classes moyennes.*
1941 (W. L. Warner and P. S. Lunt, *The Social Life of a Modern Community*).
1942 J. A. Schumpeter, *Capitalism, Socialism and Democracy.*
1945 (K. Davis, W. Moore, 'Some Principles of Stratification' in *Am. Soc. Rev.,* No. 10).
F. Heek, *Klassen-en-standen structuur.*
1947 P. A. Sorokin, 'Qu'est-ce qu'une classe sociale', *Cah. Int. de sociol.,* Vol. II.
1949 R. Centers, *The Psychology of Social Class.*
T. Geiger, *Die Klassengesellschaft im Schmelztiegel.*
R. Lewis and A. Maud, *The English Middle Classes.*
1950 R. Aron, 'Social Structure and the Ruling Class', *Brit. Jnl. Soc.*

G. D. H. Cole, 'The Conception of the Middle Classes', *Brit. Jnl. Soc.*

T. H. Marshall, *Citizenship and Social Class.*

D. Riesman, *The Lonely Crowd.*

1953 R. Bendix, S. M. Lipset, eds., *Class Status and Power*, 1st ed.

D. MacRae, 'Social Stratification', *Current Sociology.*

K. Renner, *Wandlungen der modernen Gesellschaft.*

A. Touraine, Report on 'Enquête internationale sur la stratification sociale' in *Association Internationale de Sociologie, Congrès de Liège* (ISA Liège Congress, Acts, Vol. I).

1954 D. Glass, *Social Mobility in Britain.*

G. Gurvitch, *Le concept des classes sociales* (Cours de Sorbonne).

(G. Lenski, 'Status Crystallization', *Am. Soc. Rev.*).

1955 R. Aron, *Dix-huit leçons sur la société industrielle* (Cours de Sorbonne).

1956 R. Aron, *La lutte des classes* (Cours de Sorbonne).

S. Ossowski, *Struktura klasowa w spoteoznez swiadomosci.*

1957 R. Dahrendorf, *Soziale Klassen und Klassenkonflikt in der industriellen Gesellschaft.*

1958 H. Kötler, *Landbevölkerung im sozialen Wandel.*

D. Lockwood, *The Blackcoated Worker.*

1960 S. Aaronovith, *The Ruling Class.*

G. Friedmann, P. Naville, eds., *Traité de sociologie du travail.*

A. Girard, *La reussite sociale en France.*

A. Inkeles, 'Industrial Man: the relation of status to Experience, Perception and Value', *Am. Jnl. Soc.*, Vol. LXVI.

D. Lockwood, 'The New Working Class' in *European Journal of Sociology.*

H. Popitz et al., *Das Gesellschaftsbild des Arbeiters.*

R. Zweig, *The Worker in an Affluent Society.*

1962 S. Mallet, *Les Paysans contre le passé.*

R. M. Titmuss, *Income Distribution and Social Change.*

D. Wedderburn, 'Poverty in Britain Today', *Soc. Rev.*, Vol. X, No. 3.

1963 S. Mallet, *La nouvelle classe ouvrière.*

1964 R. Blauner, *Alienation and Freedom, the Factory Worker and his Industry.*

T. B. Bottomore, *Elites and Society.*

R. Dahrendorf, 'Recent Changes in the Class Structure of European Societies', *Daedalus* (Winter).

S. M. Lipset, 'Changing Class Structure and Contemporary European Politics', *Daedalus* (Winter).

A. Touraine, 'Management and the Working Class in Europe', *Daedalus* (Winter).

1965 G. Gurvitch, ed., 'Les classes sociales dans le monde d'aujourd'hui', *Cah. Int. Soc.*

1966 W. Kraus, *Der fünfte Stand.*

G. Lenski, *Power and Privilege.*

W. G. Runciman, *Relative Deprivation and Social Justice.*

N. Smelser and S. M. Lipset, *Social Structure and Mobility in Economic Development.*

A. Touraine, *La Conscience ouvrière.*

W. Wesołowski, 'Changes in the Class Structure of Poland' in J. Szczpásnki, *Empirical Sociology in Poland.*

1967 R. Dahrendorf, *Conflict after Class: New Perspectives on the Theory of Social and Political Conflict.*

J. Goldthorpe, et al., 'The Affluent Worker' in *Sociology.*

E. Shils, 'The Stratification System of Mass Society' in B. Singh and V. B. Singh, eds., *Social and Economic Change.*

H. Steiner, *Soziale Strukturveränderungen in modernen Kapitalismus.*

(M. Tumin, *Social Stratification*).

1968 J. A. Jackson, ed., *Social Stratification.*

R. T. McKenzie, A. Silver, *Angels in Marble: Working Class Conservatives in Urban England.*

F. Parkin, *Middle Class Radicalism.*

N. Pulantzas, *Pouvoir politique et classes sociales.*

A. Touraine, 'Anciennes et nouvelles classes sociales' in G. Balandier, *Perspectives de la sociologie contemporaine.*

1969 P. Ammassari, 'The Italian Blue-Collar Worker', *Int. Jnl. Comp. Soc.*

N. Birnbaum, *The Crisis of Industrial Society.*

J. Dorselaer, 'The Belgian Blue-Collar Worker', *Int. Jnl. Comp. Soc.*

H. Mendras, Y. Tavernier, *Terre, Paysans et Politique.*

F. Parkin, 'Class Stratification in Socialist Societies', *Br. Jnl. Sociol.*

A. Touraine, *La société post-industrielle.*

Index

Accent, 13, 27, 258, 259
Achievement-orientation, 39, 47, 129
Act of Union (Ireland), 199
Advisers, economic, 45, 128; government, 248
Aegean, Greek traders in, 164; village community in, 174
Affluent Society, The (J. K. Galbraith), 388
Africa, repatriation of French from, 224
Agencies, bureaucratized, 36; land reform, 111
Agrarian reform, 126, 130, 145, 156 nn, 172, 321, 322, 330; lack of Greek, 172–4 *passim*; problems arising from, 318; shelving of Spanish, 126
Agriculture, advisers in, power of, 207; effect on of returning migrants, 224; capitalistic, 100, 106; changes in, 167, 168; *chiflik* system, 168; commercialization of, 168, 172, 174, 175; composition of, 195 n, 205; industrialization of, 28; migrants to urban jobs, 29; modernization of, 339; proportion of workers in (*see also* Workers, rural), 73, 130, 131, 173, 204, 250, 318; shift away from, 202, 205, 206, 394; stagnation of, 67; *timar* system, 168; upper class choice, 68; wages in, 83
Allardt, E., 393
Ammassari, P. 29
Andalusia, 30, 132, 133, 134, 137, 151, 153
Anderson, C., 379
Andreski, S., 63
Angels in Marble (R. T. McKenzie and A. Silver), 270
Anglo-Irish Ascendancy, 214, 215, 217, 218, 219
Arensberg, C., 204, 209–11 *passim*, 214

Aristocracy, 364, 365; attitude towards, 242; commercial interests of, 244; integration with bourgeoisie, 244; landed, disappearance of, 322, 323; ruling class, 348; *see also* Peerage
Aristocratization, 69, 70, 87
Armed forces, as channel to power, 71; as channel to upward mobility, 43, 146; component of upper strata, 71; heads of, 25; Italian, 104; privilege of, 64; training in, 159 n
Aron, R., 43, 282, 389–91 *passim*, 393
Artisans, 209, 228, 249, 331
Athens, 186, 187, 189
Attica, gross national product in, 186
Autarchy, policies of, 128, 145
Automation, 249, 261, 340, 394
Autonomy, 242, 243, 264
Avakumović, I., 311

Background, social, 13, 21, 22, 25, 35, 47, 52 n, 190, 224, 260, 326, 329, 348, 365
Balkans, the, 165, 166, 167, 168, 172, 192 n
Banking, 13, 70, 102, 103, 110, 128, 146, 151, 156 n
Barcelona (Spain), 136; Círculo de Economiá, 144
Barth, E. A. T., 14, 15
Basque country, 127, 132, 146, 151, 153
Belfast (Northern Ireland), Campbell College, 219; Methodist College, 219
Belgium, 25, 56 n
Belgrade, Institute of Social Sciences, 313; University of, 298
Bentham, J., 95
Bentzel, R., 383
Birth-rate, increase in, 226
Black Sea, closing of, 166